EMBATTLED EUROPE

Embattled Europe

A PROGRESSIVE ALTERNATIVE

KONRAD H. JARAUSCH

PRINCETON UNIVERSITY PRESS

PRINCETON & OXFORD

Published by Princeton University Press
41 William Street, Princeton, New Jersey 08540
99 Banbury Road, Oxford OX2 6JX

press.princeton.edu

All Rights Reserved

First paperback printing, 2024
Paperback ISBN 9780691225531

The Library of Congress has cataloged the cloth edition as follows:

Names: Jarausch, Konrad Hugo, author.
Title: Embattled Europe : a progressive alternative / Konrad H. Jarausch.
Description: Princeton : Princeton University Press, [2021] | Includes
    bibliographical references and index.
Identifiers: LCCN 2021011362 (print) | LCCN 2021011363 (ebook) |
    ISBN 9780691200415 (hardback) | ISBN 9780691226187 (ebook)
Subjects: LCSH: Europe—History—1989– | Europe—Politics and government—
    20th century. | Europe—Politics and government—21st century. | Europe—
    Social conditions—20th century. | BISAC: HISTORY / Europe / General |
    SOCIAL SCIENCE / Regional Studies
Classification: LCC D2003 .J37 2021 (print) | LCC D2003 (ebook) |
    DDC 940.56—dc23
LC record available at https://lccn.loc.gov/2021011362
LC ebook record available at https://lccn.loc.gov/2021011363

British Library Cataloging-in-Publication Data is available

Jacket/Cover image: Shutterstock

The author received support to complete this work from the Jean Monnet Center of Excellence at the University of North Carolina at Chapel Hill, which is supported by the European Commission. The European Commission's support for the production of this publication does not constitute an endorsement of the contents, which reflect the views only of the authors, and the Commission cannot be held responsible for any use which may be made of the information contained therein.

Co-funded by the
Erasmus+ Programme
of the European Union

This book has been composed in Arno

CONTENTS

ABBREVIATIONS

AfD	Alternative for Germany Party
ALMP	Active Labor Market Policies
BRIC	Brazil, Russia, India, and China
CAP	Common Agricultural Policy
CDU	Christian Democratic Union, Germany
CEPOS	Centre for Political Studies
CETA	Comprehensive Economic and Trade Agreement
CFSP	Common Foreign and Security Policy
CIA	United States Central Intelligence Agency
CIS	Commonwealth of Independent States
COMECON	Council for Mutual Economic Assistance
CSDP	Common Security and Defense Policy
CSU	Christian Social Union, Germany
DGB	German Trade Union Confederation
DM	Deutsche Mark
DUP	Northern Irish Democratic Unionist Party
EC	European Community
ECB	European Central Bank
ECSC	European Coal and Steel Community
EEC	European Economic Community
EFTA	European Free Trade Association

EMU	European Monetary Union
ESM	European Stability Mechanism
EU	European Union
Euratom	European Atomic Energy Community
EURODAC	EU asylum fingerprint database
FN	Front National
FPÖ	Austrian Freedom Party
FRG	Federal Republic of Germany
Frontex	European Border and Coast Guard Agency
GATT	General Agreement on Tariffs and Trade
GDR	German Democratic Republic
GHGE	Greenhouse gas emissions
HEH	House of European History, Brussels
IMF	International Monetary Fund
ISIS	Islamic State
LPF	Pim Fortuyn List, Holland
NATO	North Atlantic Treaty Organization
NHS	National Health Service
NRA	National Rifle Association
OECD	Organisation for Economic Co-operation and Development
OMT	Outright Money Transactions Fund
OOA	Organization for Information on Nuclear Power
OPEC	Organization of the Petroleum Exporting Countries
PASOK	Panhellenic Socialist Movement
PCF	French Communist Party
PEGIDA	Patriotic Europeans Against the Islamisation of the Occident
PESCO	Permanent Structured Cooperation

PIIGS	Portugal, Ireland, Italy, Greece, and Spain
PiS	Law and Justice Party, Poland
PISA	Program for International Student Assessment
PS	French Socialist Party
PZPR	Polish United Workers' Party
SEA	Single European Act
SED	Socialist Union Party of Germany
SFIO	French Worker's Party
SPD	Social Democratic Party of Germany
SVP	Swiss People's Party
TTIP	Transatlantic Trade and Investment Partnership
UDCA	Union for the Defense of Tradesmen and Artisans, in France
UEFA	Union of European Football Associations
UK	United Kingdom of Great Britain
UKIP	United Kingdom Independence Party
UN	United Nations
UNICEF	United Nations Children's Fund
UNRRA	United Nations Relief and Rehabilitation Authority
USSR	Union of Soviet Socialist Republics
WHO	World Health Organization
WTO	World Trade Organization

EMBATTLED EUROPE

The European Puzzle

FIGURE 1. Las Ramblas, Barcelona, Spain. Jan Kranendonk, Shutterstock.

On September 26, 2017, the French president Emmanuel Macron laid out a compelling vision for the European future. Speaking to students at the Sorbonne, he reaffirmed the promise of Europe as an idea of "peace, prosperity and freedom," claiming "it is our responsibility to bring it to life." Proposing a long list of reforms to strengthen "European sovereignty," he called for cooperation in security and defense; a common approach to migration; greater coordination in foreign policy; a joint effort to manage the ecological transition; more support for digital innovation; and finally, increased economic competitiveness. To implement such an ambitious agenda, he insisted on "a stronger budget within Europe," public debate in "democratic conventions" and a new Franco-German partnership as an engine of European progress.[1] While many Europhiles were inspired by Macron's lofty rhetoric, more pragmatic leaders like the German chancellor Angela Merkel worried about how to achieve these bold goals in actual practice.

In contrast to such enthusiasm, Euroskeptics consider the very concept of Europe "a dirty word." Western European populists like Marine Le Pen of France blame Brussels for all the problems of globalization and immigration. Similarly, the Eastern European authoritarians like the Hungarian president Viktor Orbán or the Polish Law and Justice Party miss no opportunity to disparage the EU, although they are dependent on its subsidies. The British prime minister Boris Johnson and his Brexiteer supporters loathed the supranational aspirations of the Continent so much that they actually left the EU on January 1, 2021.[2] In the United States, many Republicans "do not want to become more like Europe" and fuel a visceral fear of socialism so as to defend American exceptionalism. Ex-president Donald Trump's call to "make America great again" was also predicated on seeing the European Union as the enemy who had cheated the United States in trade and freeloaded to secure its defense.[3] In the rightist discourse, Europe has become a symbol for everything it detests.

Journalistic appraisals and scholarly analyses have similarly swung from enthusiastic support for the European project to severe criticism. The initially optimistic assessments of the European Union as a promising model for dealing with the challenges of globalization seem curiously antiquated due to the more recent problems that have threatened to break the EU apart.[4] Supported by the conservative media like the Murdoch press, an entire gloom-and-doom literature has instead been predicting the impending collapse of Europe—even if that has refused to happen so far.[5] Such alarmist analyses exaggerate the very real challenges of currency coherence, migration pressure, or British withdrawal in order to paint a discouraging picture of a "fractured continent" that is incapable of solving its existential problems. This largely negative portrayal has created a self-fulfilling prophecy, making the historian Timothy Garton Ash wonder: "Is Europe disintegrating?"[6]

The privilege of living in both Europe and the United States has provoked me to question such clichéd accounts of Continental decline with more accurate information and interpretation. Born during World War II, I grew up in postwar Germany, reared by my mother since my father had died in Russia. In order to understand the world better, I went to the United States as a foreign student, earning a BA in American studies at the University of Wyoming and a PhD in comparative history at the University of Wisconsin. Writing and teaching on both sides of the Atlantic, I have tried to explain the travails of the German past to Americans while explicating the convolutions of US politics to Europeans.[7] This double perspective has given me the inside knowledge of and distance to European affairs that informed my synthesis *Out of Ashes: A New History of Europe in the Twentieth Century*.[8] By following that work with a reflection on the European experience since 1990, I want to discuss which of its aspects constitute a "European way of life" as shown by the Las Ramblas boulevard in Barcelona. By addressing current problems, such a reflection aims to stimulate a transatlantic dialogue about progressive solutions.

The European Model

This European model is a form of democratic modernity, produced by painful learning from the bloody catastrophes of the first half of the twentieth century. During the stalemate of World War I, three different visions emerged that battled for supremacy on the Continent: In Russia, Vladimir Lenin propagated a radical form of socialism in the revolution by promising an egalitarian life in the Soviet Union. From the United States, President Woodrow Wilson promoted peace and prosperity through a benign form of liberal democracy. And in Central Europe, nationalist resentments inspired Benito Mussolini and Adolf Hitler to develop a Fascism and National Socialism that claimed to create a people's community. In the bitter contest between these ideological blueprints, democracy finally emerged victorious since the United States twice rescued the Continent from itself. But during the last decades of the twentieth century, the Europeans have begun to emancipate themselves from American tutelage, developing shared Western values in their own version of self-government that can serve as an example even for the United States.[9]

A first positive trait of the European model is the existence of a truly democratic election system that seeks to encourage more citizen involvement. In contrast to the vote suppression, rural overrepresentation, and flagrant gerrymandering of the American and to a degree British "winner takes all" process, proportional representation more accurately reflects the wishes of the electorate by counting all ballots equally, even those of the smaller parties. To prevent fragmentation, it sometimes includes a hurdle for parliamentary representation, which is set at 5 percent in Germany. Unlike the money-driven US campaigns, European parties are more often supported by public funds. Since this system reflects minority views, it leads to higher participation during elections. The broader range of voices in Parliament favors coalition governments, which tend toward compromise, resulting in centrist policies. Weighing each vote more fairly than the Electoral College, proportional voting, also used in the European Parliament, makes for better government in the long run.[10]

A second exemplary aspect is the generally peaceful international behavior of a Europe that has learned the lessons of two incredibly bloody wars. While individual countries still cling to national sovereignty, their cooperation in the EU is an attempt to avoid the repetition of earlier bloodshed. Though often disagreeing on foreign or security issues, Brussels speaks with a more united voice in matters of global trade, favoring a balance between free exchanges and protection of its own market. The European member states are heavily involved in international organizations such as the World Trade Organization (WTO), supporting the liberal world order that emerged after World War II. While participating in some military interventions sponsored by the United Nations (UN) or the North Atlantic Treaty Organization (NATO), they prefer to resolve problems by negotiation whenever possible. With the exception of the wars of Yugoslav succession, this civilian approach has pacified Europe and helped reduce tensions in other crisis regions, even if it had occasionally to be supplemented by force.[11]

A third worthwhile characteristic of the European model is the welfare state, which creates a sense of security and solidarity. Since neoliberals in the UK have prevented a Europeanization of social policy, it has largely remained a preserve of the EU member states. The provision of social benefits that had expanded greatly during the postwar boom ceased to grow further during the stagflation and deindustrialization following the oil shocks of the 1970s. Instead, the return to a market ideology fostered by a middle-class tax revolt led to a considerable retrenchment in government services. But far from collapsing, the welfare state has been reformed, moving from subsidizing wage replacements for client groups to enabling recipients to reenter the job market through additional training and childcare.[12] Though strained by feminist demands for equality, migration pressures, and aging populations, support for government social policy has continued, absorbing almost half of the budget of most European states.

Taken together, these traits of the European model constitute a progressive alternative because they provide a better quality of life for most citizens than the vaunted "American dream." In truth, the latter offers perhaps a higher income, bigger houses, grander SUVs—but these are purchased by job insecurity, social inequality, racist violence, and a rampant pandemic. People who have lived in Europe prize its social safety net, such as "access for all to child care, medical and parental leave from work, tuition free college, a living stipend, universal health care and generous pensions." Other attractive features are longer vacations, public transit, support for culture, gun safety, and secure employment, just to cite a few examples. Such benefits unquestionably do require paying higher taxes. But they also provide greater services that make life more agreeable for the average citizen. Even if they would have to develop their own version, many Americans might enjoy these advantages as well. In a recent Social Progress Index, the United States has therefore dropped down to number twenty-eight in the world—a scandalous decline.[13]

The Present as History

This reflection draws on theoretical discussions of a "history of the present" that go beyond journalistic snapshots by putting current events into a longer time frame.[14] Looking for bearings in a rapidly changing world is difficult since the outcome of developments is not yet known and the archival record remains inaccessible. Nonetheless, a systematic review of public debates about a series of major issues like migration can provide a more stable perspective that differentiates short-range panics from longer structural trends. The source base for such an analysis consists of speeches and interviews by political actors as well as commentary in the leading media, ranging from the *Economist* to *Die Zeit*. Moreover, statistical data from Eurostat and survey results from various pollsters provide a way to distinguish rhetorical claims from actual facts. Finally, personal statements of ordinary people offer a window on the impact of policy decisions on their changing everyday lives.

In order to address the transatlantic crisis of liberal democracy, this book explores a series of thematic and national case studies, proceeding in four chronological steps.[15] Part I begins in Sopron, Hungary, with the lifting of the Iron Curtain in 1989, which triggered the mass exodus from East Germany that toppled the Berlin Wall and provided the Continent with a chance to become "whole and free" again.[16] Chapter 2 then moves to a shopping center in the Polish city of Poznań to discuss the difficulties and successes of the neoliberal transformation of Eastern European economies and societies.[17] Chapter 3 goes on to the Luxembourg border town of Schengen to reflect on the progress of European integration due to the opening of borders, the introduction of a shared currency, and the expansion of the European Union to the east.[18] In the euphoria of the Communist overthrow, European integration seemed to offer an attractive blueprint for peace and prosperity to be emulated elsewhere.[19]

Part II aims to explain the reasons for the unexpected avalanche of problems during the past decade, which often appeared to prove the Euroskeptics right. As the epicenter of the sovereign debt crisis, the Greek capital of Athens serves as a starting point for a discussion of the advantages and liabilities of the euro as a single currency.[20] Chapter 5 then visits Italian beaches like those on the island of Lampedusa to discuss the desperate mass migration from Africa and Syria that is stoking populist fears all over Europe of terrorism by angry Muslim youths.[21] Chapter 6 moves to London to explore the shocking outcome of the Brexit referendum that has catapulted the UK out of the EU in spite of its shared business interests and historical ties to the Continent.[22] Due to these unforeseen crises, an entire pessimistic literature now flatly asserts that "the end of Europe" has come.[23]

Part III contradicts these predictions of failure by presenting examples of the continued viability of the European model. Starting with Volkswagen's car production plant in Wolfsburg, chapter 7 analyzes the adjustment of the German economy to global competition by specializing in medium-high technology such as luxury automobiles.[24] Chapter 8 then moves to the village of Högfors to explore the Swedish attempts to restructure the welfare state into an "enabling" mode that makes workers fit for a high-tech economy.[25] Chapter 9 describes a wind power park close to the island of Anholt to demonstrate the Danish effort to become independent of fossil fuels in response to global warming.[26] These examples show that Europe functions quite well in daily life, even if the project of transforming the EU into "an ever closer union" still needs, according to the French president Emmanuel Macron, a new European initiative so as to revitalize its trajectory.[27]

Part IV addresses the shared transatlantic challenges of liberal democracy, affecting both Europe and the United States. It begins with a look at the Russian annexation of Crimea and invasion of Eastern Ukraine in order to discuss problems of European military defense in a post–Cold War era.[28] Chapter 11 then goes on to Paris to explore the French "yellow vest" movement as an example of grassroots populism, which is challenging cosmopolitan elites by rejecting further integration of the EU and by demanding protection against the effects of globalization.[29] The final chapter moves to the World Economic Forum in Davos, Switzerland, to reconsider how the global role of Europe during the last several decades made it drift away from the United States in its interests as well as its values.[30] It concludes by arguing that, in order to resolve issues like defense and democratic governance, Europeans and Americans still have much to learn from each other.

Such a multifaceted approach is necessary in order to address the complexity of "unity in diversity" that characterizes contemporary life on the Continent.[31] As a geographical expression "Europe" is merely a protrusion of the Asian landmass with a paradoxical blend of nation-states and supranational institutions. Neither Russia nor the United States quite belong to it, though they have a major impact on it. The UK is itself not sure whether it is a part, being both inside and outside at the same time. The European Union has largely managed to unite the Continent, with the exception of Norway, Switzerland, and some of the Balkan states. But Europe itself is also divided into major regions like Scandinavia, the West-Central core, the Mediterranean area, and the post-Communist realm. Since the journalistic and political usage varies between the EU as institution and the entire Continent, this reflection explores their dialectic of diversity and unity. Focusing on some of the best practices, it treats Europe as a projection screen for a whole range of aspirations and behaviors that constitute the references to it.

European Lessons

It is the thesis of this book that the European experience during the past three decades provides an instructive guide to the possibilities and problems of progressive politics in the twenty-first century.[32] The failure of Soviet-style Marxism has left an ideological void that populists have rushed to fill with their dangerous nationalist and racist hatred, which appeals to many people who feel threatened by the changes of globalization. Where it works, the European model of liberal democracy, peaceful multilateralism, and social welfare provides a constructive alternative that offers freedom, peace, and solidarity. Achieving these values is far from inevitable as the crises of mass migration, sovereign debt, and nationalist egotism have shown. But positive experiences in competitiveness, welfare reform, or environmental protection also suggest that many Europeans have already begun to realize the gains of their cooperation.[33] These successful examples offer hope for a renewal of progressive politics in general.

On the one hand, Europeans themselves must redouble their efforts to live up to the standards of their own model to counter the pressures of globalized competition. The negative stereotypes of the "Brussels bureaucracy," purveyed even by leftist media, have undercut much of the prior progress of integration. Moreover, a populist group of illiberal democrats like the Hungarian Viktor Orbán is eroding human rights and opposing common solutions to vital questions like migration. Though recognizing the economic clout of the EU, foreign leaders often ridicule its diplomatic and military weakness. Concerned intellectuals like the political scientist Ulrike Guerot, the writer Robert Menasse, and the theater impresario Milo Rau have therefore issued a manifesto for a "European Republic" to be founded by citizens from below: "It is time to turn the promise inherent in Europe into a reality" by transcending the nation-state so that "a common market and a common currency can be created within a common European democracy."[34]

On the other hand, those Americans who are searching for a reasonable alternative to Trumpist populism also ought to take a fresh look at "Europe's promise."[35] While both sides share fundamental values—such as human rights, democracy, and capitalism—their implementation is increasingly diverging.[36] In contrast to the United States' frequent resort to military force, most Europeans believe in peaceful diplomacy and multilateralism. Unlike the neoliberal American faith in unbridled competition, Europe prefers to curb financial speculation so as to avoid periodic crashes. While the gap between rich and poor is widening in market-oriented America, this discrepancy is limited by the social solidarity of a generous welfare state on the Continent. While Washington has rejoined the Paris climate agreement, Brussels insists on environmental protection and shifts to renewable energies. Why do Europeans live more secure and satisfying lives according to a whole spate of criteria, ranging from health care to gun control?[37]

Both Continental skeptics and American critics need to remember the catastrophes of the twentieth century in order to make sure that such disasters will not recur in the future.[38] The populist temptation of resorting to simple solutions, repressing dissent, and attacking foreign enemies has had terrible results in the fascist and Communist dictatorships. Their ideological efforts at social engineering have proven deadly to millions of race or class victims who were excluded from the community or unwilling to go along. Moreover, the launching of nationalist wars of annihilation has claimed an immense number of lives, devastating even the victorious countries. American victories in the world wars have tended to stifle self-criticism through military success, while Europeans have been forced to learn the bitter lessons of such dangers at tremendous human costs. Fortunately, the inauguration of Joseph Biden as American president in 2021 offers an opportunity to engage in a renewed transatlantic dialogue about progressive solutions.[39]

PART I

Promising Future

With the lifting of the Iron Curtain, the European future looked quite bright in 1989/90. Facilitated by détente, the overthrow of Communism in Eastern Europe ended the Cold War, and made the Red Army withdraw, leading to the implosion of the Soviet Union. This peaceful revolution from below opened the door to a post-Communist transformation among the former satellite states, the erstwhile Soviet Empire and even in the Russian motherland, initiating an exciting transition to democracy and capitalism. Concurrently with this unforeseen upheaval, the process of Western European integration picked up speed and eventually included most of Eastern Europe in NATO and the EU. After half a century of near warfare, the reunification of Germany and the entire Continent finally offered all Europeans a chance to live in peace, freedom, and prosperity. How did this opportunity come about, what obstacles did it have to overcome and what consequences did it involve?

1

Peaceful Revolution

FIGURE 2. Pan European picnic, Sopron, Hungary. dpa.

It all started with a harmless picnic. In order to reduce Cold War tensions, Hungarian opposition groups invited their Austrian neighbors to hold a joint cookout near Sopron, opening the border for three hours on August 19, 1989. When tens of thousands of East German citizens vacationing at Lake Balaton got word, they decided to use the occasion to leave the drab SED-dictatorship of the German Democratic Republic (GDR). Even before the official press conference on the road to

St. Margarethen was finished, hundreds of pedestrians began to stream to the wooden boundary gate. Arpad Bella, colonel of the border troops, was puzzled: "If I don't stop the East Germans, I violate my orders. But the use of weapons [is] impossible without bloodshed." So in responding to the pressure of the crowd, he did exactly the right thing—nothing. The fleeing East Germans were in no mood to show any identification: "They pushed the gate open, rushed past us like lightning and caused great confusion."[1]

This pan-European picnic was a grassroots initiative, organized by a growing civil opposition in Hungary and encouraged by local Austrian officials. During a lecture by Otto von Habsburg in Debrecen, Ferenc Meszaros, a member of the Hungarian Democratic Forum, thought "that they ought to continue their conversation at the Hungarian border to Austria," allowing citizens of both countries to grill meat, drink beer, and talk about practical ways to soften the seemingly impenetrable Iron Curtain. The organizers even persuaded the Hungarian minister of state Imre Pozsgay and the Habsburg prince to assume patronage over the event, giving it official legitimacy. The East German vacationers found out about it through a German language leaflet that called on them to "tear down and take along" pieces of the border fence. In his speech during the picnic, the opposition intellectual György Konrad hoped that easing tensions would provide an opportunity "for real changes" without anyone being locked up.[2]

Though rather surprising, the breakthrough of the border was also the result of the increasing reform orientation of the Hungarian government. In the fall of 1988, the flexible Miklós Németh had taken over the reins of the Communist Party, allowing the reburial of Imre Nagy, the hero of the 1956 anti-Soviet uprising, which attracted tens of thousands of attendees. On May 2, 1989, his cabinet quietly authorized the dismantling of the outdated electronic border fence since its replacement with Western material proved too expensive. In a symbolic gesture, the Hungarian foreign minister Gyula Horn and his Austrian colleague Alois Mock then cut a piece of the barbed wire on June 27. But, by "voting with their feet," the escapees confronted Budapest with a dilemma: Should it reimpose control and alienate the West or let them out and offend the East? After much debate, the Hungarian government chose human rights over socialist solidarity and opened its border on September 11, 1989, allowing fifty thousand East Germans to escape.[3]

When the GDR prohibited travel to Hungary, other desperate refugees crowded into the West German embassy in Prague. Though the grounds of the Palais Lobkowicz were spacious, the unending arrival of East Germans created a humanitarian emergency since providing housing in tents, mass feeding, and sanitary facilities for several thousand escapees was beyond its capacity. East German efforts to persuade its fleeing citizens to return home by assuring them freedom from punishment failed to have any effect. Hence, the West German foreign minister Hans-Dietrich Genscher tried to persuade the GDR government to make a humanitarian gesture. Not wanting to let the celebrations for the fortieth anniversary of the GDR's founding be spoiled by the crisis, the chief of the Socialist Union Party of Germany (SED) Erich Honecker finally agreed to let the embassy occupants be taken by train to West Germany. On September 30, an elated Genscher announced this solution on the balcony of the embassy: "We have come to say to you . . ." The rest was drowned out by jubilation.[4]

This refugee drama signaled a loss of Communist control that ultimately led to the disintegration of the entire Soviet system. In many ways, the protests were a test of Mikhail Gorbachev's repudiation of the Brezhnev Doctrine, clothed in the appealing rhetoric of "a common European house." The rise of unauthorized mass movements in Poland, Hungary, and East Germany started a race between rising citizens' demands and reluctant party concessions that socialist reformers could not hope to win. The breaching of the Iron Curtain showed that, in the face of unrest, solidarity among members of the Warsaw Pact was crumbling since each country sought to make a separate arrangement with the West. A dramatic cascade of events, spilling over from one country to the next, first overthrew the satellite regimes in East Central Europe and then engulfed the Soviet Union itself.[5] The unprecedented downfall of the entire socialist system triggered a celebration of "people's power" that seemed to bode well for a return to democracy.

Communist Collapse

The East German mass exodus to the West suggested that the imposing edifice of Communist dictatorship in Eastern Europe had developed serious cracks. The normalization of rule after the failed uprisings of East Berlin in 1953, Budapest in 1956, and Prague in 1968 had rested on a tacit bargain between the populace and the party: The former would reluctantly tolerate the system as long as the latter provided an improved standard of living.[6] Due to the stagnation of the planned economy, the governments could not meet the expectations of their citizenry, especially when compared to the conspicuous consumption of capitalist states. Impressed by the cultural experimentation of the West, restive intellectuals also wanted more room for debate, inspiring some of them to become dissidents. "Real existing socialism" was therefore failing both the working class and the intelligentsia whose alliance was supposed to underpin the Communist experiment. Instead of waiting for an undefined future, discontented groups wanted to see changes now.

Even some members of the ruling communist parties were beginning to doubt whether their experiment in social engineering would succeed in the long run. Repeated Soviet military interventions in satellite states robbed the ideology of most of its ethical appeal since a progressive creed should not need tanks to convince its beneficiaries. Through Western travel, some of the leading cadres could also see with their own eyes that the Soviet Bloc was losing the economic competition, while the liveliness of public debate made socialist indoctrination seem paltry in comparison. The new Soviet leader Mikhail Gorbachev correctly understood that a restructuring of the economy demanded political openness, that *perestroika* needed *glasnost'*.[7] But the failure to contain previous reform efforts suggested that the challenge was how to let off some steam without having the entire pot blow away. Access to Western credits and technology required abandoning the Brezhnev Doctrine and allowing satellites to find their own way.

The downfall of Communism began in Poland, which had always been the "happiest barracks" in the Soviet Bloc. Due to centuries of partition, ordinary Poles hated the Russians almost as much as the

Germans. The hold of Catholicism over much of the populace also provided a barrier against indoctrination since the Polish pope John Paul
II offered moral support from the outside. Recurrent workers' strikes
culminated in the founding of an underground labor union that flatly
rejected the Polish Workers Party's claim to speak for the proletariat.
Inspired by Lech Wałęsa, the charismatic leader of the Gdańsk ship-
yards, millions of workers joined, calling for both higher wages and
more political freedom. The imposition of martial law in late 1981 merely
drove the movement underground, only to reemerge when the repression lifted in 1983. During Round Table negotiations in 1989, Solidarity
gained semi-free elections, which it swept on June 4, and installed a
non-Communist cabinet under Tadeusz Mazowiecki in September.[8]

The next domino to fall was Hungary, which had never completely
bought into the Soviet vision, allowing independent farms and small
businesses. As a German ally and Nazi collaborator until late 1944, Hungary had lost much of its territory, with one-quarter of its ethnic population residing in neighboring states. The Catholic Church also provided
some opposition since Cardinal József Mindszenty was a staunch op-
ponent of Communism. Moreover, the defeat of the 1956 uprising left
deep psychological scars that even the consumer-driven "goulash Communism" of János Kádár could not completely efface. During the 1980s,
an ecological dissident camp formed to oppose the building of a dam
across the Danube River. But in Budapest it was the Communist Party
itself that initiated a reform from above, permitting other parties to form
and restoring parliamentary government in 1988/89.[9] Since Hungary
shared a border with its former twin Austria, it was not surprising that
this was the place where the Iron Curtain tore apart.

Even more decisive was the destabilization of the GDR since it was
the cornerstone of the Soviet Empire in Eastern Europe. Having cost
Russia twenty-seven million dead, East Germany was a victory prize of
World War II and a bastion of the Red Army, which stationed around
450,000 soldiers there, the bulk of its forces in Central Europe. In the
competition with the West, the GDR was a showcase of the anti-fascist
East, claiming to be "a better Germany."[10] But the very existence of a
prosperous and free West Berlin, linked to the Federal Republic of

Germany (FRG), continued to present an alternative to the Soviet order, inducing around three million people to flee between 1949 and 1960. In August 1961, the SED leader Walter Ulbricht finally persuaded Moscow to stop the hemorrhaging of the population by building a concrete barrier, the infamous Berlin Wall, which cut off all escape routes to the West. In the short run, the Berlin Wall stabilized the GDR by suggesting that it was there to stay, but in the long run it produced continual escape attempts and tarnished the reputation of the Communist experiment.[11]

During September 1989, popular demands for free travel inspired increasing protests in the streets, calling for a real democratization of the GDR. Instead of demanding "We want to get out," other demonstrators who intended to reform their country intoned "We want to stay here." Sheltered by the Protestant Church, a peace movement had been slow to form since the Stasi, the infamous East German secret police, would simply ship dissidents like the singer Wolf Biermann to the West. Angered by the fraud of local elections, critics rallied at Monday night prayer vigils at the St. Nikolai Church in Leipzig. Daring to voice their opposition in public, protesters shouted "We are the people," thereby refuting the claim of the SED to represent the populace. On October 9, some seventy thousand demonstrators gathered in Leipzig, confronting the party with a dire choice: it could either suppress dissent with a bloodbath like the massacre on Tiananmen Square in China or allow freedom of speech.[12] Fortunately, nonviolence prevailed—but the recovery of human rights only increased the intensity of public protests.

A key opposition demand was the right of free travel to the West since it would allow families, torn apart by German division, to be reunited. With its conciliatory *Ostpolitik*, the FRG had long supported cross-border ties, but the GDR, afraid of losing its own people, only granted travel privileges to retirees and cadres who would return from such visits. Under pressure from the street, the SED tried to lift some restrictions in order to show its willingness to reform. But when the party spokesman Günter Schabowski was asked during a press conference on November 9 when such liberalization would start, he fumbled for a slip of paper and mumbled "immediately, right away." Western TV channels broadcast this sensational news, inspiring GDR citizens to mass at the border crossing points. Confronted with thousands of would-be travelers, Harald Jäger, the commander of the border guards at Bornholmer Brücke, decided not to resist and opened the gates.[13] The fall of the Berlin Wall not only removed a physical barrier but also sent a symbolic message that the Communist system was losing control.

The East German example inspired dissidents in other satellite states to demand the resignation of their governments since Gorbachev was apparently unwilling to intervene. Next in line was Czechoslovakia, which had never quite forgiven the suppression of the Prague Spring in 1968. Gathered in a group called Charta 77, dissident intellectuals pursued a form of "anti-politics," not directly threatening the hard-line regime of Gustáv Husák but trying to create a civil space in which they could "live in truth" within a repressive system. When the riot police repressed a student demonstration on November 17, its massive brutality had precisely the opposite effect: in the following days, up to half a million protesters gathered in Wenceslas Square in Prague and a general strike broke out, demanding the resignation of the government and the recovery of human rights. Within six weeks the mass protests forced the fall of the Communist system and a return to democracy. Ironically, by the end of the year the dissident playwright Václav Havel was elected the country's federal president.[14]

A little later, the tremors of the anti-Communist earthquake reached Bulgaria and overthrew its hard-line regime as well. After the fall of the Berlin Wall, the ruling party tried to head off protests by ousting the aged dictator Todor Zhivkov, but the change of personnel had as little effect as the change from Erich Honecker to Egon Krenz in East Berlin. Led by a pro-democracy movement, ecological protests in Sofia expanded into general calls for political reform. Responding to public pressure, the Communist Party relinquished its monopoly on power in February 1990. The first free elections in June were then won by the Bulgarian Socialist Party, composed of the more moderate segment of the Communists.[15] This peaceful repudiation of the Soviet model did bring Bulgaria into the Western orbit, but changing authoritarian habits and established power structures turned out to be quite difficult.

Only in Romania did the overthrow of Communism create bloodshed, though it is still not entirely clear what actually happened. In contrast to his deposed colleagues, the vicious dictator Nicolae Ceauşescu was not willing to resign. Riots broke out when the Securitate arrested a Hungarian Calvinist minister named László Tőkés on December 16. Seeking to reaffirm his hold on power, Ceauşescu held a mass rally in Bucharest but was shocked when the dissatisfied crowd openly booed him. As the protests spread across the entire country, the security forces tried to restore order by shooting demonstrators. Yet, on December 22, the Romanian military suddenly changed sides. When army tanks rumbled toward the Central Committee building, the dictator realized that his time was up and fled by helicopter into the mountains. However, on Christmas Day his opponents captured him, tried him on the spot, and executed him.[16] A National Salvation Front Council took over and scheduled elections, turning Romania into a titular democracy.

In retrospect, the rapidity and extent of the demise of Communism in East Central Europe from 1988 to 1990 remain astounding. The spread of protests recalls the Springtime of the Peoples in 1848, suggesting a process of contagion due to the structural similarity of problems and the role of the media in showing successful examples. But on closer inspection, each country pursued a somewhat different path in the system change.[17] In some places, like Hungary, the process resembled a collapse of self-assurance, in which leading Communists understood that reform was urgently needed. In other countries, like Poland, it was more a result of pressure from below because it was Solidarity's grassroots protest that compelled the regime change. Once again, Germany was a special case since the Eastern rejection of Communism led to reunification with the West. Most amazing was the nonviolent nature of the upheaval, which robbed the security forces of any pretext for using force.[18] Actually, all these elements worked together to spread popular unrest and make Communist rule collapse through demonstrations from below.

Remapping Europe

The democratization of the Soviet satellites in East Central Europe was only a first step in a much larger process of realignment that fundamentally changed the structure of the Continent. On the one hand, the reunification of East and West Germany in an enlarged Federal Republic restored a German nation-state, shifting the center of Europe to the East. Even in its reduced and chastened form, this new country revived the Bismarckian dilemma: Could a united and strengthened Germany fit into the Continent or would it try to dominate its neighbors? On the other hand, the dissolution of the Soviet Union itself liberated not just its former satellites but also many nationalities contained in the former Tsarist Empire. The independence of a whole belt of countries from the Baltic to the Black Sea revived a *Zwischeneuropa*, which had little experience in separate statehood and could only flourish when both Russia and Germany were weak.[19] The manifold implications of this remapping of Europe are still not completely understood.

German reunification was one of the surprising consequences of the peaceful revolution because it allowed the divided country to follow its desire for self-determination. Though the West Germans had lived well enough through their integration into Western Europe, their East German cousins chafed under Soviet control and sought prosperity as well as political freedom by joining the well-to-do and democratic Federal Republic. When he realized that Moscow might be willing to negotiate, Chancellor Helmut Kohl proposed a daring "Ten Point Plan" in November 1989 that outlined a progression from confederation to federation. Though angered by this surprising proposal, Margaret Thatcher, Mikhail Gorbachev, and François Mitterrand could find no way to shore up the tottering East German state and economy. The first free election of March 1990 rejected the Communists and disappointed the dissidents who had led the mass protests since three-quarters of the GDR citizens voted for parties favoring unification with the West.[20]

After this decisive mandate, the Two-Plus-Four negotiations between the World War II victors and the German states sought an

MAP 1. Post-Communist Europe, 1993. Cox Cartographic.

acceptable form for the unprecedented merger. Against the clamor of the refugee organizations, the West German government was forced to accept the loss of its former Eastern territories by recognizing the Polish frontier as legitimate. Due to the mediation of the American president George H. W. Bush and Secretary of State James Baker, Gorbachev realized that a united Germany would be a more secure partner, if it remained integrated in the EU and NATO than if it followed a neutralist course. Chancellor Kohl and Foreign Minister Genscher's offer of ample economic aid to the Soviet Union also helped persuade the hard-liners in Moscow to sign the Two-Plus-Four Treaty, which de jure recognized the boundary shifts of World War II.[21] At the same time, a customs union and a unification treaty regulated the domestic form of reunification that took place on October 3, 1990.

The evident weakening of Soviet power also inspired the small Baltic countries to reject Communism and campaign for independence. The former provinces of the Tsarist Empire of Lithuania, Latvia, and Estonia had only been independent in the interwar period until they were annexed by the Soviet Union in 1940. But Russification remained unsuccessful since they disliked Communism, did not speak Russian, and were mostly Catholic. Their citizens thought of themselves as Europeans like their Scandinavian neighbors. Encouraged by glasnost, nationalist feelings dared to come out into the open, calling for cultural autonomy and reasserting their sovereignty. In the early spring of 1990, all three countries declared their independence, insisting on free elections. When negotiations for a peaceful separation failed, the Soviets sent troops to Lithuania and Latvia, killing dozens of civilians. But during the collapse of the Soviet Union, Moscow recognized their separation and gradually withdrew its soldiers, setting the Baltic countries free.[22]

More problematic was the independence of Ukraine due to its language similarity to Russian and its centuries-long intertwining with Muscovite statehood. During the October revolution, various groups had striven for sovereignty but lost to the Bolsheviks, only to experience mass starvation in the *Holodomor* during the 1930s. In World War II, the Ukrainian lands became a battleground with the populace divided between Nazi auxiliaries, Communist ideologues, and nationalist fighters. After the war, Kiev enjoyed a quasi-independence to bolster the Soviet presence in the UN. In spite of these long-lasting ties, hundreds of thousands of Ukrainians demanded sovereignty in January 1990. In August 1991, the Communist government proclaimed that it would no longer follow the laws of the USSR, asserting its independence, which was approved by over 90 percent of the citizens in a referendum later that year. On December 8, Ukraine joined Russia and Belarus in formally dissolving the Soviet Union and setting out on an independent path.[23]

Despite having an even weaker national tradition, Belarus also managed to gain its independence during the general upheaval in the early 1990s. Closer in language and culture to Russia than even Ukraine, the Byelorussian Soviet Socialist Republic was a central constituent of the Soviet Union and the third quasi-independent country created to augment Soviet influence internationally, even if its borders and population had shifted several times during the twentieth century. During the Second World War, the Belarussians suffered greatly from Nazi ethnic cleansing and afterward were subjected to a rigorous policy of Sovietization by Stalin. Although the nationalist movement was weaker than elsewhere, the country also declared itself sovereign in July 1990. Since the Communist Party managed the campaign for independence, Belarus was the third signatory of the Belavezha Accord that dissolved the USSR and granted it formal sovereignty.[24] But the popular protests against the Lukashenko dictatorship show that the post-Communist transition remains incomplete.

More momentous yet was the collapse of the Soviet Union as a result of Gorbachev's effort to save Communism by reforming it. The appointment of the charismatic younger leader in 1985 was supposed to end the stagnation brought about by his older predecessors by revitalizing the economy. After the failure of his anti-alcohol campaign, the new secretary general set out to democratize the Communist Party through internal elections in 1987, creating a new Congress of Peoples' Deputies that would be chosen from among multiple candidates. But the introduction of market incentives failed to jump-start the economy and the opening of debate allowed separatism to emerge in the Baltics and the Caucasus region. Since the resistance of orthodox Communists in the apparatus hampered his "new thinking," Gorbachev was stranded between dismantling the Soviet corset and hopes for new freedoms. In the West, he was acclaimed as a "hero of retreat," but in Moscow he was identified with defeat and forced to resign late in 1991.[25]

Ironically, it was the Russian Republic under Boris Yeltsin that ultimately buried the Soviet Union, considering it incapable of reform. The rival leader, a hard-drinking bear of a man, was the mayor of Moscow and had resigned from the Politburo due to the slow pace of change, which made him popular as a resolute reformer. As a result, he was elected leader of the Russian Soviet Federative Socialist Republic, and declared its sovereignty just like the other member republics. Frustrated with traditionalist foot-dragging, he left the Communist Party in 1990 and began pushing for full independence. But in August 1991 a group of hard-liners, supported by elements of the military, staged a coup, claiming to save the Soviet Union. Immediately, Yeltsin rushed to the Kremlin and on top of a tank appealed to the populace to defend the reforms. When the putsch collapsed, the Soviet Union dissolved itself in the Alma Ata Protocol in December 1991. Only its core survived into a post-Communist era as the Commonwealth of Independent States (CIS).[26]

In retrospect, a whole host of international and internal factors was responsible for the collapse of Communism in Eastern Europe. One problem was "imperial overstretch," which extended Soviet control beyond the available resource since Moscow had to support its client regimes rather than exploiting them as it had done in the beginning. To some degree, it was also the nuclear arms race since the enormous military expenditures detracted from the development of a civilian sector of consumer goods capable of competing with Western products. Another handicap was the inherent limitation of the planned economy that functioned well enough in big projects but distorted the allocation of resources through its politically determined price structure that ignored production costs and privileged quantity over quality. At the same time, socialist internationalism had suppressed the powerful emotion of nationalism by reducing it to folkloristic irrelevance. Finally, political repression prevented open debate to correct mistakes and stifled cultural innovation.[27]

The attraction of the Western way of life also contributed to a growing disenchantment with Communist promises of an egalitarian society. Early in the Cold War, West German leaders had formulated a "magnet theory" that emphasized the attractiveness of liberal democracy and a social market economy in contrast to the dictatorship of the proletariat. The conciliatory character of Social Democratic *Ostpolitik* also undercut Communist accusations of German revisionism since partners in material trade and cultural exchange could no longer be irreconcilable foes.

The blandishments of Western consumer society with its glitzy advertising, innovative products, and fancy automobiles also exerted a considerable pull on Eastern consumers faced with drab offerings. Finally, intellectuals admired the openness of debate, which allowed daring experimentation. Though Communist propaganda harped on capitalist shortcomings such as labor exploitation, many Eastern Europeans were willing to risk their social supports for a Western lifestyle.[28]

The downfall of Communism initiated an enormously important reconfiguration of Europe whose implications are still being worked out. The upheaval of 1989 to 1991 ended seven decades of ideological competition between the liberal capitalist and dictatorial Communist blueprints for modernity, thereby concluding the Cold War. International approval for the reemergence of a reduced German state finally produced a peace treaty for World War II and restored the FRG to a key position as a bridge between East and West. The reemergence of a belt of independent countries in East Central Europe dissolved the Soviet Empire, enabled them to follow their national destinies, and opened the door for some to return to Western Europe. Finally, the disintegration of the Soviet Union freed Russia from its ideological constraints and imperial ballast, giving it a chance to obtain prosperity and enjoy freedom.[29] For the concerned region, the extent of the caesura rivals 1945—only without having required yet another world war.

Post-Communist Hopes

In Eastern Europe the overthrow of Communism created a widespread euphoria since the victory of the people over the party suggested all sorts of new possibilities. During the improbable fall of the Berlin Wall, the amazed crowds kept saying *Wahnsinn*!!!—literally meaning this must be "madness." Symbolized by the solidity of the barrier dividing Berlin, the Soviet system had seemed so massive as "to continue to exist for another 50 or 100 years, as long as the reasons for it are not removed." Or as the dictator Erich Honecker had rhymed: "Neither ox nor ass will stop socialism's pass."[30] It was all the more incredible that a system with a disciplined party, a well-trained military, and a vaunted secret police could be overthrown by its own citizens. No doubt, Western propaganda and subversion also played some role, but their effect was rather minor compared to the challenge from below. Even in Frank Räthel's later recollection, such a "nonviolent change of systems" seemed to many participants like a veritable "miracle."[31]

To the many victims of Communist dictatorship, the peaceful revolution offered a chance to resume their normal lives and seek justice. The opening of the gates of infamous prisons like the "Red Ox" in Bautzen meant quite literally freedom from further years of ideological reeducation or arbitrary incarceration. Dissident intellectuals like Adam Michnik in Poland, Jiří Dienstbier in Czechoslovakia, or Jens Reich in East Germany were overjoyed by the prospect of no longer being hounded by the secret service or betrayed by their friends. Critical journalists could now report on the crimes committed in the name of socialism and expose the scandalous lifestyle of the elite cadres who claimed to be serving an egalitarian ideal. Moreover, they could also demand some form of public rehabilitation for false accusations or material restitution for their suffering. Ironically, the human rights commitment of dissidents like Václav Havel now gave them credibility for leadership positions in the post-Communist era.[32]

The population at large was more excited by the new possibilities for consumption and travel that had long been denied them. Free access to foreign money opened up a fantasy world that had only existed in hard-currency stores like Intershop for those fortunate enough to possess that magic means of payment. Almost immediately, Western goods flooded Eastern stores, displacing locally made products and imperiling manufacturing jobs in the rush to satisfy long-suppressed consumer desires. Similarly, a spontaneous travel boom developed toward destinations of desire like London, Paris, or Rome, that had only been known through Western magazines or television shows. At long last, apolitical citizens like the physician Klaus Hübschmann could live the glamorous Western life—if they could acquire the necessary money to afford it. But for many ordinary people, the overthrow of Communism created great uncertainty because it required them to reorient their entire daily life, from schools to jobs.[33]

Many displaced ideologues and apparatchiks of the former Communist system were, however, disappointed with losing their cause and privileges. Naturally, Marxist intellectuals like the GDR philosopher Alfred Kosing were shocked that their ideological promise turned out to be illusory and the Western class enemy had prevailed. Nomenklatura members who did not succeed in privatization were also angry about the loss of their power and hard-earned privileges, having to subsist on meager pensions in a capitalist world. In veteran groups, they sought explanations for feeling cheated by history, either blaming socialist ideology as such or at least its faulty implementation, only disagreeing about whether the problem lay already with Lenin or later on with Stalin. Unwilling to abandon a creed to which they had dedicated their lives, Marxists clung to the hope that it would have another chance sometime in the future.[34] Noting the globalization problems of the West with glee, they predicted that it would soon collapse as well.

As less directly affected bystanders, Western Europeans watched the overthrow of Communism with amazement and incredulity. Commentators like Theo Sommer were gratified that the fall of the Berlin Wall validated their own system but disagreed about who deserved credit for it. While the Right emphasized the firmness of its anti-Communism and the costs of the arms race, the Left instead stressed the role of détente in creating a nonthreatening climate that allowed mass protests to form. Emigrants like the Latvian Valters Nollendorfs returned to their former homes while some Western idealists tried to help with the difficulties of the transition. Attracted by the possibilities of the "Wild East," a number of opportunists rushed eastward to make their fortune as well. Only gradually did it become clear that the post-Communist transformation would also be an expensive proposition for the West because it demanded large financial transfers.[35] Despite their initially only indirect involvement, Western Europeans slowly reforged a relationship with their cousins in the East.

In Washington the overthrow of Communism sparked a wave of "Cold War triumphalism," asserting that the United States had decisively won the ideological contest. Especially neoconservatives attributed the downfall of their primary antagonist to President Ronald

Reagan's general military buildup and the particular pursuit of "Star Wars" capability. But even most of the Left saw the dissolution of the Soviet Union and the retreat of Russia as a vindication of the American combination of capitalism and democracy. Summing up the consensus of the political class, President George W. Bush declared in 2002: "The great struggles of the twentieth century between liberty and totalitarianism ended with a decisive victory for the forces of freedom—and a single sustainable model for national success: freedom, democracy, and free enterprise." The problem with this reading of the ending of the Cold War was that it encouraged a simplistic view of history that reinforced the hubris of US decision makers.[36]

Political commentators in the United States like Francis Fukuyama celebrated "the universalization of Western liberal democracy as the final form of human government." The 1990 report of Freedom House was delighted with the spread of democracy: "The most significant advances in freedom occurred in the Soviet Union and Eastern Europe." International observers were impressed by the revival of civil society that reclaimed self-government through the foundation of opposition groups like Solidarność or the Neues Forum and mass demonstrations from below.[37] They were pleased that the existence of the shell of democratic institutions facilitated the transition since the Round Table agreement on "free elections" could be used to pass power from Communist dictatorship to popular control. But Washington underestimated the difficulties of establishing new constitutional structures in order to guarantee self-government as well as the challenge of learning a democratic culture of public life during a difficult moment of transition.[38]

In Russia reactions were rather mixed, welcoming some of the changes as liberating but seeing others as threatening losses. No doubt, reformers like Boris Yeltsin were overjoyed at having the leaden weight of the bureaucracy lifted somewhat and the priority of military expenditures questioned at last. Moreover, clever businessmen quickly figured out how to use the privatization of state resources as a foundation for amassing huge fortunes, creating a new class of plutocratic oligarchs, often above the law. Dissidents were glad to have their criticism of the repressiveness of the Communist dictatorship validated by the opening of secret government files that seemed to prove many of their worst allegations. Moreover, civil society groups like Memorial could explore the full extent of Stalinist crimes at last. Finally, the Orthodox Church was able to resume its place as the official Russian religion.[39] It is often forgotten that a considerable number of citizens initially supported the liberalization of the country as long overdue.

But when the reforms produced chaotic effects, more and more Russians looked for a restoration of order under an authoritarian post-Communism of the kind offered by Vladimir Putin. Inspired by the Washington Consensus, the radical destruction of the planned economy and shift to market competition raised prices without increasing wages, hitting state employees and pensioners especially hard. Unused to coping with the uncertainty of the new freedom, many people blamed neoliberal reforms for their problems. Nationalists and the military deplored the loss of the empire as unnecessary and were convinced that the use of force like in China would have nipped the unrest in the bud. Quite a few Russians who had migrated into outlying provinces now found themselves as an ethnic minority in newly independent states like Estonia or Moldova, calling for protection from Moscow. Finally, the oblast Kaliningrad became an isolated Russian enclave in the Baltics. All these people saw the dissolution of the USSR as a personal disaster.[40]

Surprisingly enough, many Eastern European dissidents also fell into a kind of *tristesse*, refusing to use the very term "revolution" for their achievement. For years, system critics had worked in small opposition groups, often penetrated by the secret service which complicated their struggle with disinformation. When their demonstrations suddenly caught on with thousands of protesters, they found themselves in the spotlight, and their organizations like the Neues Forum gathered innumerable signatures. Moreover, in the Round Table negotiations with the government, they were able to advocate a Third Way, a democratized version of socialism that was neither capitalist nor Communist. But with the reemergence of electoral politics, they were caught between the more resolute economic reformers and the defenders of the socialist welfare state. The East German dissident Bärbel Bohley formulated her disappointment in the classic phrase: "We longed for justice, but got only the rule of law." Many activists therefore faded away into obscurity.[41]

According to the psychologist Hans-Joachim Maaz, the overthrow of Communism unleashed a torrent of emotions, previously penned up, because their realization seemed unlikely. The mass demonstrations created a heady sense of popular empowerment when they not only toppled hated dictators but repudiated the entire "dictatorship of the proletariat" and forced the occupying Russians to withdraw their troops. For dissidents, freedom promised self-determination in their domestic affairs and a return of national independence on the international stage. For ordinary people, the revolution offered a gateway to a better life, defined as Western prosperity, enabling them to participate more fully in consumer society and popular culture. After decades of Cold War stagnation, the dramatic events of 1989/91 gave long-suppressed people a chance for making Europe "whole and free," in President Bush's felicitous phrase.[42] But such high expectations were hard to sustain when faced with the problems of the post-Communist transition.

Nonviolent Revolution

Three decades later, the momentous character of the events during 1989 to 1991 is becoming even clearer than when they occurred. The downfall of Communism in Europe was simply the most important caesura after the end of the Second World War since it ended the Cold War and liberated Eastern Europe from Soviet control.[43] On closer inspection, it was both a collapse from above and an overthrow from below because without the weakening of party resolve and the courage of dissidents, the popular contestation could not have succeeded. Especially astounding was the generally peaceful nature of the system's change, which at other times would have required a major war. A rather improbable constellation brought Communism to its knees: An international climate of détente encouraged attempts at party reform that allowed dissidents to demand human rights and ordinary people to flee for a better life. Since both sides were willing to talk, the result was a "negotiated" or "pacted revolution" that allowed a return to democracy.[44]

In spite of the nonviolent transfer of power, the Eastern European upheaval was a real revolution that overturned politics, economics, society, and culture. The French and Soviet revolutions were rather bloodier, but they were merely the most radical variant of a system change. According to Jack Goldstone, the "color revolutions" in Eastern Europe "unfolded as a series of moderate confrontations between crowds engaged in peaceful demonstrations and powerful authoritarian states that lost confidence to defend themselves. The latter conceded power to the opposition or negotiated a change of regime." In this definition, the Eastern European upheavals qualify as revolutions since they fundamentally changed the political system, replaced planning with a market economy, restratified society, and ended cultural censorship.[45] Even if the transition was negotiated, these changes were revolutionary indeed.

A key to the success of the protest movement was its nonviolent character, which also encouraged the Communist Party to refrain from using force. Both sides wanted to avoid a repetition of the enormous carnage of the Second World War, while the nuclear stalemate made a great power conflict between the United States and the USSR impractical. The bloodshed of the Chinese repression of rebellious students at Tiananmen Square also had a deterrent effect since the Eastern European governments did not want to risk international opprobrium. Though increasingly numerous, the opposition did not possess any weapons to challenge the extensively armed security services and was therefore reduced to using moral arguments and political persuasion to make its case. The Round Table successfully mediated between the two sides since the government had power without legitimacy and the protesters had legitimacy but lacked power. Free elections were therefore an ideal way to resolve the stalemate and legitimately transfer power.[46]

The medium of television also played a crucial role in the new style of nonviolent revolution since it inspired followers by spreading emotional images of exodus and protest. The effort of the East German *Aktuelle Kamera* to belittle escapees as "organized human trafficking" discredited itself since it was contradicted by actual experience. In contrast, the West German *Tagesschau* and *Heute-Nachrichten* succeeded in capturing the human drama as well as the political implications of the mass exodus. Images of desperate flight, joy of escape, and warm welcome radiated strong emotional power even to viewers far away. Seeing young families, crying children, and even older people joining a stream of refugees helped delegitimize the East German "welfare dictatorship." Pictures of peacefully protesting citizens also inhibited the GDR and Soviet Union from using force and compelled negotiations about grievances instead. It was clear that with such emotional images of flight and protest "a new and irreversible development" had begun that was to dissolve the Soviet Bloc.[47]

In spite of its inspiring character, the overthrow of Communism was but an indifferent guide to other mass mobilizations that aimed at regime change. In truth, subsequent efforts had some similar characteristics: many protesters were aroused through electronic media that circumvented government control, just as the West German TV channels and Radio Free Europe had done in Central Europe. Many demonstrators were also young people, thirsting for freedom and willing to risk their lives for a better future. But like in the case of Nelson Mandela's release in South Africa, everything depended on the response of the authorities. If they were willing to use brutal force, they could usually drown the protests in a sea of blood, but if both sides found a way to peaceful transition, the revolution would succeed.[48] The Arab Spring started with similar high hopes, especially in Egypt, only to succumb to violence. The failure of other civil contestations underlines the uniqueness of the peaceful revolution's success.

2

Post-Communist Transformation

FIGURE 3. Stary Browar shopping center, Poznań, Poland. Lucas Vallecillos /
Alamy Stock Photo.

After years of preparation, the Stary Browar shopping center finally
opened on November 15, 2004, in Poznań, an economic and administrative hub in Western Poland. Reconstruction of a huge brewery complex
built in 1874 had converted its traditional redbrick facades and industrial
interiors into a glass, steel, and concrete assembly of one hundred small

shops, offices, and apartments. Designed by the fashion-conscious lawyer Grażyna Kulczyk, the dazzling complex combined commerce with culture, sponsoring art objects, concerts, and theater productions. Already during her studies, she had drifted into the art scene and eventually become a patron of experimental artists, helping reconnect creative spirits in Poland with the outside world. In 2005 she sold the prize-winning ensemble to a German investment group for 290 million euros.[1] With its upscale shops and artistic flair, the Stary Browar became a showcase of the new cosmopolitan, consumer Poland.

The capital for this venture came from her husband Jan Kulczyk, one of the most successful businessmen to profit from the overthrow of Communism. Born in 1950 in Bydgoszcz, he had studied international law in Poznań and written his dissertation on the Basic Treaty between the FRG and the GDR. During martial law, he founded an import-export business with the help of his father who lived in West Berlin, becoming a "capitalist within Communism" by providing scarce consumer goods. As the general representative of VW in Poland, he benefited from the privatization of state enterprises after 1991 by having his company sell public assets like the national telephone company to the West. The secret of his success in the unregulated transition was access to politicians, which gave his deals a "somewhat shady aura." Diversifying from cars into oil, brewing, communications, and chemicals, he became one of the richest oligarchs before his death in 2015, amassing a fortune of about $4 billion.[2]

The precondition for the Polish revival was the open admission of the failure of socialism and its party nomenklatura. Considerable segments of society attached to the Catholic Church, the working class, and intellectuals had never liked Communism in the first place. But it took the economic bankruptcy of socialist reform efforts and the resentment against the imposition of "martial law" to turn the majority against it. According to Adam Michnik, "Nothing can be done to revive a system that promised a glorious future [but] brought terror and poverty, lies and depravity, a system that stripped people of their national culture and violated human conscience." Fortunately, the opposition, led by Solidarity, and the discredited government were willing to negotiate a nonviolent transfer of power toward parliamentary democracy in the Round Table to inaugurate the transition. The political challenge for the post-Communist government in June 1989 was to "construct an institutional order based on the ideas of dialogue and compromise."[3]

The unprecedented task of transforming a Communist economy posed a difficult choice: Should the Mazowiecki government engage in "shock therapy" as advocated by Western neoliberals or proceed more gradually as proposed by Social Democrats? The appointment of Leszek Balcerowicz as deputy prime minister suggested that the post-Communist cabinet was ready to authorize a rapid and thorough marketization, in the hope that such a "big bang" would liberate competitive energies. But other leading Polish economists preferred "a far more gradual pace of reform" and cautioned that the human price to be paid for such a rigorous transformation in terms of lower wages and unemployment would be too high. If the populace found its hopes for access to a capitalist consumer economy disappointed, it might turn against the entire project of democratization as well. Only time would tell whether freeing the energies of the market or the "deeply rooted respect for social responsibility" would be the correct course.[4]

The transformation of Eastern Europe therefore became a battleground for contending approaches to the economy, providing test cases for their respective approaches. Both political and economic aspects were intertwined since the failure of the planned economy had undercut socialism, while the success of democratization also depended on the performance of consumer society. Since the stagflation of the 1970s had discredited post-Keynesianism in the West, neoliberal approaches dominated advisers from Reagan's United States, Thatcher's UK, and Kohl's FRG. But the Scandinavian countries and the labor movement were still defending an enabling version of the welfare state that appealed to Eastern intellectuals who feared the destructiveness of unfettered markets. Instead of demanding instant privatization of state enterprises, their watchword was "industrial policy" to help ailing companies meet global competition.[5] The post-Communist transformation therefore became a real live experiment in opposing political beliefs.

A Polish Miracle

The starting position of liberated Poland in 1945 could hardly have been worse. The ruthless fighting between the Wehrmacht and the Red Army had devastated its industry, infrastructure, and housing, reducing the center of Warsaw to an enormous pile of rubble. Over one-quarter of the population had been killed in the Second World War and the Holocaust, reducing its number to about twenty-three million. Agreed to between Stalin and Churchill, the westward shift of the country's boundaries by about 150 miles lost ancient Polish territories in the East and gained German provinces in the West that needed to be purged of their historic inhabitants and resettled with displaced Poles. Moreover, the Soviet Union refused to recognize the legitimate Sikorski government in London, installing instead its own puppet regime in Lublin, controlled by the Polish United Workers' Party (PZPR). While Polish patriots were glad that the country had survived and become ethnically more homogeneous, the challenge of rebuilding was daunting.[6]

The consolidation of socialism in Poland was never complete since it was largely imposed from the outside by the victorious Soviet Union. Moreover, the stationing of Red Army troops gave it a Stalinist form that repressed national independence and domestic freedom. The rebuilding emphasized heavy industry with large nationalized enterprises, although collectivization of agriculture stalled and small businesses with fewer than five employees survived. Since economic planning failed to raise the living standards quickly enough, workers and students periodically rebelled in 1956, 1966–68, 1970–71, and 1975–76, demanding more consumer goods and freedom of debate.[7] Even the changes of leadership from Władysław Gomułka to Bolesław Bierut, and once again from Gomułka to Edward Gierek could not find the right reform formula in order to revitalize production. Instead, Poland became ever more dependent on Western loans to improve living standards, trapping itself in a cycle of increasing foreign debt.

The economic crisis of 1979–81 grew so acute as to trigger the creation of a mass opposition movement, called Solidarity. Rising inflation and declining consumption seemed to prove critics in the democratic underground and the Catholic Church right that socialism was a hopeless project. Finally, the Gdańsk shipyard workers, led by the charismatic electrician Lech Wałęsa, launched a strike and founded Solidarność, an independent trade union that rejected the Communist claim of serving the proletariat. With surprising speed, this broad coalition of disgruntled workers, intellectuals, Catholics, and farmers attracted almost ten million members in a grassroots form of "people's self-organization."[8] To forestall Soviet intervention, the Polish military under General Wojciech Jaruzelski ultimately declared martial law in 1981 but was unable to quell the popular unrest. After half a decade of stalemate, the regime in Round Table talks finally agreed to semi-free elections, which precipitated the end of Communist rule in 1989.

The first task of the new Mazowiecki government was to reestablish democratic institutions in order to revive self-government. The leading role of the Communist Party had to be eliminated and the country renamed as the "Republic of Poland." When the PZPR dissolved itself, new parties had to be founded. At the same time, civil rights had to be restored and legal rules for the transformation of the economy established. The first truly free election in 1990 was swept by Solidarity, but the broad opposition coalition dissolved thereafter into competing ideological camps. In December 1990, the symbolic head of the opposition movement Lech Wałęsa was elected president. While there was general agreement on the need to end all vestiges of dictatorship, the precise form of a post-Communist governance brought heated disputes between the successor party of the PZPR and the former opposition. Due to a splintering party system and low election turnout, the initial cabinets proved rather unstable.[9] The road to democracy turned out to be more complicated than had been imagined.

The second challenge was the transformation of the economy in order to break the cycle of reforms and crises that had brought socialism to its knees. A circle of Warsaw economists around Leszek Balcerowicz had already developed a neoliberal plan that seized the opportunity for radical marketization, popularly called shock therapy. Hence, in October 1989, the government began to dismantle socialist structures such as the planning apparatus, the privileged position of state-owned enterprises, the priority of state investment, and so on. At the same time, the Balcerowicz group sought to encourage the return of competition with actual cost pricing, currency interchangeability, and foreign direct investment so as to liberate market energies. During this dramatic changeover, the government also had to keep inflation in check and manage day-to-day expenses. Since the so-called Washington Consensus supported these neoliberal measures, foreign governments helped by restructuring and writing off parts of Poland's debt.[10]

The rapidity of change made the transition more destructive than creative, disappointing hopes for instant growth through marketization. Initially, the collapse of the socialist order produced chaos because the planning rules no longer applied, and new market mechanisms were not yet in place. Since many of the goods that had been produced to serve the Council for Mutual Economic Assistance (COMECON) neighbors were no longer competitive on the world market, industrial production fell by a shocking one-third. As a result, the GDP contracted by one-fifth and wages also dropped by 20 percent, stifling domestic consumption. With some state enterprises going bankrupt and businesses shedding superfluous employees, unemployment, previously hidden in overstaffed companies, started to rise, reaching 16.4 percent in 1993. Falling tax revenues forced cuts in social expenditures by one-quarter, just when transfer payments were most needed to help the displaced.[11] No wonder that the advent of capitalism seemed to confirm the worst socialist fears.

By 1992 the first signs of improvement had appeared and gathered so much steam that the Polish economy grew by an average of about 5 percent for the rest of the decade. Fiscal discipline gradually brought runaway inflation that had reached 585 percent in 1990 under control. The privatization of the large state-owned enterprises continued to lag and the small-scale structure of self-sufficient agriculture remained a barrier to growth. But the private sector expanded dramatically with 1.5 million new small businesses being founded during the first years. After the stabilization of the legal framework, foreign direct investment also started to pour in, taking advantage of lower wages in the East and trying to serve Poland's sizable market of about forty million customers.

Finally, credits by the International Monetary Fund (IMF) and the EU, inspired by an association agreement, also helped provide venture capital for new factories.[12] As a result, wages began to recover, domestic consumption increased steadily, and the gamble on a harsh transition appeared to pay off.

The turnaround was based on a surprising transformation of economic culture. Traditionally, Poland had been considered a problem country, full of crises and shortages. With marketization, a new group of entrepreneurs arose who were willing to use the novel freedom to expand their small businesses into midsize companies. Taking advantage of prior barter experience, these businesspeople opened their own stores, traded with each other, and founded transportation companies, supplying those consumer goods that had previously been out of reach. At the same time, Polish workers who had often procrastinated as a form of protest against foreign owners, now began to work with a will since they were trying to share in the rewards of the market. One of the new entrepreneurs told a Western journalist that Poland lacked resources, "but we have good labor. My men work hard for their money" in contrast to Western workers who "are a little bit spoiled."[13] Polish plumbers now became synonymous with diligent laborers.

The strains of the economic transition complicated the political consolidation of Poland since the electorate wavered between wanting a hard or soft transformation. In 1990 the first president to be elected was the popular Solidarity leader Lech Wałęsa, but the cabinets continued to be short-lived. By 1995 criticism of shock therapy had elevated the former Communist Aleksander Kwaśniewski to the presidency, and all parties agreed on the 1997 constitution, which defined Poland as a civic nation. In 2005 the conservative nationalists of the Law and Justice Party (PiS) succeeded in making Lech Kaczyński head of state, though his tenure was overshadowed by the airplane crash that killed him and other government members on their way to the memorial commemorating the Katyn massacre. The moderate pro-Western leader Donald Tusk was the first prime minister to be reelected, serving from 2007 to 2014. But in 2015 PiS succeeded in making Andrzej Duda president.[14] Since then, the Law and Justice Party has controlled the government with an authoritarian mixture of nationalist appeals and social support programs.

The results seemed to bear out the advocates of a harsh return to the market since Poland was spectacularly successful according to virtually all economic indicators. For instance, its GDP more than quadrupled from $250.4 billion to $1,121.0 billion between 1990 and 2017. At the same time, the GDP per person increased 4.5 times, rising from $6,557 to $29,521. Since 1992 the GDP has grown steadily, even avoiding the dot .com and financial crisis recessions of 2000 and 2008 that stalled growth in most other Eastern European countries. The initial runaway inflation was reduced to around 2 percent per annum and government debt hovered around 50 percent of GDP, a thoroughly respectable figure. No wonder that the Polish case has become a poster child of neoliberal advocates. Balcerowicz, the author of many measures, therefore claims "the larger the scope of market-oriented reforms, the better the performance in terms of growth, low inflation and environmental improvement."[15]

Critics nonetheless deplored the human cost of the rapid transformation, which created much resentment against the new order. Unemployment rose to around 20 percent for half a decade around the turn of the century and once again topped 10 percent after the Great Recession. The lack of job opportunities at home pushed about two million well-trained Polish workers into emigration, over half of them to the UK where their future remains uncertain due to the restrictions imposed by Brexit. Moreover, the rise of a new class of entrepreneurs and the poverty of the elderly have increased the Gini coefficient to 0.308, making Poland one of the most unequal countries in Europe. No wonder that some Solidarity intellectuals, like the economist Tadeusz Kowalik, see the transformation as a lost opportunity. He claims that "the failures of the Communist Party, combined with the power of the Catholic Church and interference from the United States, have subverted efforts to build a cooperative and democratic economic order in the 1990s."[16]

Patterns of Transition

Compared to the Polish miracle, most other Eastern European countries had greater difficulties in transforming themselves into capitalist democracies. Some social science theoreticians have attributed the differences to the "dilemma of simultaneity," arguing that the triple transition from dictatorship to democracy, planned economy to market competition, and Soviet domination to national independence created an overwhelming challenge for the people involved. Fundamental changes in one area inevitably had consequences in another, destabilizing institutions and creating negative feedback loops. Others have instead emphasized the path dependency of different levels of modernity, with varying traditions of governance and contrasting degrees of outside help as decisive factors. The actual pattern of post-Communist transformation reveals considerable differences of consolidation, with outcomes ranging all the way from a rapid turnaround to gradual accommodation, with other countries lagging behind and some outright failures.[17]

The hardest transition occurred in East Germany, which was both privileged and problematic, since it took the form of unification with the FRG, a successful Western state. The fall of the Berlin Wall in November 1989 shifted public sentiment from reforming a Communist GDR to unification with the prosperous Federal Republic. The first free election, agreed to during Round Table negotiations, yielded a three-quarter vote against a "third way" and for unification as a shortcut to political freedom and economic prosperity. This mandate for self-determination convinced even skeptics among the four World War II victors, letting them only determine the outside borders and military alliance of a reunited Germany. The domestic accession of the bankrupt GDR to the FRG took the form of a voluminous "unification treaty" that regulated the transfer of Western institutions to the new federal states.[18] On October 3, 1990, East Germans entered a parliamentary democracy but still had to learn how to become self-governing citizens.

The economic results of German unification turned out to be rather disappointing for East Germans who compared themselves with the West, not with other Eastern European states. Since the GDR economy was in bad shape, attaining only one-third of the productivity of the FRG per capita, no spontaneous miracle occurred as Chancellor Kohl had promised. Due to consumption pressure by the Eastern electorate, the exchange rate of the Ostmark for the hard Western DM was too generous at around 1:1.5, exceeding the real buying power that was closer to 1:4.4. Eager to expand eastward, the Western trade unions set wages too high at about two-thirds of the FRG level, making Eastern products too expensive. At the same time, the COMECON trade collapsed. Instead of yielding a public windfall, privatization via the Trusteeship Agency proved rather costly. As a result, many companies went bankrupt and about one-third of the jobs were lost. Only enormous transfer payments from the West repaired the infrastructure and kept social peace.[19]

Another example of shock therapy was the economic transition in the Baltic countries, which was closely tied to nation-state building and democratization. Mass protests against Soviet occupation and ethnic Russification finally succeeded in the recovery of independence in 1991. All three countries quickly adopted democratic institutions and attempted a cultural renationalization, discriminating against a large Russian minority. Following the advice of the IMF and World Bank, they also pursued a rapid marketization, in part to dismantle their large Soviet-style industry. As a result, GDP fell precipitously, by 45 percent in Estonia, 56 percent in Latvia, and 71 percent in Lithuania, accompanied by high inflation! The ensuing collapse of the state budget also meant a severe reduction of social services, hitting the elderly and rural population hard. In the Western-style cities, youthful elites prospered, but rural areas that started out at a lower level had further to go.[20] This pattern was also repeated in Slovakia and Slovenia but with more success.

Among a second group that took a more gradual approach, the Czech Republic was the most successful in spite of its "Velvet Divorce" from Slovakia in 1993. Less destroyed in the Second World War, the country had one of the highest standards of living in the Soviet Bloc due to its well-developed industrial base. Led by dissidents like Václav Havel, the transition to democracy also went smoothly, drawing on the nation's interwar experience of self-government. Prime Minister Václav Klaus followed a neoliberal agenda that centered "on reduced taxes, completing the privatization of banks, utilities and the railways, trimming payments for welfare and subsidies for university education" in order to complete the transition to a free-market economy. But a strong Social Democratic Party led by Miloš Zeman insisted on the preservation of the welfare state. Attracting the most foreign investment in the former Eastern Bloc, including Volkswagen's takeover of Škoda, the Czech

GNP dropped less initially and continued to grow moderately, with low unemployment and balanced budgets.[21]

Hungary had similarly favorable starting conditions, but the initial hesitation to inflict economic pain unnecessarily protracted the transformation process. Democracy had a harder time taking root since the interwar tradition was authoritarian and irredentist. But during the 1980s Hungary was ahead of the other Eastern countries in decentralizing the economy, allowing small businesses, independent farms, and trade with the West. Ironically, this head start made the public less willing to accept radical reform measures until they became inevitable in the second half of the 1990s. The country did receive the second highest foreign investment in the post-Communist East, mostly in the automotive sector—for instance, from companies like Audi—but privatization dragged on and relatively high wages did not help. As a result, Hungary remained vulnerable to international economic crises and the electorate failed to take pride in relative progress, instead supporting a resentful, xenophobic, and illiberal Viktor Orbán government.[22]

A third cluster of countries, such as Bulgaria and Romania, lagged behind and reached disappointing results in the post-Communist transformation. To begin with, these states had few democratic traditions, being used to right- or left-wing forms of autocratic governments. Their economies were also less developed, still maintaining a bigger agricultural sector and containing more socialist large-scale companies, resulting in a smaller degree of private business. Moreover, they were less open to trade with the West. In most of these countries, the old nomenklatura controlled the privatization process, taking over the ailing state-owned enterprises and thereby preserving its elite status. Though sometimes using neoliberal rhetoric, such post-Communist parties competed mainly in order to capture their states for the sake of rent-seeking, trying to use public institutions for private gain and corrupting state administration. As a result, economic growth was slower and GNP per person only half of that of the transition leaders.[23]

The transformation of Russia was even more disappointing because the collapse of the Soviet system was deeper than expected and the recovery delayed. Since the population lacked experience in self-government and market competition, Gorbachev's reform efforts led to the dissolution of the Soviet Union. But urged by the Washington Consensus of neoliberal economists, Boris Yeltsin's shock therapy cut the GDP almost in half, drastically reducing incomes and living standards. Only under Putin's authoritarian restoration of state structures did the economy recover, reaching its prior level in 2007, having lost over a decade of potential development. The key problem was the corrupt privatization that allowed Soviet managers to take ownership of firms, thereby creating an entire new class of oligarchs and making Russia a rather unequal country. As a result of such crony capitalism, the Russian economy continued to rely on the export of natural resources like oil and gas, taking pride only in its innovative defense sector.[24]

A final group of countries, located at the Russian borders, seems to have largely failed in the triple transition to democracy, capitalism, and nation-state. Still within Russia's orbit, Belarus has remained a dictatorship under Alexander Lukashenko that has continued Soviet-style control in spite of mass protests and merely developed a weak national identity. Similarly, Moldova has stayed quasi-Communist and poor, beset by ethnic Russian secessionism in Transnistria.[25] Internally split, Ukraine has vacillated between Russia and the West, seeing its economy largely collapse despite Western aid. While the Orange Revolution flashed a beacon of democratic hope, the corruption of politics and economics hindered stabilization and progress. Moreover, Russian expansionism, initiated by Putin's annexation of Crimea, inspired a struggle over the secession of eastern coal-rich provinces, thus imposing enormous strains on Kiev's budget and economy.[26] These countries bordering on Russia suffer from their Soviet heritage, and Moscow's economic dominance and political interference.

The most catastrophic transition took place in the former Yugoslavia, which dissolved in successive wars that left a legacy of hatred and destruction. After Josip Tito's death in 1980, the South Slav federation came apart due to ethnic hostilities as his successor Milošević turned to Greater Serbian nationalism. After Slovenia declared independence, the first armed conflict in June 1991 involved Croatia when Belgrade sought to protect the Serbian minority in the Kraina. The second war revolved around the independence of largely Muslim Bosnia, where Serbian nationalists wanted to create a territorial bridge to their newly founded Republika Srbska. The third fighting involved the province of Kosovo, Albanian in ethnic composition but home to a Serbian national monument. Since the international community intervened too late, these conflicts in mixed-ethnic territories cost around one hundred thousand lives and fragmented the region, hindering economic development.[27] From among the successor states trapped in nationalist mythmaking, only Slovenia and Croatia have gradually managed to democratize and resume economic growth.

These short country sketches suggest that multiple factors determined the success of the post-Communist transition. The Polish miracle demonstrates that the depth of the Communist fiasco was an important precondition for creating a resolute approach to reform. The East German case shows that much depended on external help in financing welfare costs and investing in infrastructure. The Czech example indicates that the level of prior development both in politics and economics played a rather important role in the post-Communist transformation. The Baltic and Slovakian pattern reveals the significance of a strong political will to abandon Communist practices since the populace had to be ready to bear a considerable amount of pain from the collapse of the prior order. Finally, the Ukrainian and Yugoslav stories illustrate the importance of recognized external borders.[28] In the long run, shock therapy only worked when its destruction was merely temporary and its suffering was buffered by social solidarity.

Post-Communist Experiences

For many Eastern Europeans, life after Communism turned out to be full of confusing experiences and ambivalent emotions. At first the new freedom was intoxicating since it meant the end of party control, collectivist behavior, and limited consumption. The Polish journalist Witold Szablowski likened the feeling to the disorientation of "dancing bears" whose controlling nose rings have been removed. "We have had to learn of how free people take care of themselves, of their families, of their futures, how they eat, sleep, make love, because under socialism, the state was always poking its nose into citizens' plates, beds and private lives." But taking responsibility for decisions, earning enough money became unsettling. "I'm talking about how complicated the freedom is, how painful it might be." Confronted with liberty and the market, "we weren't ready. . . . We were so spontaneous, so happy that communism is over that we probably didn't think too much."[29] Hence, many people were unprepared for the negative aspects of the new order.

Initially, the dissidents were overjoyed since they had achieved their aim of overthrowing the Soviet-style dictatorship. Adam Michnik remembers the reasons for rebelling: Socialism "was a lie, and we were searching for truth; communism meant conformity, and we desired authenticity; communism was enslavement, fear and censorship, and we desired freedom; it was an ongoing attack on tradition and national identity that we held to be ours; it was social inequality and injustice, and we believed in equality and justice." It therefore took a courageous "moral absolutism" to oppose an evil system. As a result, the peaceful revolution seemed like a dazzling, unexpected achievement. But the dissidents were not particularly suited to govern after their victory: "Many felt opposed to the very idea of party politics, which they saw as an affront to the dictates of individual conscience."[30] Glad to have escaped Stalinist prisons, regime opponents often became critics of the compromises needed in parliamentary democracy and of market capitalism.

In contrast, many new entrepreneurs seized the opportunity to expand their Communist-era small enterprises into medium-sized businesses. Marek Partala, "an energetic engineering professor," turned his "high quality carpentry workshop" into a bigger firm of "putting up and knocking down Italian-designed high-tech exhibition halls for car shows and fashion fairs." Małgorzata Żurawska, a trained linguist, "recognized that Poland was a fashion wasteland in which a growing number of women had some money and hankered after European style." She signed a joint-venture agreement with an Italian company, got a hard-currency loan, and switched production to Poland "so that her retail prices fell by half," making her clothes available to shoppers with modest means. The combination of a skilled workforce, willing labor, and geographic position between Germany and Russia made for success. While many ventures—like an effort to found a cosmetic studio—failed, enough succeeded to persuade some Polish emigrants to come home.[31]

For consumers, the overthrow of Communism also opened up fascinating possibilities, changing the face of many Eastern European cities. One British journalist from the *Guardian* noted that in Warsaw quite a few "gleaming skyscrapers" had shot up since his last visit in the mid-1980s. "There are vast numbers of cars and traffic jams." Moreover, "shopping malls and luxury blocks" had sprouted everywhere and fashionable suburbs with new houses and gardens were built in the contemporary style. All the previously inaccessible Western brand names—from IKEA to Chanel No 5, from London Fog to Apple—became available. "We can buy anything now," his elderly relatives reassured him. While they were content to keep basic supplies local, they could occasionally indulge in foreign luxuries. "But if everything is obtainable, is it affordable?"[32] In this burgeoning post-Communist consumer society, the availability of sufficient money became the new dividing line between urban and rural, young and old.

Unlike retirees on shrinking pensions, youths were the "lucky generation," since they could make use of the new opportunities. Initially, the impact of the overthrow of Communism was disorienting since it removed accustomed constraints without yet bringing liberal self-control. But, eventually, the young like Jana Hensel arrived in post-Communism, learning its new rules more quickly than their Stalinized elders. The liberalization of education offered them access to all sorts of previously proscribed knowledge. The freedom of international travel made it possible for them to explore not just Western Europe but also the rest of the world. The arrival of the internet allowed them to network with other young people in their own and foreign countries. Unconstrained by socialist customs, the young could experiment with new jobs, joining the global economy with a vengeance. Eventually, post-socialist youths also began to challenge the established politicians, trying to get rid of "candidates who have been around for 20 years."[33]

Other segments of post-socialist society were among the losers of the transformation, most notably political elites that had upheld the dictatorship. A process called "lustration"—after a Roman cleansing ritual—sought to stabilize democracy through the removal of Communist cadres from public life by exposing their crimes. But in negotiated transfers of power, the nomenklatura had exacted a promise not to be punished for its misdeeds. Only in East Germany did the dissidents succeed in keeping the secret police (Stasi) files and in having a parliamentary commission of inquiry discuss SED repression publicly. The Czech attempts at self-cleansing ran into strong opposition, and in Poland and Hungary the confrontation with the past was postponed for over a decade while post-Soviet countries like Belarus did not even make any apparent efforts. The process was so difficult since accusations of secret police collaboration served as a political weapon to discredit leaders like Wałęsa.[34] Because only the top layers were removed, the elite replacement remained rather incomplete.

When the planned economy fell apart, workers also faced mass unemployment since previously hidden underemployment now came out into the open. Many socialist rust-belt companies went into bankruptcy and even those that survived shed much of their labor in order to become competitive. The workforce shrank in all transition countries and unemployment rose to over 15 percent in Poland, East Germany, Slovakia, and Romania, with former Yugoslavia reaching more than 60 percent! At the same time, inflation soared, wiping out savings and eroding the buying power of pensions. Real wages dropped as much as one-quarter during the early years of transition. Traditional labor strategies like strikes were ineffective when companies were being shut down anyway. While older workers could retire, a "lost generation" of forty- to fifty-five-year-olds was left out since "they cannot change."[35] Only reliance on family networks, temporary emigration, and participation in an unreported "gray economy" made it possible for many laborers to survive.

Women were especially hard hit by the post-Communist transition since many lost their jobs and found their social services curtailed. The Yugoslav writer Slavenka Drakulić pointed out that under "real existing

socialism" they had been practically rather than ideologically emanci-
pated since virtually all of them worked outside the home. But the initial
contraction eliminated many service positions that struggling companies considered inessential so that fourteen million of the twenty-five
million lost jobs in Eastern Europe had belonged to women. While the
availability of Western consumer goods and appliances somewhat reduced the "double burden," performance pressure rose on those who
continued to be employed. Female life expectancy declined due to the
loss of support structures, while sexual freedom brought a steep increase of HIV infections due to the lack of condom use. Aside from the
arrival of Western feminism, the only bright spot was that a number of
female entrepreneurs capitalized on their new freedom.[36]

The transition was rather painful since "social security, one of the
advantages of state socialism, disappeared." According to the economist
Iván Berend, the severe rise in prices "eroded welfare subsidies, built
into the price of basic food products, children's clothing, books, rents,
entertainment and transportation fees." In order to achieve macroeco-
nomic stabilization as a precondition for Western credits, governments,
in response to dropping tax revenues, had to slash unemployment compensation and retirement pensions, accelerating a drop in consumption.
Previously free services such as medical treatment and drugs now had
to be paid for. Institutions like childcare were either shut down or converted to a fee basis that fewer people could afford. As a result of an
initial decline in wages, "poverty according to UNICEF became widespread" while social inequality increased.[37] Confronted with the tearing
of the social welfare net, many people fell back on the underground
barter economy and networks of family support.

Most Eastern Europeans were neither oligarchs nor destitute but
rather ordinary citizens who gradually adapted to the post-socialist
world. Neoliberal advocates like the Czech premier Václav Klaus tended
to gloss over the extent of the disruption involved in the breakup of the
Soviet system, which removed accustomed structures that provided
security even if they had been repressive. But in the transition many
people proved amazingly flexible, falling back on the survival mechanisms they had learned during the wars. While some bemoaned the loss

of state support, others became small entrepreneurs, "working for themselves for the first time in their lives," by "opening clothing stores, restaurants, bars, gas stations, hotels, hair salons, taxi companies, newsstands," and the like. The populace proved surprisingly patient with the price of transformation, just as long as progress was visible. Even the revived post-socialist parties were "not rushing to go back to Communism," campaigning instead for a kinder capitalism.[38]

Eastern European opinion surveys show that ordinary people "felt vulnerable and confused," while they hoped for a better future. Initially, the transformation seemed destructive, with three-fifths of the population finding it difficult to live on their salaries, about one-fifth unemployed, and the rest having dropped out of the economy. While two-thirds of the people considered the present situation worse than socialism, half were convinced that things would get better. As a result, many people distrusted public institutions, most still clung to collectivist values, and only three-fifths were self-professed democrats, while most expected things to improve in the future. Several years later, the mood had brightened considerably. While about four-fifths still considered a secure job "far more important than the freedom to travel or the richness of consumer choice," an increasing number "thought they were better off today than they were five years ago"; the optimists were beginning to outnumber the skeptics.[39]

Gains and Losses

Virtually all participants in the peaceful revolution underestimated the enormity of the transformation the overthrow of Communism would entail. In politics, the shift involved a transition from a late socialist welfare-dictatorship to a parliamentary democracy; in economics, it meant a change from a faltering planned economy to a competitive form of market capitalism; in international affairs, it signaled the end of Soviet hegemony and the reemergence of nation-states in the former bloc. But many commentators underrated the necessary adjustment and failed to comprehend the effects of changing from a party-sponsored, collectivist Marxism to a person-centered individualism. No wonder these multiple transitions that turned daily lives topsy-turvy proved both liberating and unsettling. Only writers like the Belarusian Nobel laureate Svetlana Alexievich were, with their part nostalgic, part inspiring stories, able to portray what these changes meant to people caught up in them.[40]

Though the Eastern European mood has become less celebratory than during the heady events, supporters maintain that the great transformation was largely a success story. In politics, the restoration of civil rights created "a return to normalcy, freedom [and] democracy," although the revival of self-government was more difficult than expected.[41] In economics, the reintroduction of competitive markets ended the stagnation of the planned economies with growth spurts that raised prosperity and began to close the gap to Western living standards. In society, the rejection of collectivism opened up space for individual life choices that widened the range of personal experiences. And in culture, the end of censorship and Marxist indoctrination reconnected Eastern Europe to international debates and intellectual styles as well as to global pop culture.[42] As a result, the former Soviet satellites have become vibrant places with impressive creativity.

Full of "frustration and resentment" against inequality, critics, however, claim that the price of the transformation was unnecessarily high. Stabilizing post-Communist governments proved to be a challenge since cynicism kept participation in elections low, party affiliations remained weak, and habits of corruption died hard. The initial economic collapse was longer and deeper than expected, unregulated capitalism provided a field day for domestic profiteers and foreign exploiters, and the economy divided into international and local sectors. Due to nomenklatura privatization, energetic individuals amassed large fortunes while the elderly, the unemployed, and rural populations sank into destitution, increasing social inequality. And the abolition of state support led to a commercialization of intellectual activity that also constrained freedom of debate in an insidious way. As a result of the transition difficulties, intellectuals like Daniela Dahn penned a whole literature of nostalgic complaint, disappointed that their project of reforming socialism had failed.[43]

The ideological outlook that emerged after the overthrow of Communism was therefore not so much Western-style liberalism as a resurgent ethnic nationalism. After decades of Soviet control, the reassertion of national identity became the common denominator that could ease the strains of transition. German unification turned out to be surprisingly benign with the orderly accession of former GDR states, but lingering frustration fueled the rise of the populist Alternative for Germany Party (AfD). In the Czech case, nationalism inspired the secession of Slovakia from Prague, albeit in a fairly peaceful fashion. In Yugoslavia, however, Greater Serbian chauvinism triggered successive wars in which the Croatian, Bosnian, or Kosovar opponents responded with equally rabid defense of their own identities. Even in those countries where the transformation was proceeding successfully, its difficulties inspired an authoritarian populism like in PiS's Poland and Orbán's Hungary. With such a defensive ethnic nationalism, an old poison has returned to liberated Eastern Europe.[44]

Three decades after the overthrow of Communism, the transition of Eastern Europe still remains unfinished. In historical perspective, the post-Communist states are just regaining their previous position at the periphery of Western Europe, returning to a new form of normalcy. The consolidation of self-government remains a challenge due to state capture by post-socialist elites and a trend toward "illiberal democracy." Similarly, the Eastern economies have yet to wean themselves off aid from the IMF or EU in order to reach self-sustained growth independent of the largesse of the West. The social service net has yet to become strong enough to lift the new underclass produced by restratification out of poverty. Finally, the cultural embrace of liberal slogans and ideas needs to go beyond superficial imitation in order to inhibit the resurgence of ethnic nationalism.[45] But anyone who travels in the dynamic East can see that it finally has a chance to develop in its own way—an enormous step forward that was unimaginable before.

3

European Integration

FIGURE 4. Schengenland open border, Italy. John Heseltine / Alamy Stock Photo.

On the murky morning of June 14, 1985, the integration of Europe took an important step forward in the tiny village of Schengen. Nestled amid vineyards on the western shore of the Moselle River, this picturesque Luxembourg town hosted a momentous meeting beyond the glare of the metropolitan media. Aboard a cruise ship named *Princesse Marie-Astrid*, moored where their frontiers converged, representatives of the adjoining nations of France, Germany, and the Benelux countries signed an agreement that promised to inaugurate "border free travel" among themselves. Since half of the members of the European Economic Community (EEC) were as yet unwilling to risk their domestic security by loosening border controls, the treaty remained outside its structure, complementing it for those five states who wanted to try a closer integration by easing travel between them. In retrospect, "the idea of open borders in 1985 was something extraordinary—like a kind of utopia. Nobody really believed that it could become reality."[1]

This Schengen Agreement was an unprecedented step since it required the signatories to yield a significant part of their sovereignty. In the development of nation-states, the imposition of borders had been an essential aspect of creating the "territoriality" that distinguished between citizens and foreigners while controlling trade.[2] In practice, "the ultimate abolition of all border controls of persons" was a complicated process that required another convention on June 19, 1990, to harmonize the "treatment of immigrants . . . the cooperation of police forces . . . and the adoption of uniform rules on arms and explosives and on traffic in narcotic drugs."[3] Due to public fears, the actual abolishment of borders took another five years to be implemented. But for travelers and truckers, the Schengen Agreement was such a boon—speeding the crossing of frontiers on highways and in airports—that twenty-two of the European Union (EU) members and four other countries eventually joined. In effect, the agreement on free movement created a "Schengenland" of about 420 million citizens.[4]

Euroenthusiasts interpret such progress as proof of the benefits of integration in overcoming the deadly legacy of nationalism. The US journalist Roger Cohen has confessed to being "a European patriot," because the EU brought international peace as well as domestic tranquility. In the post-fascist Mediterranean and Eastern European transitions, such cooperation also helped stabilize democracy. "The bond that binds the West is freedom." Coinciding with the rapid economic growth of the postwar decades, the establishment of the Common Market contributed to rising prosperity. Even if Gaullist obstruction and British resistance prevented a complete integration, the spread of wealth made it possible to pay for a generous welfare state that reduced social

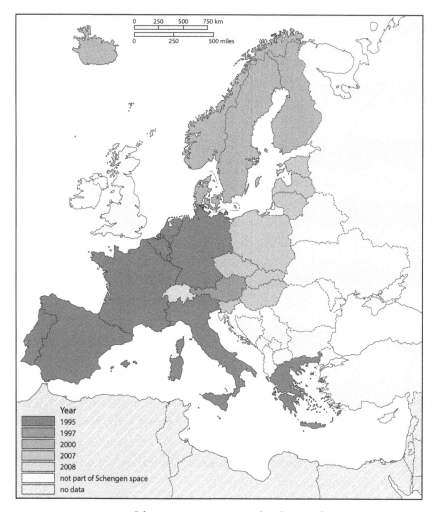

MAP 2. Schengen space, 1995–2008. Cox Cartographic.

inequality. Other commentators like Steven Hill have extolled *Europe's Promise* as "the best hope in an insecure age." But, more recently, worried intellectuals are sounding an alarm: "We must now fight for the idea of Europe or see it perish beneath the waves of populism."[5]

In contrast, Euroskeptics tend to blame many of their frustrations on Europe, accusing the EU of usurping their self-government. A whole host of anti-European parties ranging from UK Brexiteers to the French National Front, from the Hungarian Orbán government to the German

AfD have used Brussels as a whipping boy. In *The Strange Death of Europe*, the British journalist Douglas Murray argues that immigration and Islam are submerging European identity. Playing on prejudices and fears, he deplores the loss of beliefs and values that have traditionally been associated with European culture. He blames young male Muslim migrants for crime and terrorism while disparaging Islamic women with headscarves as a threat to white male dominance. Other critics, like Thilo Sarrazin, rail against the European bureaucracy as well as the euro currency.[6] Spurred by the fear of COVID-19, such anti-integration voices demand that a beleaguered Europe must reimpose its borders in order to regain sovereignty and survive.

At present the outcome of the European experiment remains open since neither side has achieved a clear advantage so far. The customary elite-driven process of "functionalist spillover" no longer works since the EU has become too controversial by intervening in the lives of its citizens. Surveys show ambivalent feelings. There is widespread agreement on the benefits of integration especially in countries with little trust in their own government but also mounting frustration with the emotional distance between "eurocrats" and citizens who feel powerless to influence their decisions. While the tide of anti-European populism still seems to be rising, the nationalists are divided among themselves, making it hard for them to cooperate. Chancellor Angela Merkel and President Emmanuel Macron are consulting more closely by signing a new Franco-German cooperation treaty in Aachen, but they are both weakened internally.[7] Perhaps a closer look at the struggles over a deepening or widening of the European Community as well as the daily life of its citizens might produce a clearer answer for the future of the EU.

Deepening the Union

By the second half of the 1970s, the original momentum of integration had dissipated, triggering widespread talk of a "Eurosclerosis." The Rome Treaties of 1957, which had created the Common Market and nuclear cooperation, had sought to build "an ever closer union" among the member states through internal free trade and common external tariffs. Charles de Gaulle's adherence to a "Europe of the fatherlands" stopped, however, the advance of supranational institutions through the "empty chair crisis" in which France blocked additional integration measures. The accession of the UK, Denmark, and Ireland in 1973 as well as the Mediterranean expansion into Greece, Spain, and Portugal in the 1980s increased membership in the Economic Community to twelve countries. But the double shock of the oil crises of 1973 and 1979 as well as British insistence on reducing the UK's contribution to the common budget and on cutting the subsidies of the Common Agricultural Policy (CAP) stalled further progress.[8]

In the mid-eighties an unlikely cooperation between Jacques Delors and Margaret Thatcher revitalized the movement toward integration. As head of the European Commission, the French Socialist was a committed Eurofederalist, using his authority to have a white paper, called the Cockfield Report, prepared that suggested about three hundred measures to abolish nontariff barriers in order to complete the creation of a single market "without internal frontiers." Though an avid neoliberal at home, the British prime minister swallowed her hostility to Brussels and permitted an intergovernmental conference that worked out a set of proposals which became known as the Single European Act.[9] Signed in February 1986 and coming into force a year later, this document was a typical compromise between advocates of further integration and skeptics wanting to limit it to free trade. But as the first comprehensive effort to reform the Treaties of Rome, it became a milestone in the deepening of the European project.

In order to make "concrete progress towards European unity," the Single European Act (SEA) sought to abolish the remaining hindrances to trade and improve the decision making of European institutions. By setting a date for the completion of the single market in 1992, the agreement provided a fixed deadline for its implementation. Its key aim was to ensure "the free movement of goods, persons, services and capital" within the EEC so that competition could function without indirect obstructions. For instance, a German car maker like BMW could design a car in Munich, have it produced in Britain, and sold in France as if the entire process were taking place within the same country. Though simple in principle, this was a rather ambitious aim in practice since different local taxes, business subsidies, health and safety regulations, and the like needed to be harmonized. At the same time, the SEA introduced qualified majority voting in the European Commission and gave the European Parliament greater powers of "cooperation" and "assent."[10]

Further progress toward a political union was, however, rudely interrupted by the overthrow of Communism and German reunification. The accession of the GDR states to the Federal Republic increased its population to over eighty million and its share of the European GDP to about 30 percent, clearly making Germany the largest and most powerful state in the EEC. Still thinking in World War II categories, Margaret Thatcher was aghast but powerless to stop the unification process. The French president François Mitterrand was equally disturbed by the increased weight of his neighbor across the Rhine but decided on a more constructive course of action, using integration to contain him. Fortunately, the German chancellor Helmut Kohl was also a convinced European who was willing to embed the enlarged Federal Republic in a more closely cooperating Europe. What might have been a divisive development therefore turned into a further impetus toward integration by transforming the twelve EEC members into "a European Union."[11]

In December 1991, a conference in the Dutch border city of Maastricht agreed to a double reform of the European treaties by creating a common currency and reorganizing community functions into three pillars. Since the 1970s, the governments had struggled with finding a way to contain currency fluctuations, eventually realizing that only a European Monetary Union (EMU) would ultimately solve the problem of the dominance of the Deutsche Mark, known as DM. Helmut Kohl was willing to give up the cherished German currency as long as its successor, the euro, guarded by the European Central Bank (ECB), would follow the anti-inflation course of the Bundesbank. The result was the formulation of three "stability criteria": inflation was not supposed to exceed 1.5 percent beyond the average of the best states; the annual government deficit must not go beyond 3 percent of GNP; and the ratio of the gross government debt ought not surpass 60 percent of the GDP. The location of the ECB in Frankfurt underlined the intended stability of the new euro currency, to be introduced by 1999.[12]

Equally important was the reorganization of the European Union that sought to streamline its structure in order to clarify its competence. The first so-called pillar brought together the three prior European treaties of the European Coal and Steel Community (ECSC), the European Economic Community (EEC), and the European Atomic Energy Community (Euratom) into one, largely supranational cluster. Added to it was a second area of a Common Foreign and Security Policy (CFSP) as well as a third leg of Justice and Home Affairs, which were merely intergovernmental, relying on the willingness of their members to cooperate. These changes created a confusing hybrid structure, offering a compromise between advocates of integration like France and Germany and skeptics of cooperation like Britain and Denmark. These agreements could only be reached by allowing some states to opt out of further advances, creating a Europe of multiple speeds.[13] As a result, the ratification process became a dramatic struggle, with bare approval in French and Danish referenda and the British Parliament, followed by the endorsement of the German Constitutional Court.

The implementation of the Maastricht Treaty turned out to be even more complicated than its initial negotiations. Due to the strength of the DM, the character of the common currency became a battleground between hard-money defenders and soft-money advocates. Meeting the convergence criteria proved rather difficult, especially since the unification costs kept even orthodox Bonn from fully living up to the standards. The inclusion of countries like Italy or Spain, whose performance was worse, became a political football, leading to a Solomonic decision of certifying movement toward the goal as sufficient. The Amsterdam Treaty of 1997 was an effort to tidy up the institutional implications of the EMU and regulate the accession of new members. Its compromise balanced the seats of small and big countries in the European Commission and strengthened the power of the European Parliament in new areas. In effect, these arrangements ratified the drift toward a "two-tier Europe which proved ever harder to understand.[14]

When the euro finally became a reality in 2002 in eleven member states, its performance surprised even the skeptics who criticized the lack of an economic government. The coins had a solid feel, showing a

European symbol on one side and a national image on the other, while the colorful bills displayed abstract pictures of well-known pieces of architecture. Tourists and businessmen were delighted with the single currency because it eliminated the unpredictable conversion into other moneys and costly bank conversion fees. Initially, traders were cautious, pegging its exchange rate at about one-quarter lower than the dollar, but soon the euro began to rise, outstripping the US currency and becoming a major global instrument. While criticism continued especially in Germany due to the loss of the DM, non-Germans like Wim Duisenberg or Jean-Claude Trichet defended the euro's value vigorously.[15] In spite of all the predictions of doom, the currency survived and grew popular while the countries originally belonging to the Eurozone became the core of the EU.

Dissatisfied with patchwork reforms, the EU then sought to draw up a new treaty, ambitiously called "constitution" for the member countries. Led by the former French president Valery Giscard d'Estaing, a convention deliberated about the articulation of a set of shared values and the inclusion of a "charter of fundamental rights." Disagreements erupted about the weight of the votes of smaller countries such as Austria, which outnumbered the bigger states like Germany, until a compromise of qualified majority voting was reached. To make the EU more visible to its citizens as well as its trading partners, the debates suggested the creation of an elected president as well as a foreign representative. Another fateful addition was a formal "exit clause," establishing a process for leaving the EU.[16] Since the media hardly reported on the complicated technical proceedings, the public remained uninvolved. As a result of dissatisfaction over domestic issues and resentment against Brussels, referenda in France and Holland rejected the draft in 2005, bringing the constitutional process to an abrupt halt.

Shocked by the defeat of the constitution, the EU leadership sought to salvage its core provisions through a less ambitious approach. Since the majority of the member countries had already ratified the document, it seemed possible to save most of its reforms by simply calling them amendments, which could be approved by parliamentary vote. The treaty nonetheless improved the EU by basing it explicitly on human rights, clarifying organizing principles such as conferred powers, subsidiarity, and proportionality while spelling out which competences were exclusive, shared, or supporting. After much wrangling, the treaty draft was signed in 2007—only to be rejected by an Irish referendum that had to be repeated so as to let it pass. While the compromises were largely hammered out during the German EU presidency, the revised text was signed in the Portuguese capital, becoming known thereafter as the Lisbon Treaty.[17] Though more modest than a constitution, this agreement endowed the EU with a clearer legal personality.

The effort to deepen European integration after 1990 can best be described as stumbling forward since progress and reverses alternated with each other. Normally, reforms started with the presentation of a white paper by European Commission experts, which would then be discussed in an intergovernmental conference before it would be presented to the Council of Ministers. With the increase in the membership, reaching agreement among countries became ever more difficult due to their disparate interests. The complexity of many of the issues also created public disinterest until a referendum campaign would provide a platform to vent domestic resentment against a government by turning down initiatives of the so-called Brussels "eurocrats." Though skeptics take this frustrating process as proof that integration is a pipe dream, more charitable observers marvel that so much has already been accomplished anyway.[18] The EU could only be deepened somewhat as long as its main task remained the absorption of new members.

Widening the EU

The end of the Cold War and the collapse of the Soviet Union offered Eastern Europeans a chance to join Western institutions. The withdrawal of the Red Army allowed the former satellite states to "return to Europe" and become part of the "free world" as contemporary clichés had it. In security matters, this desire meant gaining membership in the North Atlantic Treaty Organization (NATO), which would protect the newly independent states even if it was likely to affront Russia by bringing the enemy alliance close to its frontiers. In economic matters, the

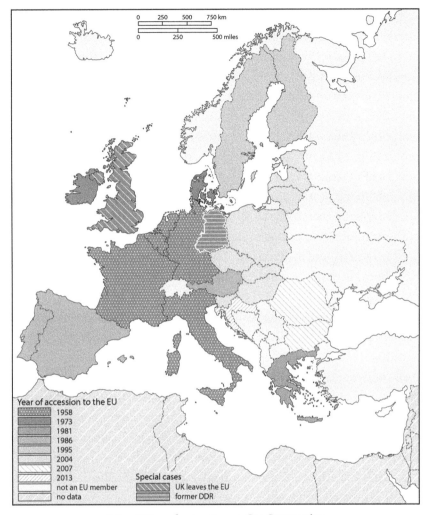

MAP 3. EU members, 1958–2013. Cox Cartographic.

hope for a better life suggested joining the European Community, whose lifestyle was attractive since it combined political freedom with consumer prosperity. These aspirations posed complicated questions about where to draw the new boundaries in the East—which countries should be accepted and which ones were to be rejected? Moreover, the wish to become part of the West also raised the issue of whether applicants would be politically stable and economically developed enough in order to be included.[19]

Hoping for American help in case of a Russian attack, many Eastern European countries lobbied for inclusion in an enlarged NATO. Founded in 1949, the transatlantic alliance had already accepted Greece, Turkey, West Germany, and Spain prior to 1990. The tense negotiations about German unification allowed the states of the former GDR to be included, albeit without the stationing of foreign troops and nuclear weapons. While some scholars maintain that further expansion was not prohibited, Mikhail Gorbachev claims that the West "gave assurances that NATO would not extend its zone of operations to the East."[20] Though liberals hesitated to affront Russia, American neoconservatives wanted to seize the chance of Moscow's weakness to expand the alliance eastward. Some Western-oriented states like Austria, Finland, Ireland, Malta, Sweden, and Switzerland chose to remain neutral, but the Czech Republic, Hungary, and Poland succeeded in becoming NATO members in 1999.

The other Eastern European applicants had to meet stringent criteria in order to be admitted. Each state had to approve a Membership Action Plan that fulfilled the following demands: the country had to "be capable of operating effectively with NATO forces" and "uphold democracy and free enterprise," since admission required unanimity. In 2004 Bulgaria, Romania, Slovakia, and Slovenia plus the three Baltic states were admitted, although Moscow was upset that its Kaliningrad enclave was now surrounded by NATO members. Albania, Croatia, Montenegro, and North Macedonia subsequently joined, while Russian-oriented Serbia remained opposed. Beyond the disputes over Georgia, Bosnia, and Kosovo, the most controversial issue was the orientation of Ukraine, as Russia particularly resented the inclusion of this former part of the Tsarist Empire, annexing the Crimea and fostering separatism in the eastern provinces. As a result of its protective stance, NATO grew from a Western bulwark into "a continent wide alliance" of thirty members.[21]

While it was less politically fraught, the EU's enlargement into Eastern Europe was technically more complicated since potential members had first to become economically and politically compatible. The process was guided by the precedent of two prior rounds of expansion. After having overcome a French veto and internal opposition, the UK,

Denmark, and Ireland had joined in 1973, adding proponents of free trade but otherwise not posing any problems. The Mediterranean round of accessions with Greece in 1981 and with Spain and Portugal in 1986 was more complicated since these countries were just emerging from right-wing dictatorships and their economic performance was considerably lower than the living standard of existing members. As a result, Brussels had to help with the transition to democracy as well as with economic development in order to make the new members capable of reaching EU standards.[22] In contrast, referenda in the wealthy democracies of Norway and Switzerland rejected formal membership, choosing instead to rely on North Sea oil and traditional neutrality.

The post-Communist widening of the EU repeated the Mediterranean experience of having to assist with political and economic transformation. The East German states entered through the back door by joining the FRG in October 1990. But for the western neutrals and other Soviet satellites, the EU formulated explicit criteria during the Copenhagen summit in 1993: "Membership requires that the candidate country has achieved stability of institutions guaranteeing democracy, the rule of law, human rights and respect for and protection of minorities, the existence of a functioning market economy as well as the capacity to cope with competitive pressure and market forces within the Union." Accession also demanded "adherence to the aims of political, economic and monetary union," spelled out in the *acquis communautaire*, that is, the body of rules and decisions compiled by the existing members.[23] This effort of "conditionality" to meet these targets helped the transition to democracy and the market through a mixture of political pressure and financial support.

The end of the Cold War also gave neutrals—such as Austria, Finland, and Sweden—the chance to join the EU because the relaxation of tensions removed objections against it. To Brussels, the accession of three wealthy democracies seemed attractive since they would be net contributors to the budget. From the applicants' perspective, the free trade zone EFTA was stagnating and the intermediary arrangement of a joint European Economic Area seemed unsatisfactory because it gave them no voice in EU decisions. But the devil lay in the details. Interests clashed in areas such as fishing rights or truck traffic through the Alps. Moreover, the addition of three new members required renegotiating the internal quota for qualified majority voting and seats in the European Parliament, diluting the power of existing members. Nonetheless, the applicants quickly implemented the *acquis communautaire* and joined in January 1995.[24] Switzerland and Norway negotiated special relationships of quasi membership instead, allowing free trade but requiring contributions to the EU budget.

The accession of Eastern European countries was much more difficult since political institutions remained unstable and the economic gap was huge. Though applicants were just establishing democratic constitutions and mustered only one-third of the GNP per capita of the EU members, they shamed the West by claiming membership as a moral imperative, based on the recognition of their "Europeanness," which would keep them out of the Russian sphere of influence. As a result, the EU signed so-called "Europe agreements" with the Eastern candidates during the mid-1990s, that initiated a "structured dialogue" about the Copenhagen criteria of democratization, marketization, and EU regulation. At the same time, Brussels offered some economic help with a European Bank for Reconstruction, though members were reluctant to open their own markets. Chancellor Kohl particularly pushed for expansion since Germany's eastern neighbors were a natural political and economic hinterland that would shift the EU center to Berlin.[25]

In spite of massive obstacles, the negotiations with the Eastern European applicants were ultimately successful, making them full members in 2004. After almost a decade of preparations, actual talks started in 1998 for the Czech Republic, Hungary, Poland, Estonia, and Slovenia and somewhat later for Latvia, Lithuania, and Slovakia. The most contentious issues were the huge cost of inclusion in the Common Agricultural Policy, the redistribution of regional development funds, and the question of mobility for workers who would undercut wages in the EU. Except for the immediate opening of the UK and Ireland, the solutions reached consisted largely of gradual phase-ins, allowing supports to be raised according to the ability of the budget to afford them, and free movement of labor only when pay levels had risen somewhat. While accepting community standards required large changes in the applicants, their accession also changed the power balance in the EU.[26] With the addition of Cyprus and Malta, the Southern and Eastern enlargement by one hundred million people was the most significant expansion of the union.

Due to instability and poverty, the potential membership of the other Balkan countries has remained an unresolved problem for the EU. Though part of the original negotiations, Bulgaria and Romania were only admitted in 2007 since their democratic performance remained questionable; their economic development lagged and corruption remained a blight. From among the wreckage of former Yugoslavia, only Slovenia (in 2004) and Croatia (in 2013) managed to convince the international community that they had shed their dictatorial past and that the economy was slowly catching up to the other new members. The remaining Western Balkan countries—such as Albania, Bosnia, Kosovo, North Macedonia, Montenegro, and Serbia—were considered "'state captures' by corrupt politicians, linked with organized crime." Their "endemic political corruption" as well as contested borders kept them from meeting the Copenhagen criteria.[27] Although the EU would like to tie them to the West, it remains unclear when, if ever, these candidates will be considered ready for accession.

Another controversy concerned Turkish membership because it raised the question of what is to be considered as "European." Reformminded leaders in Ankara pressured Brussels so much that the country was offered candidate status in 1999 and actual negotiations about the completion of various EU requirements were begun in 2004. For strategic reasons, Washington pushed for admission, while liberal Europeans wanted to strengthen the modernizers within Turkey. Resistance came from conservative circles in Austria, France, and Germany who did not consider the country culturally European, recalling centuries of conflict between Islam and Christianity. A series of unresolved issues like the partition of Cyprus, the Kurdish problem, the proximity to Syria and Iraq, and the death penalty also counseled caution. While many Europeans were afraid of adding eighty million Muslims and showed "enlargement fatigue," the initially liberal Erdoğan government moved in a nationalist, dictatorial, and Islamic direction, currently putting Turkey's membership application on hold.[28]

Such problems notwithstanding, the EU "has a splendid record concerning enlargement." Running parallel to but not identical with NATO expansion, the growth of the European Union from the original six members to twenty-seven states comprises over 450 million people and constitutes one of the world's largest trading blocs. The absorption of advanced democratic and capitalist states was already a challenge due to their free trade views, which slowed cooperation. Even more difficult was the accomplishment of postdictatorial transitions in the Mediterranean and in Eastern Europe that had to introduce self-government and speed economic development. No doubt, a number of boundary problems in the Balkans and the Middle East as well as with the Russian sphere of influence remain to be resolved. The successive inclusion of new member states has also hindered further internal integration.[29] But in spite of much criticism, the EU's peaceful transformation of the Continent remains an amazing success.

Lived Europe

Perhaps even more important than the building of European institutions is the Europeanization of daily lives, which is progressing often without conscious debate. Half a century ago the frame of reference was clearly the nation-state, reborn after disastrous wars, depressions, and genocide. In the meantime, many aspects of ordinary living in Europe are no longer controlled by decisions in national capitals but rather stem from bureaucratic guidelines or intergovernmental negotiations in Brussels. The curvature of African bananas, the consistency of Dutch tomatoes, the aroma of French cheeses, the pasteurization of German beer—all these attributes have been regulated, creating a harmonization of rules for European shoppers. Similarly, everywhere on the Continent business firms have to follow the same legal standards, allowing employees to move freely from one country to another. Though critics complain about overregulation, such rules are gradually creating a Europe from below, consisting of a transnational realm of shared experiences.[30]

One of the "greatest achievements of the EU" has been the free crossing of borders within the Schengen Area. The abolition of internal frontiers has allowed business people and tourists to "freely circulate without being subjected to border checks." The frequent backups on roads between countries have disappeared and EU passport or identity card holders now speed through the airport controls more quickly than other travelers. Of course, the removal of internal barriers has put a premium on tightening the control of external borders through a common visa policy that harmonizes rules for non-EU citizens. A separate frontier police, called Frontex, had to be established to help those countries located at the periphery of the EU with implementing rigorous external policing.[31] Unfortunately, the migration and COVID-19 crises have prompted many member states to reinstitute "temporary border checks," claiming to provide security for their citizens. An unexpected consequence has also been the transnationalization of crime, allowing gangs of beggars, burglars, and pimps to operate on a Continental scale. But where it works, the abolition of borders has created a lived sense of Europe.

A chief benefit for consumers and travelers in the Eurozone has been the common currency of the euro, even if economists like Bernd Lucke prefer fiscal independence. No longer having to exchange money at every border crossing has facilitated travel for tourists who previously had to fiddle with different coins and bills. Paying in the same currency also made it easier to judge the actual prices of a foreign hotel room, a dinner, or a present to be bought. For business people, the use of the same money has facilitated trade across frontiers since costs and profits no longer depend on fluctuations of the foreign exchange market. As part of a stronger currency, smaller states have especially benefited from the discipline of the European Central Bank in keeping inflation low and borrowing costs minimal. Because the public is convinced that the tangible advantages of the shared euro outweigh the drawbacks of a loss of fiscal sovereignty, nineteen of the then twenty-eight EU countries joined the Eurozone.[32]

The introduction of the euro has fundamentally transformed manufacturing jobs through facilitating the creation of transnational production chains. The infamous example of yogurt based on milk extracted in Holland, shipped to Italy to be cultured, and then transferred to Germany, only to be sold under a local label is but one case. More typical is the assembly of cars such as Audis in Hungary from parts made in surrounding countries, taking advantage of the low labor costs and the proximity to major markets. Similarly, the airplane consortium Airbus has its main fuselage and engine factories in France and Germany with additional parts from Britain, working as if located in a single country. This combination of pieces created in different places in a final product ignores state boundaries since it is more sensitive to labor and shipping costs than to nationality. Only somewhat tongue in cheek, the historian Karl Schlögel has therefore celebrated truckers on the Autobahn as the avant-garde of European integration while budget airlines have also linked the Continent together for travelers.[33]

As a result of the shared currency, consumption patterns have been Europeanized, even if many of the labels have achieved a global name recognition. Instead of being limited to canned or greenhouse vegetables in the winter, Northern Europeans can now enjoy produce and fruit from Mediterranean EU countries far into the fall and once again in early spring. At the same time, electric appliances—made by companies like Siemens in Germany—are sold in all Southern European countries, and once-national superstores like the French Carrefour are to be found everywhere. Similarly, Ingvar Kamprad's budget furniture made by IKEA is designed according to a Scandinavian style, made out of Nordic pine wood, and marketed to youthful consumers from the Baltic to the Mediterranean. European clothing stores like H&M or C&A also offer fashions, manufactured in Asia, in Continental pedestrian streets.[34] Even if such major brands are sold worldwide, their Continental origins and styles still reinforce European identities for consumers.

Another major effort to link European citizens has been the Erasmus Programme of student exchanges that intends to reduce national animosities through shared experiences. Its purpose is "to support education, training, youth and sport in Europe. Its budget of €14.7 billion (of 2020) will provide opportunities for over four million Europeans to study, train, and gain experience abroad." Erasmus primarily seeks to reduce youth unemployment, train young people in democracy, and promote mobility and understanding among EU partner countries. The number of annual participants is impressive with two million in student exchanges, 650,000 in vocational training, 800,000 educators, and so on. One of the important academic aspects is the support of one hundred Jean Monnet Centers that sponsor research and outreach about European integration. Combining professional development with tourism, participation in these exchanges has been a smashing success as the comedy *L'Auberge espagnole* indicates.[35] Hence the UK's decision to leave them is a regrettable loss.

More controversial has been the European effort to harmonize academic degrees and ensure equality of higher education through the Bologna Process. In 1999 many European education and science ministers met at the ancient University of Bologna in order to create a European Higher Education Area in which academic degrees would be compatible. In practice, that agreement meant the introduction of the Anglo-American BA degree as a first step, leading to the MA and finally the PhD. In German-speaking countries, this reform provoked traditionalist opposition since it meant the addition of an intermediary degree before the state examinations or the MA. This also required that some states reduce prior schooling to twelve years, while taking only three years for a BA meant that the curriculum needed to be streamlined.[36] Though it was accused of subordinating education to the economy, the Bologna Process made it possible for degrees to be recognized everywhere and allowed young professionals to pursue their careers in other member countries.

Another pleasant way to experience the diversity of Europe has been the Eurail Pass for train travel. Designed for non-European visitors, it was created in 1959 to allow the use of Western European railroads during a specified period without having to make prior reservations or learning the confusing special schedules of the various national rail companies. Similarly, the Interrail Pass was intended to offer the same flexible services to citizens of all European countries. Though the passes are not cheap, they allow hordes of young backpack tourists each summer to range all over the Continent from Paris to Prague, from

Copenhagen to Capri. One guide touts the experience: "As an American, I am always thoroughly impressed by European public transportation. The railways are an extremely convenient (and fun) way to travel Europe. The vast network of rails connects even the smallest towns to one another." Especially for young people, this "wonderful Eurail [or Interrail] Pass experience" fosters a sense of Europe as a whole.[37]

Creating a European public opinion through shared media has been rather more difficult due to the language differences. The promising magazine the *European*, for instance, folded at the newsstands and has been reduced to a shadowy internet existence. Traditional newspapers like the *London Times*, *Libération*, or the *Frankfurter Allgemeine Zeitung* are still primarily national in their language and orientation, even if they offer a few pages in English. On television, Anglo-American news channels like CNN or BBC dominate since public news coverage in France, Germany, and Italy remains national, having rather to fight commercial competitors. Feeble efforts at common programming like the Eurovision song contest for pop music have only been able to attract an event-oriented audience without lasting impact. More promising has been the Franco-German TV network Arte, but its decidedly high-brow programming mostly appeals to intellectuals. Predictions of the rise of a European public sphere may apply to lobbying in Brussels but remain somewhat premature.[38]

Competition in sports on the European level is, however, quite popular as an intermediary stage between national and world championships. In some fields—like basketball and handball—there are regular European leagues for the best teams. In other areas—like track and field, gymnastics, or football—there are also European championships alternating with world title competitions. Dominant on television are the UEFA Champions League soccer games in which the best teams from all Continental countries plus Israel are pitted against each other in a preliminary group stage, followed by a final round of single elimination. Heavily supported by advertising, these matches between professional teams can function as a kind of *ersatz* war, especially in British tabloid reporting on Anglo-German contests. In recent decades, women's competitions have also been added on the team or country level.[39]

Especially for fans, these sporting events create European heroes like Ronaldo and contribute to viewers' thinking in European frames of reference.

These scattered impressions indicate that Europe is gradually growing from below through shared experiences in daily lives. In important areas like currency, jobs, travel, education, and entertainment, Europeans are coming closer together without much fanfare. Two-thirds of respondents in a 2018 Eurobarometer survey said that their country benefited from being a member of the EU, even if a significant minority of nationalists opposed further delegation of decisions to Brussels. As a result, the 2019 elections for the European Parliament were more hotly contested than ever between pro- and anti-European parties. Since she was appointed by the Council of Ministers, the new European Commission president Ursula von der Leyen faces a stiff challenge in meeting public expectations of greater participation.[40] This contradictory evidence suggests that many people take the benefits of the EU for granted while still seeking national protection against the disruptions of globalization. Hence, Europe has acquired positive and negative connotations at the same time.

A Success Story?

Evaluations of European integration differ rather drastically. The House of European History (HEH) in Brussels presents the process as a largely successful effort to overcome past divisions. When the founding generation started to pass away, the European Parliament decided in 2007 to "present the development of European integration in a comprehensible way for a broader public. And to explain its main historical developments, motivating forces and aims, so as to enable future generations to understand how and why today's Union developed and when it did." The presentation starts with the cultural heritage, proceeds to Europe's role in the world, goes on to the destruction of the Continent, moves to its rebuilding after 1945, discusses the acceleration of integration, and finishes with the relevance of the past for the future.[41] Though public criticism of the concept has prevented the construction of a simplistic master narrative, the HEH's pluralistic approach nonetheless seeks to affirm the building of an integrated Europe.

In contrast, Euroskeptics do not just criticize individual policies but actively combat the entire project. Populist politicians of the Right—ranging from Nigel Farage to Marine Le Pen, from Viktor Orbán to Alexander Gauland—are fighting against the EU, though some of them are members of the European Parliament. They are joined by a group of publicists like Douglas Murray and academics like Hans-Werner Sinn who have discovered that Brussels can be blamed for all the problems of globalization. Their criticism focuses on several basic objections: First, nationalists fear ceding their country's sovereignty to a supranational EU, thereby losing their identity and control of their own destiny. Second, soft money advocates decry the austerity policy of the European Central Bank, which imposes fiscal discipline upon borrowing. Finally, xenophobes hate the free movement of people in the EU, which they erroneously blame for an unrestricted influx of Muslim migrants into Europe. Though often exaggerated, these phobias have a strong populist appeal.[42]

On the other side, Euroenthusiasts also berate the EU for not having created a United States of Europe, capable of common action on the international stage. From Jacques Delors to Joschka Fischer, European idealists have been frustrated with the lack of progress toward a common state. Arguing that the Brussels institutions actually hinder further integration, the publicist Ulrike Guerot and the writer Robert Menasse have called on citizens to build a European republic from below.[43] Such critics have focused on several all too real issues: First, idealists bemoan the "democratic deficit" that makes EU decisions often seem remote, technocratic, and uncontrolled by the European Parliament. Second, integration advocates decry the lack of majority voting in the European Commission, which allows a single state like Hungary or Poland to block a common policy. Finally, commentators regret the lack of concerted action in foreign policy or defense that makes the EU appear weak in the grand game of global politics.

More dispassionate analysts seek to address the complexity of the European Union through exploring its many contradictions. Instead of looking to the US model, they invoke past experiences of the Holy Roman or Habsburg Empires that better reflect diversity. In such a perspective, the EU appears both fragile and resilient, full of crises and defeats, yet doggedly pursuing further integration. Its triple structure of supranational, shared, and reserved policy fields suggests a tenuous compromise between supranationalism and intergovernmentalism, moderated by the principle of subsidiarity. Strong in community law and market competition, the EU remains weak in foreign policy, defense, and social issues, although there is a tendency toward adding competence whenever a new problem like the policing of external borders appears.[44] As a hybrid form of political cooperation that both strengthens and surpasses its member states, the EU should be understood as an unfinished project.

Belying the popular rhetoric of crisis, the transformation of Europe since 1990 has been nothing short of astounding. None of the pundits really predicted the peaceful revolution and the overthrow of Communism that reconfigured the map of the old Continent. Though the transition to democracy and capitalism has been more painful than expected, on the whole it has brought Eastern Europe greater freedom and prosperity than before. While the West has sought to deepen its integration project, the East has returned to Europe, joining both NATO and the European Union. No doubt, the post-Communist transformation has required enormous effort and disappointed many hopes for perfect democracy and instant consumer prosperity. Moreover, the public has often been frustrated by the national egotism of the EU member states as well as by the cumbersome nature of decision-making in Brussels.[45] But at the cusp of the twenty-first century, the peaceful revolution, economic transformation, and progress of integration have given most Europeans ample reason to look with optimism to a better future.

PART II

Avalanche of Crises

Just when everything seemed to be going well, an avalanche of crises descended that threw the viability of the European Union into doubt by highlighting its unresolved problems. Starting with the default of Lehman Brothers in the United States, the sovereign debt crisis spilled over to Europe through the collapse of financial lending, endangering the solvency of heavily indebted Mediterranean countries as well as the survival of the euro as a transnational currency. A few years later, a tidal wave of desperate African and Near Eastern refugees washed up on the Continental shores, straining the European capacity and willingness to help since fears of losing cultural identity and exaggerated claims of terrorism sparked xenophobic resentment. Finally, the shocking exit of a previously ambivalent United Kingdom from the European Union after a contested referendum weakened the EU by demonstrating the resurgence of nationalism. What were the causes of these reverses, what was their cumulative impact, and how have the Europeans managed to deal with them?

4

Sovereign Debt Debacle

FIGURE 5. Run on an ATM, Athens, Greece. Ververidis Vasilis, Shutterstock.

On the last weekend of June 2015, "marathon queues snaked in front of automated teller machines across Greece." Uneasy Greeks were withdrawing cash after the leftist prime minister Alexis Tsipras had called for a referendum to determine the fiscal fate of the nearly bankrupt state. Thousands of fearful customers were withdrawing the maximum amount of €600 per person since banks would be closed the following Monday for an indefinite period and withdrawals were going to be limited to €60. Within hours, one-third of the about 5,500 ATMs in Athens and all over the country were out of cash. In a veritable run on the banks, €600 million were taken out in one day, making it necessary for the institutions to stay closed until after the vote. "People are feeling very concerned . . . very insecure," one woman said. Uncertain about how the government was going to avoid bankruptcy, Greeks talked "about their fear but also about their anger."[1] Unwilling to admit their own responsibility, they only blamed the international creditors who insisted on austerity.

The fiscal crisis hit Greece especially hard since the huge debt of the preceding boom had become insupportable. Starting in 2010 two controversial bailouts had already forced Athens to reduce its 15 percent annual budget deficit by slashing expenditures to the bone. As a result, "the overwhelming majority" rejected further austerity, fearing a drastic reduction of their living standards. Endorsed by 61 percent of the popular vote against the proposed deficit reduction plan, Tsipras went to Brussels in order to renegotiate the terms of the third bailout. But he was in a weak position since the country was unable to come up with the €1.8 billion installment that it owed to the International Monetary Fund. As drawn-out negotiations went on, plans like the temporary withdrawal from the Eurozone, called Grexit, were discussed. But the EU was also under pressure since it did not want its singular accomplishment of a common currency to fail. As a result, no one was satisfied with the tenuous compromise that was worked out.[2]

The reasons for the Greek crisis lay in the problematic structure of the state, which made the economy function almost like a Ponzi scheme. Acceptance in the Eurozone had been facilitated by largely falsified statistics that painted too rosy a picture of the effort to catch up to EU levels of development. Both the conservative Right and socialist Left had sought to serve their clients through liberal spending, compounded by rampant tax evasion and political corruption. Membership in the euro made it easy to borrow funds from abroad, which fueled a building boom, creating new highways and houses all over the Greek peninsula. The solidity of the common currency reduced interest rates to a minimum, hiding the speculative risks of investment in many dubious projects.[3] When the influx of funds dried up during the Great Recession, the effect was disastrous: All over the country construction stopped, with highways ending nowhere and second stories of new houses remaining incomplete. Unable to service its debt, Greece became virtually bankrupt.

Faced with this disaster, pundits fiercely debated how to rescue the Greek economy in order to defend the euro as currency. Greece itself was only of marginal importance, amounting to about 2 percent of the Eurozone's GDP, but markets feared that other Mediterranean countries with excessive debt might also default. On the one hand, leftist economists like Paul Krugman argued for relief through additional credits so that Greece might eventually grow out of its debts, even if it could no longer devalue its currency in order to reduce its obligations. On the other hand, neoliberal creditors, personified by the German finance minister Wolfgang Schäuble, insisted on regaining fiscal discipline through austerity by cutting government expenditures in order to decrease labor costs and once again make Greece competitive.[4] Essentially, the debate raged around the question of who had to bear the pain of readjustment—the Greek people through a drastic reduction of living standards or the international creditors by forgiving much of the debt.

Beyond the specific Greek problems loomed a more general euro crisis for which neoliberals and neo-Keynesians offered contrasting solutions. Fiscal conservatives denounced the creation of a common currency of countries with different economic performance and without a shared government as an impossibility, with the *Wall Street Journal* continuously predicting its imminent failure. Soft-money advocates like the Nobel Prize–winner Joseph E. Stiglitz had more sympathy for the integrative goals of a shared currency but berated the austerity policies of the European Central Bank as counterproductive for growth and prosperity. Anti-inflationary measures that helped the export surplus of Germany, the Eurozone's largest economy, were constricting the catch-up efforts of Eastern European and Mediterranean countries.[5] This was not just an academic debate, but a highly emotional policy conflict that threatened to tear the EU apart. The euro crisis therefore became synonymous with the incompleteness of the European project.

The Grexit Threat

Unfortunately, the inclusion of Greece in the Eurozone had been based on an overly optimistic assessment of its economy and polity. The country had quite a difficult past, including a repressive Nazi occupation and a bitter civil war between royalists and Communists that led to a failed democracy followed by a military dictatorship. Even after the overthrow of the colonels' regime, Greece struggled with severe structural problems. In a habit inherited from resistance against Ottoman domination, citizens evaded between one-third and one-half of their taxes, starving the government of needed revenue. Moreover, corruption ran rampant, requiring payoffs, called *fakelaki*, in order to get official permits. Though ideologically opposed, the two dominant parties, the Panhellenic Socialist Movement (PASOK) on the left and New Democracy on the right, rewarded their followers with jobs that bloated the public payroll. As a result, the statistics reported to Brussels were inflated, making it look as if Athens would meet the Eurozone membership requirements in the near future.[6]

Initially, inclusion in the Eurozone triggered an impressive boom that rested on public borrowing and private investment. Due to the low interest rates of the euro and the solidity of the currency guaranteed by the European Central Bank, lending money to Athens looked like a safe bet that promised high returns. New hotels sprouted up at the scenic shores all over Hellas, four-lane highways opened to the Peloponnese, private houses were built with modern conveniences—the country looked dynamic and increasingly prosperous. Wages rose steeply, soon exceeding the EU norm, and after the turn of the century growth averaged over 4 percent per annum. The only problem was that the debt per GDP ratio had already reached 100 percent in 2000, eventually increasing to 175 percent, the highest in the EU. With the building of new kindergartens, schools, and other public facilities, the budget deficit widened, reaching 15.3 percent in 2009, a level that could only be sustained as long as creditors were willing to pour new euros into the Greek economy.[7]

In October 2009, this pyramid scheme fell apart when the government publicly admitted that it had misreported its household deficit and public debt figures. Because international lenders were still struggling with the default of Lehman Brothers in the United States, the markets were shocked and downgraded Greek bonds to junk status. Since Athens would be unable to pay $53 billion to service its debts for 2010, the country was effectively bankrupt. If the EU wanted to keep the crisis from imperiling the euro as a whole, Brussels had to find a way to restructure the Greek debt. In principle, there were three different ways out of the predicament: First, Athens could leave the Eurozone and devalue the drachma, repudiating many of its obligations. Second, the European Union could come to the rescue by requiring the imprudent lenders to write off part of their loans, making them accept "a haircut." Finally, the financial community could insist on Greek austerity, de facto lowering its living standard to rebalance the budget.[8]

Reaching agreement on bailing out the economy was complicated because it required clashing interests to be reconciled and EU laws to be observed. As the biggest creditor, the German government wanted to construct a firewall to defend the euro while keeping its own banks and taxpayers from having to cover the Greek debt through mutualization. The EU was hamstrung by its rules, which prohibited the ECB from trying to stabilize the market by buying up Greek bonds. Moreover, the IMF was reluctant to use funds in Europe that were needed elsewhere. But action was urgently required since the drying up of interbank lending was about to result in an acute "systemic crisis."[9] Eventually, the troika of the ECB, the European Commission, and the IMF agreed on a huge bailout loan of €110 billion both to finance the current budget deficit and service the external debt. While this rescue package bought some time, this memorandum of agreement also required the Greek government to take drastic steps to put its fiscal house in order so as to return to solvency.

In Greece the most draconian austerity program ever created great resentment since it required a complete change in fiscal behavior and a reduction of public services. The Papandreou government took a first step in 2010 and drastically reduced public expenditures by cutting officials' pay, slashing public pensions, raising the retirement age, and so on. Within months, the country had to make up an 18 percent shortfall, which could only be accomplished by an internal deflation that drastically affected individual lives—for instance, by forcing people to pay for a previously generous health care system. The Greek elite quickly moved much of its assets to safe havens like Switzerland, while ordinary citizens were forced to absorb the brunt of the reductions. Anyone with traceable income was hard-hit, while people in the underground cash economy could evade much of the pressure. The result was a public uproar from citizens who felt cheated, creating mass strikes with the slogan "We can't pay, we won't pay."[10] Due to its shocking consequences, the rescue acquired a bad name.

It soon become apparent that the first bailout was not enough since the restructuring measures deepened Greece's recession and made repaying the outstanding loans even more difficult. The markets remained skeptical, pushing interest rates for government bonds to unprecedented heights of almost 30 percent while the real GNP severely contracted at the same time. Because this declining economy made servicing loans seem unrealistic, the German government pushed through a haircut of about 50 percent for private creditors, forcing them to write off half of their claims. After complicated negotiations in 2012, the troika came up with another €130 billion in loans to make it possible for Athens to survive its short-term obligations and eventually reach a primary surplus, not counting payments on loans. The creditors hoped that the imposition of additional restructuring measures would create a turnaround by rebalancing the budget, which would restore investor confidence and lower the interest rates on bonds.[11]

For many Greek citizens, the effects of continued austerity were, nonetheless, devastating since they tore their elaborate social safety net. The government increased taxes such as the VAT and made strenuous efforts to curb the shadow economy by requiring payment for goods and services by credit card in order to make transactions traceable. At the same time, Athens further reduced formerly generous pensions and raised the retirement age. Against the resistance of a reluctant bureaucracy, it also attempted to sell off some of its property and to shed some of the excessive government jobs. The result of these measures was a deepened recession, amounting to a roughly one-quarter drop in GNP during the course of the crisis. Adult unemployment rose to 25 percent while youth joblessness reached a shocking 50 percent. In practice, this meant that many people could only survive by relying on extensive family networks and by doing odd jobs in the shadow economy.[12] Restoring competitiveness therefore exacted a high price in human suffering.

The severity of the bailout conditions inspired the astounding rise of a new party, called Syriza, that channeled discontent in a radical leftist direction. The established parties, New Democracy and PASOK, were both discredited and held responsible for carrying out the austerity cuts intensely resented by much of the population. Unlike the ossified Communist Party, this newcomer was a motley coalition of dissident leftists, ready to endorse a whole range of local protests and national strikes against the troika-imposed reductions in salaries and services. In the two 2012 elections, Syriza rose from a marginal presence to 27 percent of the vote, becoming the biggest party almost overnight. It had campaigned on refusing further austerity, demanding a debt remission, and reversing some of the welfare cuts. On this refusal platform Syriza won the January 2015 election, gained about half of the seats in Parliament and made its youthful leader Alexis Tsipras prime minister. Resentment against austerity had created a populist left-wing government.[13]

The Greek debt crisis reached its climax in the summer of 2015 when creditors insisted on additional austerity measures and Athens rejected any further cutbacks. This increased the possibility of default since the country had not yet sufficiently recovered to service its loans and needed another extension. Torn between the Syriza voters' resistance and the troika's insistence on fiscal discipline, Tsipras called a referendum on July 5 in which three-fifths of the Greeks rejected the conditions imposed. When Athens media claimed that the German government owed it reparations for its World War II occupation, the German finance minister Wolfgang Schäuble responded in no uncertain terms that Berlin would not be blackmailed. Moreover, the ECB warned that a Grexit of leaving the Eurozone would have "catastrophic consequences," thereby triggering a run on the banks.[14] Only at the last minute did the exasperated creditors and the angry Athens cabinet reach an agreement, making another €86 billion available in return for harsh spending cuts.

The subsequent recovery of the Greek economy under international oversight has been agonizingly slow. In effect, austerity has wiped out the gains of the Eurozone boom and returned the country to the level of 2000, which was one-quarter lower. By 2014 the first signs of a turnaround became visible, with GNP showing a small gain, repeated in subsequent years. But the release of bailout funds remained contingent on additional reforms to increase taxation and reduce pensions while creating an independent statistical service. Though a minority left Syriza out of protest, the Parliament reluctantly accepted the draconian measures, which reduced the budget deficit to about 2 percent per annum since it wanted to stay in the Eurozone. Armed with a permanent European Stability Mechanism (ESM), capable of lending 700 billion euros, the creditors led by the ECB also preferred to keep Athens in the euro to defend the common currency. The Greek debt has therefore plateaued at around €320 billion, allowing the country to finally return to the bond market in 2018.[15]

The blame for the near-Grexit must fall on the shoulders of all the participants in the debacle. In pre-crisis years, Greece had "built up a mountain of debt," far beyond its capacity to repay, fueling a spending spree. With this influx of funds, Athens failed to address structural problems so that "tax evasion flourished and budget shortfalls were swept under the rug." To the creditors, Greek investments looked attractive since the Eurozone guaranteed the solidity of the loans. Counting on the ECB, investors poured money into Greece, dismissing warning signs of underlying risks. When the American fiscal crisis dried up further loans, this house of cards collapsed. Since Athens resented harsh austerity while the troika protected its banks and taxpayers, the struggle over bailouts produced only half-measures of "defer and pretend."[16] In the end the creditors prevailed by imposing a draconian restructuring program that saved the euro and the banks but inflicted enormous pain on the Greeks, lowering their living standard by one-quarter.

The Eurozone Crisis

The international financial crisis had started through unrestrained speculation in the United States, dramatized in the 2015 film *The Big Short*.[17] It was a result of immense amounts of capital being invested in pension, money market, or hedge funds in search of higher profits in a low-interest environment. Although Reagan had piled up public debts, Clinton reduced an already porous regulatory framework by allowing banks not just to finance business ventures but also to speculate in the market in 1999. To satisfy this demand, the financial industry invented new derivatives, such as "the securitization of mortgage lending," which made marginal loans instruments of speculation by bundling them and detaching them from performance. Instead of calling their bluff, the major rating agencies colluded in assigning security scores far higher than their actual values and the insurance companies blithely ignored the risks. When interest rates finally began to rise again, interbank lending effectively collapsed.[18] The dramatic symbol was the default of the overextended Lehman Brothers on September 16, 2008.

The crisis quickly spread to Europe since the transatlantic banking systems were rather closely intertwined. The City of London had become a hub of offshore dollar banking, rivaling New York in the volume of transactions. Aided by Margaret Thatcher's neoliberal deregulation, European banks had also thrown themselves into financial speculation, investing heavily in American subprime mortgages. When nervous lenders called back their loans, overextended banks began to implode since they were committed way above their actual assets. In the United States, mortgage lenders were bailed out with public funds while the Federal Reserve Bank helped banks with liquidity in order keep the financial system from collapsing. On the Continent, this downward spiral engulfed the institutions that had been overeager to share in the profits of the speculative housing bubble without taking sufficient precautions against its bursting. As a result of the financial crisis, consumer confidence plummeted, triggering the greatest recession since the Great Depression.[19]

The general downturn had a special impact on Eastern Europe since it stopped the catch-up drive to achieve Western levels of consumption that had been fueled with outside investments. When the funds refused to flow, GDP declined by over 10 percent, dashing the hopes of consumers for improving their living standards. The Baltic countries were worst off since they wanted to join the euro and were therefore unwilling to follow their neighbors' practice of devaluing their currencies. But

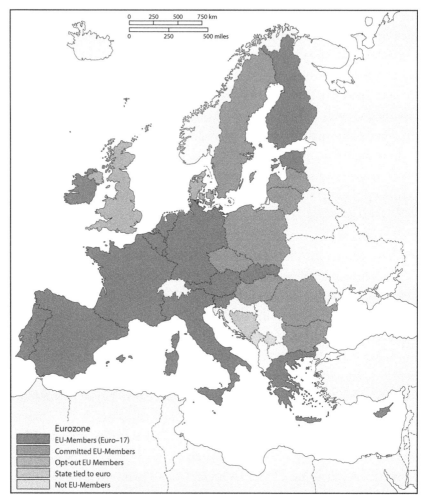

MAP 4. Eurozone members, 2011. Cox Cartographic.

everywhere private spending collapsed, taxes declined, national budgets became unbalanced, and unemployment soared. Only Poland managed to escape the downward spiral. Preoccupied with its own liquidity problems, the ECB was unwilling to intervene, handing the problem to the IMF. Eventually, modest packages of aid were agreed on to save the investments of Austrian or Swedish banks, producing a gradual recovery.[20] But the Eastern European public's disappointment in the lack of aid by the West left deep psychological scars.

The root of the sovereign debt problem was the unrestrained boom during the previous decade, which had rested on an influx of foreign loans rather than on internal productivity gains. The shared currency of by then seventeen Eurozone countries had created a splendid opportunity for borrowing money at low cost since the risk seemed minimal due to the anti-inflationary policy of the ECB. In the private realm, access to cheap loans fueled an enormous building boom of hotels, businesses, and homes along the Mediterranean shores, fed by a wave of speculative euphoria. In the public arena, the influx of foreign investment made it possible for governments to expand services, offering health care and other welfare measures that had hitherto seemed out of reach. The debts of the PIIGS states were staggering: Portugal owed $322.4 billion, Ireland $843.8 billion, Italy $1,475.3 billion, Greece $297.2 billion, and Spain $1,102.6 billion.[21] The liabilities of $2.5 trillion had grown so large that they could only be serviced with additional loans, rendering their repayment illusory.

Although French banks had lent more than twice as much as the German ones, the latter's response was crucial since they represented the largest economy on the Continent. Berlin's approach to fiscal policy was still haunted by the terrifying memory of two prior inflations in the twentieth century that had wiped out financial assets and thereby promoted political radicalism. Moreover, in response to economic sluggishness due to high wages, the red-green government of Gerhard Schröder had already pushed through painful welfare-state cutbacks, called Agenda 2010, which aimed to restore Germany's global competitiveness. The subsequent Christian Democratic Union–led government of Angela Merkel therefore rejected making the Eurozone into a "transfer union" and insisted on fiscal discipline among the other member states. Since the debtor countries could no longer devalue their own currencies externally, they were forced to do so internally by lowering their living standards. Supported by other northern countries, the German-imposed austerity helped their export surplus, but it exploded the bubble in the Eastern European and Mediterranean countries.[22]

Without a common financial policy, the European response to the sovereign debt crisis remained piecemeal and half-hearted. The turn to the "intergovernmentalism" of the 2009 Lisbon Treaty prevented the launch of a European Monetary Fund, which could have stepped in like the Fed in the United States. Instead, Germany prevailed by pulling the IMF into the Greek rescue operation, dealing with each affected country individually rather than presenting a common solution. After much wrangling in the troika of the European Commission, the ECB, and the IMF, a compromise emerged that linked the refinancing of toxic loans to strenuous efforts at debt reduction—such as the further slashing of public expenditures by cutting bureaucratic salaries, dropping services, and so on. Eventually, a temporary European Financial Stability Facility was created to which individual states would contribute funds to be used for rescuing delinquent countries.[23] The reluctant ECB decision to start buying back toxic bonds calmed the markets but failed to solve the underlying problem.

By turning bailouts into a struggle over austerity, the Eurozone crisis moved beyond the debtors into the creditor countries. At issue was the Eurozone's basic economic philosophy: Following a household model of balancing one's budget, deficit hawks demanded a drastic reduction of public and private borrowing. In contrast, leftist economists steadfastly called for additional stimulus expenditures in order to end the crisis and restore growth. In Great Britain, the incoming Conservative administration slashed public expenditures by cutting over one million jobs, mostly from local government. In Germany, the CDU-led government enacted a deficit brake, allowing the budget to grow only 0.34 percent annually, which ruled out large stimulus packages. This neoliberal orthodoxy sought to make the entire Eurozone follow the German pattern of restoring competitiveness by reducing wage increases. Berlin insisted that first expenditures needed to be brought under control and only then could one seriously consider stimulating additional growth.[24]

The next victim of the financial crisis was Ireland, whose economy had grown spectacularly since 1994 due to US multinational investments in this low-tax, anglophone country. Cheap financing as a consequence of euro membership triggered a boom in the housing sector, which created a credit bubble in the banks by borrowing sums from abroad and relending them domestically. Acting on the motto "If I have it, I'll spend it," the government failed to rein in the spending spree. When the loans had gotten too big to be serviced, the troika imposed a drastic set of austerity measures to reduce the budget deficit of 31 percent and refinance the indebted banks. These severe cuts led to a permanent loss of output of 15 to 20 percent of production, shrinking the economy by about one-tenth of the GDP. As a result, salaries were cut and jobless-ness reached 14 percent, imposing a drastic burden on individuals that reduced domestic demand.[25] Eventually, such interventions restored a primary surplus and growth resumed—albeit from a much lower level than before.

From the Greek and Irish defaults, the crisis spread so as to threaten the survival of the euro as a whole. The markets were shocked when Portugal and Spain also admitted excessive liabilities, though the Italian balance sheet did not look much better. The situation was tense since the larger economies of these states required more assistance. Ignoring a tide of popular protests, the troika demanded drastic measures, mak-ing its loans dependent on sizable deficit reductions in spite of their recessionary effects. Berlin still insisted on a fiscal compact, enshrining its austerity rules. But the pressure grew so much that a comprehensive firewall of debt restructuring, creditor haircuts, and the creation of a European Stability Mechanism began to emerge. The final breakthrough combined a Growth Pact with permission for the ESM to support gov-ernment debt in all countries in compliance with fiscal discipline. To reassure the markets, the ECB head Mario Draghi announced: "Within our mandate, the ECB is ready to do whatever it takes to preserve the Euro."[26]

This rhetorical commitment became the turning point of the acute Eurozone crisis since it succeeded in calming the markets. In effect, it rested on a compromise between deficit spenders on the one hand and fiscal conservatives on the other. With the establishment of an Outright Money Transactions Fund (OMT), the ECB became the lender of last resort. This was backed by a patchwork of "Greek restructuring, the fis-cal compact, banking union, ESM [and] the ECB's OMT facility." Bely-ing hordes of transatlantic doomsayers, the Eurozone finally showed sufficient cohesion to come up with the necessary measures to rescue the common currency. It required several years for this solution to really take hold since the crisis aftershocks continued in places like Ukraine and new compromises had to be found time and again. But in the end the combination of fiscal discipline and lending support managed to bring the debt of most PIIGS countries except for Greece under control and made them competitive again.[27]

The ultimate stabilization, nevertheless, remained contested, with Germany largely cast in the role of villain. The social crisis imposed by austerity led to the election successes of new populist parties of the Left like Syriza or Podemos in Spain as well as radical right-wing movements like the Front National in France and the Alternative for Germany. In response to the continuing Greek crisis, Mario Draghi and the ECB finally decided on a quantitative easing of Athens' credit crunch by buying back bonds in order to avert default. But in the long run, the size of the Greek debt was insupportable, triggering dramatic negotiations with the troika over additional bailouts that were complicated by a refusal to authorize further haircuts. In order not to let Europe fail, Angela Merkel finally agreed to the creation of a guarantee fund in 2015, imposing severe controls on Athens.[28] While this concession ended the short-run crisis, the piecemeal approach failed to solve the underlying problem of the creation of a joint financial policy.

The Burden of Austerity

The debate about the euro crisis ultimately revolved around the question of who should pay down the accumulated debt. During the preceding boom, it was easy to agree on the heady expansion of credit since both lenders and borrowers appeared to profit. But when the bubble burst, a fierce conflict developed over which side ought to bear the chief burden of servicing and repaying the loans. With the help of the troika, the creditors insisted on safeguarding their investments, clamoring to save the banks, even if they had engaged in irresponsible speculation in the first place. But rallying behind left-wing parties and economists, the borrowers called for a restructuring of their obligations and tried to shift the costs to the banks through haircuts that would forgive much of the debt. When the austerity policies inflicted enormous personal hardship, the disappointed people repudiated their governments and flocked to populist parties, promising anticapitalist measures on the left, or anti-globalist responses on the right.[29]

During the "golden years" before the crisis in the 2000s, it looked as if all Eurozone states were benefiting from the introduction of a common currency. The adoption of the euro fulfilled the French wish to eliminate the disliked DM, which had time and again constrained Paris's plans for expansion via deficit financing. At the same time, the larger currency area helped German businesses by eliminating exchange fees and creating a stable, low-inflation environment that aided the development of their exports. For the post-Communist countries that adopted the euro, the shared currency provided a hedge against speculation and an impetus to catch up to the rest of the members in growth. For the Mediterranean periphery, the conditionality criteria exerted pressure on economic reforms and provided access to low-interest financing for their development. A liberal interpretation of movement toward convergence aimed to establish incentives for membership that would offer benefits to all members of the Eurozone.[30]

Especially in the catch-up countries of Eastern and Southern Europe, the euro encouraged the development of a real estate boom through low-cost financing. When banks offered cheap credit, many families were only too happy to escape their cramped quarters by building new houses or apartments. Service providers in the tourist economy of the Mediterranean shores were determined to erect new hotel complexes or provide vacation apartments with swimming pools. The Spanish economist Juan Dolado explained: "Sun and bricks, this is our industrial specialization." While some of the funds went into expanding production facilities that lured high-tech firms to Ireland, much of the international investment augmented services and consumption. As a result of the competition for land and materials, housing prices more than doubled in Spain and many households took on too much debt. Offering an escape from habitual poverty, the rapid expansion was so intoxicating that participants ignored timely warnings that things were about to overheat.[31]

Ignoring their responsibilities, banks and governments colluded in supporting the continuation of the boom beyond its sustainable limits. Financial institutions began to offer low-interest loans with repayment schedules of forty years or beyond in order to inflate their balance sheets. Governments provided attractive tax breaks for home construction projects. Buoyed by increasing revenues, they also built new schools, hospitals, and highways to replace worn-out facilities. Moreover, the authorities hired many professionals in order to provide extended services, ranging from childcare to health facilities. Awash with borrowed money, they increased public salaries substantially, pricing the boom countries out of the international labor market. "Cheap money brought a burst of self-confidence and a consumption binge," finally lifting countries on the EU periphery out of poverty.[32] As a result, no one wanted to spoil the party by reminding the public that the accumulated debts would have to be repaid someday.

When the speculative bubble burst, "it was a total shock," because the hectic economic activity almost ground to a halt. House prices tumbled below the amount of the outstanding loans, but inflated interest payments continued. Consumer credit collapsed, car payments stalled, and credit cards could no longer be balanced, decreasing purchases and endangering indebted stores. Moreover, tax receipts dropped, forcing governments to curtail their expenditures just when welfare payments were most needed. Construction projects stopped, houses were left incomplete, and highways ended in the middle of nowhere since feeder roads could not be finished. Worried about their accounts, individuals made a run on the most endangered banks, forcing their governments to guarantee their deposits like in 2008 in Ireland. Overburdened states were having difficulty making their loan payments on schedule. For critics within the system, the "financial crisis was a strong warning sign that the finance sector needed to change."[33]

The neoliberal remedy for the Eurozone crisis, touted by the troika, was austerity in order once again to make the indebted countries competitive. In practice, that meant stopping the floating of new loans and restructuring the outstanding liabilities so that they could continue to be serviced. At the same time, so-called financial reform required rigorous efforts to rebalance public budgets by raising taxes and lowering expenditures. For private individuals, this often caused drastic wage cuts or even dismissals so as to reduce the bloated workforce. The key argument was that "the crisis was the outcome of a lack of discipline on the part of other governments." The neoliberal advice insisted on returning to "a prudent economic policy." A former ECB member Jürgen Stark argued in moral terms: "While others were living beyond their means, Germany avoided excess."[34] The solution was therefore a drastic reduction of expenditures to a level that could be sustained by actually earned incomes.

Leftist economists like Joseph Stiglitz countered that "austerity has been an utter and unmitigated disaster," since it led to recession rather than to recovery. Instead of being limited to a short period of intense pain, the deflationary cycle provoked a prolonged depression. "There is no other word to describe an economy like that of Spain or Greece, where nearly one in four people—and more than 50% of young people—cannot find work." Since the remedy proved worse than the disease, the GNP of the afflicted countries was reduced to the level it had reached before the boom. Many leftist commentators argued that the neoliberal prescription of making overly indebted countries once again competitive through debt restructuring and reduction of expenditures was counterproductive because it increased the proportional debt burden by destroying demand. "All the suffering in Europe—inflicted in the service of man-made artifice—is even more tragic for being unnecessary."[35]

For the affected individuals, the effect of austerity was nothing short of disastrous. Even middle-class folk like the Spaniard Luis who had worked in the legal department of a bank for years suddenly found themselves out of work. "Little could we have imagined that at 57, it would be a struggle to stay off" the unemployment lists. Barely making ends meet on a meager preretirement income, the couple had "given up credit cards, and this month their home internet connection [was] cut off." Since gas was too expensive, "our car's just gathering dust now." Their savings had "been dwindling over the past years, especially since the wife lost her job as an administrative assistant." Book clubs, union dues, and television and telephone services were no longer affordable. "The days when they could go away on holiday [were a] distant memory; the luxury of going out [was] a thing of the past." As a result, they felt "awful" since at their age there was little chance of finding a new job. Losing "a settled life," they resented "being treated like dirt."[36]

The younger generation also saw its future blocked through the debt crisis since it was impossible to launch adequate careers. Already as a fourteen-year-old, the Greek girl Joanna Ntoukaki had learned about "sovereign debt spreads" and financial haircuts. "As there were not enough jobs" she "chose to leave the country at 18 to study economics" in Great Britain. Similarly, Daniele Mondiale, a thirty-year-old Italian architect, was forced to move in with his parents, reassured by their security but feeling "a sense of failure and humiliation." He had started on a promising career in 2007, earning €2,000 per month. But when the financial crisis hit, creating a future for himself became "an illusion . . . a flash in the pan." The recession "closed the building sites" with big companies squeezing out the younger newcomers. When he could not even afford to share a flat, "he gave up." While "studying for a doctorate he packed his bags and headed back home."[37] An entire generation found itself shut out, falling back into dependence.

Even worse off were people who needed special supports that were cut "by a government determined to rein in public debt." Stuart Noden, a fifty-one-year-old from Great Britain, had worked "for more than three decades as a cabinet maker in Manchester." But when he blacked out and fell from a roof, his accustomed "life collapsed" since he had a series of strokes, rendering him unable to work. "He's been left with weakness down his left side, relies on a walking stick to get about and has regular seizures." Though he was no longer able to drive and could not return to his job, "he failed to score enough points to qualify for the welfare payment designed to assist people who are incapacitated through sickness." Lacking supplemental private insurance, he experienced the National Health Service (NHS) as a Kafkaesque "hell of people being rude and saying no," where he was being sent from one social department to another without receiving aid. Since his wife's pay as a cleaner was not enough, "the couple [were] about to lose their home after falling behind on their mortgage."[38] Austerity denied help to those people who needed it most.

In their crisis management the Eurozone governments chose to save the banks in order to preserve the financial system rather than to lessen the pain for ordinary people. As a result of the debt binge, the economists Carmen Reinhart and Kenneth Rogoff have argued that "over the longer haul, a comprehensive credible fiscal consolidation is very much needed" so as to prevent the recurrence of deep crises. But "a lot of policies are directed at keeping European banks afloat and it is crippling the credit system." As a result of excessive prior borrowing, policy makers went to the other extreme and insisted on a cautious, anti-inflationary approach that ironically created a deep double-dip recession. "Delaying debt write-downs and delaying marking to market is not particularly conducive to speeding up deleveraging and recovery." What started as a necessary effort to lance the bubble ultimately prolonged the adjustment of the Eurozone. More quantitative easing, the repurchase of bonds, and even modest inflation would have speeded the recovery.[39]

Saving the Euro

Throughout the Eurozone crisis journalists, economists, and politicians predicted the imminent collapse of the euro. Early on, the economist Barry Eichengreen had forecast a debacle due to "the limited extent of political integration in Europe," which constrained the EU's enforcement powers. In 2012 Martin Feldstein concluded even more drastically in *Foreign Affairs*: "The Euro should now be recognized as an experiment that failed." This was not a result of "bureaucratic mismanagement but rather the inevitable consequence of imposing a single currency on a very heterogeneous group of countries." Because it was based on a political decision to harness German power to European integration, the euro was far from an "optimum currency area" and would never become an international rival to the dollar since "the EU lacks the will, the ideas and the capacity to promote the Euro." Athens could only save itself by a Grexit, leaving the Eurozone.[40] Yet, in spite of so many dire forecasts, the euro has miraculously survived.

The failure of most Eurozone members to meet the Maastricht criteria revealed the enormous obstacles to the creation of a common currency in such disparate economies. Only Denmark, Estonia, Finland, Germany, and Sweden matched the 3 percent level of government budget deficit as percentage of GDP during 2009. In contrast, the amount clearly exceeded 10 percent in Greece, Ireland, Latvia, and Spain. Moreover, Belgium's national debt as percentage of GDP approached 100 percent in 2009, with Greece and Italy going well beyond it and even France, Germany, and Portugal surpassing the 60 percent level. As a result, the governments of Austria, Bulgaria, the Czech Republic, France, Ireland, Italy, and Slovakia pledged to undertake rigorous efforts to reduce their deficits. Drastic measures of tax increases and expenditure reductions attempted to rein in runaway spending—but at the cost of turning a temporary downturn in 2009 into a deep double-dip recession, with growth resuming only in 2015.[41]

Though they were right on the delayed response, most doomsayers underestimated the political commitment to European integration and misunderstood the bargaining process. Compared with the concerted action of the Fed and the US government, the vacillation of the ECB and the EU Commission did look frustrating. In effect, their response to the Eurozone crisis was a strategy of "failing forward," with members only making a minimum of concessions and settling for the "lowest common denominator solutions" due to the philosophy of intergovernmentalism. Moreover, the electorate in the fiscally sound countries resisted paying for the seeming profligacy of its neighbors. But "to date, this sequential cycle of piecemeal reform, followed by policy failure, followed by further reform, has managed to sustain both the European project and the common currency."[42] Though highly risky in postponing solutions, this decision-making process has ultimately come up with enough pragmatic compromises to reassure the markets and rescue the common currency.

Even if it was excruciatingly slow, growth has eventually returned in the wake of tough austerity measures. For example, Ireland has made a dramatic recovery since "it has slashed spending, increased taxes, reformed the economy and is now well on the road to recovery." Though not in the Eurozone, Iceland "suffered perhaps the most spectacular crash," but it also returned to growth after a tough IMF bailout. Latvia took a radically neoliberal approach as well in preparation for Eurozone membership. With a much larger economy, Spain was also forced to introduce "a series of stiff reforms and austerity measures," leaving the bailout scheme while still fighting unemployment. Having delayed restructuring before, Portugal needed similarly drastic measures to turn its economy around. Even Greece eventually resumed growth, electing a center-right New Democracy government under Kyriakos Mitsotakis in the summer of 2019.[43] While neoliberal advocates could point to austerity's eventual success, neo-Keynesians deplored the high human cost involved.

Though the efforts to rescue the euro exacted a high price, they failed to erode commitment to the common currency in the member countries. Widespread resentment against austerity led to the erosion of their support in the centrist parties and drove anti-European sentiment to new heights. In the creditor countries, populist appeals strengthened the radical right-wing parties like the Front National in France or the AfD in Germany. In the austerity-plagued states (like Greece, Spain, and Italy), new left-wing parties (like Syriza, Podemos, and the Five Star Movement) have sprung up to channel popular protest. But, ultimately, no country has been ready to abandon the euro since the EU's long-term advantages, such as support from agricultural and regional funds, promised to exceed the short-run pain of convergence efforts. Even with an initial lowering of living standards, the public ultimately accepted the need for debt reduction as a path to competitiveness. Moreover, the lessons of the fiscal crisis have inspired a more constructive response to the creation of a coronavirus relief fund, even accepting a partial mutualization of debt in 2020.[44]

5

Migration Wave

FIGURE 6. Drowning refugees, Lampedusa, Italy. dpa picture alliance / Alamy Stock Photo.

In the early morning hours of October 3, 2013, an overloaded trawler approached Lampedusa, the southernmost Italian island in the Mediterranean. After having crossed for two stormy days from Libya, the boat lost its engines and the pumps gave out. The pilot then lit a blanket to draw the coast guard's attention—but suddenly spilled gasoline caught on fire. Seeking to escape the flaming inferno, the desperate migrants from Eritrea and Somalia rushed to the opposite side of the twenty-meter-long boat, capsizing the unbalanced ship and spilling about 500 men, women, and children into the frigid waters. Though local fishermen and the Italian navy quickly came to the rescue, they only managed to pull about 155 people out alive. Not being able to swim, the rest met a grisly death. Trying to recover the sunken bodies, the divers described "seeing horrific scenes inside the wreckage." Up to this time, the sinking was "one of Italy's worst disasters involving a boat carrying Europe-bound migrants from Africa."[1]

Although twenty thousand refugees had already been lost by 2013 while crossing the treacherous Mediterranean, the size of the Lampedusa tragedy shocked politicians and the public. The dazed survivors only hoped to move on to Sweden or Germany to start a new life. The overwhelmed islanders protested against the lack of support from the Italian government: "Once again you didn't hear me crying." Pope Francis called the situation "a disgrace" and exhorted: "Let us unite our efforts so that similar tragedies do not happen again." Similarly, the president of the European Commission José Manuel Barroso was stunned by the sight of hundreds of caskets in a makeshift mortuary: "It's something, I think, one cannot forget: coffins of babies, coffins of a mother and a child that was born at that moment." To the Italian interior minister Angelino Alfano, this was not just an accident but the result of a failed migration policy: "Europe must realize it is not an Italian drama, but a European one."[2] In short, the constant drowning of refugees was a European tragedy.

In spite of the perils of the journey, African migrants and Middle Eastern refugees continued to come, propelled by the horrendous conditions in their countries. A sizable minority of the about twenty-two million people pushed by abject poverty and political repression to abandon their homes dreamed of finding a better future in Europe. When one Sudanese man got word that he was about to be killed, his friends said: "You have to leave, hide, disappear." The first obstacle was traversing the Sahara Desert, where bandits preyed on helpless refugees and extorted their meager savings. Then there was lawless Libya "where some die in transit and many are bought and sold like slaves." Smugglers who controlled the only means of reaching Europe created a further bottleneck by extorting thousands of dollars for a place on an unsafe boat. When these fragile vessels, sometimes even rubber rafts, began to sink, the scared refugees hoped to be picked up by the Italian Coast Guard or other rescue ships. In spite of dire cell phone warnings of the trip's dangers, tens of thousands remained ready to take the risk.[3]

The steady rise in refugee numbers troubled EU decision makers, because they were themselves at odds over the issue of multiculturalism. Already during the 1980s, the arrival of a sizable number of Muslims from Pakistan, North Africa, and Turkey had provoked a political backlash against their different appearance, social habits, and religious practices. Conservative politicians opposed the building of mosques and inveighed against the loss of Christian identity, even if they were willing to hire so-called guest workers. While left-wing parties tended to insist on openness, some labor unions and many workers feared losing their jobs to hardworking competitors from abroad. Eastern Europeans with but little experience in living with strangers resented the newcomers as a threat to their traditional national cultures. Even many liberals worried that Islamic fundamentalism was incompatible with diversity, gender equality, or sexual freedom. This strange set of xenophobes wanted to keep migrants out.[4]

Liberal commentators and migration experts, nonetheless, insisted on welcoming refugees as a humanitarian duty regardless of the cost. These critics argued that rescuing those who were shipwrecked was a recognized moral imperative, even if it served the business model of the smugglers. They stressed that asylum was a basic human right that could not be denied because of the practical problems of determining who had a justified claim to it. Sympathetic volunteers also helped in the migrant shelters, offering their time, work, and money so as to make migrants feel welcome. As a result, the question of how to respond to the unforeseen mass migration became highly politicized with the Right demanding the closing of borders and the Left calling for continued humanitarian aid. According to the 1990 compromise of the Dublin System, the countries of a migrant's first entry into the EU were supposed to document and separate persecuted refugees with a claim to political asylum from economic migrants looking for a better life. Moralizing observers therefore asserted that "the EU failed the test, on all counts."[5]

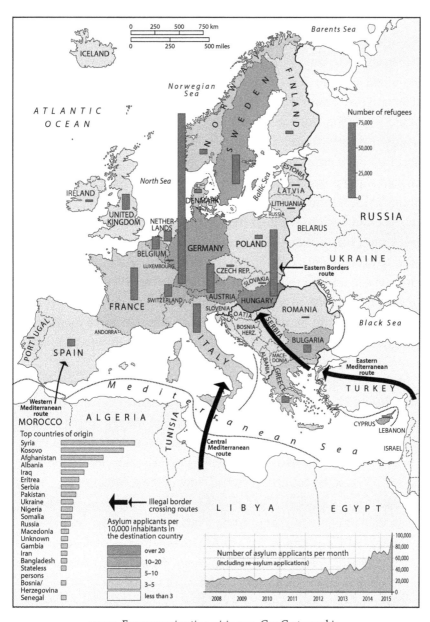

MAP 5. European migration crisis, 2015. Cox Cartographic.

Italian Responses

Italian efforts to cope with the migration crisis were complicated by the ingrained memory of the country's long history of emigration. Between 1880 and 1915, about thirteen million Italians had left their homes for work in neighboring states or for overseas opportunities in the United States and Latin America. Unrestrained by the Catholic proscription against birth control, population growth, especially in the rural South, created abject poverty from which people sought to escape by migrating abroad. While toiling elsewhere in factories and fields, they could send remittances back to support their extended families or, if they were really successful, return themselves in a chain migration that sent others away to take their place. After 1861 the newly unified Italian state tried to channel emigrations into its own African Empire in Somalia and Libya or to other established communities in which the language and culture of *Italianita* could be preserved.[6] Due to this pervasive memory of emigration, which continued after World War II, Italy was completely unprepared for the influx from across the sea.

A first inkling of a turnaround in migration patterns had already come after 1945 with the attempted repatriation of Italian citizens from the former empire. A case in point was the fascist occupation of Albania from 1939 to 1943, which brought tens of thousands of soldiers and civilian administrators as well as businessmen to the other shore of the Adriatic Sea. When the country switched sides in the summer of 1943, most of them were trapped by the newly dominant Wehrmacht, first having to do the Germans' bidding and then following the orders of the independent but Communist state of Albania. While most succeeded in eventually getting repatriated with the help of the United Nations Relief and Rehabilitation Authority (UNRRA), a significant number of essential specialists remained behind for several decades. Only after the end of the Cold War in 1990 could they return to Italy, followed by tens of thousands of Albanians who were desperate to escape a backward post-Communist country for the more prosperous and modern West.[7]

In the new migration from Africa, the preferred refugee route was the central Mediterranean with Lampedusa, seventy miles north of Libya, as the first destination. When Madrid clamped down on its border in 2006, migrants turned to Italy, almost doubling their number from 22,194 to 39,726 in 2008. Alarmed by the sudden increase, Prime Minister Silvio Berlusconi "signed a 'friendship' agreement with the Gaddafi regime" by which the dictator "sent his police on to the Tripoli beaches, arrested trafficking agents and all but halted the trade," reducing the number of migrants to 4,450 by 2010. But the overthrow of Gaddafi in 2011 "wreak[ed] havoc by opening the floodgates again," increasing the number to 64,261 during the next year! According to a British journalist, "so many immigrants have been arriving that Italy has declared it a national emergency." Angry at "a flagrant lack of solidarity from Italy's European neighbors," Berlusconi could only promise to ship the migrants on to Italy proper in the hope that they would move on.[8]

The governments at the edge of the EU were unable to stop the influx of migrants, because their efforts to police the border were undercut by criminal networks of smugglers. With dictatorial authority evaporating in the Arab Spring and various factions fighting for dominance, the prior policing of borders broke down, creating opportunities for human trafficking. The desperate migrants provided an attractive business opportunity for the smugglers since the offer of help with illegal crossing of frontiers proved irresistible, in spite of all the well-known risks involved. For West African refugees, getting through the Sahara Desert required local assistance, which placed them at the none too tender mercies of guides promising to transport them to the Libyan shore. Waiting for a boat in Tripoli turned out to be "a pure hell," since extortion was combined with imprisonment unless refugees or their families could come up with around $1,600 as an average price for being shipped to Europe.[9] The testimonies of surviving migrants are horrendous tales of enslavement and suffering.

The conflicting legal and moral implications of rescue at sea created a confusing policy that sought to stop the smuggling while aiding imperiled migrants. Italians were split between humanitarians and some Catholics who wanted to help and nationalists and racists who wanted to keep the migrants out. In 2012 the European Court of Human Rights rejected Italian efforts to return rescued refugees to Libya as a human rights violation. After the Lampedusa disaster, the Roman government launched a "Mare Nostrum" mission for its navy and coast guard that focused on rescuing migrants from their sinking boats. But capturing smugglers remained difficult since they often abandoned their unseaworthy ships when they caught sight of Italian shores, returning by speedboat to Libya. By the mid-2010s the EU had finally begun to support Italian efforts with funds for search and rescue programs such as Triton. But saving almost half a million migrants strained public patience so much, that Matteo Salvini, the xenophobic minister of the interior, refused further operations.[10]

Migrants who had survived the hazards of desert and sea faced new challenges in the overcrowded reception facilities due to delays in bureaucratic processing. "Now that the journeys are over, the survivors expressed disillusionment and disappointment about the countries in which they now live," since the reality of a refugee existence fell far short of the hopes for a better life in Europe. They had to contend with improvised migrant shelters that often lacked the most basic conveniences; they had to cope with unfamiliar food, provided by local volunteers; they had to get used to a different climate; and they had to deal with not officially being allowed to work, often idling away their days in boredom. While aid organizations like the Catholic Misericordia tried to provide essential necessities, living in crowded camps with an uncertain future was depressing. And when they managed to escape confinement, the only jobs available were physical labor, often in the fields and at the mercy of Mafiosi bosses.[11]

Bureaucratic processing aimed at sorting migrants into various categories in order to return some immediately and offer others the chance to apply for asylum. After their arrival, applicants were registered, fingerprinted, and questioned about their reasons for coming to Italy while their data was forwarded to the EURODAC fingerprint database. Since migrants coming from so-called safe countries like Tunisia, Morocco, or Algeria were shipped back to their places of origin, many "lost" their papers and rendered their fingertips unrecognizable. According to the 1951 UN refugee convention that prohibited the return of migrants when their lives were in danger, those who could prove persecution and hailed from war-torn states like Syria, were detained and transported to the mainland to reception centers. There, they had to await the outcome of their petitions, which took months or even years, suspending them in limbo between their homes and destinations.[12] Only about half were granted the coveted status of asylum and redistributed.

Italian responses to mass immigration were initially quite generous since many migrants only wanted to cross through it as a transit country on the way to Western and Northern Europe. Three kinds of foreign populations have emerged in Italy during the last two decades. First, there were about six million legally recognized immigrants, mostly from other EU countries, with official work permits by 2018. Second, due to the steep rise to over 200,000 seaborne refugees per year in 2015 and 2016 and the lax practice of deportations, the second category consisted of between five hundred thousand and one million illegal North Africans whose legal status remained uncertain and who could only work off the books. The third group comprised most of the migrants who intended to stay only temporarily in Italy because they wanted to move on to the more prosperous Central and Northern European countries. Favorite destinations included Sweden and Germany, due to their better job opportunities and extensive welfare system, as well as France for the French-speaking North Africans. English speakers preferred Great Britain, although they mostly arrived by air or across the English Channel from Calais.[13]

Confronted with such a tidal wave of illegal immigrants, the Italian public felt abandoned by the EU whose southern border it was supposed to defend. Rome resented the negative publicity of dead bodies washing up on what were supposed to be scenic beaches since such images discouraged tourism. Expressions of humanitarian regret from Brussels did not really help with the costs of processing and sheltering refugees, which rose from 1.5 to 9.5 million euros a month during 2014. In effect, other states far from the front line of the refugee crisis hid behind the Dublin rule that migrants had to register and apply for asylum in the first country in which they entered the Schengen space. "In ever harsher tones, Italian officials have protested that the EU is not helping enough," since the burden fell disproportionally on their shoulders. The Italian minister of the interior Angelino Alfano even threatened unspecified reprisals unless other countries were willing to accept more refugees.[14]

Eventually, the patience of the public wore so thin that humanitarian solidarity turned into xenophobic hatred, ending efforts at rescue and aid. Initially, the populist Lega Nord had campaigned on a platform of hostility toward the poverty-stricken and mafia-infested South, even promising to secede. But the persistent horror stories of crime, drugs, and violence spread by the Berlusconi-controlled media created a terrifying image of black immigrants threatening white Italians. Moreover, a public prosecutor charged a German ship called *Juventa*—sponsored by a youth rescue NGO—with profiting from smuggling, claiming that "contacts, meetings and understandings" had taken place. Although there was not a shred of proof for the allegation, the Lega used such claims to make electoral gains and create a populist coalition with the Five Star Movement. Invoking racist stereotypes, the minister of the interior Matteo Salvini in 2019 inveighed against the "migrant menace" and refused to let rescue ships dock in Italian ports to debark the migrants.[15]

The Italian case demonstrates that muddling through in the face of a mounting migration crisis was ultimately bound to fail. No doubt, the unprepared authorities were overwhelmed by the human throng of migrants reaching their coast. Although other ports were also involved, Lampedusa became the physical focus and symbolic referent of the refugee stream due to its proximity to the Libyan shore. The recurrent disasters of sinking ships and perishing lives were no accident but a result of a systematic smuggling strategy that used the moral imperative of sea rescue as a way to force entry into the EU.[16] Only briefly in 2010, when the Libyan dictator Muammar Gaddafi prevented the departure of smuggler boats, did the number of arrivals drastically decline. Paradoxically, the rescue ships of the Italian navy or private NGOs therefore served as battering rams against the walls of "Fortress Europe" that tried to keep migrants out. Eventually, the inability of the authorities and the lack of EU aid inspired a xenophobic backlash that undermined human solidarity.

The Balkan Route

By the mid-2010s "the Balkan overland route" leading from Turkey via the Greek islands to Hungary "replaced the Mediterranean passage as the favored route for migrants" from the civil wars in Afghanistan and Syria. The proximity of the islands of Lesbos, Chios, Samos, and Rhodes to the Anatolian shore meant that the water crossing was easier and less dangerous than going across the open Mediterranean. Moreover, the jagged coastline rendered it difficult to police the arrival of small boats or rubber rafts when smugglers tried to deposit their human freight on Greek territory during the night. While it was cheaper to obtain such a passage than from North Africa, a long and costly land voyage through various Balkan countries was still necessary to reach Austria or Germany where migrants could stay or continue on. This second leg required another set of transports and choice of different paths, depending on where border controls would be lax enough to pass. Based on family networks, a huge human trafficking business developed, delivering thousands of migrants on the European Continent.[17]

From 2014 on, migrant numbers through the Balkans exploded and obliterated all efforts of transit and receiving countries to channel the throng. After 2009 the European Border and Coast Guard Agency (Frontex) had intercepted and registered between 24,000 and 57,000 refugees on the Eastern Mediterranean route, but in 2015 the number jumped to an astounding 885,386 migrants before falling to the still impressive figure of 182,277 a year later. Commentators surmised that the pressures from the Afghan conflict and the Syrian War were largely to blame for the increased influx. Moreover, a passage through North Africa had become perilous, due to civil strife, while news images of drowned boat people also deterred migrants from crossing to Italy. This unexpected quantum leap led to a loss of control, overwhelming the bureaucratic registration procedures and humanitarian aid efforts on the way. Confronted with such human misery, the resigned authorities in Greece gave up their efforts at first registration and started to just "wave people through."[18]

Using the Balkan route was, however, not without dangers of its own since migrants were once again at the mercy of organized smuggler rings. According to the Austrian interior minister, "it has developed into a business worth billions," with local gangs cooperating by internet and handing migrants off from one country to another. Refugees "are abandoned in the woods and threatened if they complain. Still others are robbed and left on remote roadsides." In one car chase, the Viennese police succeeded in rescuing twenty-four Afghan refugees. In another case in 2015, the inmates of a Hungarian truck were not so lucky. Since they were locked in during the summer heat, all seventy-one people died. The authorities quickly established that the smugglers were a Bulgarian land-based ring, linked "both the driver and his accomplices to [the] deaths," and prosecuted them for murder. The German chancellor Angela Merkel deplored "such a tragic death," but had little success in asking Europe "to pull together and ease the migration crisis."[19]

Often lost in the media criticism of the inadequacy of the effort is the outpouring of aid to migrants, which helped them on their way and supported them in the receiving countries. NGO ships, staffed by Doctors Without Borders or chartered by the International Rescue Committee, saved tens of thousands of people in international waters off the Libyan shore. Once the refugees reached reception camps, these same organizations helped with medical services and counseling and in other ways to make up for the glaring deficiencies of care.[20] On the overland route of the Balkans, private individuals, church groups, and civil society organizations tried to help the migrants on their way. At the same time, local governments in places like Austria sought to provide food and shelter, requisitioning gymnasiums, warehouses, and schools in order to house the newcomers at least temporarily. Much of this was a spontaneous effort to cope with the evident crisis through extending humanitarian aid to those in dire need, regardless of skin color or religion.

One of the most open countries to refugees was Sweden, which provided assistance with its elaborate welfare state. In spite of its cold climate, it attracted refugees due to its reputation of being a "welcoming society," willing to help newcomers. Initially, this expectation was not disappointed since private individuals "collected clothes, food," or toys and started working in refugee shelters as volunteers. Moreover, the state offered facilities to house and feed migrants while their applications for asylum were decided. In schools, teachers improvised when confronted with a sudden influx of Arabic-speaking children who had to learn Swedish or English in order to follow instructions. This helpful atmosphere was, however, rudely disturbed by culture clashes when some young, male Muslim migrants went after Swedish girls, groping or even assaulting them. While "a lot of people reached out" to help, such incidents stoked "fears of the unknown," forcing the government to institute tougher border controls in order to keep additional migrants out.[21]

Another favorite destination of refugees was Germany due to its proclamation of a "welcome culture" that invited immigrants. Considering itself an emigration country, the FRG had a complex immigration history, previously absorbing millions of expellees, GDR escapees, Turkish laborers, Yugoslav refugees, and ethnic remigrants. In memory of the Holocaust, its constitution, called the Basic Law, contained a quite liberal asylum clause, guaranteeing refuge to anyone who was persecuted elsewhere. At the same time, reception was limited by right-wing and labor resistance to absorbing large numbers of foreigners, which tightened asylum conditions in 1993. Since the FRG had the largest economy in the EU and at the same time possessed an extensive welfare state, many refugees wanted to settle there. In 2015 the number of migrants to Germany reached more than one million, severely straining resources. But since Chancellor Angela Merkel did not want to build a new wall and felt emotionally touched by an interview with a migrant girl, she refused to close the border, declaring in August: "We can manage it."[22] Praised by international commentators, this promise of openness increased the refugee throng.

In the long run, this extraordinarily liberal reception of refugees could not be sustained for logistical and political reasons. Local governments found their resources strained by new arrivals who needed to be housed and fed, while their budgets had made no allowance for these new expenditures. Refugees were frustrated with the lengthy processing of their asylum claims since they were forbidden to work as long as their applications remained undecided. Then, during the New

Year's celebration of 2015/16, groups of young immigrant men assaulted German women in front of the Cologne Cathedral, while the police proved unable to protect them—thereby activating preexisting xenophobic fears. A year later, a terrorist from Northern Africa drove a truck into a crowd of holiday shoppers in Berlin, further stoking anti-immigrant sentiment. Pressured by the rise of the racist Alternative for Germany Party (AfD), the Merkel government sought to regain control by tightening up asylum rules and distributing refugees to other countries.[23]

As the main reception country, Germany pushed for a European solution since the problem involved the entire Schengen area and the EU. Shocked by continued shipwrecks, EU leaders insisted on reinforcing naval operations in the Mediterranean, fingerprinting refugees, and distributing migrants through all member countries. Moreover, the EU tried to stop migration at its place of origin and in non-European transit countries. In response to right-wing hysteria about "tens of millions" of refugees swamping the Continent, EU interior ministers approved an ambitious relocation plan in September 2015 that would distribute 120,000 migrants to EU states on the basis of their capacity. But the scheme was woefully inadequate since more than ten times that number of refugees from Syria, Afghanistan, and Eritrea clamored for asylum, while the Eastern European members refused to accept any refugees at all. Only the designation of so-called safe countries, the restrictive practice of granting refuge, and the threat of deportations helped reduce the number of asylum seekers somewhat.[24]

Since the EU was slow to arrive at an effective solution, the exposed frontier countries took "matters into their hands by beefing up their border defenses." Anticipating the issue, Greece had already built a border fence at its Turkish frontier in 2012, while Hungary, propelled by its xenophobic leader Viktor Orbán, created a razor-wire barrier at its Serbian frontier in June 2015. When refugees tried to circumvent this obstacle, other Balkan states like Croatia, Bulgaria, North Macedonia, Serbia, and Slovenia followed suit, also attempting to stop the migrant wave with fences and the deployment of police.[25] As a result of this tightening of border controls, tens of thousands of refugees got trapped en route, neither able to advance nor to return. When the influx shifted back to Italy, the populist government refused to permit rescue ships to land and for migrants to disembark, a policy also followed by Malta. These restrictions made human trafficking more difficult for smugglers but failed to stop the mass movement.

The shift of the migrant stream to the Eastern Mediterranean in 2015 suggested the need to curb migration through negotiations with Turkey where more than three million Syrian refugees had congregated. Talks led by Germany reached a controversial agreement with Ankara on closing the Aegean Sea route in March 2016. Irregular migrants would be sent back to Turkey based on a case-by-case evaluation of their asylum claims, but one new migrant would be accepted for each returned Syrian refugee. As an incentive, Brussels promised that visas for Turkish citizens would be liberalized, the stalled talks on EU membership would be resumed, and Brussels would pay €3 billion to finance the Syrian refugee camps on Anatolian territory. This controversial deal proved to be a game changer since it reduced migrant arrivals in Greece by 97 percent. But when in 2020 the Syrian war triggered another wave of migrants, President Recep Tayyip Erdoğan sought to extort additional EU funds and Greece used brutal "extrajudicial methods" to keep newcomers out.[26]

As a result, critics of all persuasions accused the EU of mismanaging the migrant crisis. One British journalist commented on the polarization of opinion regarding the refugee wave: "The divisions are between those who want [to] show generosity towards refugees and those who want to shut their borders." Clearly, the EU did not cause the mass migration; it was rather a product of regional wars, political repression, lack of food, and dire poverty in Africa and the Middle East. But "the EU's chaotic response to the refugee crisis has probably exacerbated the problem." Members of Angela Merkel's Bavarian sister party, the Christian Social Union (CSU), heavily criticized her humanitarian gesture of welcoming migrants in the fall of 2015, claiming that it created an unwitting "pull factor" by promising a better life for migrants. The subsequent reimposition of border controls on land and sea had a deterrent effect— but at the price of deepening migrant misery.[27] Ultimately, the EU stumbled toward a compromise that maintained the right to asylum but discouraged actual immigration.

Survival Stories

Tales of migration are a crucial aspect of the refugee experience since they not only communicate the terrors along the way but also link places of origin with eventual destinations. During illegal border crossing and long voyages, migrants share experiences in order to find out information about how to overcome the next obstacle on their path. Their heart-rending accounts of brutality and extortion also appeal for sympathy from individual helpers or international aid organizations. In a stylized way, migrant stories are an essential aspect of their asylum applications, which rest on the credibility of their narratives of escape and suffering. Tales of harrowing experiences are communicated back home by cell phone, marking progress, describing hindrances, and appealing for additional money.[28] Told and retold, these individual accounts blend together in essential aspects, creating a shocking metanarrative of migration abuses in prizewinning novels such as Jenny Erpenbeck's *Go, Went, Gone* or documentaries such as *Fire at Sea*.[29]

Refugee stories begin with the decision to leave, often long in preparation but then also sudden in execution. In many cases, this choice is prompted by an acute danger to one's life, triggering migration as a desperate attempt at survival. Especially in failing states, international strife or civil war, political repression of ideological differences, or religious persecution of a minority are the cause. Refugees have some hope of receiving asylum when they, like the Sudanese Toto, can make plausible claims that they fear for their lives due to "genocidal repression." Other migrants—like a Nigerian man called Andrew—left their homelands due to "the prospect, however slim, of a better life in Europe." Unemployed youths with few chances at home often migrate for economic reasons because they see no future in their own country. Due to an "uncertain economy, life-risking illegal migration has become an increasingly normalized option."[30] They underestimate the perils along the way and the difficulties of getting along in Europe since the likely denial of most asylum claims leads to a shadowy existence of illegality.

Especially for black migrants from sub-Saharan Africa, narratives describe finding an agent who can put them in touch with the vast network of smugglers. Illegal border crossing requires paying off guards and lengthy land travel necessitates a series of trucks and safe houses. Andrew, like other migrants, had to pay in advance without obtaining a receipt in the vain hope that his $1,750 would get him all the way to Europe. Crossing the fifteen hundred miles of the Sahara from Agadez to Tripoli was a life-and-death challenge since "if you fell off [a truck], you were on your own"; the track was littered with "skeletons and dead bodies." On the way they were robbed by bandits, forced to work, and charged more fees since "money is the point of the business all along the migration routes." According to the Senegalese Dawda, "the military, local militias, bandits and police all form a clandestine transportation system" for the migrants, a kind of Saharan mafia.[31]

Accounts also say that arriving in Libya turned out to be a nightmare, since finding a boat was often difficult for refugees who had run out of funds. The breakdown of state order after the overthrow of Gaddafi put migrants at the mercy of smuggler gangs and corrupt officials, bent on extracting every last cent from their hapless victims. As Prince Daley, a Ghanaian man, recalled: "They requested money. I only had money for transport, I was being beaten at the border" by the police. Female migrants, like Queen from Nigeria, were especially vulnerable to false promises of help when there was no work, which would lead them to prostitution in order "to pay off the 'debt' to both traffickers and local madams." Duped and destitute migrants had no other recourse than slave labor when promises were broken and families were unable to wire additional funds.[32] If they were lucky enough to be ransomed, they had to wait in crowded compounds or prisons for weeks to obtain a spot on a rickety ship that would take them across the perilous Mediterranean.

Narratives then report that on an appointed day smugglers would rush the migrants to the beach and put them onto overcrowded fishing boats, rafts, or anything that could float. Most of the refugees could not swim and lacked life vests. If they were lucky, they got a compass and a cell phone to call the coast guard. But often the motor would fail or a storm would swamp the incompetent craft. Mamadou, from Mali, recalled spending three days at sea in a raft: "We didn't have food, not even water. We thought we'd die. For one day, our motor failed. There were waves. It was very dangerous." The smugglers' plan "was dependent on forcing a rescue mission by Italian officials," who would be compelled to pick them up and bring them to a European shore. If migrants were fortunate, this strategy worked and they were rescued. But all too many were not. Tolessa, a Sudanese boy, reported that only 36 of the 150 people on his ship survived. After her boat capsized, Faven, an Eritrean girl, was similarly pulled out of a group of dead bodies in the sea.[33]

Refugees on the Eastern Mediterranean route report that the decision to leave was easier since the civil wars in Syria and Afghanistan put their lives in imminent danger. Shiar, a Kurd, had to go in order not to be drafted in Syria while his family escaped Aleppo when his street "became a frontline" with "missiles flying past." Ali Fellah, from Iraq, fled "the advance of Islamic State (IS) militants and the breakdown of services as basic as drinking water" in order to assure a better future for his son. Sara Arbini, from Syria, said she could not obtain medicine for her boys: "It's like we went back 200 years." A Somalian named Ahmed Umar tried to get away from the "violence in Mogadishu and a lack of work and education opportunities." Finally, Ali Khan from Pakistan fled "because the Taliban wanted him to join their jihad."[34] While their long overland journeys were not quite as dangerous as those in North Africa, these migrants did not want to stay in crowded camps with several million others in Turkey because they were not welcome and hoped for a better life in Europe.

Though the crossing from Turkey to Greece was shorter, survivors relate that the voyage was dangerous enough. Migrants at the Anatolian shore also had to pay with their life savings, ranging from $1,000 to $2,500, to be ferried across in old fishing boats or rubber rafts. After two days at sea, a Syrian girl named Doaa started to worry: "We will never reach the shore. We will all sink." When the refugees refused to transfer to another rust bucket, the smugglers got angry and rammed their boat, drowning three hundred people. Her fiancé fortunately found a "water ring" to hang on to, but after more than twenty-four hours in the sea, he gave up "and drowned before her eyes." Struggling to stay afloat, Doaa was approached by a woman who gave her an eighteen-month-old girl, saying "save her, I will not survive." Though she could not swim, she accepted another baby. But on the fourth day in the sea, she was rescued by a merchant boat; only one child survived.[35] Though her heroism was exemplary, the mass drowning was a shocking tragedy.

After getting registered, migrants told about the bureaucratic procedure that determined the prospects for their future life in Europe. Housed in temporary camps, warehouses, or gymnasiums, they were at the mercy of immigration officials, who were charged with ascertaining whether they had a legitimate claim to asylum or they were merely "economic migrants." After being photographed and registered, they had to produce papers or other proof of their identity and country of origin. Confronted with languages they did not understand, refugees had often abandoned their identification cards during the passage or rendered their fingertips unrecognizable for printing. Intent on staying in more welcoming countries, refugees often exchanged information with each other on how to beat the system in order to do "asylum shopping" for the best conditions. Petitioners feared being classified as coming from a "safe country" like Tunisia to which they would be sent back.[36] This was a lengthy and unequal process that frayed their nerves.

Once in Europe, the stories reveal that the vetting procedure divided migrants into three groups of different legal status and varying life chances. Best off were those who could prove persecution and received official asylum. In 2017 the EU made around eight hundred thousand positive decisions, recognizing petitioners as "having a right to protection," with about two-fifths of them accepted by Germany. Those fortunate refugees could begin to rebuild their lives, learn the local languages, send their children to school, and start to integrate into a new country and culture. An even larger number—those who remained in limbo while their applications were being reviewed or because they lacked papers—were merely tolerated rather than recognized. These folks continued to live in camps, receiving minimal subsistence without officially being allowed to work. Least fortunate were those migrants whose petitions were denied and who were supposed to be repatriated. They could only escape deportation by going underground and struggling to survive illegally.[37]

Migration narratives finally point out that the huge influx triggered increasing resentment against foreigners, making the new arrivals feel unwelcome. A Leipzig study of xenophobia showed that about one-third of the Germans felt like "strangers in their own country," fearing the cultural and religious otherness of Muslims. Xenophobic attitudes especially proliferated in East Germany among almost half of the respondents, though they had little experience of contact with people of different backgrounds. Using real or alleged crimes by foreigners, right-wing vigilante groups of youths would chase people of a different skin color in ugly incidents, such as the attacks in Chemnitz in August 2018.[38] But according to another integration survey, a clear majority of Germans "regards living together in an immigration society as preponderantly positive, if it is experienced personally." Rejecting xenophobia, this remarkably stable openness bodes well for the difficult process of integration.[39]

Migrant stories therefore show a whole spectrum of experiences in Europe, ranging from bitter disappointment to optimism about a better future. Finding no peace in Malta, Umar Silla, a mechanic from Sierra Leone, grumbled: "There's nothing good here. I feel like it's all upside down." Mahmoud Shubat, a construction worker from Syria, agreed that "life in Europe was hard," telling his friends "not to come because, here in Italy, there is nothing." Others were more sanguine. Ajmal Sadiqi, a grocer from Afghanistan, admitted: "Here, I have nothing, but I feel safe, I can walk on the street without being afraid." Nazir, an Afghan, praised Greeks as "very good people, they like foreigners," stating: "Life is much better here, we have our own space, my kids can go to school." H. R., from Pakistan, was also grateful for learning and feeling secure: "People in the shelter have opened their arms and now I can finally dream with my eyes open."[40] Most migrants were grateful for aid and, if given half a chance, were ready to integrate into a new country that would accept them.

Humanitarian Dilemmas

The continued arrival of new migrants demonstrates that "the pull of Europe" remains strong in spite of all the hazards of the journey and the uncertainty of reception. Coming from a postcolonial world, it is actually surprising that refugees should want to go to a continent that was once responsible for imperial exploitation. Yet the promise of a "safer, better life" keeps attracting migrants who are willing to risk everything in order to get a fresh start in a strange land. Their testimonies center above all on personal safety from war and persecution, considering Europe as a peaceful place, ruled by law. Many refugees are also looking for sufficient food, housing, and work that will make it possible to feed, shelter, and sustain their families. Time and again they mention the improved future of their children, like ten-year-old Younes: "I dream of becoming a doctor when I grow up." While some new arrivals hope to return home if things improve, many, like the Iraqi Karim Dhahi, are resolved to stay: "My life is in Europe now."[41]

According to refugee testimonies, the push that uprooted many of them in the desperate search for survival was even more powerful. Conditions had become so terrible in a whole belt of failing states in North Africa and the Middle East by the mid-2010s that many people were ready to flee to a neighboring country, where they would live in camps, with a minority ready to move on to Europe. According to Sadiqi, "Afghanistan has been at war for 50 years and things are never going to change." Most often, refugees mention war and civil strife, repression and dictatorship, or religious persecution as direct threats. Mahmoud Shubat left his home in Homs because "if I had stayed [in] Syria I would have to be part of one party or of ISIS. I'd have to take up arms and kill people. But I don't want that." Others sought to escape grinding poverty, mass starvation, or rampant disease.[42] The terrible conditions in their countries and refugee camps turned Europe into a symbolic gateway to a better existence where migrants could live under more humane conditions.

This unexpected pressure created a migration crisis that sparked a backlash and forced restrictive measures. The notoriously imprecise migration numbers peaked in 2015, when 1,322,825 applicants petitioned the EU for asylum; this influx only slightly declined to 1,259,955 in 2016 and stabilized around 750,000 thereafter. Most of the migrants applied in Germany with 1,444,225; followed by Italy with 335,350; France with 259,765; and Sweden with 207,565. Since border authorities in Italy and

Greece were simply overwhelmed, they shifted registration to destination countries like Germany where a new xenophobic party, the AfD, clamored for tougher restrictions.[43] The Balkan states barricaded their frontiers, and even cosmopolitan places like Sweden drastically cut down on new admissions. In September 2020, the European Commission finally proposed a new "Pact on Migration and Asylum" that sought to process migrants in centers in Turkey and North Africa, strengthen border controls of Frontex, and redistribute refugees voluntarily. Though late in coming and restrictive in intent, this package was a step toward a European solution.[44]

For those migrants who succeeded in getting into European countries, prospects did generally improve with time. Germany, for instance, speeded up its asylum decisions, recognizing well over a million refugees and tolerating several hundred thousand migrants whose status could not be determined while others yet remained because their home countries seemed too dangerous for them to be deported. More than half of the accepted migrants succeeded in gaining some kind of employment, often lower than their qualifications, but they paid taxes and gradually integrated into society. About three-quarters no longer lived in collective housing but rather in private apartments or homes. Virtually all the migrant children went to school, often learning German better than their parents who lived in Syrian, Afghan, or Iraqi language bubbles. Unfortunately, displaced youths were also more likely to commit crimes—apparently proving right-wing accusations right. But, on balance, such progress in integration made a British journalist conclude that "Angela Merkel's great migrant gamble paid off."[45]

The heated controversy about migration suggests that this issue ultimately poses an unresolvable ethical dilemma. The immigration philosopher David Miller maintains that it is impossible for a society to follow the humanitarian impulse and open the door to all newcomers who demand entry. But he also argues that closing the border to those who are in mortal danger is equally immoral since it violates the human imperative of solidarity. States have a right to defend their own citizens and to aid those who require support. But as members of the international community, they also have a duty to help people in dire need. The distinction between a universal right to asylum and a choice among different categories of immigrants is supposed to resolve the problem since it recognizes the imperative of aid while maintaining control. Unfortunately, the new "survival migration" is obliterating the distinction between asylum seekers and economic migrants.[46] Since an aging population needs immigrants to maintain the welfare state, EU policy makers can only aspire to an unsatisfactory compromise between both conflicting imperatives.

6

Brexit Self-Destruction

FIGURE 7. Brexit supporters, London, UK. Shutterstock.

At 4:39 a.m. on June 24, 2016, it was all over. The BBC announced that the British electorate had decided to leave the European Union after forty-three years of membership. During referendum day, most polls predicted that the Remain camp was comfortably ahead by several points, but when the first returns came in, 10 Downing Street became increasingly nervous since this lead failed to hold up. Though most of the political elite, media commentators, and outside observers expected the Remainers to prevail, the voting results started to swing in the direction of Leave. As the night wore on, the Brexiteers became more and more optimistic that their long-shot campaign might actually win. When the city of Sunderland showed a huge advantage for Leave, the game was up, with Brexit narrowly winning by 51.9 percent. The shocked prime minister David Cameron had no choice but to concede defeat and resign. "The British people have voted to leave the EU and their will must be respected."[1]

The pressure to take Britain out of the European Union came from the most unlikely of sources, a political fringe group called the United Kingdom Independence Party (UKIP). Founded in 1993, this party campaigned single-mindedly against EU membership, accusing Brussels of bureaucratic overregulation, mishandling the financial crisis, and unrestrained immigration from Eastern Europe. Its leader Nigel Farage was a former City trader in metal derivatives whose folksy ways and outspoken comments capitalized on a widespread dislike of British elites and established political parties. Dismissed by Cameron as a bunch of "fruitcakes, loonies and closet racists," UKIP nonetheless made steady gains in European elections, becoming the largest party in the UK by 2014 in proportional terms, even though it failed to win more than a seat or two in the winner-takes-all format of voting for the British Parliament.[2] By mobilizing an angry grassroots base with the promise to "take back control," this populist group finally forced the Conservatives to address the issue of EU membership.

The British establishment had no compelling answer to the UKIP challenge since it was itself deeply split on the issue. The only group that was unreservedly in favor of European integration was the small Liberal Democratic Party, which had lost its electoral base due to its unpopular coalition with the Conservatives. The ruling Conservative Party cooperated with the EU, but it kept the country out of the euro and was more interested in the free trade aspect of the single market than the project of creating "an ever closer union." It also contained a large minority of so-called backbenchers, who opposed any diminution of British sovereignty and considered the rules issued by Brussels to be foreign impositions. One of their key spokesmen was Boris Johnson, the charismatic but mercurial former mayor of London. Though part of the Labour

Party was rather Europhile, this opposition party provided little help for Remain because it was led by radical leftists such as Jeremy Corbyn, who disparaged the EU as a stronghold of neoliberal capitalism.[3]

Without sufficient defense of its positive contribution to life in the UK, Brussels quickly became the symbolic scapegoat for multiple, sometimes contradictory resentments. Patriotic Englishmen saw the EU as a Continental usurper of sovereignty to be resisted at all costs. The Murdoch media constantly derided Europe as a vast, faceless bureaucracy that enjoyed an easy life without sufficient democratic controls. Though the sovereign debt crisis had partially been triggered by the speculation of London bankers, the business community preferred an independent trade policy. The biggest complaint was unrestrained immigration from Eastern Europe to the UK since London had refused to restrict it for a transition period like other EU members. The influx annually brought 200,00 to 300,000 migrants who were accused of welfare tourism, even if they just wanted to work.[4] While France, Denmark, and Ireland also held referenda that rejected integration projects like the draft constitution, only in England did anti-European sentiment produce a mass movement that called for leaving the EU altogether.

Five years after the referendum, it is not yet clear how much the UK and the EU will suffer from the British exit. The promise of leaving the EU while at the same time retaining free trade with its large market is a contradiction in terms. Much of the outcome depends on the fine print in the divorce agreement, which will only become apparent with its actual implementation. No doubt, the dire predictions of the alleged Project Fear, launched by the Remainers' campaign, were exaggerated, but early business decisions on relocation to the Continent in order to preserve privileged access to the EU seem to substantiate the concern of a negative impact on Britain. At the same time, the European Union is losing a market of sixty-five million people, a leading financial center, and a large economy, which is bound to diminish the stature of Brussels in international trade. But, so far, all doomsday predictions of other members following London's example have proven rather erroneous. Since public approval of the EU has risen among its members, Brexit may yet turn into a salutary shock.[5]

Referendum Gamble

The relationship between Great Britain and the European Continent has always been rather ambivalent. In his inspiring Zurich speech of 1946, Winston Churchill had called for a reconciliation between Germany and France and the creation of a united Europe but purposely left his own country out of the appeal. When six Continental states created the Common Market eleven years later, instead of joining the United Kingdom they established a rival free trade area, called EFTA, consisting of Austria, Denmark, Norway, Portugal, Sweden, and Switzerland. Inspired by the impressive growth rates of the EC, the conservative prime minister Harold Macmillan applied for membership in 1961 but was turned down by the French president Charles de Gaulle who feared that London would be an unreliable partner. Six years later, he repeated his veto when the Labour leader Harold Wilson reapplied. Only after de Gaulle was overthrown, did the UK, Denmark, and Ireland officially manage to join the European Community in 1973.[6]

From the beginning London and Brussels pursued somewhat different aims within the EC since the former merely wanted free trade, while the latter followed a vision of further integration. To confirm the decision on UK membership, Harold Wilson held a referendum in 1975 that resulted in two-thirds approval, although such support was wide rather than deep. Then the combative Prime Minister Margaret Thatcher tried to placate Euroskeptics by demanding a rebate for Britain, considerably lowering its contribution to the EC budget from 1984 onward. But two years later, due to her neoliberal beliefs, she also supported the drafting of the Single European Act, which envisaged the completion of the internal market by 1992. London also refused to join the Schengen area and adopt the common currency of the euro in order to protect its sovereignty as a global financial hub.[7] As a result, only the cosmopolitan part of the British public developed an affective bond to the EU, while the rest had a more instrumental attitude, looking for concrete payoffs rather than a transformation of identity.

Nigel Farage succeeded in exploiting this ambivalence and made UKIP a surprising third force in British politics. Elected to the European

Parliament in 1999 on a hostile platform, he set out to dismantle the hated Brussels bureaucracy from the inside. His grassroots campaigning appealed to some upper-middle-class Conservatives who despised the EU as well as to Labour Party supporters who felt left behind in the rush to globalization. UKIP's anti-immigration message especially resonated with blue-collar workers, pensioners, and Englishmen without higher education. With each European election, this "people's army" gathered more attention and funding until it became the largest British party in Brussels with 27 percent of the vote in 2014. In the national election of the following year, the "Kippers" even won a couple of seats in Parliament through conservative renegades.[8] UKIP had risen from a marginal laughing stock to a threat to the establishment by pushing an issue that would not go away.

Aware that "public disillusionment with the EU [was] at an all-time high," David Cameron sought to head off the rebellion by way of a treaty reform that would be approved by a referendum. He laid out a road map in his "Bloomberg speech" of January 2013, starting from the premise that "for us the EU is a means to an end—prosperity, stability, the anchor of freedom and democracy." To placate critics, he admitted the problems of sovereign debt, immigration, and a lack democratic accountability but vowed to reform the union to make it more palatable. He summed up his agenda in five points: (1) he stressed the competitiveness of the single market; (2) he called for flexibility in the forms of cooperation; (3) he demanded "that power must be able to flow back" to the member states; (4) he insisted on greater "democratic accountability"; and (5) he wanted more fairness for countries not in the Eurozone. Hoping for an endorsement of his course, he promised a referendum on "a more flexible, adaptable and open EU" in which British interests would be better met.[9]

The referendum promise was quite a gamble since it required Britain to obtain reforms that were substantial enough to satisfy the Euroskeptics. But negotiations with the Continental partners turned out to be more frustrating than expected since London was out of touch with Brussels and failed to realize that unilateral demands would be of little avail. Overestimating the persuasiveness of his plea for concessions to keep the UK in the EU, Cameron demanded more "respect for the legitimate interests of non-euro members" and an "end of Britain's obligation" to work toward "an ever closer union." Describing the annual net influx of over three hundred thousand EU citizens as "unsustainable," he called for a brake on immigration and a waiting period before migrants would be eligible for welfare benefits. Struggling hard to overcome the insistence of Eastern European states on free movement of people, Cameron finally managed to gain some assurances that he could sell as "a qualified success." But the Euroskeptic media savaged the result, turning the deal into a signal defeat.[10]

Two well-oiled machines confronted each other in the referendum campaign, employing the latest advertising techniques and mobilization strategies. The Leavers were funded (with Russian help?) by the financier Arron Banks and used the polling expertise of Dominic Cummings in order to launch a grassroots campaign as well as a strong media appeal. Since they wanted to take Britain out of the EU, they mounted consistent attacks in a come-from-behind effort that spread misinformation and pushed all sorts of emotional buttons. The Remainers were slower to get started, relying on the government's presumed advantage and using Andrew Cooper as their chief pollster. Their problem was the internal division of the Conservative Party, which could not be relied on to back its prime minister. In order to hold his cabinet together, Cameron allowed its members to support different sides of the referendum. But the government lost its advantage of authority when prominent figures like Boris Johnson and Michael Gove joined the Leavers.[11]

The Leavers' campaign was more aggressive in directing widespread public resentment of whatever did not seem to work against the EU. Their imaginative slogan "Vote Leave. Take Back Control" appealed to a deep-seated nationalism that promised to return to a simpler time in which Britain was a major power, capable of standing alone. One poster promised to regain control over "our money, our economy, our borders, our security [and] our taxes." Playing on fears about the refugee crisis, they claimed that the biggest issue facing the UK was the influx of migrants from the new Eastern European members of the EU because it would take jobs away, strain housing as well as health services, and make the British strangers in their own country. The Leavers also attacked the rulings of the European

Court of Justice and ridiculed bureaucratic regulations, such as prescribing the curvature of bananas, in order to call for a return to national sovereignty. Boris Johnson rejected integration in populist terms: "Now is the time to believe in ourselves and in what Britain can do."[12]

In contrast, the Remainers had a harder time making their case since they were trying to defend an imperfect status quo. Their slogan "Britain Stronger In" emphasized the multiple benefits of remaining in the EU, such as "more jobs, lower prices, workers' rights," in short, "a brighter future IN Europe." In a video the entrepreneur Lord Alan Sugar called leaving the European Union "a daft idea and a duff proposal" since its consequences for the British economy were likely to be disastrous. In addition to emphasizing the positive aspects of EU membership, the Remain campaign also embarked on Project Fear, which highlighted the probable losses in jobs and markets should Britain leave its highly networked relationship with the European Union. "Less trade plus less investment plus lower confidence equals fewer jobs, lower wages, less growth and a weaker country." While the Leavers appealed to emotions, the Remainers argued more rationally that the disadvantages would be greater with Brexit.[13]

The Leave campaign was ultimately more effective because it was more mendacious in making unsubstantiated claims. A case in point was the famous red bus with the incendiary slogan: "We send to the EU £350 million each week. Let's fund the NHS instead. Vote Leave. Let's take back control." This pitch connected hatred of Brussels with the funding of the National Health Service, implying that if this money did not go to the EU, medical treatment at home would be improved. Critical journalists quickly pointed out that the figure was greatly exaggerated since it neither included the British rebate nor the return money from the EU in support of such projects as the funding of scientific research. Various financial authorities sought to prove "how spectacularly wrong the Brexit bus £350 million lie was." But the emotional damage was done once Farage and Johnson cynically repeated the rather inflated figure since media like the *Sun* and the *Daily Mail* refused to correct it.[14]

The Brexit campaign won the popular vote by 51.9 percent to 48.1 percent not only due to the complacency of the Remainers but also because it put together a surprising coalition of supporters. Convinced that Remain would win, some voters did not go to the polls at all. First, in regional terms only Scotland (62.8 percent), London (59.9 percent), Northern Ireland (55.8 percent), and most cities voted to remain, while the English heartland chose to leave. Second, most Leavers were also older than 45, while younger voters between 18 and 44 overwhelmingly chose to remain. Similarly, most of those with little or modest education supported Brexit, while voters with advanced degrees tended to vote for remaining. Whereas the Leavers were motivated by concerns about immigration and sovereignty, the Remainers responded to worries about the economy and to appeals for civil rights.[15] This split between the pensioned and less-educated English and the young and better-educated cosmopolitans revealed a fundamental cleavage with people who felt threatened by globalization opting out while those who saw chances wanting to stay in.

The Brexit decision shocked an international community that had counted on Britain to remain in the EU. The French president François Hollande and the German chancellor Angela Merkel regretted the outcome: "There is no doubt that this is a blow to Europe and to the European unification process." Similarly, the presidents of the European Commission, Council, and Parliament tried to control the damage by expressing their "hope to have the UK as a close partner of the EU also in the future." But the Dutch Freedom Party leader Geert Wilders and the Front National chief Marine Le Pen were delighted with this "victory for freedom," concluding that "now we need to have the same referendum in France and in the countries of the EU." Interpreting the move "as a wake-up call for Europe," other member states rallied around Brussels and declared that they "remain[ed] committed to the EU." Promising to respect the British decision, prior critics vowed that "the EU must go through fundamental changes."[16]

Implementation Mess

Referenda have played an important role in European integration since governments asked their populations whether to join or to accept major policy changes. While twenty-eight electorates voted to become EU members, only Norway and Switzerland refused, relying instead on

North Sea oil and a tradition of neutrality. But even these states signed a series of association treaties that provided indirect membership in the EU. More problematic was the rejection of the draft constitution by French and Dutch voters, who sought to punish their national governments by berating the bureaucracy in Brussels. These negative votes did not, however, threaten the survival of the EU since the European Commission decided on a less ambitious form of the Lisbon Treaty that did not require popular ratification. In Ireland, a second referendum approved the agreement with a two-thirds majority. Since the withdrawal of Greenland was only a minor stumble, the unprecedented Brexit decision posed a whole new set of challenges.[17]

The legal procedure for an organized withdrawal was spelled out in Article 50 of the Lisbon Treaty: "Any Member State may decide to withdraw from the Union in accordance with its own constitutional requirements." This provision had emerged as a bit of an afterthought from the constitutional discussion since the Eastern European states, the UK, and Denmark wanted to include a formal way out of the EU, even if it contradicted the spirit of "an ever closer union." The leaving member was to notify the Council of Ministers and negotiate a formal withdrawal treaty as a kind of divorce settlement, undoing the rights and obligations previously incurred. On the European side, the European Commission was to work out the conditions of leaving, the council needed to approve the treaty with a qualified majority and the European Parliament had to agree as well. The task of managing an orderly exit from the EU would have to unravel decades of cooperation and integration in personnel, funding, and institutions.[18]

The actual implementation of the decision to leave turned out to be rather more complicated than the somewhat naive or rather cynical Brexiteers had promised. The referendum campaign left a deeply polarized country in its wake with large segments of the public having second thoughts and hoping for another referendum to reverse the original decision. Moreover, Leavers themselves were divided about which form the withdrawal should take: On the one hand, business groups and academic specialists advocated a "soft Brexit," which would keep as many of the existing ties to the Continent as possible in order to preserve the advantages of their largest market and scholarly contacts. On the other hand, UKIP and conservative backbenchers demanded a "hard Brexit" that would rupture all connections with the EU and get rid of its hated rules and regulations, no matter what the economic cost might be.[19] Reaching agreement proved well-nigh impossible since these battle lines cut across the political parties.

Faced with having to find a way out, commentators began debating which of the competing models would satisfy the Brexiteers. Remaining in or renegotiating a new common market seemed unacceptable since this would maintain many onerous EU regulations and require arbitration for legal disputes except for the Schengen opt-out. A hard Brexit instead meant escaping EU rules but losing all market advantages since merely following World Trade Organization (WTO) procedures would still raise new tariffs. A temporal custom union might do for a transition period by temporarily maintaining most ties, including EU citizens' rights in the UK, without prejudicing the future. Finally, a permanent custom union might give the UK more leeway in controlling immigration, limiting the European Court of Justice, and maintaining separate deals for services.[20] Since neither the Norwegian nor the Swiss model of association quite seemed to fit, a special British way of reconciling independence with access would need to be worked out.

To end the confusion, the new prime minister Theresa May unambiguously pledged in her Birmingham speech of October 3, 2018: "Brexit means Brexit and we are going to make a success of it." The anti-immigrant former home secretary had only tepidly endorsed remaining in the referendum campaign, voicing areas of frustration with Brussels without joining the Leavers. This studied centrism, which promised to keep the Conservative Party together, allowed May to win the succession struggle against all rivals because she was seen as someone more capable of affecting a controlled transition. May also succeeded in seizing power since other contenders like Johnson and Gove attacked each other, while she brought them into the cabinet so as to control them. In no uncertain terms, she accepted the mandate of leading Britain out of the EU in order to fulfill the democratic wish of the electorate. In a rather forceful speech, she promised strong leadership to obtain the best withdrawal terms as well as a "bold, new positive vision" for the future.[21]

In Brussels, responding to the British withdrawal turned out to be exceedingly difficult due to the complexity of the issues and the strong emotions provoked by them. After the first "sorry and good riddance" reaction, calmer heads prevailed, with the head of the European Parliament Martin Schulz accepting the decision by saying "who leaves, leaves." To the surprise of many Anglo-American skeptics, European capitals quickly closed ranks and agreed on a common strategy: "Brexit means one member leaving, not the club falling apart." The EU leaders agreed that Britain would need to invoke Article 50, negotiations would have to be completed within a two-year period, and both sides would have to approve the final divorce settlement. The chief EU negotiator Michel Barnier, a former French minister, indicated that the "four freedoms of the internal market were indivisible" and the "final deal would have to be worse than EU membership." Only after achieving "a clean divorce" could a new relationship be worked out.[22]

Starting on March 29, 2017, formal negotiations on "an orderly withdrawal" soon revealed the enormity of undoing over four decades of close UK integration into the EU. While both sides vowed to proceed in good faith, the very issues that had fed the Brexit campaign continued to prove highly contentious. One such problem was the size of the "divorce bill" of obligations owed by Britain to the EU as budget contributions as well as funds for contractually agreed-upon enterprises that ultimately amounted to €41.8 billion. Another bone of contention was the right of residence for 3.7 million EU citizens in the UK as well as for 1.3 million British nationals in Europe while allowing future immigration restrictions. Then there was the irresolvable Irish question, which sought to avoid reimposing a hard border between Northern Ireland and the Republic of Ireland lest historic hostilities might erupt again. After settling scores of other technical issues, an equitable Withdrawal Agreement was finally completed on November 14, 2018.[23]

The chief motivation for reaching a compromise in the Brexit talks was the threat of a "no deal" exit, which would produce unforeseeable chaos. Such an uncontrolled withdrawal was favored by hard-line

Brexiteers who overestimated the strength of the British economy and were frustrated with the increasingly negative impact of leaving the EU, which they had so studiously denied. Financial estimates put the probable cost for business at about €65 billion, split between the Continent and Great Britain. No-deal warnings painted scary scenarios of endless truck queues at border crossings such as Dover, job losses due to interrupted production chains as well as relocated financial institutions to Dublin or Frankfurt. To avoid such an unnecessary disaster, governments began some contingency planning in order not to be "falling over the cliff edge." While London claimed "no deal is better than a bad deal," Barnier countered "a fair deal is better than no deal" since the UK would suffer more.[24]

Facing a deeply divided nation, Theresa May sought parliamentary approval of the Withdrawal Agreement by promising to make Britain "a fully independent, sovereign country." She failed to get the controversial treaty draft through Westminster since the snap election she had confidently called in 2017 produced only a conservative plurality. Her coalition with the Northern Irish Democratic Unionist Party (DUP) effectively gave the small, Protestant, and right-wing unionists veto power over any deal and made May vulnerable to obstruction from her own party.[25] When she tried to deliver "the Brexit that people voted for," May lost the first parliamentary vote in January 2019 by a stunning margin of 230 votes. Even after gaining some modest concessions from the EU on the Irish custom border, she lost a second ballot in mid-March by 149 votes due to the opposition of both the radical Brexiteers and moderate Remainers. Gambling on a promise to step down if she did not succeed, May lost the third vote by 344 to 286 votes.[26] Having failed three times, she had no choice but to resign in June 2019.

Her successor in the intraparty struggle turned out to be the former mayor of London, Boris Johnson, who promised "to get Brexit done." Though he initially wavered on the issue, he won a new election in December 2019 by a landslide of eighty seats since the public was tired of the wrangling, the Labor Party remained divided, the Conservative backbenchers seized the chance to beat UKIP, and the party leadership's campaign focused on Johnson's popularity. As a result, on January 31,

2020, the UK formally left the EU, seeking to go it alone. During the protracted divorce negotiations with Brussels, Trump's election loss and the chaos of the COVID lockdown in Dover weakened the position of the no-deal faction.[27] Finally, on Christmas Eve 2020, the talks produced a compromise that avoided a hard Brexit. While Johnson crowed about regaining control, Ursula von der Leyen was relieved that the agreement "recognizes Britain's desire to leave . . . while preserving tariff-free, quota-free trade in goods with the EU." Both sides could claim success in concluding "a fair and balanced deal."[28]

Because Britain's exit "immediately brought a litany of headaches and lost business," the 1,246-page treaty suggests that the larger EU ultimately prevailed in many respects. In truth, London succeeded in reducing access of the Continental fishing fleets to its own territorial waters. And Johnson proudly announced the UK's withdrawal from the Erasmus student exchange program even if it hurt British universities more than their European counterparts. But on the issue of the Irish border, London had to give in and create a partial custom frontier between the UK and Northern Ireland in order to avoid restoring a land border on the Irish island. And in the crucial area of technical and social standards of production, the EU succeeded in maintaining its rules, with disputes to be settled by arbitration. Moreover, the financial services sector, the core of the British economy, was not even addressed in the divorce agreement, denying "passporting" access to the city of London.[29] Since many Scots want to stay in the EU, the deal appears to be a Pyrrhic victory for the Brexiteers the consequences of which might haunt them in the long run.

Ultimately, the Brexit mess was a product of the failure of the British political class to come to terms with the pressures of globalization. The EU had little choice but to stand fast on its four freedoms as the cornerstone of a single market, even if the UK wanted special exceptions to limit it to a free trade area. But the Westminster elite underestimated the resentment of its own provincial, white, male, and older constituency, represented by the grassroots populism of the UKIP as well as the traditionalist resistance of the small-town Conservative backbenchers. Misled by Corbyn's radical Marxist appeal to "the many not the few" and his critique of the EU as a neoliberal project, the Labour Party lost because it failed to provide a credible pro-European alternative. Since the Liberal Democrats were just too small to count, the Remainers lacked a personality and party to rally around. The prolonged ratification deadlock in Parliament showed an appalling lack of willingness to compromise, typical of emotional identity politics.[30] Only another election finally created a legislative majority due to the single-member-district system, which ignored the strong but dispersed sentiment of the public for remaining in the EU.

Withdrawal Symptoms

Since the economic effect of the exit from the EU is still unclear, its impact on the lives of ordinary people remains in dispute. Continuing their confrontation from the referendum battle, both British camps are vigorously making their respective cases. On the one hand, cheerleaders of departure are celebrating the concluded divorce from the Continent as a long-wished-for "moment of national rebirth" that will liberate Britain from all sorts of nasty restraints, allowing the island to recover its glorious past. On the other hand, convinced Remainers and the majority of experts are predicting "a severe economic shock and shortages of food, fuel and medical supplies." The protracted four-year struggle over the implementation of Brexit has already begun to have adverse effects like an initial drop in the stock market and a weakening of the pound. While hard-line Leavers look forward to a glorious future, skeptics are afraid that both the UK and the EU will lose in the end.[31]

Sunderland voters were rather "pleased" and "happy" with the outcome of the referendum, which sent a critical message to the political class. With coal mining and shipbuilding gone, even the arrival of a Nissan factory and the influx of EU money could not counteract their sense of being let down by the powers that be. Rising unemployment created a feeling of "being left behind" and of "utter alienation" from the politicians in the capital. While resentment against immigration played some role, the Brexit vote was as much a revolt against the London elite as a rejection of the EU. The voters of this northeastern city, which produced one of the highest results for Leave, were therefore motivated by the hope of "getting our own back," resuming control of their own lives, which they had somehow lost. According to random Sunderlanders interviewed by a TV journalist, this was "a vote which has really changed things."[32] To them, the EU came to symbolize the betrayal of their expectations for the future.

Other Brexiteers in the provinces adduced additional reasons for voting to leave the EU, though most were profoundly ignorant of what really went on in Brussels. Confusing EU freedom of movement regulations with Commonwealth rules, a middle-aged man proclaimed: "It's all about immigration," it's about "stopping the Muslims from coming into our country." An elderly woman was glad for "England to be free," since her grandparents had fought for this cause in the world wars and it had now been realized once more. Yet another older man explained how he "disliked foreign officials telling us what to do" because they were not elected and could not be dismissed. Moreover, the "Brussels bureaucrats" were spending taxpayers' money without sufficient supervision. Finally, a young woman of foreign background but British citizenship was gratified by having restored the position of "England on the globe."[33] Showing the impact of the Leavers' propaganda, such spontaneous opinions suggested a nationalist groundswell, convinced that England and Wales would be better off going it alone.

During the protracted negotiations, many Leavers began to hope for a hard exit in order to escape EU obligations no matter what the cost. "If no deal is struck, that would please the staunch Brexiteers." The euphoria about leaving gradually turned into widespread "dismay over how long it has taken to achieve the promise of the historic split from the EU." May's withdrawal agreement "was deeply unpopular" among politicians and the public due to the size of the exit bill of over €42 billion and the length of the transition period in which ties to the EU would continue. Although he had initially waffled about the issue, Boris Johnson considered the draft to be "a national humiliation" and "a real stinker" that had to be repudiated. More and more Leavers were willing to risk the dire economic consequences, predicted by the Bank of England, in order to get out. One commentator opined: "We could use that money to patch up whatever problems arise from a no-deal, also we could start making proper trade deals with the rest of the world."[34]

To justify their global role, Brexiteers invoked a warped sense of history presented as a celebratory national narrative. Nigel Farage claimed that the Norman conquest was "the last time we were invaded and taken over." The historian David Starkey rebranded the Reformation as "the first Brexit," even if its theology had come from the Continent. The Brexiteer Jacob Rees-Mogg celebrated the "glorious Revolution" as "a great liberation" but forgot that it was a Dutch king who captured the throne. Cameron's claim that "the former colonies [were] better off thanks to British imperialism" elided its racist repression and exploitation. Finally, the glorification of the Second World War as the "'finest hour' in which Britain stood alone in defiance of Nazism," ignored the Soviet and American contributions to allied victory. According to the leftist historian Christopher Kissane, "by refusing to confront its complex and difficult history, Britain is turning its back on decades of shared progress, to the dismay of its friends."[35]

But when "the Brexit hangover kicked in," some "bregretters" who had voted to leave reversed course and started to campaign for a second vote. Though many had bought into the sovereignty argument, they were shocked by the political chaos the referendum had unleashed. Upon checking the facts of Brexiteer propaganda, they realized that they had been manipulated by simple lies or outright falsehoods such as the assertion that there would "be no money for the NHS" if they stayed in the EU. Moreover, the image of the EU as a faceless bureaucracy was misleading since Brussels had protected peace and provided "benefits of free trade and regulatory alignment with our neighbors." To correct his mistake, "Andy" founded a website called "Remainer Now," while other disillusioned folks called for a new "peoples' vote." Though hundreds of thousands of old and new Remainers protested in the streets, the Conservative leadership claimed to defend a democratic decision and refused to hold a second referendum, putting party before country.[36]

Vowing "We won't be fooled again," pro-Europeans tried to build a case for staying in the EU, based on the multiple benefits of being in a larger trading block. Feelings of "national liberation" were fine but could not "compensate for [the loss] of jobs, for economic growth, for living standards, for businesses, none of them." The blogger Tom Foudy argued: "Firstly, Britain will fall behind Europe and the rest of the world" in growth, making it poorer by comparison. "Secondly, investors prefer a single market of 450 million people to one of 65 million people" since with so many more potential customers the larger EU looked more attractive than the smaller UK. "Thirdly, Trump is not an alternative and stop pretending he is" because his defeat by Joseph Biden made counting on a special relationship with the United States as an anchor for British prosperity "a botched fantasy."[37] Even if Project Fear had overstated the case, promises of concluding better bilateral trade deals were likely to turn out to be hollow since by going alone Britain would lose leverage with potential partners.

Gary Wrights, a fish-and-chips store owner from Norfolk, explained the negative impact of Brexit on small businesses. After the Leave vote, his seafood prices soared 25 percent, making his food more expensive and indicating that "he and other small business owners will be worse off out of the EU." Resenting that Brexit was "sprung upon us," he claimed to have fallen for "lots of fake news" and voted to leave so as to "feel British again." But when reality hit, he figured out that this was not the best decision in a globalized world which had opened up chances for the younger generation to work on the Continent. The fifty-two-year-old was convinced that "the government has never done what the British people wanted." It was foolish to try to return to the 1950s and 1960s because the world had fundamentally changed since then. Simon Cowley, a worker in the North, also reported that "no one ever explained the simple stuff the EU does for us" and that "the cost of leaving is starting to outstrip the cost of staying."[38]

Similarly, Dr. Charles Gallagher, an emergency medicine physician in London, considered Brexit "a huge disaster" and called for a second popular vote. Though he thought the EU was too neoliberal, he believed that leaving would have a rather detrimental impact on the National Health Service. First, the huge NHS organization would not be able to staff its 100,000 vacancies without EU workers who made up 5.6 percent of personnel, 7 percent of nurses, and 10 percent of physicians. Second, the medical system would be starved of revenue once tax receipts started to decline as was predicted under most Brexit scenarios. Third, research was likely to suffer and the waiting times for availability of new medicines would significantly increase. He claimed in no uncertain terms that "it would be the end of NHS as we know it." Emma-Jane Manley, who had a handicapped daughter, considered her care to be absolutely vital, while Ben testified that their premature baby had only survived through the efforts of a male nurse from the EU.[39]

The vice president of the National Union of Students Sorna Vieru also predicted that Brexit would especially hit the younger generation, which had "enjoyed the freedom of Europe" before. For the fifteen thousand British students enrolled on the Continent, British withdrawal from the Erasmus program would make it "harder to get visas and fees may be more expensive." At the same time, the number of twenty thousand EU students in the UK was "likely to dwindle" due to a steep increase in fees. Moreover, "if Brexit does prompt a recession, it is young people who are most likely to suffer" from decreased hiring, lowered wages, and rising youth unemployment. Brexit would make it also more difficult to "travel, live or work in Europe" since the British would lose their insider status and be treated like any other foreigner. Henry Saker-Clark, a journalist conducting a survey of young voters, therefore concluded: "The effect of Brexit on the economy is the key reason for many young people supporting remain."[40]

European Union citizens who made their home in the UK as well as British nationals living in Europe also faced an uncertain future. Without new agreements, Brexit would strip them of their legal protection, relegate them to becoming second-class citizens, or risk their deportation. "Some feel they've been used as bargaining chips in the negotiations and cannot understand why it is taking so long to provide them with the reassurances they want." The German-born Maria Bates, a former deputy head teacher from Kendal in the Lake District, "fear[ed] for the future," saying "the referendum created a them versus us mentality which is completely unnecessary." Many EU citizens already "felt ostracized and unwelcome."[41] The Leavers' campaign played on xenophobic sentiments rather than acknowledging the sizable contributions of

Polish workers to the functioning of the British economy or the role of German academics like Wolfram Kaiser to maintaining the high intellectual standards of leading UK institutions.

Such personal statements indicate that, even after the conclusion of the implementation battle, the British public continued to be polarized. Feeling betrayed by the interminable negotiations, Dennis and Pat Murray of Stoke-on-Trent argued "the sooner we come out the better," willing to risk a no-deal withdrawal just to get the question settled. Others, like Andrew James from Newcastle, who had "voted leave because of the EU red tapes and the European Court of Justice," now "changed [their] mind[s]." Frustrated Remainers hoped that a second vote could avoid a crash landing since polls showed them to have a slight lead.[42] The European election in 2019 was therefore won by the extremes with the new Brexit Party gaining 30.5 percent and the pro-European Liberal Democrats 19.8 percent, while the discredited Conservatives finished in a distant fifth place behind Labour and even the Greens.[43] Though the final withdrawal agreement settled many of the disputed issues, it brought new restrictions on movement and increased paperwork for trade with the Continent.

Out of Europe

Skepticism about involvement in Europe has been an essential part of British history in both insular and imperial terms. Beginning with the Magna Carta, the national master narrative of "forging the British nation" has always emphasized distinctiveness from the Continental chaos. The combination of Scotch, Welsh, and Irish populations with the English in one country is seen as a signal achievement, based on a common Crown, an unwritten constitution, and parliamentary representation. Moreover, the grand story of the once vast imperial domination over areas like the entire Indian subcontinent tends to justify a sense of cultural superiority, unrivaled by other countries. From this perspective, Continental Europe has been seen as a related but distinctive place, to be engaged in specific aspects but kept down as a rival, whether led by the Spanish, French, or Germans. The Brexit campaign drew on this ambivalent legacy, expressed in the "balance of power" tradition of being involved in but separate from the Continent.[44]

Feeling somehow threatened, many Brexiteers were woefully ignorant of the EU, seeing it through the tabloid headlines that decried the financial and migration crises. One favorite cliché, repeated time and again, railed against the "fact that unelected bureaucrats have got power over what goes on in this country." Resenting rules imposed by Brussels, one Leave voter was rather angered by "e-cigarettes being branded evil." Others were unimpressed by the EU's halting response to the sovereign debt crisis, which hampered the financial transactions of the City of London. Another favorite criticism was the lack of immigration control since Britain was a small island that already had "too many people." Because "all our resources [like the NHS] are pushed to the limits," the UK ought to "be concerned with its own children" rather than welcoming hordes of foreigners. Taken together, such complaints added up to a sense that "we are losing our identity."[45]

The Brexit campaign became a battle for Britain's soul since the Remainers had a more cosmopolitan and optimistic vision of the future. They believed that "the EU has improved the lives of its citizens through being part of it." Instead of being a "eurocratic" monster, it had guaranteed peace and prosperity, allowing different peoples to live together in harmony. Sim, a first-generation immigrant from India, took "pride in a diverse Britain," seeing it as an inclusive place that offered a plurality of life chances. With his "finance and technology background," he supported free trade rather than protectionism and immigration rather than nativism. "Where I wanted cooperation with the EU, others wanted hostility." Hoping to "transform the UK into a further services economy," he represented the liberal and youthful part of society that saw Europeanization as an opportunity. In order for the EU "to reach the aspirations of its citizens we must seriously consider fully integrating."[46]

Most experts agree that leaving is likely to harm the UK more than the EU due to the disparity in negotiating power. The freelance journalist Christopher Oram put the issue in metaphorical terms: "The idea of Brexit was sold to us like a mystery box. The Leave campaign list all the things they think are inside"—such as more money for the NHS, control of immigration, a trade deal with Germany, the ability to make one's own laws, and so on. Unfortunately, "upon looking inside, we discover that it is actually a Pandora's box! Full of lies, misery, betrayal, sickness, poverty, hunger, deception and greed." The divorce bill would swallow all potential savings for the NHS, migration could be controlled with existing laws, making trade deals with a single EU member was impossible, and Scotland was threatening to secede.[47] While 6.6 percent of EU goods exports (3 percent of its GDP) went to Britain in 2014, a whopping 51.4 percent of UK exports (12 percent of its GDP) went to Europe. The potential impact could hardly be any more asymmetrical.

Ironically, the Brexit shock seems to have had the opposite effect on the EU from what was anticipated. Many Anglo-American media interpreted the withdrawal of the UK as the beginning of "the disintegration of Europe." Quite to the contrary, the European Commission of the remaining twenty-seven countries was able to develop a common negotiating position and to stick to it, even in the vexing issue of the Irish border. Since Theresa May failed to pit various member states against each other, the "no-deal" threats of her successor Boris Johnson, weakened by COVID, only managed to extract a few symbolic concessions from a Brussels that was still working toward a compromise. While negotiations remained deadlocked, approval ratings of the EU in the member countries have noticeably improved to around 75 percent during the Brexit crisis. The threat to the unity and prosperity that had been achieved has apparently had a sobering effect on Europhobe sentiment.[48] The cascade of financial chaos, migration pressure, and UK withdrawal actually reinforced cooperation by showing Europeans what they stood to lose.

PART III

Continuing Strengths

In spite of all the predictions of doom, Europe is still functioning quite well in many respects—perhaps even better than the United States. Most Europeans, for instance, can enjoy high-speed train service, low-cost higher education, or long vacations while many Americans are stuck in traffic jams and have to pay high tuition or work lengthy hours. Contrary to neoliberal complaints, countries like Germany are highly competitive and have a huge trade surplus. Criticisms of social service fraud notwithstanding, states like Sweden enjoy a reinvigorated welfare system, including ample child care, that creates more equal life opportunities. And in contrast to Republican denials of global warming, some societies like Denmark have abandoned nuclear power and switched almost exclusively to renewable energy. Why are these Europeans more fortunate in issues such as gun control and what might Americans be able to learn from the Continent?

7

Economic Competitiveness

FIGURE 8. Volkswagen exhibition, Wolfsburg, Germany. imageBROKER / Alamy Stock Photo.

On June 1, 2000, Chancellor Gerhard Schröder and Ferdinand Piech, CEO of Volkswagen, formally opened "Car City" in Wolfsburg, Germany. Complementing the already huge VW factory, this *Autostadt* aims to be a "world forum of automobile mobility" and a showcase of technical innovation. The seventy acres along the Mittelland Canal provide a park-like environment with trees, ponds, and theme buildings, displaying the different brands of the Volkswagen corporation. The grand glass, steel, and concrete entry hall welcomes visitors with a soaring globe so as to suggest VW's many different production sites around the world. The park's practical purpose is to serve as the pick-up point of deliveries for over 150,000 proud owners of new VW cars each year. But at the same time, "Car City" constitutes a forum for debates about mobility and a site of entertainment for over two million tourists, demonstrating the success of a company that aspires to be the largest automobile producer in the world.[1]

The rise of Volkswagen was by no means foreordained but rather a result of the company's surprising resiliency in overcoming crises. Even before Ferdinand Porsche's odd but utilitarian car design could reach Labor Front subscribers in the Third Reich, World War II had transformed the prototype into a simple but indestructible Jeep. In 1949 the British occupation authorities returned the factory to civilian purposes and handed it over to the Lower Saxon state and German national government. Meeting the demand for simple but reliable transportation, the *Käfer* became the car of Germany's Economic Miracle, while the "beetle" and microbus attracted a counterculture following in the United States. For their successors, VW developed a whole range of different cars such as the "Rabbit," took over Audi in Germany, SEAT in Spain, and Škoda in the Czech Republic and expanded production to Brazil, Mexico, China, and the United States. Time and again, the company had to weather problems like the test-cheating in the "dieselgate" emission scandal and the slow start in "electro-mobility."[2]

In many ways the VW corporation is typical of Continental European business practices, which differ somewhat from the Anglo-American pattern. While listings of the "top 20" EU companies by revenue include energy providers like British Petroleum or financial services like Paribas, they still contain a large number of manufacturing giants like Siemens and Bayer. In contrast to the American reliance on borrowing, Continental firms more frequently resort to self-funding and executive positions are held by engineers who believe that "in the morning we create technology and in the afternoon we talk about costs." Their workers are usually unionized and tend to have considerable influence on labor issues as well as business decisions. Especially in France, firms like Renault are state supported and subject to political control. Nevertheless, many giants, like Nestle, are transnational with corporate headquarters in low-tax states and production sites in different countries. The result is a more stable and sustainable European business culture.[3]

In contrast, different neoliberal assumptions inspire the prevailing Anglo-American criticism of slower growth on the Continent. Not only businesspeople but also journalists and academics tend to be products of an MBA culture that is based on an implicit faith in the superiority of individual initiative and the benign effects of unfettered competition. This market mentality is driven by short-term considerations of quarterly profits on balance sheets rather than by the basic health of a company's future business prospects. Decisions tend to be made by financial officers who have an eye to shareholder value in the stock market rather than on the underlying vitality of a company, thus making long-term planning difficult. Though also helped by a supportive state, this pervasive mindset produces a highly dynamic environment—but at the cost of lowering wages and generating periodic crises such as the savings and loan crisis, the dot-com bubble, and the Great Recession.[4]

Ultimately, the key question is whether European or American approaches are more successful in coping with the competitive pressures of globalization. Since each has its own advantages and drawbacks, they tend to succeed in some areas and fall short in others. Aided by deregulation, the start-up climate in the United States is more conducive to developing new technologies like personal computers and smartphones or to creating software like Microsoft or Google. But the horrendous American current account deficit suggests that, in terms of international investment and trade, the Europeans and especially the Germans are more than holding their own. While New York and London lead in financial transactions, Continental countries are doing well in high-end manufacturing such as the production of Airbus, the chief rival of scandal-ridden Boeing. Finally, the outcome should not just be measured in terms of GDP growth but also needs to take into consideration the greater satisfaction with the Continental quality of life.[5] What is the reason for this European success?

Social Market Economy

The core philosophy of the Central European economic model is the social market economy, the ideological motor of German prowess. Rejecting wartime dictatorial control, a group of ordoliberal economists around Alfred Müller-Armack suggested a compromise that would provide both competition and order. Their key axiom of "as much market as possible, as much state as necessary" aimed to combine the dynamism of individual enterprise with the constraints of public solidarity. Promoting "prosperity for all," the rotund West German economics minister Ludwig Erhard gambled on freeing the market with the currency reform of 1948 and thereby unleashed the spectacular growth of the Economic Miracle. The labor unions also kept wage demands down in exchange for codetermination, offering workers seats on the company boards.[6] Known as "Germany Inc.," this neo-Keynesian cooperation between capital, labor, and government as well as the interlocking network of industry, banking, and insurance faced neoliberal challenges with deindustrialization and reunification.[7]

While Germany has its share of world-renowned companies, it is really the midsize firms, called the *Mittelstand* that are the secret of its economic success. Large corporations like Siemens, Bayer, Bosch, Daimler, and BMW are known around the globe and account for a good part of German export earnings. But it is smaller firms—like the robot maker KUKA, the washing machine producer Miele, or electronic controls maker Beckhoff—that are less famous but nonetheless global leaders in market niches that provide one-third of Germany's GNP and three-fifths of its jobs. Hundreds of these "hidden champions" are provincially based and still family owned, without ambition to make a financial killing but rather following an outlook of wanting to hand over a flourishing business to the next generation.[8] As a result, relations with skilled labor are often paternalistic, with workers treated well even in recessions, generating loyalty and pride in having an assured future.

Another dimension of the German model is the unique combination of advanced engineering with a dual system of vocational training. The creation of technical universities in the nineteenth century elevated practical tinkering with technology into a more systematic pursuit of innovation. At the same time, the founding of independent centers like the Max Planck or Helmholtz institutes supports much basic and applied research.[9] This academic endeavor is matched with a practice-oriented vocational training on the job, supplemented by attendance at technical schools. This *duale System* is a modernized version of traditional apprenticeship, complemented with instruction in the theory of a given pursuit. For young people tired of formal schooling, it provides an entry into the working world and a chance to earn a bit of money while acquiring necessary occupational expertise.[10] The high reputation of German products not only derives from innovative design but also from quality service.

The strong and responsible role of labor unions in obtaining gains for workers while respecting company profits is also typical of Rhenish capitalism. In contrast to the fragmentation of labor seen in other countries, the German Trade Union Confederation (DGB) is a comprehensive body with sections like the powerful metalworkers' union IG Metall. The socialist project of nationalizing industries failed after World War II since the US occupation authorities rejected such labor efforts. Instead, a system of codetermination developed in which unions in large companies with over five hundred workers are able to elect representatives to the company board, making their voice heard in general business decisions. Even in smaller enterprises, they are allowed to create "works councils."[11] While not avoiding wage conflicts, this system of representation has moderated collective bargaining by providing pay increases and shorter working hours with fewer of the crippling strikes that afflict neighboring countries like France.

Right from the start, the German economy has also been export oriented, providing a higher degree of international trade than its size would indicate. Since the production of its industry exceeded the absorption capacity of its domestic market, the FRG had to rely on selling its goods abroad. As a result, it is the country with the highest export dependency among the G-20. Initially, the focus was on Continental neighbors, successively expanding with European integration to the West, the Mediterranean, and the East. The strict anti-inflation policy of the Bundesbank turned the DM into one of the hardest currencies in the international monetary system, with upward revaluations making German products hard to sell. As a result, Germany reluctantly supported the creation of the euro as a regional currency, facilitating its Eurozone exports with stable prices. Eventually, German firms expanded their reach farther afield and became truly global.[12]

This high wage and benefit system was hit especially hard by deindustrialization because many of its products were simply becoming too expensive. With the rise of the "Asian tigers," who had lower costs and just as efficient machines, mass production of labor-intensive goods such as textiles disappeared since even further automation proved insufficient. Initially hidden by the "oil shocks," this structural transformation met with vigorous resistance by the trade unions, who wanted to protect the traditional industrial jobs of their members. The extensive social plans that cushioned the transition with early retirement benefits helped the affected workers but did not sufficiently fund the development of new high-tech occupations. For a while, outsourcing to cheaper neighboring countries like Italy, Eastern Europe, or the Balkans helped, but ultimately entire sectors—like shipbuilding, coal mining, camera production, and consumer electronics—were lost.[13] Only through additional specialization and labor union cooperation in wage restraint did high-end manufacturing—for instance, in the car industry—manage to survive.

The soaring cost of reunification compounded such difficulties since it turned the assets of the social market economy into liabilities. Buoyed by Chancellor Kohl's promise of "flourishing landscapes" in the East, the reconstruction boom of the early 1990s proved to be rather short-lived since the costs of bringing the new states up to Western levels turned out to be prohibitive. Repairing rotten infrastructure and supporting unemployed workers, who amounted to up to one-third of the Eastern labor force, devoured trillions of DM from the public purse. The fire sale of East German companies, lands, and forests that was supposed to reap huge profits for the Trusteeship Agency instead turned into a black hole because enterprises that did not find buyers had to be practically given away or shut down. Around the turn of the century, half a decade of weak growth was followed by another recession. As a result, the neoliberal commentators of the *Economist* called Germany "the sick man of Europe."[14]

The social democratic solution to this problem was the "new labor" paper of Tony Blair and Gerhard Schröder of 1999, which propagated a "Third Way" between neoliberalism and Marxism. This appeal to modernize labor policies departed from the premise that "ever higher levels of public spending" would not solve social problems but rather hurt "competitiveness, employment and living standards." Instead, they maintained, "the real test for society is how effectively this expenditure is used and how much it enables people to help themselves." Breaking with the tradition of trying to protect workers against the vicissitudes of life like disease or unemployment, the manifesto argued: "The most important task of modernization is to invest in human capital: to make the individual and businesses fit for the knowledge-based economy of the future." In order "to modernize the welfare state, not to abolish it," Europe's Social Democrats "must together formulate and implement a new supply-side agenda for the left."[15]

The legislative form of this reform of the labor market and welfare system was the "Agenda 2010" passed by the red-green coalition of Gerhard Schröder and Joschka Fischer in 2003. Alluding to the EU's Lisbon future strategy, this comprehensive set of measures was intended to improve the "conditions for more growth and employment" by easing the founding of small businesses, loosening job protections, and lowering nonwage labor costs. The core provisions—called Hartz IV after the union representative on the VW board—were the reduction of long-term unemployment benefits to the level of basic welfare coupled with a needs test of possessions and a tightening of job assignments in order to qualify for support. Moreover, some health insurance reimbursements were also cut.[16] The purpose of pruning the welfare state's extensive benefits was to push the unemployed back to work by creating new low-paying mini-jobs that would reduce taxpayer costs and mainstream recipients of support.

The impact of "this most far reaching national economic reform" remains highly controversial since experts debate whether it has gone too far or not far enough. Most trade unions and workers felt betrayed by what they saw as a dismantling of labor gains during the previous decades. Moreover, leftist economists denounced the underlying neoliberalism as counterproductive and claimed that positive developments were more the result of wage restraint, which put the average hourly wage of twenty-six euros back below the EU average. Conservative commentators pointed to the halving of unemployment figures and the creation of thousands of jobs, while neoliberal skeptics claimed that the labor reforms had been too timid to revitalize the economy. The political price was huge because it cost the Social Democratic Party (SPD) the 2005 German parliamentary election. The new Christian Democratic Union (CDU) chancellor Angela Merkel, an East German physicist, thanked her predecessor for "courageously and decisively having opened a door, a door to reforms" and for pushing them through against tough resistance.[17]

The tone of appraisals changed markedly after a few years with the *Economist* proclaiming that Germany's economy was "back above the bar again." By 2007 GNP growth reached almost 3 percent per year, company profits rose, and even long-term unemployment declined. While exports in machine tools, cars, and other medium-high-tech items hummed, domestic demand finally rebounded since more people were working and as consumers had money to spend. The modest increase in labor market flexibility and rise in mini-jobs, coupled with a reduction of relative wage costs and corporate taxes, managed to reinvigorate Germany as an economic powerhouse. Trade unions were willing to compromise their pay demands since employers threatened to relocate their jobs overseas. Even if the reforms were limited, the greater flexibility resulted in "a marked improvement in German industry's competitiveness."[18] Due to cooperation between management, unions, and government, the social market economy was able to compete after all.

Globalization Challenges

The survival of the European social model depends on the response of its coordinated market economies to the pressures of globalization. The attendant intensification of trade, financial transactions, labor movement, and cultural exchanges is both a threat and an opportunity, contingent on how the Europeans use it. The Continental response is, however, rather circumscribed by their comparatively high salaries and extensive benefits, which price many goods and services that they provide out of the market when competing with laborers in low-wage countries. Though the precise mix varies across the Continent, all EU members possess co-ordinated market economies that pursue some combination of market freedom and social solidarity, which provides such an attractive living standard that refugees from many countries are desperate to reach their shores. The political challenge is therefore to find a way of competing on a global scale while maintaining a welfare state.[19] How do different styles of economies and companies seek to accomplish this task?

As a classic liberal market system, Great Britain is itself one of the promoters of globalization, feeling both its negative and positive effects. The imperial past and remaining connections to the former colonies have given the UK a worldwide horizon, balanced by strong national pride. Pushed by the energetic "Iron Lady," Margaret Thatcher, London in the 1980s embarked on a fairly radical form of neoliberalism, deregulating and privatizing its economy where it could. Though she did not dismantle the National Health Service and other social provisions like council flats, this marketization did keep UK social expenditures to one of the lower levels in the EU at 20.54 percent of annual GDP. The negative consequence of such a resolute embrace of globalization has been the deindustrialization of the Midlands, which destroyed coal mining and much classical manufacturing. Continued by David Cameron's austerity cuts, its benefit was the creation of a speculation-driven world financial center in the City of London and a flourishing southwest. However, only Ireland followed a similar path.[20]

The opposite extreme among the coordinated market economies is the Nordic Model, which offers "a unique combination of free market capitalism and social benefits." On the one hand, the Scandinavian countries possess vigorous industries based on provisions for easy shedding of employees and implementing transformative business models. On the other, they provide a generous social welfare program for the unemployed and free education as well as universal health care. These extensive benefits are made possible through progressive taxation rates that fund high social expenses of around 28 percent of annual GNP. The public accepts this system because "citizens willingly choose to pay higher taxes in exchange for benefits that they and their family members will get to enjoy." As a product of a social democratic consensus culture, the Nordic Model has reduced income inequality as well as gender differences, trading slower economic growth for a distinctly higher quality of life.[21]

Somewhat similar is the hybrid French style of coordinated capitalism, which is based on a mercantilist tradition of state direction of the economy. The system is run by an elite network with common training in the *hautes écoles,* which is located both in business and the bureaucracy. This shared outlook and personal connection leads to a close relationship between corporate boardrooms and government offices that facilitates communication and cooperation between the private and public sectors. Typical of France is also a strong emphasis on *dirigisme* in which the state sets broad goals to be achieved by business enterprise, sometimes with considerable financial aid. To succeed in international competition, Paris also encourages rival companies to merge into "national champions" that are big enough to prosper globally. The extensive welfare and childcare system requires a high degree of public spending, which limits growth, but the populace only minds when its expectations exceed actual benefits.[22]

More problematic are the mixed market economies of the Mediterranean countries, such as Italy and Spain. Their ancient agricultural structures favor small producers, while some regions also have impressive industrial sites, initially based on low labor costs. These countries contain a well-developed tourist sector, serving as a playground for sun-starved Northern Europeans. Unfortunately, the sovereign debt crisis turned the impressive building boom of the 2000s into a deep recession. One of the chief problems of this model is the low productivity of workers, which requires long hours of toil without appropriate rewards. In spite of early retirement ages, the paternalistic protection of older laborers has created an enormous unemployment problem for the younger generation, which has been unable to obtain jobs.[23] Though some regions like Northern Italy or Catalonia are flourishing, the resistance of a tradition-bound system has kept these economies from reaching their true potential.

Since the Eastern European transition is still underway, the precise features of post-Communist capitalism are only beginning to crystallize. The failure of the planned economy also led to a collapse of the extensive welfare system of "real existing socialism." The hectic and unprecedented nature of the conversion to a market economy created an opening for a free-for-all capitalism, unrestrained by a legal framework that would moderate market competition. As a result, the heady hopes for a people's capitalism, based on shares in the erstwhile state enterprises, have collapsed. Instead, in many countries a group of oligarchs has managed to amass breathtaking fortunes by taking advantage of its connections to old and new political leaders or secret service insiders. Especially in the Balkans, post-Communist politics have concentrated on capturing the state apparatus for the rent-seeking of client parties.[24] While the initial impulse has been a neoliberal removal of state controls, rising prosperity gradually allowed some prior welfare features to return.

On the level of an individual company, neoliberal rhetoric promises to enhance performance and thereby also competitiveness. Construing a firm's purpose as "to make a profit," raise its stock price, and augment the executives' paycheck, focuses policy on those measures that promise a short-run return. In contrast to the production ethos of engineers, this accounting outlook "financializes" a company, turning it into an instrument for making money irrespective of its actual activities. One favorite measure for impressing investors is to cut costs by firing workers, cutting the labor force down to the bare minimum needed to continue to function. With few if any local ties, CEOs are ready to move production to new locations where government incentives reduce taxes or labor costs are cheaper. Hedge funds are forever looking to take over companies in order to sell off their pieces for financial gain.[25] This neoliberal definition of competitiveness ultimately threatens to destroy what it claims to enhance.

The French retailer Carrefour, however, shows that new concepts such as the *hypermarché* can also be successful, even if they are launched from a coordinated market economy. Founded in 1959 as a series of modest grocery stores, the chain expanded into the "big box" concept of creating huge shopping centers, supplementing the core food and fruit business with anything else a customer might want to buy. With French style and panache, the Carrefour group rapidly expanded into Belgium, Spain, Italy, and Poland and then also into Latin America and even into China. Moreover, it diversified its offerings, ranging from small "eight to eight" outlets to massive stores with tens of thousands of square meters of retail space. By 2015 the chain was present in 35 countries, had sales of about €100 billion in 12,000 stores, and employed 380,000 workers![26] While Carrefour failed to get a foothold in Germany or Austria, its red, white, and blue arrow logo can be found in shopping centers all over the world.

A more traditional leader in incremental technology is the electronic giant Siemens, which makes more than half of its profits outside of Germany. The firm was founded in 1847 in order to facilitate electric lighting, power generation, and motor construction, which made it a major part of German military production during both world wars. Although losing its patents after the defeats, it recovered quickly and spread into 190 countries with €83 billion in sales and 378,000 employees by 2018. Though the structure and products of the firm have changed time and again in response to technical and business developments, its core areas have consisted of power generation, train construction, health care equipment, and household appliances. Some of its ventures have failed because the bureaucratized enterprise was too unwieldy to keep up with changes in the manufacture of television sets, personal computers, or cell phones.[27] But Siemens continued to succeed in enough areas through innovative engineering, quality production, and on-the-ground service that it has become a household word.

The Royal Dutch Shell oil company is an example of a multinational corporation that blends elements taken from liberal and coordinated capitalism. It originated in 1907 as a result of a merger of the British Shell Transport and Trading Company and the Koninklijke Nederlandse Petroleum Maatschappij, incorporated in London but with the firm's headquarters located in a traditional brick building in The Hague.

Though the Dutch held 60 percent of the shares, Shell was listed on the London and New York stock exchanges. The joint company is active in the exploration, extraction, refining, and distribution of oil products. In 2018 it employed 81,000 people and had $388.4 billion in sales in 25 million filling stations in more than 140 countries. Due to environmentalist criticism of scandals like the planned sinking of the Brent Spar platform, Shell has also begun to invest heavily in renewable energy.[28] Hence, the company's culture seems to be combining traditional and neoliberal styles.

Firms within the coordinated market countries have enhanced their competitiveness by working within the framework of the single EU market and its international trade policies. Succeeding within the "largest economy in the world" and "the world's largest trading block" required much managerial foresight and labor productivity to prepare businesses for global competition. Profiting from its free trade regime of modest tariffs, these corporations made the EU "the world's largest exporter of manufactured goods and services" as well as "the biggest export market for around 80 countries." Though social policy adjustments like the Agenda 2010 remained a national preserve, Brussels helped companies by signing dozens of trade agreements with countries like Canada, Japan, Singapore, and South Korea. With patient research and systematic outsourcing, firms like the chemical giant Bayer acquired a leading global position, enabling them to make controversial purchases of competitors like Monsanto.[29] Through a careful balance of neoliberal initiatives and social supports, many European companies are mastering the global challenge.

The Impact on Jobs

Proof of the superiority of one or another version of the coordinated market economy depends on its impact on the actual lives of its workers. A liberal system offers high rewards for successful managers and space for dynamic start-ups but often at the cost of insecurity and big differentials in earning power. The coordinated variant provides more modest remuneration but offers more security of positions as well as less income disparity between top and bottom earners. During the last decades of neoliberal ascendency, the job protections that had been won by trade unions have come under increasing pressure, making it easier to hire and fire depending on the business cycle. Moreover, technological innovations in computing and communications have eroded traditional manufacturing jobs, lasting a lifetime, and replaced them with more precarious patchwork careers.[30] While some trends like greater gender equality were positive, the dissolution of the industrial work model has left especially young immigrant workers behind.

Typical of the liberal market economies is the genre of CEO success stories, which celebrate a business turnaround due to vigorous executive leadership. The rescue narrative proceeds according to the following plotline: The company is unprofitable, management is demoralized, and customers are unhappy; in short, the firm is on the verge of bankruptcy. In comes a new manager who vigorously cuts costs by dismissing workers, eliminating redundant layers of management, improving the quality of products, and shifting to "just in time production," according to the credo of "thinking lean." After a suitable interval, the company miraculously returns to profitability, the stockholders are delighted, and the CEO basks in his success. "The fast realistic action of an Interim Executive Manager has prevented an insolvency case."[31] This stylized account justifies a generous remuneration, sweetened by stock options that are much higher in the UK and the United States than on the Continent.

The counterpoint to such self-affirmation is the story line of dismissed workers or managers who cannot find new jobs because they are over fifty years old. One "successful, experienced, and ambitious" executive, codenamed Martin Maler, agreed to resign from his company, which had run into difficulties, since he believed "good people are always needed" and he would have another position within three months. "He had never been so wrong" in his life. Ten months later, after fifty rejections of responses to advertisements, his unemployment benefits were about to run out and he would have to "live on his savings," selling his stocks, cashing in his life insurance, and so on. Once the money was gone, descent into welfare threatened. The psychological impact of his failure was devastating: "No matter what I do, nobody wants me any longer." Another half year later with his assets depleted, he finally landed another job but had to leave his family and move to Frankfurt 250 miles away.[32] Many others were not so lucky.

The chief advantage of a coordinated market economy is the higher degree of job security guaranteed by both legal protections and social custom. Two French middle managers were satisfied enough to admit, "I have been at the same company for twenty years," rejecting the implication that they ought to have moved on in the meantime. Thierry, the director of a vacation center, had gradually worked his way up from a summer job after training in hotel management, while Laurent, the manager of a clothing shop, had responded to an advertisement and enjoyed the contact with his customers. Having tried a couple of other options, the former always returned to his present job since he preferred his colleagues. With long-term experience came satisfaction. "I am happy like that. I don't regret anything." The latter explained: "I liked the comfort and stability, which have not kept me from developing, quite to the contrary. Being loyal to one business also has a financial advantage of seniority."[33]

In contrast to liberal hiring and firing, companies in a coordinated market economy tend to engage in "labor hoarding," which keeps staff on shorter hours rather than letting them go in a downturn. The business rationale of this approach is the high cost of finding new workers and training them for particular tasks to replace those dismissed. Reducing fears of losing employment, the retention of employees during a recession sends a signal of appreciation, even if their hours are cut. While peripheral personnel can be shed without any loss of company coherence, maintaining a core staff also preserves essential expertise. Caring for such a *Stammbelegschaft* not only preserves peace with labor unions but also reinforces a sense of belonging beyond a particular pay scale. During the Great Recession of 2009, 7 percent of Belgian, 5 percent of German, and 4 percent of French workers kept their jobs by being put on shorter hours.[34] Such a positive relationship between unions and management also encourages investment in lifelong learning to upgrade labor skills and productivity.

Workers in a coordinated market economy often show more job satisfaction than in a neoliberal system since they enjoy considerable security. The responses of four thousand Siemens workers to an ongoing survey reveal many positive comments. Employees called the German electronics giant "very good," found "everything terrific," or felt they had a "solid job." Many workers liked "the excellent conditions" of "a top employer," which was "the best in its business." Satisfied staff praised "the splendid company offering extras" because they liked the work atmosphere with "nice colleagues, super friendly treatment of superiors" and "quite open communication." For young employees the company offered "many possibilities to develop yourself. Managers are well prepared and can mostly implement things well." The pay and fringe benefits were good, there was "open and honest dealing with one another," and the "work-life-balance was positive." Being part of "a terrific team" made Siemens "an employer to be recommended."[35]

Employee comments, however, also reveal the difficulties of maintaining labor market control against the pressures of globalized competition. Frustrated workers in the same survey complained about "bureaucracy, servility and reporting mania" that blocked innovation. "Continual restructuring and rampant red tape" created much insecurity: "Today we are supposed to do one thing, tomorrow another and day after tomorrow something else again." The constant "financial pressures" led to "years of reductions, reductions and reductions" that made planning and specialization difficult. The "aimless activism, few investments and rigid chain of command" of such downsizing produced increasingly precarious forms of jobs with "temps, interns, [and] work students instead of regular employment." In a similar vein, the French government wanted "to make it easier to fire workers" so that companies would actually hire more since they would not be stuck with employees "for life."[36]

The protection of labor markets for insiders has led to an unprecedented level of youth unemployment in some Mediterranean countries. In Greece, Spain, and Portugal, about half of all the young were not finding jobs after graduation during the Great Recession. For instance, despite having a "postgraduate degree in industrial science," Lorene

Rodrigues was unable to obtain a position. Similarly, Linnea Borjars remained jobless and frustrated a year after finishing her studies in eco-tourism and cultural history. "I feel in some ways that I'm of no use anymore." One scholar commented: The "process of becoming self-sufficient through employment is taking longer than it did before" because too many young people studied academic subjects instead of receiving practical training. About a quarter of those who were fortu-nate enough to get some kind of job were underemployed, working below their qualifications. Since the EU's effort to combat youth unem-ployment remained ineffective, the head of the European Parliament Martin Schulz warned: "We are creating a lost generation."[37]

The difficult entry into the working world forced millennials to re-adjust their goals, no longer sure that they would have a better life than their parents. According to a Spanish survey in 2018, thirty- to thirty-four-year-olds had a "30 percent lower disposable income" than the previous generation. Many were still living with their parents or had few children since rents were eating up half of their pay. Simply going to college and getting a degree was no longer a guarantee for a job. Many millennials "have had to make alternative plans, deviating from the model followed by prior generations." Able to get only unpaid intern-ships on TV with her training in documentary filmmaking, Cristina Robles joined "a bicycle service offering scheduled deliveries" since she loved to ride the streets. Anatoliy Gatt had to move all the way from Malta to Holland to get a decent IT job. A sociologist concluded that "the economic constraints faced by millennials are slowing down their progress through major life milestones."[38]

Another way to surmount frustrating job searches was to create a start-up that would then provide employment. In an EU portal, found-ers talked about their entrepreneurial spirit, business plans, and so on, in order to encourage others to follow their successful examples. Born in China but living in Berlin, Chanyu Xu combined an inherited interest in food with her own aesthetic sense to create a line of health supple-ments to enhance beauty, called "her1." The Swedish CEO Sebastian Siemiatkowski worked out a solution for the e-commerce problems of selling "in a simple and safe way for consumers" and founded the global company Klarna as a clearinghouse. In order to fund such startups, the Israeli Shmuel Chafets helped create Target General, "a pan-European venture capital firm," which assisted quite a few businesses to market readiness. The EU supported startups with its own website in order to show that new ideas could also flourish in the somewhat restrictive environment of Europe.[39]

The data on job satisfaction indicates that people in coordinated capitalism are more pleased with their lives than those in pure market systems. In one survey of work contentment, Denmark led the list, while four of the top five states had a social market economy (Britain was the only outlier). At the top end of the scale were established EU members or affiliates, and on the bottom the post-Communist countries and Turkey. Not just the level of pay but a broader measure of well-being made the key difference. Another study argued that "the secret to happiness" was "health, housing, and job security." All these dimensions had "nothing to do with personal choice or destiny. Rather, they are social and, as such, inescapably political." It was not income alone, since "North America underperforms relative to its GDP," but social spending that buffered the vagaries of the market. In the final analysis, what made the difference in how people felt was the direction of "decades of public policy."[40]

Competition and Solidarity

The social market economy is an attempt to reconcile the contradictory principles of a dynamic market with the support of social responsibility. According to a formulation by the Commission of the Bishops' Conferences of the European Community, it "links the principle of freedom on the market and the instrument of competitive economics with the principle of solidarity and with mechanisms of social compensation." After the excesses of government regulation during dictatorship and war, free market advocates like Ludwig Erhard first had to reestablish the principle of competition based on individual gain, in order to unleash the creative spirit. But then the trade unions and Social Democrats also needed to insist on sharing the spoils of the Economic Miracle with the underprivileged widows, refugees, and bombing victims so as to restore social cohesion.[41] From the beginning the social market economy was therefore a contested effort to balance individual gain with collective solidarity.

The implementation of this model in Germany shows a number of peculiarities that can only be explained by the path dependency on prior experiences. In contrast to the British preference for financial services, the German economy remains rather production and export oriented. After the collapse of mass manufacturing of cheap goods like textiles, German companies have focused on the upper market segment, relying on quality and design. Since their venture into IT hardware and software with Infineon and SAP was only moderately successful, they have specialized in medium-high tech—such as the making of machine tools and luxury cars with Mercedes, BMW, Audi, and Porsche. At the same time, they are leaders in green technology and alternative energy. Much to the chagrin of some neighbors, the Berlin government favors fiscal discipline due to its negative recollections of two inflations. Finally, Germany also supports a generous welfare state in order to help the underprivileged segment of society.[42]

In the Anglo-American media, this German model has provoked a considerable amount of criticism for unnecessarily slowing down growth. Neoliberal commentators argue that protections of employees against arbitrary firing create a rigid labor market. They also emphasize that the many rules and regulations as well as the layers of bureaucracy inhibit risk-taking. The "non-market coordination, supplemented by a generous system of welfare protection," makes German goods often rather expensive. The "substantial inter-firm collaboration in research and development" tends toward an oligopolistic division of markets that inhibits outright competition. "Extensive cross-shareholdings, long term bank finance and co-determination" reduce the flexibility of the economy in responding to opportunities.[43] If such criticisms are justified, why then is Germany one of the leading export nations that amasses an impressive balance of payments surplus?

Even if growth is sometimes slower than in liberal market systems, German employees enjoy numerous benefits that create a high quality of life. Working time in major companies is generally limited to around 37.5 hours per week and overtime is compensated by time off. The many religious holidays, demanded by the Catholic and Protestant churches, create long weekends if they fall on a Monday or Thursday. Workers are also protected from being reached at home after hours, even if a degree of home-office work is gradually being accepted especially for white-collar occupations. Moreover, vacations are rather generous, amounting to an average of 30 days per year—exactly twice what most US employees receive! Although Americans work 1,778 hours per year, Germans do so only for 1,419 hours and yet receive salaries that are roughly equivalent.[44] Since these extensive perks raise the cost of labor, they can only be tolerated if work intensity and productivity are equally high.

A coordinated market economy also helps slow down the increasing gap between rich and poor in all European countries that have adopted it. An international research team, led by the French economist Thomas Piketty, found that the richest 1 percent of the globe has "more than doubled" its share of wealth in the last decades. "Since 1980 the income inequality in North America, China, India, and Russia has risen rapidly." The top 10 percent own 47 percent of the resources in the United States whereas in Europe it is only 37 percent. The disparity has also grown in Germany, although the middle class was able to hang on while the share of the lower half decreased from about one-third to one-fifth. Due to a high rate of social transfer payments, according to a CIA estimate the German Gini coefficient was the lowest among the G7 states at 0.27, but in the United States it was the highest at 0.45.[45] These alarming numbers indicate that recent gains in prosperity have taken place on the back of the poor. While it is not a magic wand, a social market economy does offer an effective way to curb the effects of rampant neoliberal greed.

8

Restructured Welfare State

FIGURE 9. Childcare, Stockholm, Sweden. AP.

On August 31, 2004, the leaders of four center-right parties announced the creation of an "Alliance for Sweden" that set out to reshape the welfare state. Meeting in the village of Högfors, Göran Hägglund of the Center, Lars Leijonborg of the Liberals, Maud Olofsson of the Christian Democrats, and Fredrik Reinfeldt of the Moderates agreed to put their differences aside in order to break the dominance of the Social Democrats whose unique position had become coterminous with the Swedish welfare state. Elaborated in half a dozen working groups, their election manifesto promised to "create new hope for Sweden" by restoring confidence in the success of the country. "We want to lay the cornerstone for a long-term healthy economic development, for more prosperity and power for individuals and families in their everyday lives." In contrast to the social democratic emphasis on benefits, this neoliberal program claimed to be "a job manifesto" by cutting income and property taxes.[1]

Surprisingly, this makeshift alliance narrowly won the 2006 election, gaining 178 out of 349 seats in the Riksdag. Since the Social Democrats and their allies had held power for 65 of the previous 74 years, the victory of the bourgeois opposition was a shock. Defeated, Prime Minister Göran Persson resigned but vowed: "We will never accept the Right's change of system—we will hit back." His successor, Fredrik Reinfeldt, countered by emphasizing the moderation of center-right parties: "We have won the election as the New Moderates and will also together with our Alliance friends govern Sweden as the New Moderates." The alliance claimed that "changes to Sweden's rigid labor market and high cost welfare system are long overdue" so that "the country can continue to compete in the global market." Trying to allay fears, the new prime minister nevertheless asserted that he would not abolish the "Nordic welfare model" but rather fine-tune it so as to make it more efficient.[2]

Other liberal market advocates have gone much further in opposing the egalitarianism and collectivism of welfare states in general. Time and again, libertarian commentators have railed against the "socialist nanny state" whose paternalist intrusions were taking away personal liberties—for example, by imposing seat belts in cars. During the Cold War, many Anglo-Americans like Vice President Richard M. Nixon also mistook social democracy for Communism, creating a stark alternative between "democratic freedom and state socialism." Recently released papers show that the British prime minister Margaret Thatcher "secretly tried to press ahead with a politically toxic plan to dismantle the welfare state" by proposing to charge for public education and introduce compulsory private health insurance. Condemning the "European social welfare state" has become a staple of the Anglo-American Right, inducing President Donald Trump to back welfare reform so as to supposedly eliminate abuse and compel people to go back to work.[3]

Defenders of the welfare state have countered that it is not the problem but rather the solution to numerous social ills. No doubt, organized interests like trade unions seek to influence public opinion in favor of social services because they want to keep their hard-won gains. But Christians, Marxists, and social scientists adduce more fundamental moral and pragmatic arguments: "We are for state welfare because properly funded, universal state services free at the point of use, combined with a commitment to full employment, can provide the minimum needed for people—young and old—to exist and actively take part in social and political life." Based on the democratic Nordic Model rather than the dictatorial Soviet Union, they assert that welfare states can be competitive, provide a high standard of living, limit income inequalities, and also avoid dependency on charity, family, and the like. To refute clichés like "welfare queens," they tout the many impressive benefits of a welfare state.[4]

Ultimately, the debate about the welfare state revolves around the question of how to craft a "sustainable modernity" for the future. In many ways, the dichotomy of unbridled capitalism versus social solidarity is too simple since what is needed is not one or the other but a combination of competitive and cooperative strategies. In many countries, a middle-class tax revolt has created strict limits on the further expansion of monetary transfers or services to new client groups. Moreover, the charge of debilitating psychological effects of living on public support rather than by individual work even convinced the Clinton administration in the United States. But at the same time, the steep rise in income inequality is beginning to tear societies apart since the poor and those just scraping by are realizing that the system is stacked against them. The challenge therefore consists of creating a "well-being society" that is both productive and humane.[5] How have European countries tried to resolve this dilemma?

The Swedish Example

The Swedish welfare state was a constructive response to the sociopolitical turmoil of the interwar period. In a 1928 speech in Parliament, the Social Democrat Per Albin Hansson rejected class conflict and instead proposed building a "people's home" that would include workers, farmers, and the middle class. The engaging family image became a social democratic hallmark since the party also signed a compromise with the Agrarian Party to help small farmers. While the Great Depression exacerbated the social cleavages of other countries, the Swedish Social Democrats initiated a cooperation between labor and employers in the Saltsjöbaden Agreement that reduced strikes and other wage conflicts. With the success of these practical underpinnings, the *folkhem* concept came to express "the Swedish people's deep feeling of community" that carried the country through a contested neutrality during World War II.[6] This appeal to national unity produced a consensus on the need for social reform.

It took a series of incremental steps to create the complex web of benefits that are commonly called the Swedish welfare state. The initial impulse followed the Bismarckian example of providing basic security against life's risks by offering unemployment, health, and retirement insurance. Promoted by trade unions, the system targeted male industrial workers rather than women or agricultural laborers. Assuming that the middle class could take care of itself, this effort to provide insurance started with a limited number of laborers who could afford to pay the premiums. In the postwar period, this system was expanded by introducing a compulsory national pension plan, a child allowance, support for home construction, and a national health program. Centralized collective bargaining for "a solidarity wage" compressed pay differences and generated a sense of social equality.[7] These expanded benefits and new clients gradually conditioned the Swedish people to expect welfare benefits from the state.

During the booming 1960s and 1970s, the extension into new areas initiated a change of philosophy toward universalization of social services. The welfare goal shifted from aiding the needy to creating greater equality of opportunity and income for all. Prime Minister Olof Palme called for a steep increase in productivity in order "to help people who are hurt" and "reduce social cleavages in Sweden." This approach implied a decommodification of social services like health, removing them from payment in the market to a tax-supported right for all citizens. An American observer claimed that "Sweden's health care is second to none; it boasts the world's highest investment in medical services [and] the lowest infant mortality rate." Similarly, free secondary and higher education expanded opportunities for upward social mobility. Coupled with a higher income floor and benefits tied to work, such services assured "the least privileged of its population a higher standard of living."[8]

Women especially gained from the shift to equality since it defamilianized their status, treating them as independent adults. No longer were they dependent on their husbands' incomes and tied to caring for infants and the elderly at home. The expansion of access to education provided them with appropriate credentials for the job market. The provision of free childcare and the establishment of all-day schools made it possible for women to pursue careers of their own. At the same time, a generous parental leave policy allowed mothers (and even some fathers) time to recover from birth and to bond with their children while having a guaranteed job to return to. Moreover, individualized taxation increased their financial independence by considerably reducing their tax burden. Finally, the creation of hundreds of thousands of jobs in education, health care, and social services also provided ample career opportunities in white-collar fields that were particularly attractive to women.[9]

It took a severe economic crisis in 1991 to shake this consensus on the universalist welfare state and to remove the Social Democrats from power. Beforehand, real per capita income had already begun to erode, private sector employment had stagnated, and current account deficits had led to currency devaluations. But in 1993 a deep recession lowered the GNP by 4 percent and raised unemployment from 2.03 percent to 11.15 percent with an additional 5 percent of the labor force in retraining schemes. "The employment rate fell by 12 percentage points from its previous peak." This downturn pushed "government spending above 70 percent of national income" and raised the annual budget deficit to well over 10 percent. Moreover, the ratio of debt to GDP doubled between 1990 and 1994. These fiscal difficulties also forced a contraction of the public workforce. Since "the Swedish model was no longer anyone's envy," the political elite had to search for "painful policy reforms to correct" the mounting problems.[10]

Different ideologues offered contradictory solutions to the mounting problems of the Swedish welfare state. Neoliberal experts complained about the cost of the services, raising the tax burden to one of the highest levels in the Organisation for Economic Co-operation and Development (OECD), and argued that these charges inhibited economic growth. Some prominent individuals—like the movie director Ingmar Bergman or the tennis star Björn Borg—even left the country to escape the steep marginal income tax rate. Reformist defenders of the welfare state argued that general government expenditures needed to be reduced since they exceeded 60 percent of GNP while budget deficits approached 15 percent in 1993. International Monetary Fund observers therefore concluded that the "government was generally agreed to have become too big by the late 1980s." Such bureaucratization and regulation created rigidities in the labor market that made industry less competitive. Only confirmed leftists who wanted to preserve the achievements of the welfare state opposed drastic reforms.[11]

In order to keep most gains, the social democratic administration that returned to power in 1993 initiated a fairly radical retrenchment. Stockholm adopted flexible exchange rates and inflation targeting, which softened the krona and led to a sustained export growth. It also initiated a tax reform that lowered the top rate, expanded the base, and eliminated inheritance and wealth taxes, making Sweden more attractive as a place to live and do business. At the same time, the government deregulated traditional monopolies like the railways, airlines, and telephone and postal services. This opening allowed new companies to enter and increase competition thus raising productivity. Finally, the reforms included a reduction of the public sector and a drop in the generosity of the social insurance system that decreased the government share to 52 percent of GNP and cut the debt burden in half. International observers concluded "that inequality and poverty did rise, but by remarkably little."[12]

Supported by a "robust recovery," the bourgeois coalition that assumed power in 2006 continued the transformation of the Swedish welfare state in a neoliberal direction. During the preceding decade, the economy had grown by 2.4 percent, somewhat above the OECD average. In order to encourage people to work, the government reduced the rate of unemployment benefits as well as their length. At the same time, it focused the Active Labor Market Policies by insisting on actual job searches and participation in retraining. It also added an income tax credit that was supposed to motivate low-wage laborers to reenter the workforce. Finally, it slashed taxes for firms so as to make them profitable again. A US National Bureau of Economic Standards report therefore argued: "Sweden's recovery shows that it is possible to run a reasonably successful market economy while still devoting considerable resources to a welfare state that maintains economic equality."[13]

This readjustment was successful until the arrival of a wave of refugees in 2015 severely strained public support. Since Sweden had prided itself on openness and development aid, both Conservatives and Social Democrats had welcomed refugees as a moral duty, an economic opportunity, and a demographic necessity. But when 160,000 Syrians, Afghans, and others arrived within one year and pushed the proportion of foreign born from 11 percent to 19 percent, the welfare state consensus collapsed because the need for resources for the migrants outstripped solidarity. Cultural differences with often illiterate and unskilled refugees who did not speak the local language eroded the initial goodwill since they were unable to work immediately. With integration taking longer than two years, the financial commitment appeared interminable, while the creation of "lower wage service sector jobs" was rejected by the unions.[14] A welfare state designed for white, Lutheran Swedes found it hard to cope with darker-skinned Muslims from abroad.

Such "welfare chauvinism" fueled the rapid rise of "a xenophobic, racist and right-wing populist" party, called the Sweden Democrats. After this originally neo-Nazi group grew a bit more moderate, it gained representation in the Riksdag in 2010 and became the third largest party in 2018 with 17.5 percent of the vote. One of the key resentments driving its popularity was the conviction that "people don't want to pay taxes to support people who don't work," because "many refugees will rely on welfare for years." Moreover, the party was propelled "by revulsion over multiculturalism" and the conviction that immigrants "have different religions, different ways of life" that would make them incapable of integrating. While liberals continued to be optimistic about absorbing the refugees, the all-too-real problems of dealing with trauma, dislocation, violent crime, and drug use fed into populist resentment. The strain of integration was threatening to imperil "faith in the system" of welfare as a whole.[15]

In spite of these severe challenges, the Swedish welfare state has shown surprising resilience in adjusting to new conditions. After an impressive buildup of benefits, it had to acknowledge that due to the recession of the early 1990s, assistance could not be expanded forever because it rested on the competitiveness of the underlying economy. The social democratic consensus of support depended on the sense that all citizens would receive tangible returns for their willingness to tax themselves. Though salaries were compressed, everyone understood that there was an obligation to work and contribute rather than to sponge off the efforts of others. Once the homogeneous national solidarity was questioned by the arrival of numerous refugees, this unwritten social contract began to erode both "symbolically and materially."[16] But since reforms have made the Swedish welfare state less exceptional, there is some reason to believe that it will continue to weather global competition in the future.

Welfare Patterns

Other European welfare states have developed according to a similar pattern, though the timing and extent of coverage differ from country to country. Starting with Bismarck's insurance initiative in the 1880s, public provisions gradually replaced private care and religious charity, becoming a regular task of government in the interwar period. Due to the massive suffering in World War II, the protections against life's risks for needy groups were deepened and widened after 1945. These benefits became universal during the boom years of the 1960s and early 1970s and governments shifted their focus to the more ambitious goal of creating social equality through financial transfers. But with the faltering of growth during the stagflation of the later 1970s, an aging population and long-term unemployment, states had ever more difficulty with funding the expansion of services. As a result, social democratic optimism about social engineering vanished and a neoliberal discourse emerged that pilloried "the crisis of the welfare state."[17]

Reflecting cultural traditions and political conflicts, each European country has produced a distinctive form of the welfare state. Closest to Sweden are the Nordic neighbors who are considered "brotherly peoples" due to the similarity of culture and language. All of them possess an elaborate welfare state with extensive benefits, use centralized collective bargaining with strong unions, and believe in competitive market economies. Due to the happy accident of discovering North Sea oil in the 1960s, Norway has a high degree of state ownership of companies, provides generous services, and collects its revenue surplus in a future fund for the time when raw materials will run out. Less fortunate, Denmark is more of a trade economy with big investments in alternative energy. Linguistically different Finland is trying to escape the shadow of Russian dominance by pushing education and cutting-edge technology.[18] They resemble each other so much that in many comparisons the Nordic states receive similar scores.

At the opposite end of the welfare spectrum lies the British welfare state, which started out like the Nordic Model but ended up as a neoliberal shell. During World War II, the Beveridge Report proposed a comprehensive insurance scheme to combat the five evils of "squalor, ignorance, want, idleness, and disease." In 1945 the victorious Labor Party promised protection "from the cradle to the grave" and eventually ventured into redistribution for the sake of greater equality. Its crowning achievement was the creation of the National Health Service, which provides free health care to the entire population. But a middle-class tax revolt against the high costs, amplified by neoliberal economists' theoretical objections, inspired severe benefit cuts that culminated in Margaret Thatcher's massive assault on the unions and on welfare expenses in the name of competitiveness.[19] The odd result of this contradictory trajectory is a mixture of universalist entitlements with neoliberal anti-welfare austerity.

Between these two extremes is the corporate version of welfare of the Continent, which began as occupational insurance. It combines an element of Catholic subsidiarity with a Bismarckian insurance approach and a democratic participation claim. In France, cooperation between Gaullists and Socialists has created a *protection sociale* that began from an attempt to protect people against the four fundamental risks of "illness," "accident," "old age," and "family." A special branch of insurance addresses each of these threats, with people divided according to their work into a general, bureaucratic, agricultural, and independent scheme. Originally based on employee contributions, this network has expanded so as to provide a considerable amount of protection to the entire population. This shift from individual payroll charges to general taxes has raised the state quota to over 30 percent.[20] While family benefits have been exemplary, critics like President Macron argue that the size and complexity of thirty-two different systems are a drag on competitiveness that needs to be removed.

As a pioneer of social insurance, the German *Sozialstaat*, which was widely imitated, faces similar problems of high public-sector and non-wage costs. After World War II, a unique combination of Catholic social teaching, bargaining strength of trade unions, economic prosperity, and rivalry with Communist East Germany produced extensive coverage. Five pillars characterize its institutional arrangements: public insurance against vital risks (pensions, health insurance, etc.); tax-financed income subsidies for the indigent; employer contributions to health insurance; free education; and tax exemptions for families, savers, and others. The insurance structure largely pays out benefits according to prior contributions, but there is also a considerable amount of redistribution in *Sozialhilfe* (social assistance) and health care. Ensuring "prosperity for all" worked reasonably well as long as there was full employment, but with the costs of unification, an aging population, and unemployment compensation the financial burden has become more difficult to bear.[21] As a result, the Schröder government cut back benefits in the Agenda 2010.

The Mediterranean version of the welfare state developed later and remained more incomplete than the corporate model. Since Greek, Spanish, and Portuguese dictatorships ended only in the 1960s and 1970s, social services took more time to emerge, while Italy remained divided between an advanced North and a lagging South. In Southern Europe, the impact of the Catholic Church remained stronger, while the labor unions were less powerful. Nonetheless, the labor market was more strongly protected, leading to a higher degree of segmentation. Though pension systems became widespread, the family remained the central safeguard against risk and provider of social care for children and the elderly. Instead of looking to the government for help, many citizens appealed to aid from powerful networks of relations in a clientelistic pattern.[22] While welfare provisions expanded during the boom, many benefits were cut and people were thrown back on familial support during the Great Recession.

For the Eastern European welfare states, the market transition was especially brutal and disruptive due to their inability to maintain a high benefit level. The prior Communist version had relied on a welfare dictatorship whose hallmark was full employment and wage compression in the name of social equality. Prices were fixed and rather low; housing, transportation, food, and products of daily need were heavily subsidized, while health care, childcare, and education remained free of charge and companies sponsored an array of social and cultural activities, including sports. In the transition, this entire system collapsed since obtaining services now demanded payment and providers shed social burdens. During retrenchment, the states used a mixture of dismantling, cutting of benefits, and retargeting on the really poor to maintain a minimum of protection. Only with the gradual economic recovery did they manage to restore some benefits like public pensions and child allowances through taxes and insurance contributions.[23]

During the 1980s the difficulties of paying for increasingly elaborate services in the West triggered a whole raft of criticisms, aiming to reduce the scope of welfare or to abolish it altogether. To begin with, remnants of a moral critique resurfaced, accusing recipients of support of being lazy and profligate, unworthy of public assistance. Then, in the hardworking middle class, a revolt arose, spreading from the United States to the UK and then to the Continent; it refused to pay ever-increasing taxes or contributions for government programs that chiefly benefited others. This resentment was theoretically justified by a strong neoliberal current emanating from the monetarism of the Chicago School, which considered the state to be inept and preferred market competition as more effective in allocating goods and services.[24] Taken together, these charges changed the public perception from welfare as a worthy product of solidarity to a bottomless pit of public expenditures, calling for a drastic change of course.

Defenders of the welfare state rejected these criticisms by pointing to its multiple benefits and suggesting a new activating approach. Leftist intellectuals, trade union leaders, and beneficiaries insisted on preserving public provisions and were at best willing to make minor adjustments to bring costs into line. But more progressive commentators focused on reforms that would draw welfare recipients back into the labor market, considering their activation more beneficial than transfer payments. Pioneered in Nordic countries, these efforts were intended to help women go to work by defamilianizing care for infants and elderly family members. And Active Labor Market Policies (ALMPs), such as retraining and job search assistance, would steer unemployed low-skilled workers back into the labor market. The Scandinavian experience suggested that "access to paid work is the best guarantee against poverty, marginalization, and exclusion, and a way of securing an economically sustainable welfare state."[25]

Unfortunately, the electorate has been reluctant to reward those political leaders who were willing to reform the welfare state in order to save it. Already in the early 1980s, François Mitterrand had to recant his radicalism in order to retain his presidency in France. Moreover, during the late 1990s, proponents of "the third way" like Tony Blair and Gerhard Schröder did succeed in gaining power in the UK and the FRG with slogans of "New Labour" or *die neue Mitte*. But after the turn of the millennium, the social democratic parties suffered "a remarkable electoral decline" all over Europe, almost disappearing in the process. Apparently, the labor market reforms had "sacrificed their core constituency" of blue- and white-collar workers who resented giving up their hard-won gains.[26] Prodded by dislike of Muslim immigration, much of the protest vote migrated instead to right-wing populist groups like the

Front National, UKIP, or AfD. Only in Sweden, Denmark, Spain, and Portugal have Social Democrats recovered somewhat.

In spite of such backlash, welfare states remain quite popular in Europe since efforts to defend against risks and work toward equality have been accepted by a broad range of people. As an expression of humane solidarity for the less fortunate, they are one of the great social achievements of the second half of the twentieth century. The exact form of programs and benefits varies according to the political culture and resources of the country involved. But surveys show high levels of approval everywhere for the core aspirations of social security and equal opportunity. Undertaken in response to the competitive pressures of globalization, the reforms of the last decades have shown that "such adjustments are a necessary part of a welfare state operating in a market economy." While the burden of taxes and contributions is high, the quality of life is superior to that in neoliberal countries like the United States where "welfare" is a dirty word. As a result, welfare states come out on top in many comparisons of health or education.[27]

Welfare Experiences

For both defenders and detractors of the welfare state, the Scandinavian quality of life has become a symbolic battleground. While the former hail the region as an exemplar of "sustainable development," the latter counter that for economic reasons the Nordic "model is simply not sustainable." To many liberal observers, "Sweden seems to have it all. It combines a high living standard with a strong social security net, some of the most progressive values in the world, and generous systems of paid sick and maternity leaves." Yet conservatives claim that many Swedish voters are "dissatisfied with the trajectory of their society," citing "immigration, rising crime, sluggish economic growth, and, perhaps surprisingly, the welfare model itself." Supported by a false claim of civic violence by former president Trump, "in the nationalists' message making, Sweden has become a prime cautionary tale, dripping with *Schadenfreude*."[28] That attack raises the question: What is living in a welfare state really like?

Neoliberal critics argue that "European welfare discourages work," leading to a culture of dependency on public handouts. For instance, the Cato Institute cited "the case of Carina, a 36-year-old Danish single mother who had been on welfare since she was 16" and reaped €2,300 per month in benefits. Similarly, Robert Nielsen, who had been unemployed for a dozen years, claimed: "Luckily I am born and live in Denmark, where the government is willing to support my life." But a commentator warned "when benefit levels get this high, they create a significant disincentive to work." To help recipients escape the trap of long-term joblessness and lower costs, Denmark has eliminated permanent disability benefits, making a return to employment essential. The Swedish "program lowers jobless assistance the longer [one] is on welfare" but assists with a "rapid transition from unemployment to work."[29] Such reforms have retargeted support from social maintenance to reintegration into the workforce.

Another right-wing charge is welfare fraud that abuses the system to extract illegitimate benefits. In recent years, reports of fraudulent claims in Sweden have multiplied, amounting to "10,300 welfare benefit offenses" during 2015. This is not because their number has actually risen but because the reporting has improved. A classic scandal focused on an immigrant woman who accumulated $200,000 in "parental benefits, child benefits, maintenance support and housing support" even after she moved back to Algeria. Only once the Tax Agency "deregistered [her] as a Swedish resident," did benefits stop and the insurance company try to reclaim its money. The Social Insurance Agency received thousands of denunciations of welfare fraud by envious neighbors but, on closer inspection, found only "a small group of people we strongly suspect of committing a crime."[30] More thorough investigation and tougher enforcement of the rules were actually able to reduce incidents of abuse.

In contrast to such complaints, most Swedes are quite grateful for the quality of services they receive for their high taxes. In international comparison, "Sweden is the best place in the world to give birth." In Uppsala, Carmen Helwig, aged thirty-eight, had her first child by Caesarean section since she worried about a difficult birth. The baby was born three weeks early and a bit underweight, but mother and child were fine.

Similarly, Lisa Klecker was flown by helicopter to a hospital when her baby's heartbeat dipped during a prenatal checkup. The secret of Swedish care was putting women at the center: "We have everything technology can offer but, even more importantly we treat mothers as individuals," even providing them with a "baby box" of essentials for infants. Compared with steep US hospital bills, the entire birth process and pre- as well as postnatal care are free of cost. As a result, maternal and infant survival rates are among the highest in the world and confident Swedish mothers have an average of 1.7 children.[31]

Nordic countries are also some of "the best places to have children," since young families are extensively supported. Swedish parents have 480 days of potential leave with 80 percent of their regular pay, evenly split between mothers and fathers, which gets the latter more involved in their offspring's upbringing. Moreover, they receive a child allowance of $113 per month that helps with infant expenses but continues all the way to college. There is also an extensive system of public nurseries beginning with eighteen-month-olds, followed by all-day preschools. This low-cost provision of infant care helps children from underprivileged backgrounds as well as immigrant families to make up for learning deficits at home. At the same time, this daycare system allows women to return to their previous jobs, boosting gender equality.[32] Since they do not have to make great sacrifices for their children, Scandinavian mothers are also more willing to have babies than women in other advanced countries.

Nordic welfare states also do exceptionally well in international comparisons of educational achievement. In the OECD-sponsored PISA assessment of the performance of fifteen-year-olds, Finland received top scores in areas like mathematics, literacy, and science during the early 2000s. Denmark and Sweden placed among the top four countries as well in another study of civics knowledge. Key reasons for such success appear to have been the educational reforms of the 1970s, which improved teacher training in academic subjects at the universities. Moreover, classroom instruction was refocused on problem solving rather than on rote memorization, making pupils better able to apply their knowledge. Instead of teaching to the test, the focus has been on

"developing the capacities of schools" as well as "some non-school policies associated with the welfare state."[33] In contrast to big disparities in
outcomes, the Nordic school systems not only promote excellence but
also foster social equality.

The Scandinavian model of health care has also been the envy of
many other countries since it provides high quality care to the entire
population on fairly equal terms. Its guiding principles of universalism
and equality require a large public role in ownership and control of hospitals and physicians. Though their form differs a bit, they all rely on a
single public insurance provider that covers everyone, though recently
some private supplements and modest copayments have been introduced in order to keep the system solvent. Most hospitals are publicly
owned and many doctors as well as other health professionals are public
employees. Costs as part of GNP are only slightly above the OECD
average at around 9 percent, but access remains independent of income,
in stark contrast to the financial barriers of the United States.[34] The standard of medical care is high as is evident in the lengthy life expectancy.
When they get sick, Scandinavians can concentrate on getting well
rather than worrying about how to pay.

Yet another advantage of full-fledged welfare states is the humane
character of the workplace, which makes work more tolerable. Most
Continental countries have elaborate protections against firing workers
that create job security, even if this system makes the labor market less
than flexible. Though declining, the still-powerful unions have also succeeded in limiting weekly work to under forty hours, requiring overtime
pay for any time beyond that. Many European companies have early
retirement plans, allowing their employees to stop working before the
age of sixty-five. There are also provisions for sick days, which allow for
a full recovery from minor illnesses. Similarly, there are quite a few religious and national holidays that interrupt the normal work rhythm. Finally, most states mandate a minimum of twenty-five vacation days a
year, with the Danes even receiving six weeks of time off. For stressed-
out Americans, such a system seems too good to be true—which makes
conservative commentators predict its imminent demise.[35]

In contrast to neoliberal assumptions, high welfare support can even
help reduce unemployment. Recent research shows that the widespread

notion that generous benefits will serve as a disincentive to work is actually erroneous. On the one hand, if the labor market is highly segmented and protected, the lowering of benefits forces the jobless into a new low-wage sector as in the German Agenda 2010. But on the other, higher levels of initial support can help in job searches and in maintaining skill levels, provided that the labor market is more flexible. Such a system, called *flexicurity* in Denmark, does not freeze the jobless out of positions but rather allows the unemployed to upgrade their qualifications and wait for a suitable opportunity that matches their training. Surprisingly enough, "people are willing to work despite generous benefits, if there are good job opportunities."[36] By preventing a de-skilling, sufficient support apparently stabilizes job biographies.

Pensions in welfare states have also tended to be more publicly funded and generous than in the liberal market economies. Most European countries use an insurance-based system with employee and employer's contributions that replicates past earning power in retirement. In the Scandinavian and coordinated market systems, retirees receive about one-half to two-thirds of their previous salaries in contrast to liberal economies where the public provision is much lower. Even in countries like France and Italy, the demographic crisis of insufficient children has pushed retirement age to sixty-seven in order to receive the full amount. The gradual decline of benefits has opened up a supplementary private pension sector where additional coverage—called *Riester Rente* in Germany—can be bought. Only the less prosperous Mediterranean and Eastern European systems provide lower payouts, relying more on family support. In general, European retirees are only half as likely to be poor as pensioners in the United States.[37]

On the whole, developed European welfare states are therefore prosperous societies that reward individual initiative and at the same time provide remarkable social equality. Norway, Luxembourg, and Switzerland surpass the United States in OECD income statistics, and their poverty gap is considerably lower as well. Whereas only about 8 percent of the populations of European welfare states are considered poor, that distressing number is twice as high in the United States, with child poverty approaching one-quarter! Though in liberal market countries the discrepancy between top and bottom earners is drastically increasing, welfare states tend to slow down the polarization of society. The reason for these striking differences is simply the divergence in public expenditures: While taxes and transfers of one-fifth of the GNP moderate the poverty rate in France and Germany, the United States spends only half that amount on such efforts![38] Whereas America rewards individual initiative, Europe provides a more equal and humane society.

Well-Being State

The purpose of the welfare state is best expressed by the Finnish term "well-being state," which offers equal opportunities for a dignified existence to all its citizens. In contrast to the American disdain for welfare as a sign of failure, the Nordic conception of solidarity is more positive, allowing citizens "to pursue happiness, enjoy freedom, achieve success." In neoliberal countries, the public is horrified by high taxes, whereas in Nordic states it understands that "the system is clearly in everyone's self-interest" because everyone benefits from it. The Finnish writer Anu Partanen explains: "It supports your own personal freedom, your own autonomy, and each individual's ability to determine his or her own fate, since we don't need to depend on the financial largesse of parents, spouses, or employers for the fundamental services—health care, education and aid during times of crisis—that each of us requires to fulfill our potential."[39] Instead of being one's enemy, the state is seen as one's friend.

As a result of this attractive vision, the quality of life in the Nordic and Central European welfare states is quite high. In 2003 a team of IMF economists praised the "considerable achievements" of the Swedish welfare state. "Sweden ranks very highly in almost all indicators of the quality of human life." As a result of government efforts, "Sweden's public health, educational attainment, employment, and participation indicators are among the best in the world." In spite of massive state involvement, "Swedish business conditions are remarkably favorable" since there is virtually no corruption and little labor strife. The country scores high on living standards, income compression, and gender equality, all of which create "dynamic advantages" in international competition. Even if it followed the wrong herd immunity goal in the COVID crisis,

Sweden is also a leader in environmental protection and foreign aid.[40] While not all other European welfare states reach quite this level of performance, in general their quality of life surpasses that of liberal market economies.

Increasing global competition has, however, called into question the maintenance of this "miraculous welfare machine." The difficulties of high-wage countries competing with lower-wage Asian competitors have fostered the emergence of a neoliberal discourse that denounces the excesses of the welfare state. While a middle-class tax revolt rejects the high level of taxation and insurance premiums, economists complain that this "tax wedge" creates "strong disincentive effects on effective labor supply" as well as "a sizable black market economy." Neoliberal experts charge that the bureaucratization of the welfare state has ballooned the public workforce and hampered innovation by preventing the start-up of new businesses. They assert that welfare states are growing too slowly, being outpaced by the market-oriented competitors. Hence, a new consensus has emerged "that it is both necessary and possible to streamline the Swedish model, while preserving its key elements."[41]

The reform of the welfare states has focused on their long-term fiscal sustainability by shifting from maintaining income to activating labor policies. On the one hand, governments have reduced top rates of income and inheritance taxes so as to stem capital flight into tax havens. The ensuing budget shortfalls have forced cutbacks in benefits, lowering the replacement rates of unemployment insurance from around 80 percent to 60 percent. Some countries have also limited public payments to a basic security level, leaving additional coverage to private insurance or pension plans. On the other hand, governments have also invested in activating labor market policies to retrain the jobless and make it easier for women and immigrants to enter the labor force. Both policy changes were inspired by the belief that it was necessary to abandon a high level of income maintenance in favor of a speedy reentry into work, even if on a lower wage level.[42] Such reforms have not abolished but rather refocused European welfare states.

Due to such adjustments, many European countries are at or near the top in international comparisons of life satisfaction. In one Gallup poll of 2016, the Nordic states plus the Low Countries had the highest scores. In another survey, Sweden topped the list while Germany came in fourth. An analysis of the reasons showed that higher income, good health, and a sense of cultural identity—all of which were closely tied to the welfare state—made a key difference. No doubt, for the successful elites, neoliberal market societies are more rewarding, promoting the United States also to high values. But for the populations as a whole, the more egalitarian European welfare systems do better because they are more inclusive and do not leave the bottom third of society behind. While the repeated crises of deregulated market systems call their sustainability into question, "the Nordic countries have undeniably created a model for what a high quality of life and a healthy society can look like in the twenty-first century."[43]

9

Protected Environment

FIGURE 10. Fridays for Future, Stockholm, Sweden. Per Grunditz, 123RF.

On September 4, 2013, Queen Margrethe of Denmark "pushed a big red button" that put 111 giant Siemens wind turbines on line. Located in 14–17-meter-deep water between the mainland and the island of Anholt, this wind farm was at the time one of the largest in the world for producing electric energy. With a record speed of one and a half years, the DONG energy consortium had managed to construct a 20-kilometer-wide and 5-kilometer-deep generation field, linked by a 26-centimeter-thick cable from transformers to the land from where its power was distributed. Navigating the difficult winter conditions of cold and choppy water, a special ship had driven the huge monopiles into the soft ground of the Baltic Sea and attached 120-meter-long rotors to them that were turned by strong and reliable ocean winds. The new turbines generated 400 megawatts of power, enough to supply the needs of four hundred thousand households. Though it cost over a billion dollars, this massive installation made Denmark one of the world's leaders in renewable energy.[1]

The Danish drive toward abandoning fossil fuels was the result of an enlightened attempt to gain energy independence with its own resources. Its limited oil and gas reserves in the North Sea were not sufficient to replace dirty coal, and a strong antinuclear movement had already succeeded in banning atomic energy in 1985. Because there was not enough sunshine for solar energy, Copenhagen recalled the traditional reliance on windmills since wind was free and plentiful, while new technological developments had lowered the operational costs of turbines once the initial investment was amortized. In a series of energy plans, the Danish government heavily subsidized wind farms as a clean power source, triggering a first wave of construction in the 1990s. After a neoliberal pause, all major parties agreed on a new energy plan in February 2008 in order to simultaneously speed up wind power construction and lower energy usage.[2] The Anholt wind park was one of the first fruits of this renewed dedication to alternative energy.

Powerful business circles and bourgeois parties nonetheless remained skeptical about the costs of efforts to combat climate change. As head of a Liberal-Conservative coalition, Prime Minister Anders Fogh Rasmussen called for an "environment worth the money," while the neoliberal think tank CEPOS issued a critique of wind power. Its objections focused on the technical problems of "highly intermittent" wind generation, which required "large-scale electricity storage" by the pumping of water into higher-level reservoirs in Norway or Sweden, which would be released when needed. The memorandum claimed that Danish taxpayers subsidized the export of surplus wind electricity to neighbors while saving "neither fossil fuel consumption nor CO_2 emissions." The cost to consumers was much higher than that of conventional power generation, while the subsidy for "green jobs" merely shifted employment to a different sector.[3] Though it might help reduce greenhouse emissions, wind power was therefore bad for business and consumption.

In the long run, supporters of environmental protection overcame these objections and convinced the public that such expenditures were worthwhile. A group of academic researchers for "Coherent Energy and Environmental System Analysis" attacked the neoliberal claims as highly misleading. They charged that the CEPOS report was "based on an incorrect interpretation of statistics and a lack of understanding of how international electricity markets operate." No taxes were supporting the wind turbines "and the net influence on consumer electricity prices [was] as low as 1–3 percent in the period [between] 2004 [and] 2008." Similarly, the assertion that the country was exporting half of its electricity was false since "on the contrary, almost all wind power is consumed in Denmark." Though household costs were the highest in the EU, "the Danish electricity prices for industries (excl. tax and VAT) are the 7th lowest out of 27 [EU] countries."[4] Moreover, green technology exports had become a growing sector of the Danish economy.

Emblematic of a much wider struggle over sustainability, the Danish case offers some "slow hope" by suggesting what can be done to stop global warming. In contrast to apocalyptic scenarios like Rachel Carson's *Silent Spring* or the Club of Rome's predictions of running out of fossil fuel, this story shows that sufficient public pressure can actually make progress toward halting the increase of greenhouse gasses through the use of renewable energy. It took a conceptual and organizational transformation of traditional nature conservation into a broader effort at environmental protection to reverse the exploitation of natural resources. The demand for clean air and water in one's neighborhood also had to grow into a wider, transnational vision of ecological concern in order to generate a willingness to pay the price of larger-scale solutions.[5] Although many initial impulses, such as California's antipollution standards for cars, came from the United States, the EU and some of its member countries ultimately took the lead in moving toward carbon neutrality.

Environmental Pioneer

In the 1970s Denmark hardly looked like it was predestined to become a pioneer in environmental protection because its high standard of living had created much pollution. Since 60 percent of the land surface was used by intensive agriculture for growing barley and industrial animal farming, the use of fertilizer and pesticides produced much nitrogen runoff. Moreover, the expansion of the chemical industry and transoceanic shipping by the world leader Maersk also harmed both air and water. At the same time, the prosperity of the Nordic Model created one of the highest outputs of municipal waste in the EU. Finally, much of Denmark's power generation took place in coal-burning plants that fouled the air, while the increase in car traffic in cities like Copenhagen raised small particulate and CO_2 levels.[6] It therefore took a major effort at rethinking lifestyles as well as a multilevel transformation of the economy to repudiate this high industrial model and make progress toward a greener future.

Initially, the Danish turn to renewable energy was a result of the desire for security, triggered by the oil shocks of the 1970s. Because Denmark had explicitly supported Israel, it was one of the countries singled out by the OPEC embargo. Since it had no coal deposits or water generators and too little sunshine, the country cast about for alternatives. Unlike in France or Sweden, nuclear power was no longer an option since a strong antinuclear movement, called OOA, agitated against it with the image of a smiling sun and the slogan "nuclear power, no thank you." Inspired by fear of a potential meltdown, the resistance against building atomic reactors for power generation was so strong that the Parliament passed a law in 1985 that prohibited the construction of such facilities. In the wake of the Chernobyl disaster a year later, the decision was made to decommission the three existing research reactors around the year 2000.[7] Due to the lack of alternative energy sources, wind power won out largely by default.

The transition to cleaner energy sources took place in a succession of national plans that taxed conventional generation and subsidized alternative forms of production. The first energy plan of 1976 laid the groundwork by encouraging engineering research that came up with the successful model of a "three blade upwind machine on a tubular tower with an induction generator." The second plan of 1981 "established a strong home market for renewable energy and a local industry associated with it." By increasing taxes on oil and coal consumption, the Social Democratic government got consumers used to paying higher prices, thus making alternative energies more competitive. Moreover, Copenhagen subsidized the installation of wind parks with 30 percent of the initial costs, which helped establish a local wind-generation industry that made Denmark a leader in the field. The construction of several 100-megawatt wind parks also allowed wind power to outstrip natural gas and biomass as a power source.[8]

The third energy plan of 1990 signaled the shift to combating climate change through sustainable forms of alternative energy. Responding to the growing international concern about global warming, the Danish government pledged a 20 percent reduction of CO_2 emissions as well as a 15 percent decrease in energy consumption by 2005. These ambitious goals could only be reached by increasing wind power to 10 percent of energy generation during the same time period. The creation of a Danish Energy Agency helped overcome local resistance against siting through a planning process that included hearings and shifted the location of bigger wind parks offshore. Moreover, "a fixed feed-in tariff for electricity production . . . decoupled power purchase price from existing electricity rates," thereby guaranteeing a positive return on wind power investment. The fourth energy plan of 1996 continued this trajectory by raising conservation and construction targets, making Denmark even "a net exporter of energy."[9]

The election of a Liberal-Conservative government in 2001 stalled progress toward renewable energy since its sympathies leaned toward skeptics of climate change. The new prime minister Anders Rasmussen was more sensitive to the complaints of industry that wind power was imposing a competitive handicap and to criticism of consumers that electricity prices were too high. As a result, several offshore wind park projects were canceled and construction virtually ground to a halt between 2001 and 2008. Intent on increasing market competition, the neoliberal cabinet sought to privatize energy production, relying on companies like the Danish DONG, the Swedish Vattenfall, the German EON, or on local cooperatives to provide power. A "renewable portfolio standard (RPS) mechanism" of tradable energy certificates never really got off the ground. The action plan for "A Green Market Economy" was a better election slogan than a practical solution.[10] The result was a pause in wind power construction at 3,000 megawatts.

The Danish drive for renewable energy nonetheless resumed on February 21, 2008, with another political initiative to combat climate change more broadly. When Prime Minister Rasmussen finally acknowledged the problem of global warming, all parties agreed on a framework that set a bold goal of reaching a 20 percent supply by renewable energy by the year 2011, increasing to 30 percent by the year 2025. Achieving such ambitious targets required the resumption of construction on two 200-megawatt wind parks offshore as well as the building of smaller wind turbines on land that would be closer to the actual usage of electricity in local communities. Moreover, the government raised feed-in tariffs for wind power and biomass generation so as to make a switch to alternate energy sources financially attractive. Aside from providing "incentives and a compensation scheme for local residents," Copenhagen also proposed a 4 percent reduction of actual energy usage in order to decrease the emission of greenhouse gases.[11]

While the shift to wind power was helpful, the protection of the environment required a much broader effort to change the lifestyles of a prosperous high-consumption country. The growth of organic farming reduced the nitrogen load on the land, but industrial agriculture found it hard to decrease its dependence on pesticides. A report from 2015 stated that "air quality is overall improving, but remains a challenge in densely populated areas" since driving cars and using wood pellets for heating created high levels of CO_2 emissions. Water usage decreased by more than one-quarter, and stricter purification improved the quality of lakes and streams, but mercury levels remained excessive. "Denmark's global ecological footprint has also decreased slightly, but remains one of the world's largest." Similarly, the high levels of municipal waste production were only partly alleviated through recycling and incineration.[12]

A much wider transformation of lifestyles was therefore necessary in order to combat global warming.

The election of a leftist government in 2011 accelerated planning for a "green transition" that would decouple economic growth from energy usage. The key target of its Climate Change Act was a 40 percent reduction in greenhouse gas emissions by 2020, an aim that seemed utopian at the time of its formulation. A newly created Climate Council was to coordinate a multitude of individual steps toward carbon neutrality. On land, afforestation and reduction of pesticides were the key initiatives. Water quality would be improved by closer control of chemical runoffs. At the same time, a CO_2 tax would encourage a drastic decrease in carbon emissions. Similarly, public investment in rail transportation, electric cars, and buses as well as the use of bicycles for commuting was supposed to reduce the particle pollution in the main cities. Tax support for better insulation would lower the amount of energy used for heating. It was this multidimensional strategy that made Denmark "a cognitive and exemplary pioneer."[13]

Denmark therefore played a leading role in the international efforts to combat climate change, far above the size of the country. During the 1990s, the ambitious energy minister Svend Auken of the Social Democrats committed to a 21 percent reduction of greenhouse gases, pushing the EU to embrace a progressive stance in preparing for the Kyoto Protocol. After a neoliberal pause, the conservative minister of climate and energy Connie Hedegaard initiated a Greenland Dialogue of fifteen leading countries that focused on "an emerging consensus on the two-degree target" of global warming. Unfortunately, the Copenhagen conference of 2009 "failed to live up to even the lowest expectations" since it produced only a vague "letter of intent" due to US and Chinese resistance. Undeterred, Denmark continued to advocate a drastic reduction of CO_2 emissions, which inspired the Paris Agreement of 2015 where 195 nations pledged to restrict global warming to 1.5 degrees through reducing greenhouse gas emissions.[14]

Inspired by such past successes, the city of Copenhagen sought "to become the first carbon-neutral capital in the world." By 2019 it had already cut its emissions by an astounding 42 percent, cleaning the air and reducing noise. Its energy was supplied by sixty-two giant wind turbines with more to come and supplemented by burning trash for heat and electricity. Diesel cars were being banned and buses shifted to electricity while the subway ran every two minutes and public transit was slated to become free of charge. The new suburb of Nordhavn was designed as a "five-minute city" where every place could be reached quickly on foot, rendering automobiles superfluous. An amazing 62 percent of the residents were commuting to work by bicycle, encouraged by a dozen new bike and pedestrian bridges and special lanes. Old buildings were being retrofitted and new ones built to conserve energy. According to the mayor Frank Jensen, "Copenhagen's green transformation goes hand in hand with job creation, a growing economy, and a much better quality of life."[15]

The Danes achieved their pioneering role by overcoming daunting obstacles with resolute determination. The business interests of intensive agriculture, global shipping, and resource extraction put up a valiant fight to preserve their prerogatives. But several farseeing politicians from both the Social Democrats and the Conservatives were courageous enough to make decisions that advanced the greening of the country. The gradual shift to organic production in farming was one step. The switch to wind power was another crucial move that was facilitated by the formation of local cooperatives and the development of offshore fields that circumvented siting opposition. On balance, the public was willing to pay the higher costs of the transformation because it was convinced that it would produce a better quality of life. While the reduction of the carbon footprint sometimes imposed annoying duties, it ultimately became part and parcel of the Danish national identity, giving the small Scandinavian country a sense of collective pride.[16]

European Efforts

Though the EU had been founded to promote "a harmonious development of economic activities," the protection of the environment eventually became a central concern as well. It was the accumulation of problems like the Chernobyl nuclear disaster, the increase in acid rain, the depletion of the ozone layer, and global warming that moved ecological issues to the forefront. Brussels was also intent on reducing its energy dependence on Russia from which it got 30 percent of its crude oil, 40 percent of its natural gas, and 39 percent of its coal. The Single European Act of 1987 provided the requisite authority by stating that "environmental protection requirements shall be a component of the Community's other policies." Promoted by the Brundtland Report of the UN, the novel concept of "sustainable development" inspired a systematic effort to address pollution from greenhouse gases.[17] Supported by increasing public awareness, the European Commission created a dense web of regulations in hundreds of binding directives from standards for drinking water to the elimination of chemical hazards. To level the competitive playing field, Brussels also set out to advocate global remedial action.[18]

Especially after the United States decided to reject binding measures, the EU tried "to take a strong and leading role" in the international arena. Brussels called for action by the UN since the pollution of air and water crossed national frontiers. To set a good example, it promised to freeze the emission of CO_2 at the level of 1990. As a first step, the EU signed the UN framework convention on climate change at the Rio "earth summit" of 1992. Moreover, it redoubled its efforts to get its own member states to observe the lofty international proclamations by working toward the European Climate Change Programs in 2000 and 2005. But the United Kingdom vetoed the innovative proposal of an EU-wide carbon dioxide tax on grounds of sovereignty. Instead, the EU settled for a piecemeal approach of increasing energy efficiency, promoting renewable energy, and monitoring greenhouse gas emissions. Since implementation depended on the member states, the EU continued to confront a "capacity-expectation gap."[19]

The EU was, however, a key activist during the negotiations for the Kyoto Protocol that tried to fight global warming through the reduction of six greenhouse gases. Held in the old Japanese capital in 1997, this UN-sponsored conference sought to achieve "quantified emission limitation and reduction commitments" from the signatories. Brussels proposed a 15 percent reduction based on 1990 levels, but when the United

States was only willing to agree to 7 percent, the EU settled for 8 percent as a first step. It also accepted the American suggestion for a flexible implementation that was designed to overcome the resistance of developing countries through emission trading schemes and help for the poorer nations. When the Bush government rejected ratification of the accord, the European Parliament voted 540 to 4 to ratify it and lobbied Russia, Japan, and Canada to agree to it so that it could enter into force in 2005.[20] As a result, the EU was also the first to install an emissions trading scheme that offset increases by paying for reductions elsewhere.

Undeterred by the Great Recession of 2008, the EU decided to forge ahead on its own, hoping that the big polluters, such as the United States and China, would follow suit. In 2007 Brussels proposed a 20/20 scheme to compel its member states to take action before the year 2020. It consisted of a binding commitment to reduce greenhouse gas emissions by 20 percent while increasing the use of renewable energy to 20 percent. It also suggested a nonbinding 20 percent improvement in energy efficiency while making an additional 10 percent decrease in greenhouse gas emissions conditional on "comparable efforts" of other developed countries. Over the objections of car-producing states, the EU also adopted legally binding CO_2 limits for automobiles in order to reduce particle pollution in inner cities. Finally, it offered €7.22 billion to developing countries to help them with climate adaptation measures. But since skeptics from the United States and the BRIC countries had drafted it, the Copenhagen Accord was a failure due to its vague and weak provisions.[21]

The Paris Agreement of December 15, 2015, put the environmental effort back on track since 195 countries committed themselves to reversing the increase in greenhouse gas emissions. In preparation, the European Council adopted a "2030 climate and energy package," which raised the greenhouse gas emissions (GHGE) reduction target to 40 percent and the share of renewables and energy savings to 27 percent. Based on voluntary country pledges, the Paris meeting produced "the first-ever universal legally binding global climate deal." In order to reach the "global emissions peak as soon as possible," it called for keeping "global average temperature to well below 2 degrees Celsius above pre-industrial levels." This agreement was successful since it used a "bottom-up approach," letting individual countries set their own targets and creating a fund to help the developing states. Instead of demanding change, the EU "lediated," leading and mediating at the same time.[22] While renewable energies also made local progress in the United States, the climate-change denier President Trump rejected the entire deal.

The realization of ambitious ecological goals depended entirely on the economy of individual countries as well as the resoluteness of their policies. The Nordic neighbors did well in international rankings of sustainability, although they still faced considerable problems. Sweden ranked "first in the EU in the consumption of organic foods, [led] the way in recycling drinks cans and bottles, and [got] the highest share of its energy from renewable sources." However, it still struggled with acidification of lakes and massive timber harvesting. Similarly, Norway had an outdoor culture, the *friluftsliv*, and drew 95 percent of its energy from hydropower but was one of the largest oil and gas exporters with all the environmental damage that entailed. Finally, Finland started relatively late to combat the nitrogen runoff from its commercial agriculture and the air pollution of its industries, though it has made considerable strides.[23] Even an explicit commitment to the environment had difficulty in overcoming economic realities.

Among the larger EU countries, Germany has repudiated fossil fuels and nuclear power in an *Energiewende* and become a world leader in the production of green technology. Since Germans had a tradition of protecting nature, hiking in the countryside, and allotment gardening, they were shocked by the *Waldsterben* during the 1970s when entire forests were dying due to pollution from coal-fired power plants. Similarly, fear of Armageddon, reinforced by Chernobyl and Fukushima, sparked a revulsion against nuclear power that led to an unprecedented shutdown of all reactors. The success of the Green Party in the 1980s put pressure on the political system to reduce greenhouse gases as well as limit energy consumption. In spite of a large manufacturing sector in the car industry, which complained about rising emission standards and increasing energy costs, the FRG has met its international targets due to the dismantling of much of East German industry. Though it has succeeded in decoupling growth from energy use, the remaining dependence on hard and brown coal shows that "considerable further efforts are needed."[24]

On paper, the French performance also looked quite good, albeit on the basis of problematic sources of power. Its tradition of control over nature is evident in the highly stylized approach to trees and plants in parks. France has the largest agricultural sector in the EU, producing fabled wines and cheeses but also using much fertilizer. Since the country has no oil and little coal, 80 percent of its power generation stems from nuclear reactors, one of the highest levels in the world. Much of the rest depends on hydropower, produced by huge dams of rivers like the Rhône. Deindustrialization has helped reduce greenhouse gas emissions by 13 percent between 1990 and 2012, but the increase in urban sprawl has eaten up much rural land. The government has been quite active in trying to reduce automobile emissions in inner cities, cleaning up water in rivers, promoting organic agriculture, and the like. But the high living standard has time and again limited progress. "Pollution from diffuse sources such as agriculture and transport has not fallen."[25]

In Great Britain, progress in environmental protection has been slower since the government took less drastic action and responsibility was decentralized. Centuries of grazing impoverished the soil, while leadership in industrialization produced much noxious pollution of cities. Legal efforts like the 1984 environmental law and its 2008 successor have been impressive, but they have had to go further in order to repair the damage. Greenhouse gases had fallen by one-quarter and energy use had shrunk by 7 percent by 2015, largely due to neoliberal deindustrialization that shut down many factories. The country has made special efforts to diminish waste production and clean up rivers and shorelines in order to safeguard drinking water, enhance recreation, and preserve fisheries. But due to the exploitation of large oil and gas reserves in the North Sea, the target of only 15 percent renewables by 2020 was rather modest.[26] In a competitive market economy, the romantic adoration of country life has had a harder time making the case for sustainability.

The environmental record of the Mediterranean countries has been even more disappointing since the material and political obstacles have been greater there. Centuries of deforestation have led to desertification of parts of the countryside, while mass tourism has created new strains in ancient cities and overcrowded beaches. One commentator bluntly concluded: "When it comes to the environment, Italy is a notorious laggard," with the waste disposal crisis in the Naples area only one egregious example. The European Commission has often warned Rome to stop violating EU environmental guidelines. In spite of being well suited for solar energy, "the country is not on track to meet requirements for renewable energy, the air pollution in some cities is above EU limits, and it has poor rankings for water quality." Since these problems have had low priority, the necessary funding and staffing have not been there. Unfortunately, the performance of Spain and Greece has hardly been any better, leaving the Mediterranean region seriously at risk.[27]

Though still struggling with the Communist legacy, the Eastern European countries have been making "significant progress in the area of environmental protection" during the last decades. But Poland and the Czech Republic depend on Russian gas and continue to rely for more than 50 percent of their electrical energy on the burning of coal, which is also used predominantly for home heating. Although the Soviet Bloc states had a nominal environmental policy, smokestack industries dominated manufacturing, emitting large amounts of pollution and creating much industrial waste. While deindustrialization helped somewhat, it has taken considerable effort to improve air quality. Similarly, raising water quality and reducing waste has been difficult, though EU standards have helped local efforts meet targets. Ironically, the catch-up in economic development is creating new pollution sources through traffic congestion and conspicuous consumption as part of a throwaway society.[28] Progress toward a clean environment has therefore been frustratingly slow.

Green Initiatives

During the recent past, Europeans have undertaken countless efforts to transform their neighborhoods and states so as to practice their growing environmental consciousness. Already in 1992, the EU had adopted a

Council Directive "on the conservation of natural habitats and of wild fauna and flora" to promote biodiversity. This approach was expanded into a community-wide "Natura 2000" program that created an "ecological network of protected areas, safeguarding against potentially damaging developments." When Commission president Jean-Claude Juncker tried to water down these standards in 2015, half a million Europeans called for the laws to be left alone since nature protection was popular. Alice Puritz, a lawyer for the NGO ClientEarth was delighted: "This is a huge win for wildlife. These laws work and should be celebrated. Now we need to see strong implementation and enforcement to make sure Europe's nature gets the protection it needs to thrive."[29] Such nature conservation was a first step toward a cleaner environment.

One attempt to stop global warming has been recycling, which lessens the pressure on overflowing landfills by making waste "safely managed as a resource." When traveling in Germany, tourists see multiple recycling bins outside of houses for "paper, glass, metals, [and] plastics." With its Waste Framework Directive, the EU has set "a target of 50 percent of municipal waste to be recycled and prepared for reuse by 2020." In a Green Recycling plant in the UK, Jamie Smith proudly claims to be producing two to three hundred tons of recovered material a day: "Our main products are paper, cardboard, plastic bottles, mixed plastics and wood." A gigantic artificially intelligent sorting machine, called Max, picks items tirelessly from a conveyor belt. But much waste was sent to Asia for reprocessing, with destinations shifting from China to Malaysia. Hence, a better approach was to bring back "the milkman" to reduce packaging by reusing containers in a system called "the loop." Recycling therefore was not a climate cure-all.[30]

Another approach to reduce an individual carbon footprint has been decreasing energy use in the home since it ultimately also saved money for consumers. "Households make up around one-quarter of Europe's total energy consumption and produce a fifth of the EU's greenhouse gas emissions." The leader of an Irish research project, Professor Eleanor Denny, urged banks to provide financing to save more energy in homes "by installing more efficient boilers, solar panels, insulating homes or changing windows." Such a strategy "increases the value of the property . . . because it is cheaper to run and also more comfortable." Similarly, buying more energy-saving appliances like refrigerators or washing machines would reduce both energy and costs. A 2019 European Energy Agency report concluded that "over the period 1990–2016, the energy efficiency of end-use sectors improved by 30 percent in the EU-28 countries at an annual average rate of 1.4 percent." Only the higher initial purchase price still deterred many consumers.[31]

Yet another effort to reduce greenhouse gases has been the EU's 1992 decision to set increasingly stringent fuel efficiency requirements for automobiles, which were blamed for the congestion and pollution in inner cities. For 2015 the EU mandated a reduction to a fleet-wide level of 130 grams of CO_2 per kilometer, decreasing to 95 grams by the year 2021. Eric Jonnaert of the Automobile Manufacturers Association called the targets "extremely demanding" especially for larger luxury cars. To compel the makers to meet these aims, Brussels set up an elaborate system of penalties and incentives. Predictably, the "car industry reacted with fury," calling the standards "totally unrealistic." But their threat of a loss of thirteen million jobs rang hollow due to the widespread cheating with tests in the diesel scandal. Though the targets were among the highest in the world, and could only be reached by shifting to electric cars, environmentalists like Greg Archer denounced the progress as insufficient since it was "not fast enough to hit our climate goals."[32]

A green version of mobility is cycling, which is vastly more popular in Europe than in the United States since bicycles are not considered toys or exercise equipment but a means of transport. One anonymous transatlantic observer notes: "In Denmark and Holland cycling is the norm for both general transportation and commuting to work or school." In Copenhagen about half of the residents use bicycles as transportation, while in Amsterdam there are slightly more bicycles than there are people! "Cycling is common across all demographics—men and women, old and young—who commute regularly by bike all year round." In contrast to the high-tech machines in the United States, most people "ride heavy cruiser bikes with wide fenders, large baskets and heavy racks." The popularity of cycling is enhanced by a system of bike lanes and by ample parking provisions near train stations.[33] Since there are no EU requirements, there are still problems with obeying traffic laws and rider safety. But cycling is popular because it also provides health benefits.

Another form of clean transportation is mass transit in which the elaborate European systems put the United States to shame. While the old Continent is "far more densely built" in its historic cities, it has also experienced an automobile boom in the postwar period. But countries "never stopped building rail systems" in order to provide a viable alternative to cars. The traffic scholar Jonathan English notes several traits that make the European system more successful: (1) commuter rail, subways, streetcars, and buses are highly interconnected, conveniently linking with each other at transfer stations; (2) service is frequent, with trains arriving every five to fifteen minutes so that there are no long wait times, and a reduced service runs all night long; (3) tickets are integrated across various methods of transportation and comparatively cheap, making it less expensive to ride than to drive; and (4) trains tend to be clean and pleasant, attracting middle-class ridership in spite of some graffiti.[34] As a result, there is much public support for adequately financing rail.

Concern about health has also inspired a move toward organic farming as well as a shift toward more natural foods. Disappointed in the laxity of the French government concerning glyphosate, Monsieur Cueff, mayor of a town in the Bretagne, "banned the use of pesticides within 450 feet of any dwelling" as an "ecology in action." Similarly, the European Food Safety Agency has issued dietary guidelines in the form of national food pyramids to inspire healthier eating. As a result, 70 percent of Europeans have begun to purchase healthier foods, 53 percent organic products, and 39 percent vegetarian items. In contrast to Americans, EU consumers take more time when preparing food, eat smaller portions, and consume more "fresh and unprocessed" items. They also eat less meat and prefer local fruits and vegetables while drinking mineral water rather than sugary soda. Though pork and poultry still produce much waste, there is less methane than from beef and foods are not shipped as far.[35] Ironically, what reduces obesity also helps protect the environment.

Another health-related aspect of urban life is the availability of green spaces, which reduce pollution and offer recreation. Surprisingly enough, according to satellite images, as much as 40 percent of the surface of European cities is covered by plants. This figure includes trees lining streets, yards around houses, public parks, and even urban forests. Berlin has many allotment gardens—called *Schrebergärten* after the nineteenth-century physician Moritz Schreber—which allow apartment dwellers to cultivate their own bit of nature, be it flowers, vegetables, or grass. Moreover, half of the city area of Vienna actually consists of one large forest. In recent years, many wild animal species such as foxes or boars have returned to the cities, restoring their biodiversity. These green areas "can help make cities more sustainable and contribute to solving many challenges, such as air pollution, noise, climate change impacts, heat waves, floods, and public health concerns." Many studies therefore conclude that "urban green spaces increase happiness."[36]

A by-product of the ecological turn is the rise of an entirely new category of jobs based on green technology that provide technical solutions to environmental problems. A recent survey claims that "many industries have realized that investing in resource efficiency . . . actually saves them money." During the last decades, employment in the green sector has rapidly grown and "now provides 4.2 million jobs" in the EU, surpassing the workforce in automobile manufacturing. European companies have been leading the innovation, providing about one-third of the global production. One success story is the Belgian company Umicore, which moved from mining to recycling metal waste such as extracting gold from discarded circuit boards. Similarly, the German manager Hennig Joswig changed Innogy from coal mining to "a totally different approach to power generation" with wind turbines.[37] In contrast to US business complaints about environmental protection killing jobs, the EU figures show an impressive increase in employment in the green sector.

While the European environment is gradually improving, nations differ considerably in the implementation of EU standards. A 2014 environmental review of the European Commission found not only more light but also much shadow. Traffic with diesel automobiles in densely settled areas like Belgium was still creating much air pollution, while heating and power generation from coal continued to foul the atmosphere in places like Poland. Similarly, agricultural runoff from pesticides and fertilizers was undermining water quality and contaminating groundwater in otherwise green countries like Denmark and the Netherlands. Waste management also remained a problem in states such as Croatia and Greece, which failed to make much progress in collecting trash and recycling raw materials. Even some environmental leaders like Austria and Luxembourg were falling short of sufficiently protecting endangered species.[38] Safeguarding the European environment has therefore been a difficult process that is still far from complete.

Europeans have found out that leading a sustainable life is not easy because it requires a fundamental change in lifestyle to reduce levels of resource use. Although Continental structures encourage a more modest footprint than in the United States, Professor Ricardo Garcia Mira cautions that "the challenge in changing actual behaviors . . . lies in overcoming our ingrained notions about consumption, success, and happiness." Pro-environmental consumers have to be willing to pay higher costs for organic groceries in order to limit pesticides and fertilizer. More shoppers must give up habits of convenience such as plastic bags and bottles. Many people also have to be ready to spend considerable effort to use stairs instead of elevators or bike to work and take public transportation, fitting themselves to prearranged schedules. EU-sponsored research shows that a commitment to ecological living requires a conscious decision to change one's habits. "Our pro-environmental identity can be strengthened when the individual is part of a likeminded community."[39]

Climate Catastrophe

In August 2018, the fifteen-year-old schoolgirl Greta Thunberg started protesting against global warming in front of the Swedish Parliament, calling for "a school strike for the climate." Small but determined, she attracted attention with the claim: "I want to feel safe. How can I feel safe when I know we are in the greatest crisis in human existence?" Her blunt accusation "You adults are shitting on my future" went viral on social media since it dramatized the danger of global warming and suggested that young people had a special responsibility to save the planet. The call to action quickly caught on, inspiring a series of strikes called "Fridays for Future" that spread around the globe, mobilizing hundreds of thousands of young people. Her message emphasized the existential threat of climate change, the need for youths to mobilize, the urgency of immediate action, and the importance of listening to concerned scientists.[40] As a result, Greta became a media celebrity and climate activists were happy to use her as a poster girl for their cause.

Warning that the "climate catastrophe comes for Europe," committed environmentalists paint horrific images of an impending "climate apocalypse." They can cite ample evidence of unprecedented heat waves leading to drought as well as unheard-of storms unleashing floods, suggesting that "clearly something has gone haywire in the heavens." Laboriously assembling time series, climate scientists conclude that the increase in temperature has exceeded normal fluctuations, but the size and impact of the increase remain open to debate. In shrill tones, political activists warn of "potential doom" since "America and the world [are] on a glide path to Climate Apocalypse." While gradually becoming more concerned about global warming, the public is rather confused about the seriousness of the emergency because some prior predictions of catastrophe, such as the end of oil extraction or global hunger, have turned out to be exaggerated. Even if it has recently been overshadowed by the COVID crisis, a growing movement is calling for "a green new deal for Europe."[41]

A formidable array of populist climate-change deniers, however, rejects scientific evidence and clamors for "environmental deregulation" in the European Parliament. As part of a transatlantic network funded by oil companies and reactionary donors like the Koch brothers, they denounce climate action as "collective hysteria" since it threatens to cut into their profits. Leading populist politicians like Boris Johnson of the UK, Václav Klaus of the Czech Republic, and Santiago Abascal of Spain call global warming into question "despite the fact that 97 percent of climate scientists, and virtually all scientific literature confirms the idea that humans are causing climate change." With massive publicity campaigns they try to sow doubt in the public mind by stating that "if it is a natural change, if it is a change that obeys the human being, then it is something that

[we] really don't know." By banding together the populists, especially those in poorer Eastern countries, are now trying to "deconstruct the European Union's long-held leadership on global warming."[42]

Yet the evidence of climate change in Europe is so massive that denial of its effects is no longer a convincing tactic. In an EU study, climatologists have ascertained that the decade from 2002 to 2011 "was the warmest on record in Europe, with European land temperature 1.3 degrees Celsius warmer than the preindustrial average." Heat waves have become more frequent and longer, drying up rivers and ruining crops in Southern Europe. At the same time, increasing precipitation in Northern Europe has created flooding of towns and farmlands. Due to the warming of the Arctic, Greenland's ice sheet has melted rapidly, while "glaciers in the Alps have lost approximately two-thirds of their volume since 1850." In Switzerland, the Morteratsch Glacier has retreated a shocking 2.8 kilometers since the 1880s. During the last decades, changes like the rise of sea levels have become so extensive that many scientists now claim that the earth has entered a new geological epoch, called the "Anthropocene," in which human beings have actually begun to transform the global environment.[43]

Even if they have not always lived up to their own standards, the Europeans are on the right track in fighting global warming through reducing their carbon footprint. Although the United States initially played a leading role in the climate discussion, Trump's shift to outright denial left the EU as the only major power pushing for a reduction in greenhouse gas emissions. Public opinion is solidly behind this commitment since "more than nine in ten respondents (94 percent) say that protecting the environment is important to them personally." One key challenge for Brussels is to get all the EU members to follow the Scandinavian and Central European example by improving recycling, reducing energy consumption, and avoiding plastic packaging. Another task is to convince major polluters—such as China, India, Brazil, and the United States—to follow its example in combining economic growth with environmental protection.[44] At least Europe is trying to respond effectively to the problems of competitiveness, welfare reform, and climate change.

PART IV

Common Challenges

The liberal democracies will only be able to master the unprecedented challenges around the globe if they once again work more closely together. Hamstrung by an unpredictable president, American leadership has been faltering while the Europeans have not always overcome their national divisions with resolute action. The Russian annexation of Crimea and occupation of Eastern Ukraine as well as the continuation of Muslim terrorism have revived the need for NATO, though its mission remains unclear in a post–Cold War environment. Similarly, an ugly wave of populism has threatened democratic self-government on both sides of the Atlantic, pushing politics to right-wing or left-wing extremism. Finally, Europe's role in the world remains unclear since the transatlantic relationship has moved ever closer toward divorce while the rise of China is transforming the international order. How can the EU and the United States put aside their quarrels and once again work together to address the global problems?

10

Defense Disagreements

FIGURE 11. Russian irregulars, Crimea, Ukraine. Andriy Kravchenko, 123RF.

Shouting "Putin is our President," an angry crowd of demonstrators gathered in the city of Sevastopol to protest the overthrow of the Ukrainian president Viktor Yanukovich on February 2, 2014. Four days later "little green men" in combat uniforms without insignia, riding on Russian trucks, crossed into Crimea and deposed the Ukrainian provincial government in the capital Simferopol. Buoyed by the approval of the majority of ethnic Russian speakers, local rebels and special forces, directed from Moscow, installed a pro-Russian administration on the peninsula. Since half of Kiev's military had deserted, armed resistance proved impossible. On March 16, the new Russophile government declared Crimea independent of Ukraine and two days later the province and the naval base Sevastopol formally voted to join Russia.[1] While demonstrators in Kiev chased away the pro-Russian cabinet, ethnic nationalists and Russian commandos detached Crimea from Ukraine, ratifying the separation with an overwhelming vote in a rigged plebiscite.

The Russian annexation of Crimea had all the hallmarks of a well-choreographed clandestine action, using covert force just shy of a classic war. After the breakup of the Soviet Union, relations between the newly independent states had been cordial until the "Orange Revolution" in 2004 had installed a pro-Western government in Kiev.[2] When the Euromaidan protests a decade later ousted the pro-Russian president, Putin decided, as he later proudly admitted, "We must start working to return Crimea to Russia." Assured of Moscow's support and helped by Russian special forces, pro-Russian insurgents succeeded in deposing the legitimate Ukrainian government of the peninsula. The camouflage of Russia's military invasion only served to shield the action with sufficient deniability so as to prevent outside intervention. In a manner reminiscent of Hitler's and Milošević's use of ethnic "self-determination," Putin violated the territorial integrity of Ukraine, boosting his popularity at home and lowering his reputation abroad.

While the invasion of Crimea created an international outcry, the protests failed to halt the secession. Western media were originally confused by the claim that the 1954 transfer of Crimea to Ukraine had merely been a Soviet administrative reassignment. Russian propaganda rejected the term "annexation," stressing instead the right to protect the two-thirds of the population that spoke Russian as their first language. But Ukrainian critics claimed that the Moscow-inspired secession violated a whole raft of international treaties such as the Belavezha Accords that had set up the Commonwealth of Independent States (CIS) in 1991 and a later Russian-Ukrainian Treaty of Friendship, Cooperation, and Partnership. Growing international condemnation led to the suspension of Russia from the G-8 and the imposition of sanctions on Moscow. Moreover, the

MAP 6. Ukrainian conflict, 2014–present. Cox Cartographic.

United Nations General Assembly condemned the "temporary occupation" by a vote of 100 to 11 with 58 abstentions. With the Crimean coup, Putin created another "frozen conflict" at Russia's borders.[3]

The overthrow of Communism therefore did not end war on the European Continent—it only changed its form, creating new challenges for defense. The ugly bloodshed during the breakup of Yugoslavia had already involved militias and ethnic cleansing along with conventional warfare. Similarly, the Muslim terrorist attacks in London, Madrid, and Paris—just to mention the largest incidents—were directed against civilians rather than military combatants. Speaking to the National Defense University in June 2014, the Ukrainian president Petro Poroshenko claimed: "Ukraine is in a state of war. This is a new type of warfare—with the use of professional subversive groups, mercenaries, volunteers, and the local population." This shift toward irregular warfare caught the West by surprise since Cold War–style tank armies and fighter-plane air forces as well as battleship navies were ineffective against civil conflicts and nonstate actors.[4] Not wanting to risk conventional or nuclear war, governments were often at a loss as to how to react.

Instead of reaping a "peace dividend" after 1989, Europe was forced to develop new responses to irregular warfare. Initially, military expenditures did go down but by the end of the decade they rose again. A first surprise was the ethnic struggle during the breakup of Yugoslavia, which created the conundrum of how to pacify the EU's own backyard. A second threat was the attack by Muslim terrorists like the 9/11 assault as well as the bloodshed in Continental countries that raised the issue of how to defend innocent civilians and pursue perpetrators through "out of area" NATO actions. A third dispute revolved around whether to undertake humanitarian interventions to end the dictatorships in Iraq, Libya, and Syria, which might dissolve order and security in these failing states. A final question was how to deal with the reassertion of Russian power, cyberwarfare, and autocracy promotion that claimed to protect its own citizens.[5] Within Europe and across the Atlantic, therefore, a debate developed that revolved around the relative efficacy of hard or soft power in meeting these new challenges.

Ukrainian Troubles

The Russo-Ukrainian conflict has deep roots in the contested nationhood of Ukrainians, whom many Russians consider as "little brothers." After all, Kiev had been the center of the medieval Rus' commonwealth and thereby the core of the later Russian state. Only in the nineteenth century did a national movement propagate a separate Ukrainian language and aim for independent statehood, which was briefly attained during the Russian Civil War between 1918 and 1921 and the breakup of the Austro-Hungarian Empire. The experience as a Soviet republic was rather unhappy since several million peasants were expropriated and died of hunger in the so-called Holodomor of the 1930s. Initially, the Ukrainian national movement led by Stepan Bandera collaborated with the Nazis, but eventually it fought both the Wehrmacht and the Red Army. While Stalin's westward expansion after 1945 added Polish territories, Russification continued since both Moscow and Warsaw considered Kiev as Russian.[6] Only during the breakup of the Soviet Union did Ukraine finally achieve separate statehood.

This turbulent past left fundamental cleavages in Ukrainian society between a western and an eastern orientation that have fueled the current conflict. While most Ukrainian speakers live in the West, Russian speakers dominate the East, whereas the Center is largely bilingual. The Donbas, once one of the showcases of Soviet coal mining and steel production, has now turned into a rust belt, while the agricultural western regions have adapted more quickly to global competition. These differences have also been exacerbated by religious distinctions since the West is predominantly Byzantine Catholic while the East and Center are Eastern Orthodox. As a result, the nation-building project has drawn more support in the former provinces, while the citizens of the latter regions retain a "Novorossia" identity.[7] These differences have created a contest for control of the center between a Russian orientation in the East and a European outlook in the West that remains unresolved.

The post-Communist transition in Ukraine was slower and less complete than the rapid transformation of the Visegrad countries of the Czech Republic, Hungary, Poland, and Slovakia. Even after the Ukrainian declaration of independence in 1991, much of the political class as well as the bureaucracy consisted of careerists trained in the Soviet Union. Kiev was also dependent on Moscow for its oil and natural gas, making it vulnerable to Russian pressure, while much of its industry relied on trade with the eastern neighbor. There was also a dense web of personal relationships through intermarriage and about one-third of the population remained bilingual, code-switching between both languages as needed. The two-term president Leonid Kuchma therefore tried to combine good relations with Russia with a partial opening to the West. But investment was hindered by extensive corruption, domestic scandals, and human rights violations.[8] Though Ukraine started out at about the same economic level as Poland, its development stagnated and it fell ever further behind.

The Orange Revolution of November 2004 was a civil society attempt to turn the "competitive authoritarian regime" into a true democracy. The flagrant electoral fraud of the authorities in favor of the pro-Moscow faction led by Victor Yanukovich in the presidential runoff election sparked a growing series of mass protests. Moreover, the dioxin poisoning of the opposition leader Viktor Yushchenko indicated that the Russian secret service had attempted to incapacitate the Western-oriented rival. Incensed by President Kuchma's muzzling of the press, hundreds of thousands of youthful protesters heeded internet calls and took to the streets in Kiev, displaying the color orange to mark their dissent. This unprecedented wave of peaceful mobilization inspired the Supreme Court to order a new election that was decisively won by the nationalist appeal of Yushchenko.[9] But the hopeful victory of the democracy movement ended in disappointment and accentuated the regional division of the country that continued to pull its urban center between East and West.

The EU's "flawed approach" to defining its relationship with Ukraine contributed to the struggle over the country's future orientation. Due to a certain "enlargement fatigue," Brussels hoped to strengthen its relations with Kiev but did not wish to provoke a reforming Russia by expanding its reach into Moscow's backyard. Although the pro-Western faction wanted Ukraine to join the EU, the country was farther from fulfilling the Copenhagen criteria of democratic politics, human rights, and a market economy than its Visegrad neighbors who were admitted in 2004. Because these new members had to be integrated first, lofty declarations of intent during summit meetings produced little concrete action, leaving Kiev suspended between the EU and the CIS. Brussels initially planned just to include Ukraine in its neighborhood policy, like other countries that wanted to improve relations with the EU.[10] The subsequent proposal of an Eastern Partnership in 2009 was a compromise, offering closer cooperation that improved economic relations and kept the door open to future membership.

In the fall of 2013, protests aiming to prevent an alliance between Russia and Ukraine exploded again in the Euromaidan Independence Square. In part, the Westernizers were themselves at fault since their corruption gave Yanukovich a second chance to be elected president. For two years, the EU had been negotiating an association agreement with Kiev, demanding an end to favoritism and politicized justice.

When President Yanukovich refused to sign the treaty and instead wanted to accept Russian aid, hundreds of thousands of protesters took over the central square in the capital, staunchly resisting the violence used by the security forces. Instead of disbanding, the encamped opposition formulated demands such as freedom for the arrested, the end of oligarch corruption, the signing of the EU agreement, and Yanukovich's resignation. Due to the determination of the resistance, the president fled to the Donbas and then on to Russia. The Euromaidan aimed to become the birthplace of a democratic and national Ukraine.[11]

Afraid of losing the most important member of his own project of creating Eurasian integration, Putin decided to secure at least the Russophile part of Ukraine by military force. His method was the same as during the annexation of Crimea, namely, a revolt by local separatists in the Donbas, which is adjacent to the Russian Federation. According to telephone intercepts, Moscow encouraged pro-Russian nationalists with financing, up-to-date weapons, and special forces support. The armed uprising against the Kiev government centered on the coal and steel industry provinces of Donetsk and Luhansk in which the rebels deposed the representatives of the central government. The subsequent proclamation of independent republics was not recognized by the international community. When it looked as if the Ukrainian army forces were putting down the separatist rebellion, Russia sent in more regular troops, claiming to be "volunteers on vacation."[12] The ensuing military stalemate reinforced Ukrainian nationalism and alarmed NATO.

The downing of a Malaysian airliner in July 2014 brought the Eastern European conflict to broader international attention because many of the victims were Dutch citizens. On the way from Amsterdam to Kuala Lumpur, Flight 17 was hit by an antiaircraft missile in an international air corridor over eastern Ukraine, killing all 298 passengers aboard and scattering debris and bodies over a wide area. The Buk rocket came from a Russian launcher that had mistaken a civilian flight for a Ukrainian reconnaissance plane that was trying to record separatist movements. While the West immediately accused Moscow, the Russian government blamed the Ukrainian military, although the latter lacked such sophisticated weapons. By reassembling pieces of the plane, Dutch investigators subsequently proved that the missile had been fired by Russian forces from Kursk. The Australian minister of foreign affairs Julie Bishop warned that such an incident "should be of grave international concern."[13] Brazen Russian disinformation was reducing Moscow's credibility.

The struggle over the soul of Ukraine nonetheless continued since neither the military occupation nor the political confrontation could be resolved. In the wake of the Euromaidan, an association agreement with the EU was signed and the oligarch Petro Poroshenko was elected president. To reaffirm the country's Western orientation, Brussels intensified its contacts, the United States increased its military aid, and NATO held maneuvers in neighboring states so as to warn Putin against further adventures. But Crimea remained in Russian hands and Donetsk and Luhansk under the control of separatists who gave no signs that they would relinquish their hold. Moreover, about one-third of Ukraine's trade continued to involve Russia, giving Moscow a sizable economic leverage. While the great majority of Ukrainians rejected the occupation, most people grew tired of the continued corruption of the political class. As a result, in 2019 the political neophyte and comedian Volodymyr Zelensky won the presidency in a landslide, offering Moscow a chance to reassert its influence in a new administration.[14]

The Ukrainian troubles raised the conceptual and practical question of where the eastern border of Europe was to be drawn. The pro-Western ex-president Yushchenko pronounced that "the Ukraine which we strive to create will be an integral part of a truly united Europe," while pro-Russian separatists claimed that the country was "a brother nation" of Russia that belonged in the "Russian world." Economic interests also pulled both ways since trade with the EU and the CIS was about equal and Kiev would have a tough time surviving without Moscow's natural gas. While the West sought to respond to the aspirations of newly independent countries at the Russian periphery, like Armenia and Georgia, for closer relations with Europe, Russia tried to reconstitute its prior sphere of influence by strengthening economic and military cooperation in the Commonwealth of Independent States.[15] In this identity conflict, the West has been using the indirect appeal of its prosperous lifestyle while Russia has countered with military force.

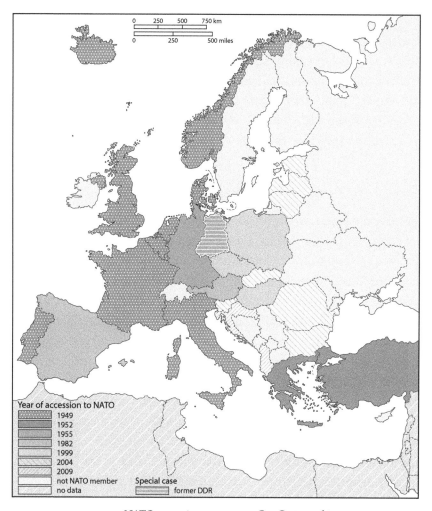

MAP 7. NATO expansion, 1949–2009. Cox Cartographic.

For European defense, the Ukraine crisis posed the vexing problem of how to respond to covert military invasions supported by Moscow. The incontrovertible proof that "Russia continues to supply separatists with equipment, fighters, and funding" has led numerous international organizations to condemn such irregular warfare. According to the NATO secretary general Anders Fogh Rasmussen, "what Russia is doing in Ukraine poses a threat to [a] rules-based international system and the sovereignty and territorial integrity of its neighboring states." In the case of Ukraine, this violation was especially egregious since Kiev had received treaty assurances of its independence from the West and Russia when giving up its nuclear arsenal. President Putin "has said that Russia reserves the right to take military action in any country where Russian citizens live. That includes countries within NATO" such as Estonia.[16] Supported by cyberwarfare and disinformation, this ethnic effort to revive the Brezhnev Doctrine has triggered economic sanctions as a measured reaction from the West.

Lagging Responses

Relying on American protection, Europe has been slow to respond to new security threats that have used "irregular warfare" methods like in Crimea. The end of the Cold War and attempts to befriend a democratizing Russia made it popular to reduce defense expenditures and draw down the conventional tank armies of NATO. The stunning US victory in the Persian Gulf War reinforced complacency, though the militia fighting and ethnic cleansing of the new Balkan Wars ought to have served as a warning. The rise of Muslim terrorism and the spectacular 9/11 attacks inspired a burst of Continental solidarity with the United States that demanded armed support for a punitive invasion of Afghanistan. But only a "coalition of the willing" participated in the second Iraq War, splitting the Continent into an "old" and "new" Europe in Donald Rumsfeld's misleading description.[17] Due to the "absence of a unifying existential threat," not even the Russian invasions of former Soviet countries have prompted the Europeans to overcome their reluctance to employ military means to protect their interests.[18]

The end of the Cold War decreased incentives to fashion a common European defense policy since it suggested that the superpower struggle for hegemony had ceased. With the breakup of the Warsaw Pact and the withdrawal of Soviet troops from the former satellites, Europe's major antagonist had evaporated, allowing a hesitant NATO to restructure its posture in order to cooperate with post-Communist Russia as a partner. During German unification, the East German National People's Army was dissolved and the West German Bundeswehr drastically reduced in size. The suspension of conscription left less than two hundred thousand men as a German armed force, hollowing out NATO's land defenses. The disappearance of the Communist threat made tank-led armies obsolete, shifting defense doctrine to the buildup of a rapid intervention force. Continental taxpayers who had long chafed under the Cold War fiscal burden were relieved to be able to limit military expenses. Since the United States refused a similar drawdown, Europeans became even more dependent on American protection.[19]

The new Balkan Wars during the disintegration of Yugoslavia quickly punctured the illusion of peace on the Continent and exposed the disarray of European defense. Prior cultural ties to the belligerents inclined the West to favor maintaining the Serbian-led federation, while Germany and Austria supported the recognition of Slovenian and Croatian independence. In practice, the reluctance of the European NATO members to get involved in the ground fighting helped Serbian separatists create a new Republika Srpska in Bosnia and Herzegovina. Cyrus Vance and Lord Owen's efforts to mediate the conflict unfortunately failed since they were not backed up with sufficient force. Only after the Clinton administration decided to bomb Belgrade did Slobodan Milošević accept the Dayton Accords that largely ratified his military gains. But NATO did intervene more quickly with air strikes in the subsequent struggle over Kosovo.[20] The Yugoslav wars showed that the Europeans lacked both the capacity and the will to meet force with force so as to preserve peace in their own backyard.

The Balkan conflict underlined the need for a common defense, going beyond NATO and national military forces. One such initiative was the Eurocorps, the brainchild of François Mitterrand and Helmut Kohl, which built on the existing Franco-German brigade. Composed of soldiers from five countries (including Belgium, Luxembourg, and Spain), it was an attempt to create the core of a future European military force. According to its commander General Helmut Willmann, "the Eurocorps can react when the Americans don't want to be involved. That is the most important thing." Headquartered in Strasbourg, the brigade comprised about 4,500 bilingual soldiers, drawing on up to 60,000 troops as a European rapid reaction force. But British skeptics considered it to be merely "Franco-German hot air," stressing cooperation within NATO instead.[21] The Eurocorps proved moderately useful in peacekeeping missions, such as in Bosnia or Kosovo, but failed to live up to its aspiration of constituting the start of a common European defense.

In contrast, the European reaction to the terrorist attacks on September 11, 2001, was more rapid and decisive, expressing a "swift and heartfelt solidarity" that helped repair transatlantic relations. Part of the strong response was due to the gruesome pictures of the collapse of the Twin Towers, part of it also to a guilty conscience for having harbored many of the terrorists beforehand. While the EU dithered over the development of a common defense policy, the European NATO states, led by the UK, agreed to invoke Article 5, which interpreted the "attack on one as an attack on all" and made them duty bound to assist the United States in hunting down the perpetrators. Swayed by alarmist media reporting, even a generally pacifist Germany was willing to support an "out of area deployment" of NATO forces, going beyond peacekeeping and into actual combat.[22] The 9/11 shock ran so deep that it drew the European NATO members into an irregular war against al-Qaeda terrorists in Afghanistan, which they could hardly win by conventional means.

The European involvement in the campaign against Islamic terrorism triggered a series of retaliatory attacks in several Continental countries that brought the struggle home to them. The first was a 2004 bombing of suburban trains in Madrid that claimed 193 lives and wounded 2,050 in a massive carnage. A year later, the subways of London were hit with the murder of 56 people and the wounding of 784 others. In November 2015, it was Paris's turn, when terrorists killed 128 youths in the Bataclan theater and other venues, wounding 413 others. And in July 2016, a fanatic drove his truck along the coastal boulevard in Nice, claiming 87 victims and injuring 434 others. Among the major European countries, Germany was largely spared except for a smaller copycat attack on a Christmas market later that year which killed 12 people and wounded 56. These attacks were in part organized by cells of al-Qaeda or ISIS, but some were also undertaken by internet-inspired radicalized Muslims who were born in Europe.[23] They presented a novel security threat since they could strike anywhere people congregated.

Since Islamic terrorists operated across frontiers, the EU gradually assumed responsibility for coordinating the fight against them. Initially, member states tightened criminal laws and police surveillance in order to stop attacks before they could be carried out. Moreover, social scientists started to research the causes of the radicalization of young men in mosques and held fundamentalist imams responsible. But the terrorist networks that cut across frontiers suggested that international cooperation was necessary to stop violence in the future. The EU issued a Directive on Combating Terrorism that proscribed any acts "which seriously destabilize the political, constitutional, economic, or social structures of a country or an international organization." In practice, that led to an intensification of the exchange of information and the establishment of a European arrest warrant. But human rights activists worried that anti-terrorism efforts would lead to a loss of freedom.[24] Such measures nonetheless considerably reduced the number of attacks.

In contrast, the US-led intervention in Iraq "exposed the stark division within the European Union." In Continental capitals like London, mass demonstrations protested against the second Iraq War, using the catchy slogan "no blood for oil," which suggested economic motives rather than humanitarian reasons for the invasion. Neither in France nor in Germany was the general public ready to believe the Bush administration's bogus claim that Iraq had "weapons of mass destruction." The EU failed to develop a common response since only the new Eastern European members plus Britain, Denmark, Italy, and Portugal were ready to send troops, based largely on their gratitude for past American protection and hope for future NATO membership. Believing in unilateralism, the Republican establishment in Washington accepted help from a "coalition of the willing" but fumed at the refusal of Paris and Berlin to join in the effort to depose the dictator Saddam Hussein. In spite of the quick military victory, "bitter resentment" remained since restoring civil peace continued to remain elusive.[25]

While calls for a common defense policy were increasing, the reality of actual shared measures continued to fall disappointingly short. The Maastricht Treaty intended to create a European Defense and Security

Policy, but the institutional rivalries between NATO, Western European Union member states, and national governments prohibited its effective development. The Lisbon Treaty increased the mandate of a Common Security and Defense Policy (CSDP), but the "member states [continued to] dominate the EU military policies." Their lack of European "coherence and capabilities" was starkly evident in the Libyan debacle in which France and Britain intervened with US help to overthrow the dictator Muammar al-Gaddafi while Germany remained on the sidelines. When the Western forces withdrew, civil war and chaos ensued. In spite of the establishment of a European Defense Agency, even the effort to unify weapons procurement has proven difficult since member states, including the United States, favored their own industries. As a result, the EU's CSDP remains far from an effective bulwark for European defense.[26]

The election victory of Donald Trump in 2016 deepened transatlantic disagreements on European defense. Articulating the frustration of the American Right with the burden of military expenditures, the president unceremoniously demanded that "Europe should first pay its fair share of NATO, which the US subsidizes greatly." To the alliance members, Secretary of Defense James Mattis insisted that European defense spending be raised to 2 percent of GNP, which only the United States, Estonia, for fear of Russia, and Greece, due to its hostility toward Turkey, were meeting in 2018. Five more Eastern European countries plus Great Britain promised to reach the target in the near future. The laggard was Germany, whose big defense budget did not even come close to 1.5 percent of GNP because its grand coalition between the CDU and SPD made drastic increases unlikely.[27] The core of the disagreement was the American failure to understand its self-interest in remaining a European power as well as the German reluctance to fund the military for historic reasons. Even under a more conciliatory Biden administration, this conflict is not likely to go away.

A final bone of contention between the EU and the United States was the right response to the Iranian nuclear program. Insisting on the nonproliferation of atomic weapons, the West was afraid that such an arsenal in the hands of radical Muslims posed a grave danger. The Bush administration worked with Britain, France, and Germany to negotiate the Tehran Declaration of 2003 with Iran that allowed the peaceful development of nuclear power while prohibiting its military use. But lack of cooperation with inspectors of the International Atomic Energy Agency and reports of clandestine arms development led the UN to impose sanctions on Tehran in 2006. In 2015 subsequent negotiations, including the United States and China, reached a new agreement on the peaceful uses of the reactors that were being built. But President Trump repudiated the deal as an Obama legacy because he did not trust the Iranian assurances and initiated more extensive sanctions even on European firms doing business with Iran. In contrast, the Europeans preferred even a controversial treaty to outright confrontation with Tehran.[28]

Personal Impact

The irregular nature of the warfare involved individuals as perpetrators or victims in increasingly terrifying ways. The ethnic cleansing during the civil war in Bosnia between Serbs and Muslims created a new paroxysm of violence through irregular gangs. One of the infamous leaders was Milan Lukić who returned to Visegrad in April 1992, gathering a group of men who called themselves "the Wolves." Escalating from "pillaging and looting Muslim homes," his thugs started killing and terrorizing their neighbors, driving around in a red VW Passat, "a harbinger of death." They used the famous bridge across the Drina River as a stage to taunt their victims, making them stand on the walls "before pushing them into the river and opening fire with automatic weapons," laughing all the while. They also set some houses on fire, burning seventy-one people with only one woman escaping. "When we saw poor Zara yelling in terror and pain, we knew that Visegrad had descended into some kind of hell."[29] Arrested in Argentina, Lukić was condemned to life imprisonment by the International Criminal Tribunal for the former Yugoslavia.

The Russian invasion of Eastern Ukraine involved a similar mixture of conventional warfare and irregular militia action. Dorji Batomunkuev was a contract soldier in a tank brigade hailing from Ulan-Ude in the Far East who was told he was going on maneuvers. He was sent to the

Donetsk Republic to reinforce the amateurish pro-Russia militia with professional armor. Before going into battle, his comrades painted over the Russian insignia and left their identification cards and phones behind. He explained the stealth approach of the fighting with the rationalization: "Our government does realize it has to help, but officially sending the troops in would rile up Europe and NATO." Initially, his unit had some successes, but eventually his tank was hit, there was blinding light, he pried the manhole cover open, and fell to the ground where a comrade put out his flaming clothes with a fire extinguisher. In a field hospital, the badly burnt youth continued to defend his actions: "If Donetsk wants independence, you gotta give it."[30]

The heated propaganda that forced everyone to take sides inspired Ukrainian nationalists to take up arms as well. Anatoly Gorbenko, aged thirty-seven, volunteered to defend his country "against Russian aggression." He told a journalist: "Of course it's a war between Ukraine and Russia . . . they just don't admit it." He was captured by separatists and held prisoner for four months before being freed in an exchange. When he returned to the front at the outskirts of Donetsk, he stepped on a mine. "There was an explosion and I saw both my legs were gone." His comrades carried him to a field hospital. "If it wasn't for Russia, this war would never have begun." Tatiana Grubenyuk, aged thirty-four, gave up her advertising job to volunteer as a nurse for wounded soldiers. "The Ukrainian government is providing soldiers and ammunition, but we volunteers are doing everything else." She explained her involvement as a defense against outside attack: "We just want to determine our own future as an independent country."[31]

The violence of Islamic terrorism had a different character since it was both global in inspiration and local in execution. The Hamburg cell of Jihadists who carried out the plane hijackings of 9/11 ironically gathered at the city's technical university, the al-Quds mosque, and a Muslim bookstore. Supported by a car mechanic named Mohammed Zammar with direct ties to al-Qaeda, the group was led by Mohamed Atta, "a disciplined student and pious Muslim" who spoke fluent German but could also be "a hectoring moralist." While fifteen of the nineteen attackers were Saudi citizens, the seven foreign students of the Hamburg cell were united in their hatred of "'world Jewry' and the United States" since they considered the so-called civilized world "the worst terrorists." Though the German authorities were aware of their increasing radicalization, the police failed to intervene since it had no proof of any actual actions that the cell had taken.[32] As a result of this misplaced tolerance, the group could complete the technical preparations for its airborne attack on the World Trade Center and the Pentagon.

The November 13, 2015, attackers on the concert hall Bataclan, the restaurants, and the soccer stadium in Paris were dissatisfied young men from Brussels and Paris, indicating the rise of a generation of indigenous terrorists. Most of the dozen youths involved in the massacre were born in Europe. "We're still in shock," a local acquaintance mused. "They were friends of ours, big smokers, big drinkers, but not radicals." As petty criminals with police records, they blamed European prejudice for their lack of social acceptance or professional success. The mastermind of the attacks, Abdelhamid Abaaoud, grew up in the Brussels neighborhood of Molenbeek, a breeding ground of radicalism, whereas others hailed from the *banlieues* of Paris. Many of them had been to Syria, Turkey, or other Muslim countries but had come back to Europe even though they resented the fact that Islam was being looked down on like in the satirical cartoons of *Charlie Hebdo*.[33] Vulnerable to Jihadist appeals from ISIS, they were ready to blow themselves up in a grand gesture of defiance intent on taking as many "crusaders" along with them as possible.

Yet another form of violence was the anti-Islamic terrorism of the Right that has been called "a lone wolf syndrome." On July 22, 2011, the Norwegian Anders Breivik first killed eight people with a bomb in Oslo and then executed sixty-nine helpless youths at a Labor Party retreat on the island of Utoya. A product of divorce and child abuse, he was a troubled young man who embraced the very medieval crusader fantasies that Muslim extremists railed against. He stated his white nationalism in a manifesto, called "2083: A European Declaration of Independence" in which he blamed the "suicide" of the Continent on "cultural Marxism/multiculturalism." Rejected by the Norwegian army, he was a gun enthusiast and a neo-Nazi sympathizer who believed that he could wake Europe up to the danger of "Islamic colonization" with one spectacular killing spree. Though acting alone, he was part of a right-wing "resistance" network on the web that admired his resolution, inspiring imitators like the perpetrator of the 2019 attack on a Jewish synagogue in Halle in East Germany.[34]

These novel forms of ethnic and religious violence also created a whole new group of civilian victims, with men subjected to torture and women as objects of rape. In the spring of 1992, victorious Serb militias rounded up 3,500 "Muslim Bosniaks and Roman Catholic Croats" in a concentration camp in Prijedor. Among the women was the young Muslim judge Nusreta Sivac. During the days of forced labor, "the women listened to tortured prisoners screaming, calling for help" until their voices went silent. In the morning, the guards forced them to clean up the interrogation rooms and dispose of twenty to thirty bodies. "At night, guards would come to take the women away, one by one—to rape." Sivac recalled that "there were days when she prayed for a bullet to end her suffering." She was saved by foreign journalists whose outraged reports eventually forced the Serbian government to release the prisoners. She helped prove that "between 20,000 and 50,000 Bosnian women were raped, forcing the UN to recognize rape as a "war crime."[35]

As a result of unleashing such violence, "ethnic cleansing" returned to Europe's backyard half a century after the defeat of the Nazi perpetrators. Though the practice is ancient, the term itself was a neologism intended to mark the compulsory population shifts during the wars among different ethnic groups in the former Yugoslavia. Already by the summer of 1992, 2.3 million people had been displaced by Serbian aggression and Croat complicity—most of them Bosnian Muslims caught in the middle of the fighting. But unlike in earlier wars, ethnic cleansing was not just a collateral by-product of "raids, arson and executions" but the very purpose of the fighting, which aimed to change the national population balance in the Balkans. This unmixing of ethnicities sought to purge settlement areas of diverse inhabitants in order to create a homogeneous Serbian or Croatian nation-state. Essentially, Europe and the West proved incapable and unprepared to defend "the suffering from nationalistic aggression and ethnic purging."[36]

The terrorists' victims were not enemy soldiers as in the case of Eastern Ukraine but random civilians, selected for the greatest media impact. The casualties of 9/11 were normal airline passengers, World Trade Center and Pentagon employees, and policemen as well as firemen seeking to rescue others. The Bataclan fatalities were youthful revelers at a rock concert who only gradually realized that the popping sounds they heard over the music were shots. Breivik's victims were teenage campers of a Socialist Youth League on an island from which there was no escape. Since the choice of such targets was unpredictable, attacks engendered horror because there was hardly any defense against them. In contrast to nineteenth-century anarchism, recent terrorist actions have often ended in suicide by bombing or shooting, which has made it more difficult to prevent them than before. Though the Council of Europe has recognized "that the suffering of victims of terrorist acts deserves national and international solidarity and support," many survivors have felt materially impoverished and psychologically traumatized.[37]

While it remained reluctant to enter into actual combat, the EU did assume responsibility for international peacekeeping efforts once conflicts had reached a stalemate. When called on by the UN or NATO, members of the European Union were willing to offer troops in places like Chad to prevent the renewal of civil war. Propelled by the failure of Dutch peacekeepers to prevent the Serbian massacre of Muslims in the Bosnian safe haven Srebrenica, the EU made a concerted effort to stabilize the Balkans after the Dayton Accords by committing 36,000 troops and 800 policemen to guarantee security against a resumption of ethnic strife. At the same time, the EU tried to encourage the recovery of the Balkan economy, investing €4.5 billion by the year 2000. In effect, this two-pronged involvement turned Bosnia and Kosovo into wards of the EU, which tried to make them into a "peaceful and viable democracy."[38] Similarly, the German Bundeswehr preferred reconstruction work to anti-Taliban combat in Afghanistan.

The International Criminal Tribunal for the former Yugoslavia has been another, largely European, effort to bring perpetrators to justice, indicating that such violations would no longer be tolerated. Created by a UN resolution in 1993, this special court addressed violations of the

Geneva Convention, war crimes, genocide, and human rights breaches. The EU used its diplomatic leverage to compel Serbia and Croatia to extradite major offenders as a precondition for any eventual acceptance into the European Community. As a result, the Serbs turned over the insurgent leader Radovan Karadžić and the military commander Radko Mladić while the Croats offered up General Ante Gotovina. Karadžić and Mladić as well as their associates were condemned for multiple transgressions. The trial of Slobodan Milošević was still ongoing when he suffered a heart attack.[39] Following the Nuremberg Trial precedent, this effort to punish perpetrators was a hopeful step toward justice, but, unfortunately, major powers like the United States and Russia refused to have their own citizens tried in the more broadly conceived International Court of Justice.

Finally, European-based NGOs have played a major role in the prevention of conflict and the resolution of disputes. Founded in 1971 in France, Doctors Without Borders "provides medical assistance to people affected by conflict, epidemics, disasters, or exclusion from healthcare" around the globe. Similarly, Greenpeace, headquartered in Amsterdam, tries to "ensure the ability of the Earth to nurture life in all its diversity" by pressuring governments to fight more energetically against global warming and other environmental problems. Located in the United Kingdom, Amnesty International "campaign[s] for a world where human rights are enjoyed by all," issuing annual reports about violations. The Association of European Journalists also promotes "critical journalism" and "defends the freedom of information" in Europe and in other regions. As civil society organizations, these associations propagate a European understanding of world problems and actively work for their solution on the Continent and around the globe.[40]

Difficult Choices

During the post–Cold War decades, Europe was surprised by a series of new security threats that called the pacification of the Continent into question. While the lifting of the Iron Curtain and the withdrawal of Russian troops ended the East-West confrontation, a surprising series of ethnic conflicts broke out at Europe's borders. Relieved by the return of the East to Europe, the public was shocked by the violence in the wars during the breakup of Yugoslavia and appalled by the Russian occupation of the Crimea and Eastern Ukraine. Through their solidarity with the United States, the European NATO members were dragged into a global confrontation with radical Islam that triggered an unforeseen spate of terrorist attacks at home. Moreover, a resurgent Russia did not develop into a constructive partner but became a destabilizing factor by supporting authoritarian regimes and issuing electronic disinformation from troll farms. Blurring the distinction between external and internal dangers, these unforeseen threats provided new challenges to European security.[41]

Unsure about how to react, Europeans have been ill prepared to protect their interests by force. The final responsibility for defense continues to reside in sovereign nation-states, which only band together for common action in NATO. While the passing of the conventional warfare threat allowed forces to be drawn down, the remaining military had to refocus its resources on developing rapid response capabilities to meet global threats or support human rights interventions. Due to its memories of war, the European public has been reluctant to use military force unless led by the United States or authorized by the United Nations as a peacekeeping mission. By 1999 the EU had understood that to "assert itself on the world stage" it needed to create a common security and defense policy represented by a strong leader like Javier Solana. While Brussels had some success in counterterrorism cooperation, a discrepancy remained in defense between the wish "to take more joint action" and the priority of national interests.[42] Hence, the implicit conflict between a transatlantic NATO and a Continental defense remains unresolved.

Time and again, US leaders have been frustrated by Continental foot-dragging, not realizing that the reason for it was a fundamental difference in military cultures. While in European memory war was immediate, devastating, and personally deadly, in American recollections war was overseas, technological, and generally victorious. As a result, Washington has been more willing to employ military force, entering a series of wars in Afghanistan, Iraq, and the like, while European NATO members have remained split on whether to support them. But the United States is also hampered by a strong isolationist current that refuses to get entangled in foreign wars and insists on bringing the troops home. Resentment at the costs of global leadership fueled Trump's insistence on greater burden sharing while resentment against Germany motivated his decision to reduce troops stationed there by nine thousand five hundred men; this decision has already been reversed by his successor.[43] Though the technological sophistication and massive resources of the United States have brought spectacular victories, excessive reliance on force has often lost the peace when confronted by sectarian antagonists.

In contrast, most Europeans have developed a decided preference for employing soft power in order to achieve their objectives. Opinion surveys show that the Continental public considers war as a last resort for direct self-defense rather than a method for interventions around the globe. As a result of their terrible history in the past century, they generally favor conflict prevention through public diplomacy and economic incentives rather than the use of force. Unlike Washington's recurrent tendencies toward unilateralism, the Continentals try to work through international organizations like the UN, or NATO, even if reaching compromise is an exasperating process. Except for some limited interventions in former colonies, they prefer to invest in mediation, peacekeeping, and aid for reconstruction. President Macron's call to develop an independent European defense needs to be taken seriously so that dictators like Milošević or Putin cannot count on European inaction when devising aggressive strategies.[44]

Both approaches are interdependent and complementary in maintaining peace and guaranteeing security in the twenty-first century. Washington's hard-line behavior has imposed enormous costs in social inequality and deteriorating infrastructure on its own country as well as provoked worldwide hostility from its enemies. The European preference for diplomacy has often been misconstrued as weakness since it has proven incapable of stopping bloody wars at its own borders. Fortunately, the newly elected US president, Joseph Biden, has promised to return to multilateral negotiations, to respect international agreements such as the Paris climate treaty, and to reevaluate the accord to stop Iran's development of nuclear weapons. At the same time, Ursula von der Leyen has started to push EU members to integrate their CSDP further and improve the actual readiness of their military capabilities.[45] Only when both transatlantic partners resume their resolute cooperation will they have some chance of success in addressing the world's endless problems.

11

Populist Backlash

FIGURE 12. Yellow Vest protests, Paris, France. Benoit Tessier / Reuters Pictures.

On May 29, 2018, an angry petition appeared on the internet that complained about the "hike in fuel prices" and "the lack of transparency" of how taxes were spent in France. Its unlikely author was the black cosmetic businesswoman Priscillia Ludosky, who hailed from Martinique but lived in the Île-de-France. Her fifteen specific points were a motley collection of resentments against "the widening gap between rich and poor, and the rise in living costs." Her appeal condemned the increase in gas, diesel, and electricity prices, called for the reduction of various taxes and charges, and demanded an increase in education and unemployment funding. The petition was deeply hostile toward the governing elite, insisting on the reduction of its privileges, salaries, and numbers, suggesting the creation of a grassroots democracy, and proposing a referendum on President Emmanuel Macron.[1] This ideologically incoherent set of demands nonetheless struck a popular chord, attracting almost a million supporters during the summer.

Half a year later, this web protest became an actual social movement that shook France to the core. To disseminate the petition, the trucker Eric Drouet proposed "that angry drivers deliberately block or slow traffic" in a nationwide action on November 17, 2018. Someone else "had the brilliant PR idea of dressing everyone up in the yellow hi-vis[ibility] vests that French motorists must by law carry in their cars." The call to arms resonated due to the shrinkage of disposable income and "other grievances in rural and outer suburban France." For instance, the mandated reduction of the two-lane speed limit from ninety to eighty kilometers per hour to save gas made commutes more onerous. Though the protests lacked central coordination, they mobilized 283,000 people during the first weekend by occupying the roundabouts that substitute for traffic lights in much of France. Spanning the entire spectrum from hard right to radical left, the supporters came mostly from a lower-middle-class section of society, demanding "that we should feel recognized and valued."[2]

The clash between such "white hot anger" and the government's defense of order triggered an explosion of violence in Paris and the provinces. When protesters destroyed property, the police resorted to rubber bullets and stun grenades. The escalating protests turned into street battles in which members of both sides were hurt and a dozen people killed. Incensed, President Macron denounced the mobs as "a hate-filled crowd who target elected representatives, security forces, journalists, Jews, foreigners, and homosexuals." But aware that rebukes would not heal the lack of trust, the government promised tax cuts, higher pensions, and a reform of the civil service, pledging €17 billion to improve the living standard of the lower classes. In response to being roundly criticized, Macron initiated a "national dialogue" with regional forums in which angry citizens could vent their grievances.[3] With this mixture of measures, the president restored order, though he continued to defend the direction of his economic reforms in order to make France more competitive.

In many ways, the Yellow Vests were a classic populist movement from below that sought to overturn sociopolitical hierarchies. Lest the term "populism" has become so ubiquitous as to lose its meaning, Cas Mudde and Christobal Kaltwasser define it as "a thin-centered ideology that considers society to be ultimately separated into two homogeneous antagonistic camps, 'the pure people' versus 'the corrupt elite,' and which argues that politics should be an expression of the *volonté generale*." The petitions, appeals, and slogans of the *gilets jaunes* showed a strong antipathy toward the elite as well as an insistent claim to represent the true populace. Both economic disparity and cultural resentment fueled the protests, even if hostility toward immigrants and criticism of the EU had already been adopted by the right-wing Front National. Also, the ideological confusion of the movement, with two-fifths of the protesters on the right and one-quarter on the left was typically populist.[4] Finally, the role of the internet in mobilization was another method of protest, even if a single charismatic leader failed to emerge.

The rise of populism has been an unanticipated challenge to liberal democracy since its demand for greater citizen participation has paradoxically opened the door to new illiberal politics. While initially only a few countries such as Italy or Austria were affected, by 2020 the populist wave had engulfed not only the United States but also virtually every European state, ranging from the Brexit Party in the UK to the Alternative for Germany (AfD) and from the Sweden Democrats to the Pim Fortuyn List in the Netherlands. The Great Recession spurred the formation of left-wing populism in Greece and Spain, whereas racist xenophobia, fear of terrorism, and resentment against the EU triggered right-wing agitation from the Fidesz Party in Hungary and the Law and Justice Party (PiS) in Poland. In order to explain the underlying crisis of liberal democracy, it is necessary to discuss the French case, take a look at comparable developments in other countries, and probe the individual motivations.[5] How has Europe dealt with this illiberal mobilization so far?

Street Protests

The Yellow Vests drew on a particular French tradition of street protests stretching from the revolution in 1789 through a turbulent nineteenth century to the youth rebellion of 1968. The centralization of power in Paris and the domination of an educated elite in the capital over the provinces often made politics unresponsive to the local needs of the lower social classes. Since the system did not respond to their wishes, enraged citizens time and again took to the streets to voice their demands. Trade unions led the charge whenever neoliberal reforms imposed cutbacks on the extensive welfare system that threatened pensions, increased the retirement age, or facilitated firing workers. But the people would take matters into their own hands, when political parties or organized labor failed to address their grievances, with farmers outraged by cuts in subsidies simply dumping manure on the *autoroutes*, shutting down traffic.[6] Expressing an anarchist strain, such *manifs* rarely led to lasting change since the governments would make specific concessions without changing basic structures.

The forerunner of postwar populism in France was the movement led by Pierre Poujade, which sought to protect the "small people" against the modernization imposed by Parisian elites. The leader hailed from a monarchist family in Saint-Céré, where he ran a stationery store, typical of modest businesses and farms that felt threatened by large retail chains and big trade unions. In 1953 Poujade organized a tax revolt by founding the Union des Commerçants et Artisans (UDCA), which quickly caught on in small towns and agricultural regions, the self-styled *France profonde*. Denouncing the corruption of the "system," this insurrectionist movement was full of anti-elite rhetoric and given to "spectacular stunts designed to discredit the administration." During the 1956 election, the Poujadists gained a surprising fifty-two seats in Parliament but eventually fizzled when the Algerian crisis put Charles de Gaulle back in power.[7] Echoing the anti-Semitism and corporatism of Vichy, this revolt prepared the ground for a future rightist mobilization.

Its successor was the Front National (FN), which collected various right-wing groups into one populist party. In 1972 the media-savvy Jean Marie Le Pen founded a new movement that took a more radical right-wing stance than the governing Gaullist Party. Traumatized by the loss of Algeria, his followers hated Islam, disliked Arabs, and rejected immigration to France from former colonies in North Africa. Reviving the old slogan "France for the French," the FN also opposed European integration and flirted openly with anti-Semitism. It remained a marginal protest force in electoral contests until François Mitterrand's victory in the early 1980s gave it an anti-socialist platform that led to local breakthroughs. More recently, Marine Le Pen, the daughter of the erratic founder, has sought to "de-demonize" the party, making it a more respectable electoral alternative, thus netting her about one-quarter of the popular vote in the presidential elections. As a form of "heritage populism," the renamed Rassemblement National has come to represent an "ecosocialist" response to globalization fears.[8]

Right-wing populism also profited from the surprising collapse of the French Communist Party (PCF), which had been the primary left-wing alternative for political protest. Benefiting from its prominence in the resistance, the PCF was the strongest party in France at the end of the Second World War, winning almost 30 percent of the popular vote. Though it was soon shut out of the government, it succeeded in building a "countersociety" of its own through working-class and rural support as well as the involvement of leading intellectuals and artists who admired the Soviet Union. Nonetheless, it failed to connect with the student rebellion of 1968 and lost credibility after the Soviet repression of the Prague Spring, which made even the fellow traveler Jean-Paul Sartre reconsider his support. The party leader Georges Marchais remained too inflexible in the debate about Eurocommunism, allowing the Socialist Party under Mitterrand to surpass the PCF and demote it to the role of a junior partner in government.[9] With the collapse of European Communism in 1989, the party lost its appeal and shrank to a marginal role.

Though initially helped by the decline of its leftist rival, the French Socialist Party (PS) did not fare any better in the long run. Founded in 1969 out of the remnants of the venerable French Workers' Party (SFIO), the PS pursued a "union of the left" policy, combining forces with the PCF in order to break the Gaullist stranglehold. This strategy paid off when François Mitterrand won the 1981 presidential election, putting the Socialists into power for the first time in the Fifth Republic. The new president started with a decidedly leftist program but could not maintain it because the weakness of the franc and his desire to stay in the European Monetary System eventually compelled him to adopt neoliberal policies. Mitterrand gained reelection in 1988, and Lionel Jospin became prime minister with a left coalition, but Ségolène Royal lost the 2007 presidential contest. The PS returned to power with a stunning victory in 2012, but the weak leadership of François Hollande alienated its supporters, leading to its collapse in the election of 2017.[10]

At the same time, the French Center-Right also splintered since its ideological mooring of Gaullism had eroded. As a presidential regime, the Fifth Republic was oriented on principles such as "France's right to a major, independent role in world politics; dirigisme, a kind of Keynesian economic policy with a major role for the French state; and anti-Communism." In the succession of presidents from Georges Pompidou to Jacques Chirac, this odd blend of assertive nationalism, technocratic modernization, and paternalist social policy gradually lost its hold on the electorate, allowing the Socialist Party access to power. In 2007 Nicolas Sarkozy's presidency sought to revive the original dynamism through a series of neoliberal reforms once again to make France competitive—but his welfare cutbacks and obnoxious style angered the electorate.[11] In the struggle among potential successors, the rival candidates were hampered by scandals, leaving a political void in the center and moderate right.

In the election of 2017, the widespread discontent with *la politique bloquée* allowed Emmanuel Macron, a relative newcomer, to gain the presidency with a campaign that emphasized "youth and renewal." A product of an elite education, Macron was a banker who had served as finance minister in the Hollande government. Within a single year, the thirty-nine-year-old managed to create a centrist reform coalition out of the remnants of previous parties, by founding a new grouping called "La République en Marche!" Learning from Barack Obama, Macron ran an American-style grassroots campaign focused on new media and the internet that featured his stylish personality and suggested change in contrast to his discredited rivals. In the first round of the presidential election, he barely overtook the Radical Left (Jean-Luc Mélenchon) and Center-Right (François Fillon) candidates, but most of their supporters rallied around him in the second round to prevent Marine Le Pen from winning. Followed by a parliamentary triumph, his victory was "one of the most spectacular hold ups in the history of the Fifth Republic."[12]

Already before Macron's meteoric rise, the widespread discontent of the lower classes had erupted in periodic mass demonstrations. When Prime Minister Alain Juppe announced "sweeping austerity measures" to cut the public debt in November 1995, between one and two million people took to the streets. But he had to abandon his plans when the railroad unions and public-sector workers also went on strike to defend their privileges. Similarly, over a million protesters demonstrated against pension reforms in 2003 but were unable to stop the changes. When Sarkozy raised the retirement age from sixty to sixty-two in 2010, incensed crowds blockaded oil refineries, fuel depots, and port terminals, shutting down car traffic. Nonetheless, Parliament passed the law. Finally, when Hollande aimed "at loosening France's rigid employment rules," hundreds of thousands protested in the streets in 2016, but they were unable to prevent the changes.[13] The continuation of such mass protests against Macron signaled that his election had not ended popular alienation.

Much of the discontent was the result of actual economic problems faced by shop-owners, artisans, and farmers who were having difficulties facing the pressures of globalization. The Yellow Vests' anger against the rise in energy prices was but an indication of a deeper social malaise of people feeling left out of rising prosperity. One statistical study argued that "the stagnation and the erosion of buying power during the last decade is a major explanatory factor." It expressed itself in "the growth of fixed household expenses" such as "rents, insurance costs, bank fees and telephone charges." Between 1960 and 2018, the "dedicated expenses of disposable income ha[d] risen from 12.6 to 29.2 percent." This burden fell most heavily on the modest households, which had 61 percent of their income eaten up by fixed costs.[14] Even small changes in daily outlays had a disproportionate political effect, but they were often ignored by the wealthy urban classes that controlled politics.

Another, largely overlooked, dimension of resentment was cultural opposition to the metropolitan elites. Édouard Bergeon's film *Au nom de la terre* dramatized the travails of a farmer who could not cope and committed suicide. It was an indictment of the "drifting apart of center and periphery, the ignorance and the disinterest of elites in politics, culture and media vis à vis the suffering of the countryside." Many people in the rural areas and outer suburbs resented the success of the cities, feeling denigrated as "yokels or rednecks." The British journalist John Lichfield observed: "It is true that energy, life, and local sources of wealth have been sucked out of large swaths of France in recent decades" due to globalization. "All this adds up to an existential conviction that peripheral France is not only being left behind but mocked and cheated by those who are forging ahead." He concluded that "this resentment—a sense of being slighted or ignored or despised or abandoned or humiliated—explains the yellow-vest movement more than any particular grievance."[15] Many people felt slighted by the elegant and sophisticated Macron.

Both the rise of protest movements and the erosion of political parties were indicators of a crisis "of public engagement with party-based liberal democratic politics." Voter turnout, party membership, trust in politicians, and interest in politics were declining in many European countries, signaling that "representative democracy looks exhausted." Propelled by the internet, new forms of grassroots mobilization were starting to take its place. "The mood is not contemplative or deliberative. It is angry and resentful." The resulting mass protests in France were often directed against changes that seemed to threaten established lifestyles and accustomed privileges. On the one hand, populists of the Right such as Le Pen or the Left such as Mélenchon promised to protect people against the effects of globalization. On the other, single-issue campaigns like Fridays for Future represented committed minorities who were intent on forcing the passive majority to follow their lead.[16] It is not yet clear if these initiatives will undercut or strengthen democracy.

Politics of Anxiety

Surprising politicians and commentators alike, the politics of resentment has spread with amazing speed throughout the European Continent, creating a seemingly irresistible wave. A generation ago, the extreme Right and Left were easy to ignore since they existed merely at the margins without much public resonance. But with the help of social media, populist movements have rapidly grown in size and brazenness of their antiestablishment message. What had seemed like private anger has made the transition into public life, and transformed chat groups into mass protests in the streets, coalescing into veritable social movements. When led by charismatic figures, like the comedian Beppe Grillo in Italy, such groups have even created political parties, like the Five Star Movement, that have scored electoral successes, either entering government coalitions or at least moving the agenda of established parties in their direction. With the help of Donald Trump, some movements—like the Brexit campaign of Nigel Farage—have overturned the entire politics of a country, like in the UK.[17]

One of the first leaders of what is now called a populist government was the media magnate Silvio Berlusconi in Italy. Born in 1936, he grew up during the war and eventually obtained a law degree. After trying his hand at various jobs, he bought a cable TV network in 1971 and developed it into Italy's biggest media empire of TV stations, newspapers, and publishing houses. When the traditional middle-class parties collapsed, he founded a party of his own in 1994 with the nationalist name *Forza Italia*, which won the following election and made him prime minister in alliance with the regionalist Lega Nord. His *contratto con gli Italiani* promised to simplify taxes, decrease unemployment, provide public works, raise pensions, and reduce crime. His appeal also rested on his machismo style, his unabashed nationalism, and his media presence. But Berlusconi was plagued by endless scandals, sexual affairs, and charges of corruption.[18] Moving in and out of government, he achieved few of his promises but prepared the ground for Matteo Salvini of the Lega Nord to follow in his far-right footsteps.

Another early populist leader was the charismatic and chameleon-like Jörg Haider of the Austrian Freedom Party (FPÖ). Founded in 1955 out of remnants of Nazi supporters, the party led a marginal existence until Haider became chairman in 1986. The good-looking lawyer came from a Nazi family and was a member of various right-wing groups. His regional base was the state of Carinthia, which borders on Italy and Slovenia, where he refused to put up street signs for the Slavic minority when he was governor. His fluctuating ideology consisted of xenophobic, anti-Semitic, and anti-European pronouncements that sought to capture widespread pan-German resentments. In 2000 the FPÖ made it into Austria's government, provoking censure from the international community, which was afraid of a resurgence of Nazism. Due to his authoritarianism, the party split several times until he died in a traffic accident in 2008.[19] Although fears of the FPÖ were exaggerated since it self-destructed through various scandals, the party poisoned Austrian politics by catering to the rightist fringe.

Yet another populist politician was the Dutch professor Pim Fortuyn, who claimed to defend liberal Western values against the onslaught of Islam. A gay Catholic, he worked as a sociologist and publicist until he began to turn to politics by criticizing the failure of multiculturalism, the rise in immigration, and the threat of crime. Profiting from the resentment of immigrants, his Pim Fortuyn List (LPF) won 36 percent in the Rotterdam election in 2002, making it the strongest party. Favoring immigration restrictions, he called for a "cold war with Islam," denouncing it "as an extraordinary threat, as a hostile religion" because it was "backward" and did not want to accept Dutch standards of diversity. On May 6, 2002, he was assassinated by a left-wing animal rights activist, making him an instant martyr. After the filmmaker Theo van Gogh was also shot by an Islamic radical, Geert Wilders and the Party for Freedom picked up their anti-elite, anti-EU, and anti-Muslim legacy, moving Dutch politics further to the right.[20]

Xenophobic attitudes have even seeped into Scandinavian politics and supported the rise of nativist political parties. "The Nordic countries have long been viewed as among the most tolerant countries in the world, with exemplary protection of minorities." But during the past decade, new anti-immigrant parties have won a growing share of the vote in Sweden (Sweden Democrats 17.5 percent in 2019), Finland (Finns Party 17.5 percent in 2019), and Norway (Progress Party 15.2 percent in 2017). Only in Denmark did the Danish People's Party, which had gained 21.1 percent of the vote in 2015, collapse again to 8.7 percent four years later. With such increasing returns, they have entered bourgeois governments and pushed the programs of mainstream moderate parties to the right. In white and Lutheran populations, popular right-wing parties have exploited the rise in immigration and refusal to integrate to feed a racist resentment of "Muslim culture that threatens us and we have to send them away." Commentators have attributed this surge to the "consequences of neoliberal globalization— mass immigration and a deterioration of welfare services."[21]

Populism has also managed to combine with various anti-globalization protests on the left as exemplified by the Greek Syriza movement. Founded for the 2004 election, this loose coalition of various ecological and Marxist groupings initially gained only 3 percent of the electoral vote. Its platform consisted of a decided rejection of neoliberalism, an endorsement of people's power, workers' rights, and protection of the environment. Syriza achieved its breakthrough in the financial crisis by articulating popular opposition to the austerity measures imposed by the troika of the IMF, the European Commission, and the European Central Bank. The drastic reduction of salaries, the campaign against corruption, and the attempt to collect taxes provoked a public outcry since it reduced living standards. In the 2015 election, the party won 36 percent of the vote and entered government under the popular leader Alexis Tsipras.[22] But when he was compelled to implement drastic cuts to balance the budget, Syriza lost some of its luster, slipping into second place in 2019.

Another fairly successful example of left-wing populism is the Spanish party Podemos, which promised "We Can" bring about political change. It grew out of the Los Indignados youth protests against austerity in May 2011, which called for an end to corruption, inequality, and unemployment. In 2014 the political scientist Pablo Iglesias turned the populist movement into a political party opposed to the austerity measures of the Popular Party of Prime Minister Mario Rajoy that followed neoliberal prescriptions to restart the Spanish economy. Instead, Podemos advocated the renegotiation of debts with international creditors, called for a universal basic income, and demanded guaranteed welfare for families hit by unemployment as well as the end of evictions of bankrupt homeowners. At the same time, it campaigned for measures of grassroots democracy, such as referenda, in order to increase public participation. In the 2015 elections, Podemos won 21 percent of the vote, but unlike Syriza, it initially refused to enter the socialist government though it has eventually become part of the ruling coalition.[23]

Rejecting both socialism and neoliberalism, post-Communist populism combines social policies with a strident neo-nationalism. A case in point of such illiberal politics is Hungary, which initially rejected Soviet Communism but subsequently repudiated Western democracy as well. Its charismatic leader, Viktor Orbán, was a former student radical who had founded a liberal Fidesz Party that helped propel the peaceful revolution. Yet, as prime minister between 1998 and 2002 and again from 2010 to the present, he steadily moved in a more authoritarian direction and cemented his power by curtailing human rights in a revised constitution. Supporting a "crony capitalism," he has been "milking billions from Brussels" while at the same time "blaming the EU for every imagined indignity or interference in Hungarian affairs." Claiming that "to defend borders is a national responsibility," he tried to stop the rush of Balkan refugees with a razor-wire fence. Unconstrained by a divided opposition, Orbán's "illiberal democracy" is nonetheless the prototype of "heritage populism."[24]

The Polish government of the PiS contains a similar paradox. "Despite unprecedented prosperity and a firm grip on the country's security, Poland has been susceptible to the siren call of populism." The Polish version draws on fundamentalist Catholicism and strong ethnic nationalism so as to promote an "anti-globalization, anti-immigrant, anti-abortion, and anti-gay rhetoric." Offering attractive social policies such as child support, PiS is supported by small towns and the countryside in the eastern part of the country. Led by Jarosław Kaczyński, it used anti-Communism to denounce the liberal supporters of the former prime minister Donald Tusk, reduce the independence of the judiciary, and curb free speech. Supplanting Russia as its chief enemy, it has made the EU its principal target for insisting on women's equality and LGBT rights, which are rejected by traditionalist Poles. Moreover, PiS has pursued a reactionary memory policy, styling Poland as an innocent victim of outsiders rather than accepting responsibility for crimes of its own.[25]

German populism, represented by the Alternative for Germany (AfD), also combines post-Communist and anti-globalization nationalism. The party was founded in 2013 by the economist Bernd Lucke who wanted to return to the hard DM. The AfD achieved its breakthrough by resentment against Chancellor Angela Merkel's opening of the doors for about a million refugees in 2015. Growing out of local protests in Dresden by Patriotic Europeans Against the Islamisation of the Occident (PEGIDA), it sought to occupy political space to the right of the governing CDU, which Angela Merkel had moved to the center. Since the revival of National Socialism was formally forbidden, the party flirted with neo-Nazi propaganda, relativizing the Third Reich—in its chairman Alexander Gauland's phrase—as "a mere drop of bird shit on German history." Resenting economic deprivation and cultural liberalism, supporters of the AfD's barely concealed racism came mainly from Eastern Germany, making it the strongest opposition party with 12.6 percent of the vote in the 2017 federal elections. But with the passing of the migration crisis, its populist appeal has begun to fade.[26]

In spite of a great diversity of movements, populist parties in Europe share important traits with each other and their American counterpart. Their members dislike the elites, distrust the official media, and believe in a national mission; they also feel that their way of life is threatened by liberals, gays, and foreigners, especially Muslims; invoking neo-Nazi symbols, they see themselves involved in a heroic struggle against uncontrollable forces of globalization, represented by the WTO or EU. Yet there are also significant transatlantic differences. In the United States, the libertarian strain of anti-government rhetoric is stronger, and it merges with an assertive gun culture; the racism of white supremacists is directed more against Blacks than Jews, expressed by references to the Confederacy and supported by a sanctimonious evangelical moralism. While in Europe such populist resentments motivate an array of radical but limited parties, in America the Trump presidency has given populism control of a superpower government. One can only hope that his electoral defeat will help reverse this populist ascendancy.[27]

Roots of Resentment

Many politicians, journalists, and scholars are puzzled by the rapid rise of populist movements and are desperately trying to find a way to stop them. One favorite explanation is a combination "of real problems as well as unreal claims," based on "widespread feelings of being left behind and losing out." This social marginalization thesis blames populism on the resentment of white and male losers of globalization who feel that their concerns are not taken seriously by the existing political parties, which they consider to be part of the problem. But another interpretation stresses the cultural anxieties over multiculturalism, feminism, and homosexuality as a threat to traditional family values, received religious beliefs, and accustomed social norms. Economic and cultural concerns have revived ancient anti-Semitic prejudices and fed racist fears of Islamic immigration by focusing on the different skin colors and customs of newcomers.[28] Does the evidence of individual cases bear out the economic or the cultural version of the causes of populism?

Surprisingly enough, some populist nationalists are themselves members of the elite who disagree with its concessions to liberalism. In the UK, one controversial leader is Jacob Rees-Mogg, a product of Eton and Trinity College at Oxford. Having achieved financial success in the City of London, he is a high Tory, and a fundamentalist Catholic with staunch anti-feminist convictions for whom David Cameron's support of abortion and same-sex marriage is anathema. According to one left-wing journalist, "he is the real deal. The real deal is not a charming, upper-crust throwback, but a thoroughly modern, neoconservative bigot."[29] A rabid British nationalist, he opposes EU membership as an infringement on the UK's sovereignty, denouncing the lack of democratic accountability. In spite of his unabashedly elitist style, his vigorous attacks on Brussels have made him the leader of the House of Commons, adored by his followers but despised by his liberal opponents.

Other versions of nationalist populism play on racist fears of immigration and cultural subversion by Islam. In France, a leading spokesman of Islamophobia is Eric Zemmour, a provocative columnist who hails from a family of Berber Jews. In his 2014 book *The French Suicide*, he prophesied the decline of France due to uncurbed Arab immigration: "Today we live in a de facto colonization from the populations that come from the south of the Mediterranean and who impose—through numbers and, sometimes with violence—a de facto sharia." His prediction of a "new civil war" between the "Christian, and white identity" of his country and supporters of "the Islamicization of France" appealed especially to the *pieds noirs* settlers who returned from Algeria after its independence. Marion Marechal, the granddaughter of Jean-Marie Le Pen, has been trying to forge a new alliance between the extreme and moderate right by stressing "our right to the primacy of French culture over that of imported cultures."[30]

Cultural resentment and economic frustration have sparked populist nationalism even in countries without Muslim immigration. Led by Jarosław Kaczyński, the Law and Justice Party (PiS) in Poland has created a narrative of "Poland in ruins," although the country has shown continual economic growth since the overthrow of Communism. The PiS was able to exploit the discrepancy between rising expectations and uneven performance by offering extensive social programs such as family and housing subsidies. One of its supporters Anna Malinowska explained: "What I always liked about them was that they have represented Christian values." She defined them as "one of the unofficial mottos of Poland" such as "God, Honor, Fatherland." While young urban Poles were eager to accept the liberal social norms of the West, rural and small-town people rejected such cultural changes as "feminism and LGBT rights."[31] After winning the election of 2015, the PiS has gradually rescinded many human rights, such as the independence of the courts, and introduced an authoritarian version of *demokratura* that clashes with EU norms.

Xenophobic nationalism and covert racism have filled the ideological void left by the collapse of Communism in other Eastern European states as well. In Hungary, Prime Minister Victor Orbán shut down the Balkan route of refugees with a metal fence in order to defend "ethnic homogeneity." Though most of them had never met a migrant, Fidesz supporters like Maria Pulai viewed immigrants as a danger: "We are enough as we are. We don't need migrants." The state-controlled media claimed that the government was only "standing up for national interests." Since educated Hungarians were becoming concerned about restrictions on public debate, "the party has gained ground with the less educated and pensioners" through social handouts. Its support was "strongest in the small towns and villages where jobs are scarce." In spite of much financial support from the EU, Orbán claimed that Hungary had to be defended from "external forces and international powers" such as the Jewish financier George Soros and that Hungarians were being "treated like second-class citizens everywhere."[32]

A strong contributing factor to such cultural populism has been real or imagined economic deprivation, inspiring the resentment of those left behind. Though they have created well-educated winners, the structural transformations of globalization and high technology have shut out many workers who are unable or unwilling to meet their competitive pressures. As a result of neoliberal policies, the economic disparity between rich and poor has grown in all European countries during the past decades. The impact of fiscal crises like the sovereign debt debacle and the shift of much manufacturing to Asia have cost many traditional industrial jobs. As a result, entire regions like the British Midlands, the French North-East, and the German Ruhr Basin have been devastated. At the same time, people in the countryside feel cut off from the cosmopolitanism of the World Wide Web. "These changes and the perceived displacement of traditional social values have caused a sense of resentment among segments of the population in the West, particularly among white men, older people, conservatives and those with less formal qualifications."[33]

Right-wing populists have had surprising success in mobilizing "angry white men" from the working class who feel abandoned by the cosmopolitanism of leftist parties. Some commentators stress general "structural factors like globalization and postindustrialism, value change, and female emancipation." But more probing analysts claim "that the widespread feeling among populist voters that decision makers care little about their interests is actually justified." Empirical data show that working-class voters often abstain from voting since they do not believe that their interests are taken care of. Moreover, "if they vote, members of the working class disproportionately vote for right-wing populist parties." Their interests are less represented in Parliament since leftist parties are more and more concerned with the wishes of white-collar employees. As a result, actual legislation also tends to favor the rich or the middle class. "Given this pattern, the perception that politics is biased against the working class is well founded."[34]

Neo-Marxist rhetoric has failed to mobilize the alienated working class because anti-capitalist promises have not improved its lot. One typical left-wing populist was the Greek minister of economics Yanis Varoufakis, who denied the existence of a debt crisis but sought to persuade the creditors to grant debt relief. He ran on a platform that promised he "would tear up the memoranda, restore salary and pension cuts, roll back tax increases, and demand immediate and total debt forgiveness." More than one-third of the Greek electorate initially responded to the promises of Syriza, which painted "his EU colleagues as cold-blooded predators lacking sensitivity and a spirit of solidarity." But once in office, the leftist movement quickly found out that offending the creditors would not secure their cooperation, forcing the party to renege on its promises. Instead of being just an "innocent victim" of predatory lending, Greece suffered from irresponsible borrowing, "widespread corruption . . . a feeble rule of law . . . and bureaucratic malaise."[35]

Ultimately, the success of populist movements stems from a fusion of economic worries and cultural resentments into racist and sexist phobias. Already in 2010, the right-wing Social Democrat Thilo Sarrazin had articulated racist fears in a book that warned of the Islamization of Germany. While the AfD started as an anti-European party, it achieved its electoral breakthrough by capitalizing on ethnic anxieties about Chancellor Merkel's open door to immigration in 2015. The influx of more than a million Muslim refugees made ordinary folks worry about the security of their jobs, the shift of welfare payments to newcomers, and the loss of cultural cohesion through Islamic fundamentalism. One sexist election poster read: "Burkas? We like Bikinis." Such concerns were strongest in the post-Communist East, where the AfD gathered as many as one-quarter of the votes in regional and national elections. Led by the history teacher Björn Höcke, the radical wing of the party shockingly flirted with neo-Nazi racism by claiming that Germany ought no longer to apologize for its brown past.[36]

Populism has also spread by ingenious use of the media in creating "a parallel universe" of identity politics that is no longer open to rational challenge. Driven by strong emotions, many populist followers reject official newspapers, radio broadcasts, or television programs as the "lying press" when the factual approach to the news disagrees with their preconceptions. Instead, mass tabloids like the *BILD-Zeitung* simplify events, report selectively, and provide entertainment rather than serious reflection. Through the privatization of stations, talk radio also appeals to small listening groups without bothering to check facts since it is intent on creating identity communities through self-approving communication. Moreover, the younger generation turns to the internet as a forum for venting its frustrations, using the new social media and the dark net to fashion fan bases, reaching all the way to racist rants and militant terrorism.[37] Often spreading conspiracy theories, these alternate media also hinder rational decisions by supporting anti-scientific protests against COVID vaccinations.

Suspicion of established politics leads populist supporters to opt for outsiders as new and seemingly more genuine voices of public sentiment. In the UK, Prime Minister Boris Johnson has become popular in the media due to the entertainment value of his tousled mop and Etonian wit rather than the consistency of his political stances. In Italy, the comedian and blogger Beppe Grillo founded the Five Star Movement in 2010 in order to campaign for honesty and direct democracy, criticizing the political class in general. Winning about a third of the electorate, his followers first entered a coalition government with the right-wing Lega Nord but then joined the Democratic Party they had opposed so as to get rid of Salvini. In Ukraine, the populace was so disgusted with the corruption of politicians that it chose the actor Volodymyr Zelensky as president, whose sole qualification was appearing in the role of the Ukrainian president in a popular television series.[38] As a result of such choices, the policies of most populist leaders like former president Trump have been erratic and their results minimal.

Post- or Neo-Democracy?

The liberal media are full of laments about the crisis of liberal democracy, predicting its imminent demise. Many citizens feel buffeted by impersonal forces, such as economic globalization or electronic digitalization, over which they have little or no control. Party politics seems to be a theater played by the political class in the capital, supported by remote media that has little to do with the cares and aspirations of the common folk. Yet time and again, the public mobilizes around causes such as environmental protection in which activists demand immediate action. Inspired by appealing leaders like Greta Thunberg, engaged minorities call for direct representation, bypassing the cumbersome structures of democratic self-government. Emphasizing such negative developments, the British political scientist Colin Crouch has coined the concept of "post-democracy" to predict its decline. However, the German theoretician Klaus von Beyme has countered with the label "neo-democracy" to denote the possibility of increased participation.[39]

The impact of populism on contemporary democracy is therefore ambivalent since it "can work *either* as a threat to *or* a corrective." In weakening dictatorships, popular mobilization can strengthen the process of democratization through public liberalization, regime transition, and constitutional reform. The peaceful revolutions of 1989/90 in East Central Europe are a classic case of the benign effects of contestation from below. But in weak democracies, populism can also hasten the erosion of self-government by diluting civil rights, undercutting representative institutions, and leading to repressive systems that maintain only the shell of democracy while losing its substance. The nationalist regimes of Kaczyński in Warsaw, Orbán in Budapest, and Babiš in Prague that have developed in the wake of disappointments with Western democracy are an example of the dangers of populist degeneration.[40] Dramatized by the Washington insurrection in January 2021, it is this fear of de-democratization in established democracies that the wave of right-wing movements has been inspiring during the last decade.

The fundamental problem of populism is its moral claim to be acting in the name of the people. Drawing on the ideas of Jean-Jacques Rousseau, populists assert that they represent the "general will" of the populace even if they are in the minority, therefore ignoring Montesquieu's reliance on institutional checks and balances. Since such leaders and their followers tend to be dissatisfied with the compromises of the established parties and the cumbersome mechanisms of majority rule, they want to directly implement their understanding of the *volonté generale* without constitutional restraints. "Exactly this is the central danger of the present day: Populists struggle against the complex and contradictory conditions of modernity." According to Paul Nolte, "they long for clear situations and quickly blame what they dislike," such as neoliberal capitalism, European integration, or social liberalism.[41] Their participatory impulse favors a sense of acting in the name of an exclusive people, even if that tramples legal constraints and minority rights.

Combating populism is difficult because democratic politicians also appeal to the people and mass protests are a legitimate form of political participation. Since berating populists does not make them go away, representative democracy has to engage its own broken promises and provide solutions for popular frustrations. Overcoming the alienation between the political elite and the masses necessitates addressing the sources of popular resentment. Closing the growing gap between the winners and losers of globalization requires a correction of neoliberal policies that favor the wealthy. Reducing the fears of metropolitan modernity demands sensitivity to the traditional values that are being displaced by liberal cosmopolitanism. Lessening racist anxieties about immigration from other cultures calls for limitations on accepting migrants and a systematic effort at integration as well as tolerance for different religious practices.[42] There is no magic solution for reducing the allure of populism. Liberal democrats can only try to point out its illusions, dry up its multiple sources, and reinforce democratic institutions.

The unresolved problem that lies beneath the populist challenge is the form of individual participation in mass democracy. The postwar establishment of constitutions, parties, interest groups, and media created an intermediary structure of political representation that proved successful in the boom years. But it failed to cope with disruptions of economic globalization, ecological degradation, cultural postmodernization, and the like that make citizens feel remote and powerless. The emergence of new social movements like environmentalism, feminism, and pacifism challenged the established order from below by developing alternate methods of direct civic mobilization beyond parliamentary representation. Similarly, the mass protests of the peaceful revolution that overthrew Communism in Eastern Europe also suggested new forms of nonviolent protest that revived democratic institutions. The challenge of revitalizing pluralist democracy is therefore to widen civic participation in government without succumbing to pipedreams of authoritarian populism.[43]

12

Global Role

FIGURE 13. World Economic Forum, Davos, Switzerland. Epa.

On January 21, 2020, three thousand members of the World Economic
Forum gathered in Switzerland to discuss the prospects of global business for the coming year. They met in Davos, a picturesque Alpine resort
renowned for its ski slopes, such as the downhill race course Parsenn.
This was the fiftieth meeting of political leaders, business CEOs, academics, and journalists who listened to speeches, socialized in bars, and

sought to make deals with each other. But this year the atmosphere was different since the Swedish schoolgirl Greta Thunberg had succeeded in dramatizing the climate crisis with her youth protests, putting the prevention of further global warming at the top of the agenda. Lambasting the fossil fuel industry, she and her followers called for an immediate end to greenhouse emissions: "Today's business as usual is turning into a crime against humanity."[1] Amplified by the media, the demonstrations of Fridays for Future had refocused the Davos agenda from business profits onto environmental protection.

During the meeting, the new president of the European Commission, Ursula von der Leyen, repeated her action program for a European Green Deal. Warning that "humanity faces an existential threat," she announced: "Our goal is to become the first climate-neutral continent by 2050." At the same time, she reassured the business community by claiming that this was really a growth strategy: "It will cut emissions while also creating jobs and improving our quality of life." In practice, the shift to environmental priorities would require a huge investment of a trillion euros, combining support for "clean energy" with an extension of "emission trading." Europe would become a global leader by cutting carbon pollution and creating green industries. Discovering sustainable solutions would give EU members a "first mover advantage." Even if its implementation might take decades, von der Leyen's bold plan was an attempt at "Europe's response to our people's call."[2]

In contrast, the US president Donald Trump's Davos speech "sharpened his break from the international community" by repudiating the urgency of climate action. Sounding like a campaigner, he cited positive economic statistics such as a soaring stock market and record low unemployment: "Today I am proud to declare that the US is in the midst of an economic boom the likes of which the world has never seen before." Though he endorsed the worldwide goal of planting one trillion trees, he touted the extraction of "traditional fuels," such as coal and gas, which had contributed to global warming. Instead of sharing an emerging concern about climate change, he polemicized: "We must reject the perennial prophets of doom and their predictions of the apocalypse." With this "hymn to [US] nationalism," he rejected international cooperation and placed himself "out of step with the rest of the summit's goals." While business leaders liked his tax cuts, critics maintained that "his politics have been extraordinarily damaging."[3]

The lessons of Davos therefore remained hotly contested between advocates and opponents of drastic changes in environmental policies. The German chancellor Angela Merkel called the limitation of global warming to 1.5 degrees centigrade "a question of survival" and claimed "the world has to act together," with each country making its contribution. The European attempt to reach climate neutrality by 2050 would be "a transformation on a gigantic and historic scale" that would require "new forms of generating wealth." But the German business economist Daniel Stelter countered that "the Davos consensus [was] an illusion." He opposed government mandates of green programs, trusting in the higher efficiency of the market to produce technical innovations. Though global warming was a pressing problem, renewable energy would only prevail if it were financially feasible enough to attract investments. "While the Europeans praised their vision of a Green Deal, outside of Europe it was seen skeptically."[4]

The climate debate exemplifies the special role Europe is currently trying to play in the world. While only a few remnants of its former imperial possessions remain, the old Continent still claims a leadership position on issues such as international trade, self-government, and public health. This aspiration for a greener future has been creating ever more tensions with the United States since Washington has become more self-assertive and nationalist rather than cooperative in recent years. Because the EU is more of an economic giant than a political force, the Europeans themselves have had difficulty defining their own policies, vacillating between cultivating trade profits and supporting human rights. As a collection of nation-states, they favor multilateralism and international organization. But with the stream of migrants, the world is also coming to the Continent, changing its skin colors and religions.[5] What global part can Europe continue to play as a partner of or alternative to the United States?

Transatlantic Divorce

In ending the Cold War, the transatlantic partnership scored impressive successes with complementary actions based on shared liberal values. The careful management of détente by the George H. W. Bush administration made it possible for Mikhail Gorbachev to accept the popular pressure for self-determination of Eastern European client states. The Western example of a free and prosperous life provided Eastern dissidents with a model to emulate. Similarly, Americans and Germans worked as "partners in leadership" during the transformation of the post-Communist countries by including them in Western organizations. While Germany accepted five new states into the Federal Republic, the newly liberated Eastern countries revitalized the institutions of representative democracy. Even the economic transition to a market economy was animated by a shared belief in the efficacy of neoliberal solutions.[6] But within a few years, disagreements in foreign policy, economic priorities, and domestic choices made this cooperation crumble, eroding the transatlantic relationship and dividing it internally as well.

This breakdown has been propelled by a cultural process of drifting apart, based on contradictory interpretations of shared values. Most people on both sides of the Atlantic believe in free elections, a fair judiciary, and unbiased media. But for Americans, freedom means "to pursue life goals without state interference," while Europeans think that the "state guarantees nobody is in need." In the United States, people claim that the path to personal success leads through individual effort, whereas on the Continent folks are more conscious that it also depends "upon forces outside of their control." Many conservative Americans understand security as the right to bear arms in self-defense, but Europeans tend to rely more on resolving conflicts without violence. While in the United States many citizens practice a fundamentalist version of religion, on the Continent the majority of the populace sees itself in a post-Christian age.[7] In these and many other issues, misunderstandings are multiplying because the Cold War generations are passing away, fraying the civil society bonds that underpinned the transatlantic relationship.

As a result of this growing value gap, mutual perceptions of Americans and Europeans have deteriorated during the last decade. While Angela Merkel topped the favorable ratings, Donald Trump was the least popular world leader due to his lack of international cooperation in tariffs and migration. Though the majority of Americans consider transatlantic relations to be good, most Europeans see them as becoming poor. Differences "are especially stark on defense spending and security issues" since many US citizens support the use of military force whereas Europeans prefer peaceful diplomacy. While Washington is proud of its strength, in Brussels it looks militaristic and adventurous, no longer to be trusted. Many conservative Americans fail to understand the project of European integration, whereas among the Continental Left Trump's blustering has inspired a revival of anti-Americanism.[8] Positive European examples still appeal to progressives in the United States and American cultural creativity continues to fascinate the European Left. But these increasing signs of cultural distance are undermining cooperation across the Atlantic.

In many ways, the recent tension between Washington and Brussels has been a classic conflict between American unilateralism and European multilateralism. Trump's "America First" agenda is but the latest version of a tradition of exceptionalism that considers the United States to be different from and superior to the rest of the world. In contrast, the project of European integration is itself an effort to overcome the deadly consequences of nationalism on the Continent. Though American internationalists have founded a set of liberal institutions like the UN, IMF, WTO, and WHO, the conservative part of the public has always been skeptical of their policies, resenting them as a limitation of American sovereignty. While Europeans were initially reluctant to join these transnational efforts, ultimately they have embraced them because they have found out that they could advance their democratic and capitalist values through them. The Continental public is shocked by alt-right efforts to force America to withdraw from institutions like NATO because it sees them as guarantors of peace and prosperity.[9]

These cultural differences have complicated the resolution of conflicting interests and created serious foreign policy disagreements between the United States and the EU. Riding a triumphalist high after the defeat of Communism, Washington considered itself the sole remaining superpower and was ready to make unilateral decisions without consulting its allies. In response to the rising threat of Islamic terrorism, it embarked on a series of regional wars in Iraq and Afghanistan that proved costly and inconclusive. Though willing to help against terrorism, most Europeans were determined to reap the peace dividend after the conclusion of the East-West confrontation, rejected military adventures abroad, and sought to contain terrorist attacks through domestic police measures. They focused instead on reconnecting the Continent by expanding successful Western institutions like NATO or the EU into the East. These contrasting priorities soured the political climate between Washington and Brussels, gradually turning the European unwillingness to follow the American lead into a more fundamental estrangement.[10]

Another typical disagreement between the US penchant for the use of force and the European preference for negotiation has been the dispute about how to stop the Iranian nuclear program. In 2015 the Obama administration and the Europeans had reached an agreement with Tehran that it would stop enriching uranium and developing a military nuclear capability in exchange for the lifting of economic sanctions and the reintegration of the country into international trade. But suspecting that Iran was circumventing the arrangement, President Trump unilaterally withdrew from the agreement while the Europeans sought to rescue its substance, considering an imperfect deal better than no deal at all. Washington thereafter threatened European companies with sanctions if they continued to trade with Tehran, prompting a Continental effort to shield its business from American retaliation. As a result of mutual provocations like Iran's shelling of Saudi oil tankers or the US drone strike that killed General Qasem Suleimani, the Middle East has teetered on the brink of war.[11]

Yet another diplomatic dispute has centered on the appropriate Western response to Vladimir Putin's expansionism into the post-Soviet space. While the Obama administration resorted to economic sanctions after the annexation of Crimea, many Central European partners sought to shield their considerably larger trade with their eastern neighbor, with Berlin continuing to build the Nord Stream Two pipeline. In contrast to conservative anti-Communism during the Cold War, President Trump apparently admired the autocratic style of the Russian president, and enjoyed the help of Russian-sponsored internet trolls during his own campaign. As a result, the American reaction to Moscow's support for separatists in Eastern Ukraine was surprisingly moderate. But the frontline Baltic States and Poland worried more acutely over Russian strong-arm policies that might threaten their independence.[12] The disagreements within the American leadership and the division of the Europeans between pro- and anti-Russian camps have offered Putin ample opportunities for continued brinkmanship.

The question of how to deal with China has been a further bone of contention between the United States and the EU. In recent years, Washington has started to see Beijing as a geostrategic rival and economic competitor, vying for control of Southeast Asia. In contrast, the EU and especially the FRG, have tried to expand their trade with and investment in the huge and growing Chinese market. De-emphasizing disagreements on human rights, Berlin has stressed political stability as a basis for long-term partnership of the two export-oriented economies. As a result of the profit dependency of firms like VW on Chinese sales, the Europeans have grown unwilling to follow American leadership in confrontation, preferring persuasion instead in order to have the Chinese accept WTO trade rules, respect copyright protections, and abandon forced technology transfer. Though the EU is also beginning to see China as "a systemic rival," the difference of interests between Washington and Brussels will continue to hamper a united transatlantic response.[13]

On the one hand, Trump's "Make America Great Again" protectionism has added to tensions with the European Union. The president's resentment against being taken advantage of scuttled the unpopular Transatlantic Trade and Investment Partnership (TTIP) agreement that had been negotiated under the Obama administration. Instead, the Trump government imposed steel and aluminum tariffs in the spring of 2018 in hopes of reviving the domestic industry. The EU retaliated by raising import duties on products such as Harley-Davidson motorcycles and Jack Daniel's whiskey—commodities that would hurt Trump's electoral base. The waging of a trade war with China and the conclusion of a revised trade agreement with Canada and Mexico helped curb further escalation of the tensions with the EU. But Trump kept threatening higher levies on European luxury cars even though many of them were built in American factories and exported from there.[14] This protectionist wave that claimed to revitalize US manufacturing so as to please labor has disrupted trade and investment with America's largest partner, the EU.

On the other hand, European efforts to regulate and tax American tech corporations like Apple and Google have also created transatlantic resentment. One bone of contention was Europe's different approach to privacy protection for data, to which EU members assign a much higher priority than the US public. Another issue was the competitive advantage that Silicon Valley firms had over European rivals by denying access to their platforms, thus provoking the EU to levy antitrust fines of €1.5 billion against Google. A third problem was the huge profits that US firms reaped in Europe by locating their Continental headquarters in Ireland to take advantage of its 12.5 percent corporate tax rate compared to the EU average of 21.9 percent. Apple had to "pay back billions of euros to Ireland" in evaded taxes. In 2017 Google "recorded a profit of 1.2 billion euros on revenue of 32.2 billion euros" while the firm paid merely 167 million euros in European corporate taxes. The French-led EU effort to create a digital-services tax created much ill will in Washington.[15]

The incoming Biden administration faces the challenge of renewing the partnership that has helped pacify the world for decades. Due to Trump's erratic "America First" rhetoric, "the transatlantic relationship is in a worse state . . . than at any other point in recent history." Aside from "serious policy disagreements" on tariffs or defense spending, Trump's aversion to the EU and the liberal world order has created "an unprecedented sense of ideological drift between the transatlantic allies." The "impulsive" and "unpredictable" nature of US leadership and the "frequent mismatch between the president's rhetoric and that of the foreign policy professionals" made dealing with Washington difficult.

Fortunately, President Biden is a convinced Atlanticist whose foreign policy experience will help him repair some of the transatlantic damage. Since he considers the "alliance with Europe as his priority," he is likely to explore common interests in dealing with Russia, Iran, and China. But the frequency and depth of prior disputes points to a deep-seated alienation in attitudes that will be difficult to reverse.[16]

Worldwide Involvement

Often overlooked, the Europeans play a considerable global role as individual countries and as a collective of the EU. Due to the growing tensions with the United States, Europe has been gradually emancipating itself from Washington's tutelage. On the one hand, the larger Continental states like France and Germany have tried to coordinate their own foreign policies, specializing in areas where they had a particular impact. On the other, with the Lisbon Treaty, the EU has developed its own instruments for external relations, such as the European Commission president, the high representative for foreign and security policy, and its own diplomatic service. Though these efforts only work when there is basic agreement, there is little doubt that Brussels is a regional power, having a major voice in the affairs on the Continent. Beyond that, in special areas like trade, the EU has sizable clout. Due to a different interpretation of liberal values, Europe is stepping out of the American shadow, aspiring to be "a global actor, ready to share responsibility for global security."[17]

What makes Europe unusual as an international protagonist is the civilian nature of its power that rejects military means. Just a few years after the end of World War II, the effort by Robert Schuman, Konrad Adenauer, and Alcide de Gasperi to create the European Coal and Steel Community was quite daring since it established collective supervision over the production of war material. A decade later, the Jean Monnet–led initiative of the Common Market sought to make war impossible on the Continent through interweaving the industrial and agrarian economies. The driving engine behind this pacification was the reconciliation of the hereditary enemies France and Germany through youth exchanges, city partnerships, and the like. The economic success of the Common Market rested on an informal condominium of Paris, responsible for political leadership, and Bonn, backing it with economic power.[18] In spite of some quarrels, this cooperation has succeeded in preventing another war on the European Continent and fostered peace beyond it through its positive example.

The EU's most successful policy has been its successive enlargement, which has united almost the entire Continent. In this process, Brussels gradually worked out a series of membership criteria for candidates in order to be accepted in the EU—such as being European and democratic.[19] The enlargement began with Britain and Denmark in the 1970s, stabilized the postdictatorial transition in Greece, Spain, and Portugal during the 1980s, and facilitated the admission of Austria, Sweden, and Finland in the early 1990s. The EU formalized this conditionality in Copenhagen in 1993, requiring a market economy of sufficient promise to be able to reach the EU level as well as a system of self-government stable enough to function. After the fall of Communism, Brussels extended its reach into Eastern Europe, helping its economic and political development. Except for Slovenia and Croatia, this process proved less successful in the Balkans and with Brexit it has been reversed in the UK. But even nonmembers like Switzerland and Norway conform to EU standards for the sake of trade and further applicants want to join.

Countries on the southern shore of the Mediterranean in North Africa could only hope for some special trade treaty since they were considered too different and undemocratic to join the EU. The existing members did not want to accept states with an Islamic culture that lacked a common Christian basis and had economies that would compete directly with their own. As part of France's colonial legacy, President Georges Pompidou launched a North Africa initiative with the Lomé Convention of 1975 in order to maintain trade ties and cultural relations. But the other EU members were less interested in this venture and agricultural lobbyists opposed the direct competition of products like wine from the southern shore of the Mediterranean. Similarly, the problem of Turkish membership could not be resolved since conservatives in the EU did not want to risk the accession of such a populous and culturally different country.[20] President Erdoğan also lost interest, preferring instead to turn Turkey into a leading Islamic state. Finally, Mediterranean issues got caught up in the Middle Eastern wars, dominated by the United States rather than the EU.

Another civilian policy has been foreign aid for economic development or in response to humanitarian crises. Simply put, the EU and its members are "the largest donor in the world," offering more than twice the amount of assistance that the United States does. The chief donors are Germany with €147,328 million, followed by the European Commission with €133,668, Britain with €121,848, and France with €92,238. Smaller countries like Sweden and the Netherlands donate even higher per capita amounts. The funds are disbursed to North African countries and other states such as Turkey, Afghanistan, and India. No doubt, much of the money is tied to trade with the donors. Part of it also disappears into the hands of local elites and does not reach its destination. And metropolitan bureaucracies control the disbursement, insisting on their own ideas of worthwhile projects. Nonetheless, European foreign aid is an effort to share wealth and to help less fortunate developing countries since it goes primarily into civilian projects.[21]

The most powerful lever of Brussels is its trading policy since the EU is a leading export and import bloc with 450 million inhabitants amounting to one-fifth of global trade. From the Common Market on, its stance has been contradictory—supporting free trade among its members and protecting its producers through tariffs to the outside. While duties on industrial goods have remained modest as a result of various General Agreement on Tariffs and Trade (GATT) rounds that abolished trade barriers, agricultural products continue to be heavily subsidized by the CAP to save family farms, leading to dumping of surplus production abroad. The establishment of the Single European Market in 1992 created more internal growth and attracted much foreign investment by the United States, Japan, and China. But the EU played rather a reactive role in the globalization of production and distribution since many of the new developments in digitization came from Silicon Valley while the hardware was produced in Asia. Brussels was able to conclude favorable bilateral trade agreements like the Comprehensive Economic and Trade

Agreement (CETA) with Canada, but the TTIP negotiations ultimately failed due to US neoprotectionism and internal EU resistance.[22]

At a time when Washington was slipping into blustering unilateralism, the Europeans were also the key players in trying to uphold the norms of a liberal international system. Although the United Nations headquarters is located in New York, some of its founding members were European powers like the UK and France that have permanent seats on the Security Council, even if the old Continent was regularly outvoted by more numerous newly independent postcolonial states. In the World Trade Organization, the EU has pushed for fair trade through the maintenance of European standards of pay, health, and environmental protection in order to stop labor exploitation in developing countries like Vietnam by creating a more level economic playing field. Similarly, Europeans have continued to play an important role in the International Monetary Fund and the World Bank through leadership and financial contributions. Since they were too small to go it alone, their states have understood that they need to work through multilateral channels in order to protect their own national interests.[23]

Another important normative dimension of EU external policies is the commitment to human rights and democratization in its trading partners. The Lisbon Treaty made the promotion of these values a significant priority of its new External Action Service. Moreover, Brussels has created a European Instrument for Democracy and Human Rights, supplemented by election observation missions and direct support for human rights defenders. At the same time, the EU has added labor standards and environmental considerations to bilateral trade agreements, using market access as a tool in order to improve conditions in trading partners. Critics nonetheless have complained about a significant "delivery gap" between high-flung human rights rhetoric in Brussels and actual observation of such considerations in trade with authoritarian regimes or dictatorships.[24] Since the EU cannot force democratization outside of its borders, it has only been able to defend individual human rights activists and advocate a gradual liberalization.

Europeans have also played a significant role in peacekeeping missions and efforts at civilian reconstruction, seeking to end regional conflicts. Smaller countries, like Sweden or the Netherlands, have been willing to offer their soldiers as "Blue Helmets" in the United Nations' efforts to separate warring factions. On the ground, it has been difficult to maintain neutrality such as in the civil war in the Congo, which cost the UN secretary general Dag Hammarskjöld his life, or in the massacre of Srebrenica in which the Dutch failed to protect Bosnians from mass murder by Serbian nationalists. But in 2020 the EU supported six military and civilian missions with about five thousand people involved in peacekeeping, conflict prevention, international security, and human rights support. The EU has also started to fund deployment of African forces as credible mediators in local conflicts.[25] For "advancing the causes of peace, reconciliation, democracy and human rights in Europe," the EU was awarded the Nobel Peace Prize in 2012.

Though attractive, soft power alone has not sufficed to deal with the many violent conflicts around the globe. The EU operates from the assumption "that multilateralism, openness and mutuality is the best model not just for our continent, but also for the entire world." But the high commissioner for external and security policy Josep Borrell warned: "We Europeans must adjust our mental maps in order to deal with the world as it is and not as we have hoped it to be." The disastrous course of the Balkan Wars after the breakup of Yugoslavia is one example of friendly persuasion failing to maintain peace unless it is backed by the military force of NATO. Similarly, the Russian annexation of Crimea and the incursion of so-called separatists into Eastern Ukraine is another case in which moral condemnation was not enough and a credible threat of military intervention would have been necessary to stop the Russian aggression. The problem was not missing resources but "lack of political will to combine these power factors" into coherent and capable instruments.[26]

The growing unreliability of the United States as a NATO ally therefore compels the Europeans to develop, in President Emmanuel Macron's words, a more effective "defense culture." Living in the shelter of the American nuclear umbrella has been convenient for NATO members, but Washington's new unilateralism has made this security guarantee problematic. The head of the Munich Security Conference

Wolfgang Ischinger cautions that "the world is getting more dangerous, ranging from classic military security and regional crises to modern dimensions like climate, energy, global health." Due to the "fundamental loss of trust" in the international system, the Europeans have to make greater efforts to defend their own interests. This task requires developing the promising beginnings of the Permanent Structured Cooperation projects (PESCO) into a creditable joint defense force.[27] While the foreign policy community understands the new dangers, it remains to be seen whether the EU can learn to speak with a single voice.

A Distinctive Lifestyle

Europe also exerts some of its soft power through an engaging lifestyle. To the casual traveler, much of Europe looks like it has become thoroughly Americanized. The golden arches of McDonald's can be seen in ancient city squares and other outlets like Starbucks proliferate as well. In the downtowns, global chains offer their homogenized wares while, at the outskirts of towns, huge shopping centers beckon with their internationalized offerings. The streets are full of cars and even SUVs are starting to crowd out traditional sedans in the competition for parking spaces. The popular music that is blaring into the headphones of the young is either from the United States or at least pretends to come from there. At the same time, movie theaters compete in showing the latest Hollywood trash and television programs air American sitcoms. Moreover, garish cigarette advertisements are calling on people to "Go West" or praising the "Marlboro man."[28] To traditionalist critics it seems that the old Continent has turned into a commercial and cultural colony of the United States.

On closer inspection, however, it becomes clear that Europe is still fundamentally different, maintaining a distinctive lifestyle that provides an attractive alternative to Americanization. To begin with, the Continent has a much older high culture than the United States, having developed writing over several thousand years. As the leading destination in the world, "tourist Europe" is replete with ancient castles, inspiring churches, lovely townhouses, and other remnants from the past.

Half-timber houses line cobblestone streets and market squares with statues or fountains, creating a picturesque sense of earlier times. Many architectural gems have been elaborately restored as a sign of local pride and an attraction for tourism. Continental towns are an open air museum of architectural styles, social systems, and religious beliefs. Of course, observant travel writers like Tim Leffel also encounter many signs of violence, such as "the bullet holes in Bosnia and Hercegovina."[29] Taken together, such ensembles create a European connection to the past that contrasts with the hectic American preoccupation with the future.

As a consequence of its ancient pedigree, Europe is much more densely settled than the United States. While there is some overlap between the most crowded American states and the least populous European countries, the population density on the Continent of 300 persons per square mile is 3.7 times as high as the US figure of 81. In contrast to the American preference for large single family homes, two-fifths of Europeans live in apartments, with another quarter in semidetached houses. According to the journalist Joe Pinsker, "US houses are among the biggest—if not *the* biggest—in the world," while European dwellings have remained smaller on average. Due to the greater availability of land, laxer zoning, and higher motorization, there is more urban sprawl through suburbanization in the United States than in the EU since on the Continent it is more expensive as well as bureaucratically difficult to build single family homes. Hence, most Europeans are content with less personal space, which is more sparing in the use of natural resources.[30]

As a result, Europe has developed a more humane kind of urbanism in which people interact more in public spaces. Since the core of Continental cities predates the automobile, folks do much more walking to and from work or as a leisure activity—making them less overweight than in the United States. Moreover, many Europeans of all social strata use tax-subsidized mass transit in order to move about since service is frequent, dependable, clean, and attractive. Because the old inner cities are becoming choked, environmental activists are trying to limit the presence of automobiles in the downtowns with special fees. Foot traffic, cycling, and scooter use bring people into the open, encountering each other on pedestrian streets, in historic squares, or in city parks and encouraging them to sit in outdoor cafés or restaurants. According to the architect Timothy Beatley, the result is a less car-driven "green urbanism" that fosters public interaction and invests in mass transit—a healthier choice in the long run.[31]

In spite of its high population density, Europe is also much less violent than the United States. No doubt, there are urban ghettos, racial tensions, religious differences, and organized crime on the Continent as well. But the journalist Nurith Aizenman shows that among developed countries, US violence is "completely outsized." The murder rate per 100,000 US inhabitants is 5.9 compared to 1.71 among Europeans, making the United States 3.45 times as deadly as the old Continent. Similarly, in gun deaths the United States ranks thirty-first in the world with 3.85 per 100,000 compared to only 0.12 in Germany. On the one hand, this discrepancy can be attributed to much tougher gun control in Europe, licensing weapons and permitting them for hunters or sportsmen only after appropriate instruction. On the other hand, it is the product of the lobbying power of the National Rifle Association (NRA) and a simpleminded gun culture, based on a misreading of the Second Amendment of the US Constitution.[32] With regard to deaths from gun violence, the United States is a third world country while Europe is among the safest places in the world.

Another stark difference between the United States and the EU is in social inequality since "Europe stands out as a positive exception" to its rise. In 1980 the distribution of wealth on both sides of the Atlantic was similar with the top 1 percent earning 10 percent of national income and the bottom half about 20 percent. Four decades later the top 1 percent of Europeans took in 12 percent of income in contrast to 20 percent in the United States, while the poorest received 22 percent in contrast to only 10 percent in America. The economist Lucas Chancel asserts that Europe remains "a global leader in preserving a degree of fairness in the social fabric." The Gini coefficient, which measures the amount of inequality, was around 0.45 for the United States compared to only 0.33 for the EU, with the gap between the two steadily widening. Neoliberal economics and tax breaks have produced growing inequality in the United States while welfare state policies and the rebound of post-Communist economies have attenuated the differences in the EU.[33] As a result of greater equality, Europeans are more content with their material lives.

Similarly, many European countries outperform the United States in most available measures of healthcare delivery. Based on a market mentality, the American system is the costliest among advanced countries since it is driven by clinicians, drug companies, and hospitals with few checks on spending. The European approach rests on a belief in social solidarity, offering basic coverage for everyone through mandatory payroll contributions, augmented by taxes. In most Continental countries, consumers can add on private insurance if they want more extensive protection. The journalist Olga Khazan claims that the United States performs well in "doctor-patient relationships, end-of-life-care, and survival rates after major issues," but badly on "measures of affordability, access, health outcomes, and equality between rich and poor." The European system does "relatively well in terms of outcomes, life expectancy and other critical indicators in comparison to resources consumed." Not surprisingly, most Europeans are happy with the extent and cost of their coverage.[34]

The workday reality of many employees is also more attractive in Europe than in the United States. According to the Finnish academic Ari Harjunmaa, "we could probably have higher salaries in the United States, but our expenses would be much higher in comparison." Due to a stronger trade-union tradition, jobs are more protected since employers cannot hire and fire at will. Working hours are somewhat shorter because coffee breaks and lunch breaks are included in work time rather than added on as unpaid requirement. Moreover, Continental workers have more holidays and time off, ranging from four to six weeks per year, while vacation days in the United States tend to be limited to only two weeks. Similarly, all businesses in Europe have to provide pension benefits to their workers, whereas saving for retirement in the United States tends to be the responsibility of the employee in smaller companies. Finally, health insurance is mandatory for everyone, not just available in better firms.[35] On balance, these advantages make for a higher quality of life for many Europeans.

The American model has set the global standard in education, but the European system also has compensatory strengths. The United States has pioneered all-day schools, which make working easier for women; it has developed comprehensive high schools for everyone; its undergraduate degree, the BA, has been exported to the EU with the Bologna Process; and its research institutions lead the world in Nobel Prizes. But the quality of the instruction is rather uneven between institutions; the different resources of districts make for economic and racial segregation; and much money is spent on entertainment with sports. Critics of comparative costs maintain that "we lose hands down," citing deep class differences. The European system is largely free of charge and more accessible; the quality of education is more uniform; the supervision is public, making the experience more democratic; and in German-speaking countries, vocational schools provide occupational training.[36] Many Americans have great faith in teaching for tests with machines while most Europeans believe in learning problem-solving and foreign languages.

The transatlantic contrast is also considerable in public support for culture. In the United States, market dominance considers government funding "a complete waste of taxpayer money," instead relying on private philanthropy, encouraged by tax deductions. The National Endowment for the Arts can only play a limited role in stimulating projects by offering seed money. Commercialized offerings tend to produce pop culture in music and film, providing entertainment for the masses. In contrast, state support for culture in Europe could almost be called "the fourth pillar of the modern welfare state," since preserving cultural heritage is thought to be a national task. Municipal, state, and national governments offer huge subsidies and the fame of museums, symphony orchestras, operas, and even clubs is a matter of pride. According to the artist Karen Stone, "if you want to sing opera, learn German" since there are more opportunities to perform in Germany or Austria.[37] While the lively US arts scene is struggling financially, the more secure European cultural establishment can count on greater public support.

Ultimately, much of the difference in quality of life revolves around the balance between taxes and services. While statistical comparisons are notoriously difficult due to the variety of levies, most surveys agree that "the US is actually on the bottom end of the scale compared to other developed nations." With taxes consuming only 26 percent of GNP, public services are also poorer than in most European countries where the tax bite is around 40 percent. Many roads and bridges are in disrepair, schools are underfunded, one-fifth of the population lacks health insurance—the list of deficits goes on and on. Individual responsibility for one's own well-being works well when one makes enough money, but "bootstrap narratives" fail when there is too little cash. In contrast, the European Quality of Life Survey for 2016 shows "general progress in . . . quality of life, quality of society and quality of public services."[38] As an innovative superpower, America may be a great place for capitalist winners, but a chastened and peaceful Europe takes better care of those in need.

After Empire

Europe's current global role is both hindered and helped by its imperial legacies since some remnants of its former political domination persist. The process of decolonization after the Second World War was stunning in its speed and completeness, which created a host of newly independent countries that constitute the majority of the UN. Among the former colonial masters, the loss of possessions has left a contradictory welter of largely suppressed emotions, ranging from pride to shame and disappointment. Among the previously colonized peoples, the withdrawal of their lords has created much resentment about prior suffering and exploitation, blaming of Europeans, and demands for repentance as well as restitution. Even various kinds of EU programs or IMF efforts at providing economic aid, political assistance, or occasional military intervention have not been able to repair the damage.[39] Nonetheless, traces of former empires abound, securing the continuation of European influence around the globe.

One set of such ties is economic since corporations from developed countries continue to dominate the terms of trade with the former colonies. Multinational companies like BP with headquarters located in

Europe still organize the extraction of raw materials such as oil or precious metals from the global south. Similarly, agribusiness giants like Nestle maintain plantation economies to produce cotton or cocoa beans, benefiting from cheap indigenous labor. Ostensibly aiding development, much of the foreign aid goes into the coffers of local elites who are interested in maintaining such relationships since they profit from the unequal exchanges. Critics denounce the asymmetry of the trade as a form of neocolonialism that keeps the former colonies in a state of dependency.[40] International organizations and NGOs struggle hard to break this negative cycle by assisting in economic development in order to complement the achievement of political independence.

Another group of connections is social since migration between former metropoles and colonies has created a multicultural mixture of populations. During decolonization, not all Europeans returned to their mother country like the *pied-noirs* from Algeria to France. Wherever they were not dispossessed, like in Zimbabwe, some whites retained their farms and other businesses, remaining part of an economic elite in the independent countries. In the reverse direction, an unanticipated stream of migrants has flowed to Europe, initially composed of subaltern helpers of the colonists like the Harkis to France in order to escape retribution. More recently, many asylum seekers have sought to flee civil wars, religious persecution, or sexual exploitation by moving to Europe while other refugees have tried to escape dire poverty by seizing job opportunities in developed countries.[41] Showing no sign of abating, this migration wave has added new minorities to European countries with different skin colors, food preferences, and religious practices.

Often overlooked is also the global impact of European culture since the "unity in diversity" of its varied manifestations is difficult to grasp. The EU itself has just begun to establish a cultural policy in order to show to its members the common European aspects by annually designating "capitals of culture" and supporting festivals to reinforce a sense of shared heritage. Toward the outside, the leading European languages dominate global communication since English has become the lingua franca that facilitates exchanges in economy, technology, and pop culture. French also remains prominent due to its historic role and *francophonie*, orienting North Africa to Paris, while Spanish is becoming more important as a global tongue as well. The academic scholarship, political media, and popular entertainments that use these languages indirectly perpetuate European influence.[42] Moreover, the hundreds of thousands of foreign students who flock to the Continent also carry aspects of the European model back home.

Although Europe no longer rules the world, it is too early to write off the old Continent as a global player. In truth, the EU is not a military force and may never become a superpower due to its underlying diversity. But Europe's cultural dynamism has made a central contribution to the emergence of the modern world, spreading such values as scientific research around the globe. Moreover, with 450 million prosperous inhabitants, the EU remains one of the top three economic powerhouses and a leading trading bloc with a global reach. At the same time, the Continental lifestyle is so attractive that millions of refugees and economic migrants are desperate to move there, proving that the Europeans must be doing something right. And finally, the EU and its member states are essential defenders of democratic governance and guardians of human rights. While the two World Wars have reduced Europe's power and populism is testing its democracies, the Continent continues to play a constructive role around the globe.

A Progressive Alternative

FIGURE 14. EU Headquarters, Brussels, Belgium. jvdwolf, 123RF.

Thirty years after the overthrow of Communism, Europeans have mixed feelings about the implications of that dramatic event. Conservative commentators have constructed a success narrative that points to many aspects of life that have improved for Europeans, especially in the East. In anniversary speeches, they like to point to the fall of the Berlin Wall as a symbol of the gain of political freedom from the Communist one-party dictatorship. At the same time, they stress the general rise of living standards in the entire Continent that have made the blessings of consumer society available to more citizens. They also emphasize that people in the former Soviet Bloc are happy about the withdrawal of Russian domination that has lifted the Iron Curtain and made it possible to recover their national sovereignty. Most of them are happy about the end of European and German division, which allowed them to "join the West," represented by NATO and the EU at last. During the thirtieth anniversary celebration, the federal president Walter Steinmeier therefore claimed, "We are living today in the best Germany that there has ever been."[1]

Especially on the left, critics view the last three decades as a record of failures instead, emphasizing both the decrepit legacy of Communism and the mistakes of the transition. Since their efforts to find a third way between the ideologies failed, Eastern intellectuals accuse the West of a conspiratorial takeover that has robbed them of the chance to develop their own ideas. Many resent the influx of foreign capital and experts that has dominated the economic transition, creating a new group of business oligarchs. Especially pensioners and women stress the losses in social services and complain about the rise in social inequality since they lack the resources to afford the glitzy consumer goods. In the small towns and the countryside, many people feel threatened by the cosmopolitan liberalism of the West, clinging instead to traditional religious and social values. In the "hearts and minds of people who cannot and will not just abandon their history," the post-Communist period is being told as a story of disappointments.[2]

Scholars have conceptualized these popular narratives in contrasting interpretations that emphasize disparate pieces of evidence. On the one hand, social scientists who have engaged in "transformation research," depart from the assumption that the East wanted to become like the West in a kind of "catch-up modernization." Their studies try to assess the progress toward convergence, focusing on benchmarks of political democratization or economic marketization. They treat current problems as challenges likely to be overcome.[3] On the other hand, critical historians have proposed the notion of a "co-transformation" in order to stress the deleterious impact of neoliberalism that not just transformed the post-Communist East but also created new problems for the liberal democratic West. Cultural critics warn of tendencies toward "illiberal democracy," rising social inequality, and growing xenophobia.[4] Which of these interpretations is ultimately more convincing in capturing European developments since 1989/90?

The Return of the East

A quick review of the last three decades shows that the evidence supports parts of both the critical and optimistic accounts. Triggered by the oil shocks, Western governments faced an ugly stagflation during the 1980s that combined inflation with weak growth. The shift of much manufacturing to Asia deindustrialized entire regions like the British Midlands, the French Northeast, and the German Ruhr Basin. When neo-Keynesian policies of pump-priming no longer worked, neoliberal prescriptions of returning to market competition became popular, cutting back welfare supports just when they were most needed. At the same time, the spread of digitalization made service jobs more precarious by reducing long-term security. Such reverses destabilized trade unions and hurt social democratic parties. But contrary to the leftist warnings of a "delayed crisis of democratic capitalism," the Western system ultimately managed to cope with its multiple problems, whereas it was state socialism that eventually collapsed.[5]

In spite of the strains of globalization, the European model continued to prosper in the West since it gradually adjusted to international competition. Optimistic observers could cite positive trends. Eventually, the recycling of petrodollars restarted economic growth by selling European luxury goods to OPEC elites. The restructuring of the welfare state from living subsidies to job training for enabling a return to work reduced unemployment. Moreover, the progress of European integration brought multiple benefits: the continual rise of living standards improved material conditions; the suspension of border controls speeded travel by abolishing waiting at frontiers; and the introduction of the euro facilitated trade by easing the calculation of international transactions. Since democratic governments found solutions to global challenges, most Western Europeans continued to live free and satisfying lives.[6] Hence, the Western lifestyle exerted a magnetic attraction to many Eastern Europeans who also wanted to enjoy its blessings.

Hastened by such aspirations, the part collapse and part overthrow of Communism ended the ideological confrontation of the Cold War and fundamentally transformed Europe. In the late 1980s, a surprising erosion of confidence among the ruling communist parties opened up space for a revolt from below and prevented the Chinese example of stopping the popular movement by force. On the one hand, various dissidents campaigned for human rights such as freedom of speech and assembly in order to be able to voice their criticism of the regime. On the other hand, workers demanded an improvement in living standards so as to reach Western levels of prosperity. Once Gorbachev had opened the door to free discussion, popular demands became unstoppable and soon transcended the goal of merely reforming Communism. What had started as an effort to salvage the ruling ideology turned into a broader contestation for the return of human rights, initiating a wave of democratization in the East.[7]

This peaceful revolution led to a fundamental reconfiguration of the Continent, lifting the Iron Curtain and creating a Europe "whole and free." In the former Soviet Bloc, the clients became independent nation-states, largely restoring the interwar map. The independence movements of the Baltic countries, Belarus, and Ukraine pushed the Russian state back to its ethnic core, leaving behind some minorities and the district of Kaliningrad. When Moscow pulled back, the Eastern European states were able to reconnect to the West as intellectuals had demanded in championing the concept of *Mitteleuropa*. As a result of regaining national independence, many of the liberated countries were able to join Western institutions like NATO in order to enhance their security. At the same time, they also managed to enter the EU and profit from its economic development programs to increase their prosperity.[8] Only in the former Yugoslavia did the resurgence of nationalism result in a bloody civil war.

The country that profited most from these changes was the Federal Republic of Germany since it was finally able to reunite with its Eastern rival, the German Democratic Republic. Initially, the process of incorporating a separate, post-Communist country created administrative nightmares, imposed heavy costs, and provoked endless discussions. But moving the capital from the Rhenish city of Bonn to the metropolis of Berlin restored a governmental tradition reaching back to Prussia. The united Berlin Republic also signified a shift of the center of gravity of the entire Continent, from the French-speaking West to the German-speaking center. Moreover, the FRG now became the most populous country with the largest economy, increasing its weight in European affairs. Yet seeking not to antagonize its neighbors, the reunited Germany tended to tread carefully, becoming at best "a co-leader" that retained its pacifistic and multilateral stance.[9]

The Eastern European transformation from a planned to a market economy, however, turned out to be more difficult than expected since it took place under the pressure of global competition. Post-Communist policy makers debated whether to follow neoliberal shock therapy and institute drastic changes or to proceed gradually, lifting protections one step at a time. The reintroduction of competitive markets did unleash a founding wave of small businesses and individual farms, spearheaded by people with experience in these trades. But the privatization of large public enterprises demanded more capital and therefore depended on foreign investment. In global competition, Eastern Europe had some advantages of location close to the West, a high level of technical education, and low wages, which enticed a number of Western companies to move production facilities like automobile plants there.[10] In general, countries like Poland that were willing to inflict initial pain did better than states like Romania that protected its outdated industries.

To individual Eastern Europeans, the return of capitalism offered both opportunities and dangers due to the steep initial recession. Astute businessmen with access to funding and political connections made large fortunes, creating a new class of oligarchs populating Western resorts. Also, energetic young people who were willing to go abroad for study or work could gather new know-how and become successful entrepreneurs. But many workers of failing companies faced unemployment at a time when welfare-state provisions were being cut back due to falling tax revenue. Especially women, virtually all of whom had worked under state socialism, lost their jobs since struggling enterprises shed the social auxiliaries like childcare or cultural circles in which they had been employed. The elderly, whose meager pensions did not keep up with inflation, were also hard-hit.[11] The neoliberal economic transition therefore restratified society, creating new winners but also leaving many vulnerable people behind.

As a result of this dislocation, many people lost faith in self-government and turned to an "illiberal democracy," advocated by authoritarian leaders, instead. In the heady rhetoric of the peaceful revolution, it had seemed that the Eastern Europeans were at last embracing Western-style liberal values—but that turned out to be an illusion since the underlying cultural differences remained large. While many young people and intellectuals embraced progressive lifestyles and pluralist politics, most small-town and rural residents were intent on returning to traditional customs and religious values, advocated by the Catholic Church. People feeling threatened by globalization sought refuge in a reassertion of nationalism that would reject the influx of refugees with different skin colors or religious beliefs, even if their actual number remained small. Populist leaders like Viktor Orbán in Hungary, Jarosław Kaczyński in Poland, or Andrej Babiš in the Czech Republic were able to capitalize on such widespread resentment.[12]

The return of the East to Europe has nonetheless inspired some convergence of values on the Continent. A Pew survey a generation after the peaceful revolution showed that "on balance, people across the former Soviet Bloc nations approve of the changeover to a multiparty electoral system and a free market economy." This strong support for "democratic rights, including a fair judiciary, gender equality and free speech," was not just ideological but rather the response of "dramatic increases in the shares of people who say the changes of the past 30 years or so have led to improved living standards." Including Western countries, "life satisfaction has improved across Europe" to a considerable degree. While on many social indicators such as gay rights the East scored lower, dissatisfaction with the practice of democracy also included France, Spain, Italy, and the UK due to the ineptness of their governments. This agreement on basic values and criticism of their performance shows that much has been achieved but much still needs to be done.[13]

Unresolved Challenges

In order to remain viable in the future, the European model has to deal with several fundamental challenges that threaten its survival. Most importantly, the EU needs to integrate beyond intergovernmentalism by facilitating majority decision making in crucial areas such as foreign affairs and fiscal policy. Similarly, Brussels has to do better in enforcing its own laws and regulations so as to defend human rights, sustain democracy, and prevent corruption among some of its new members. The Brexit shock should be a wake-up call for overdue reforms in deepening cooperation since it has demonstrated what would be lost if the EU collapsed. At present, the European Union is caught halfway between a collaboration of independent nation-states and supranational authority in areas like international trade. This asymmetrical deadlock needs to be broken by a "return of politics" and by strengthening shared institutions.[14] It remains to be seen if the new European Commission president Ursula von der Leyen will succeed in rising to this difficult challenge.

Another task is the improvement in European innovation in the face of fierce global competition. According to the World Economic Forum, "the EU tends to perform better than other advanced economies in ensuring inclusive and sustainable solutions." But it also "lags behind in terms of becoming a smarter place" in high tech. The Scandinavian countries manage to combine both imperatives, and Central European states like Germany, Austria, and Holland are engines of export-driven growth in medium-high technology. But the Mediterranean and Eastern European countries have yet to recover from the devastating impact of the Fiscal Crisis of 2008. Having lost the manufacturing of textiles and electronics, much of the EU is also falling behind in the growth of "knowledge-based" technology. In order to retain its high standard of living and extensive safety net, Europe needs to invest more in raising up the lagging countries and in promoting innovative technologies. In short, "Europe must become more competitive."[15]

Yet another unresolved problem concerns European defense since the EU member states remain dominant in this core area of national sovereignty. The Common Security and Defense Policy has made some progress, but it is far from complete due to being overshadowed by the transatlantic relationship of NATO and confronted with the loss of the UK. The US nuclear umbrella remains indispensable since the atomic weapons of France and Britain are too weak and Germany is excluded for historical reasons. So far, national economic rivalries have largely prohibited the development of a common procurement policy. Moreover, efforts at creating a shared military force, such as the Eurocorps and coordination in PESCO, remain underdeveloped. In spite of many attempts, a common command structure has yet to be articulated more fully. Finally, the defense doctrine needs to shift from anti-terror protection and out of area deployment to hybrid capability and cyberwarfare to stop potential Russian aggression.[16]

Other issues like migration have proven similarly intractable since the refugee pressure from the war in Syria has resumed and Europe remains an attractive destination for economic migrants. Disagreement between liberal countries like Sweden and illiberal states like Hungary has so far prevented the shared distribution of refugees demanded by the European Court of Justice. The intensification of the military struggle over the last Syrian rebel cities has unleashed another migration wave. Intent on extorting more money from the EU, Turkey has opened its border, confronting Greece with a new stream of petitioners for asylum. Feeling insufficiently supported by the EU, Athens has created overcrowded refugee camps, intensified sending migrants back to Turkey, and used force to prevent refugees from reaching its shores.[17] Caught between humanitarian impulses and populist xenophobia, Brussels has yet to come up with a policy that is humane and practical beyond paying Ankara more for closing its Syrian border.

Yet another challenge is the implementation of environmental protection in order to combat global warming more effectively. The

European Commission president Ursula von der Leyen's announcement of a European "green deal" is an important step in the right direction because it sets a laudable goal and also promises considerable funding. But first the EU needs to clean up its own backyard by reforming its farm policy, which still eats up 40 percent of the common budget and favors large-scale commercial agriculture, based on machines and fertilizer. At the same time, the transition to renewable energy has to be expanded by having reluctant member states like Poland and France abandon burning dirty coal or using nuclear power generation.[18] Only if the EU itself takes resolute steps, will it also have more success in persuading notorious polluters such as China or the United States to follow its example. The Europeans therefore need to go beyond promising rhetorical appeals and take concrete action to make their system fit for the future.

Finally, Europe has to improve its response to the COVID-19 pandemic in order to show that it is capable of concerted action in an emergency. Though infection figures are difficult to compare, they suggest that the US and EU responded differently to the health emergency. While the epidemic began in Italy and Spain, their radical lockdowns eventually reduced infection numbers to a mere fraction. Though Sweden followed a misguided policy of herd immunity, Germany responded more effectively, generating many fewer fatalities per capita because of more testing, more contact tracing, and a sufficient number of intensive care beds, facilitated by universal health insurance. Another reason for a better outcome has been a higher level of trust in the "rational decision making" of the government. While in the winter of 2021 the United States faced a disastrous third wave due to its irresponsible leadership, with over 550,000 patients dead, Europe was still confronting a second wave since its relative success during the previous summer had led to premature pressure for reopening. Though its population is larger than the US, the Continent has seen proportionally fewer cases and less loss of life due to more rigorous lockdowns.[19]

In the vaccination effort, the Europeans have, however, fallen behind. The transatlantic cooperation between the US and the EU to develop and distribute COVID vaccines has been a "small miracle" due to its astounding speed. The first to receive emergency authorization was the

German-American collaboration of the developer BioNTech and the distributor Pfizer; the second to be approved was the US product Moderna, financed by Operation Warp Speed; and the third was the British serum of AstraZeneca from Oxford. In the US and the UK, vaccinations started earlier and immunized more people than on the Continent, since the number of infections per capita was considerably higher. But in the EU the central review took longer and national bureaucracies slowed down the distribution. While European countries like Germany continued to implement a rigorous "contact limitation" so as to reduce the spread of the infections, the American response emphasized "a national effort" of vaccinations to stem the disease.[20] Ultimately, both the behavioral and medical forms of prevention appeared necessary to win the public health battle.

The European reaction to the accompanying economic downturn was however more effective than the American response. In the severe recession, over forty million workers in the United States lost their jobs, becoming dependent on local charities until Congress approved a massive 1.9 trillion American Rescue Plan to jump-start the economy. In France and Germany, the unemployment rate remained lower, since companies retained more employees by putting them on short-time work that was subsidized by the government. Though the frugal EU members opposed outright grants, Merkel and Macron eventually "agreed to back the idea of collective European debt to help those countries that have been hit hardest by the pandemic." The creation of a common recovery fund of €750 billion broke with German and Dutch opposition to EU borrowing by issuing pandemic bonds. Though in vaccinating member states tried to go it alone, the final agreement on a new budget of more than €1 trillion was a "hugely symbolic demonstration of solidarity" that might constitute "a major step toward a more unified Europe."[21]

Progressive Choices

In September 2019, the European Commission proposal to create a new vice president "to protect our European Way of Life" created an uproar in the European Parliament. Liberal Europeans called the initiative "an abomination," while von der Leyen replied, "The European way of life is built around solidarity, peace of mind and security." Part of the problem stemmed from the fact that "even Europeans don't agree on what the 'European way of life' is." But Article 2 of the Lisbon Treaty clearly states that "being European means peace, freedom, equality, democracy and respect for human dignity."[22] While there was some disagreement on gay rights or treatment of immigration, statisticians were able to find common patterns in daily life like the use of public transportation that made the Continental lifestyle more egalitarian, healthy, ecological, and nonviolent than its American counterpart.[23] In spite of some unresolved problems, the best practices of this European way of life are therefore exemplars of progressive politics.

As a result, the European model is the only serious alternative to the Anglo-American way of life. By embracing neoliberalism, populism, and unilateralism the United States and less so the UK have increased social inequality, curtailed the rights of participation, and heightened global conflicts. Trump's and Johnson's disparagement of Europe is fueled by fear that the Continent is providing a better quality of life than their own overblown rhetoric claims. In truth, the Mediterranean and Eastern European countries still have a considerable way to go in order to catch up to the EU's standard in prosperity, self-government, and cooperation. But Scandinavian and Western European states have already produced a way of life that is well-to-do, peaceful, and democratic. Nine of the top twelve countries in the Social Progress Index are European while the United States has dropped precipitously during the recent past![24] Progressives who are frustrated with the deficiencies of the Anglo-American system have to look no further for potential solutions to many of their own problems.

The Europeans and Americans should therefore help each other to live up to their shared social, political, and cosmopolitan values. To begin with, they ought to reject the temptations of neoliberalism in order to reinvigorate the social solidarity of the welfare state. Moreover, they should resist the lure of populism in order to develop a form of participatory self-government appropriate to the present media age. Finally, they had better refrain from xenophobia in order to maintain a multicultural diversity, reopen the borders closed by the COVID-19 pandemic, and develop an immigration policy. On both sides of the Atlantic, many members of the younger generation are already searching for a new progressivism that would embrace gender equality, ecological consciousness, and tolerance for diversity. For them, neither the traditional Marxist nor the current neoliberal prescriptions are valid guides to the future.[25] Only a renewed transatlantic dialogue between the Biden administration and a reformed EU can produce a roadmap for what might replace them.

ACKNOWLEDGMENTS

Since books are products of intellectual exchanges, I would like to acknowledge a few of the intellectual debts for this book. Most importantly, my colleagues in the Center for European Studies, including Lisbeth Hooge, Katie Lindner, Gary Marks, and John Stephens, have supported European topics at the University of North Carolina at Chapel Hill. Christian Ostermann of the Woodrow Wilson Center for International Scholars also helped by setting up a manuscript review workshop in which Jackson Janes, Arpad von Klimo, Sonya Michel, and Samuel Wells commented on the draft. Moreover, Roger Cohen from the *New York Times* supported its arguments in a public lecture. For the past few decades, Karin Goihl has also hosted interesting US dissertation work in the Berlin Program for German and European Studies. The European History Portal of clio-online, chaired by Hannes Siegrist and supported by Rüdiger Hohls, was another source of inspiration.

Many colleagues read parts of the manuscript and commented on them, helping keep the project on track. For extensive reactions, I am indebted to Björn Dämpfling, Björn Hennings, Hartmut Kaelble, Klaus Larres, Christiane Lemke, Paul Nolte, Kiran Klaus Patel, Susan Pennybacker, and Helga Welsh, just to name a few. Moreover, the Department of History at the University of North Carolina has facilitated my writing through a research and study leave. Max Lazar also helped with the pre-editing of the manuscript, and Michael Skalski prepared the index. Brigitta van Rheinberg and Eric Crahan of Princeton University Press were willing to take on a somewhat unusual project for a historian. Finally, during over five decades of teaching, dozens of graduate students have with their questions kept Europe alive as a problematic subject.

NOTES

In order to keep the notes short, they either refer to quotations and sources of information or they suggest articles and books for further reading.

Introduction: The European Puzzle

1. M. Emmanuel Macron, "Initiative for Europe," September 26, 2017, https://international .blogs.ouest-france.fr/archive/2017/09/29/macron-sorbonne-verbatim-europe-18583.html; Pierre Briançon, "Five Takeaways from Macron's Big Speech on Europe's Future," *Politico*, September 26, 2017.

2. Tony Barber, "Boris Johnson, Hungary and Rightwing European Populism," *Financial Times*, January 7, 2020.

3. Nicholas Kristof, "Why Is Europe a Dirty Word?," *New York Times*, January 14, 2012; Mitt Romney, "European Socialist Policies Not Right for US," *Telegraph*, September 23, 2011; David Frum, "Trump's Plan to End Europe," *Atlantic*, May 2017.

4. Jeremy Rifkin, *The European Dream: How Europe's Vision of the Future Is Quietly Eclipsing the American Dream* (New York, 2004).

5. Douglas Murray, *The Strange Death of Europe: Immigration, Identity, Islam* (London, 2017); Claus Offe, *Europe Entrapped* (Cambridge, 2015); Ivan Krastev, *After Europe* (Philadelphia, 2017).

6. William Drozdiak, *Fractured Continent: Europe's Crises and the Fate of the West* (New York, 2017); Timothy Garton Ash, "Is Europe Disintegrating?," *New York Review of Books*, January 19, 2017.

7. Konrad H. Jarausch, "Contemporary History as Transatlantic Project: Autobiographical Reflections on the German Problem, 1960–2010," *Historical Social Research*, supplement no. 24 (2012), 7–49.

8. Konrad H. Jarausch, *Out of Ashes: A New History of Europe in the Twentieth Century* (Princeton, NJ, 2015).

9. Konrad H. Jarausch, "Rivalen der Moderne: Amerika und Deutschland im 20. Jahrhundert," in Volker Benkert, ed., *Feinde, Freunde, Fremde? Deutsche Perespektiven auf die USA* (Baden-Baden, 2018), 21–38.

10. Sonia Alonso, John Keane, and Wolfgang Merkel, eds., *The Future of Representative Democracy* (Cambridge, 2011); Selen A. Ercan and Jean-Paul Gagnon, "The Crisis of Democracy: Which Crisis? Which Democracy?," *Democratic Theory* 1 (2014), 1–10.

11. Christopher Hill, "The Capability-Expectations Gap, or Conceptualizing Europe's International Role," *Journal of Common Market Studies* 31 (1993), 5–38.

12. Mel Cousins, *European Welfare States: Comparative Perspectives* (London, 2005); Rune Ervik, Nanna Kildal, and Even Nilssen, eds., *New Contractualism in European Welfare State Policies* (Farnham, UK, 2015).

13. Thomas L. Friedman, "Biden, Not Bernie, Is the True Scandinavian," *New York Times*, March 11, 2020; Nicholas Kristof, "We're No. 28! And Dropping!," *New York Times*, September 10, 2020.

14. Thomas Lindenberger and Martin Sabrow, eds., *German Zeitgeschichte: Konturen eines Forschungsfeldes* (Göttingen, 2016).

15. Andreas Wirsching, *Der Preis der Freiheit: Geschichte Europas in unserer Zeit* (Munich, 2012); Andreas Rödder, *21.0: Eine kurze Geschichte der Gegenwart* (Munich, 2015).

16. Konrad H. Jarausch, *The Rush to German Unity* (New York, 1994).

17. Philipp Ther, *Die neue Ordnung auf dem alten Kontinent: Eine Geschichte des neoliberalen Europa* (Berlin, 2014).

18. Kiran Klaus Patel, *Projekt Europa: Eine kritische Geschichte* (Munich, 2018).

19. Desmond Dinan, *Ever Closer Union: An Introduction to European Integration*, 4th ed. (Boulder, CO, 2010).

20. Joseph E. Stiglitz, *The Euro: How a Common Currency Threatens Europe* (New York, 2016).

21. Cornelia Wilhelm, ed., *Migration Memory and Diversity: Germany from 1945 to the Present* (New York, 2017).

22. Lee McGowan, *Preparing for Brexit: Actors, Negotiations and Consequences* (Cham, 2018).

23. James Kirchik, *The End of Europe* (New Haven, CT, 2017). Cf. Heinrich August Winkler, *Zerbricht der Westen? Über die gegenwärtige Krise in Europa und Amerika*, 2nd ed. (Munich, 2017).

24. Anthony J. Nicholls, *Freedom with Responsibility: The Social Market Economy in Germany, 1918–1963* (Oxford, 1994).

25. José Antonio Ocampo and Joseph E. Stiglitz, eds., *The Welfare State Revisited* (New York, 2018).

26. Stephen Milder, *Greening Democracy: The Anti-Nuclear Movement and Political Environmentalism in Germany and Beyond, 1968–1983* (Cambridge, 2017).

27. M. Emmanuel Macron, "Transcription du discours du Président de la République au Parlement européen," April 17, 2018, https://www.elysee.fr/emmanuel-macron/2018/04/17/speech-by-emmanuel-macron-president-of-the-republic-at-european-parliament.en.

28. Timothy Snyder, *The Road to Unfreedom: Russia, Europe, America* (New York, 2018).

29. Jan-Werner Müller, *What Is Populism?* (State College, PA, 2016).

30. Konrad H. Jarausch, "Drifting Apart: Cultural Dimensions of Transatlantic Estrangement," in Hermann Kurthen, Antonio Menendez, and Stefan Immerfall, eds., *Safeguarding German-American Relations in the New Century: Understanding and Accepting Mutual Differences* (Lanham, MD, 2006), 19–34.

31. Winfried Eberhard and Christian Lübke, eds., *Die Vielfalt Europas: Identitäten und Räume*, 2 vols. (Leipzig, 2009).

32. For the origin of the concept, see Daniel T. Rodgers, "In Search of Progressivism," *Reviews in American History* 10 (1982), 113–31.

33. Mark Gilbert, "Narrating the Process: Questioning the Progressive Story of European Integration," *Journal of Common Market Studies* 46 (2008), 641–62, versus Andrea Mork and Perikles Christodoulou, eds., *Creating the House of European History* (Luxembourg, 2018).

34. Ulrike Guerot, Robert Menasse, and Milo Rau, "Manifesto" of the European Balcony Project, November 10, 2018, https://europeanbalconyproject.eu/en/manifesto.

35. Steven Hill, *Europe's Promise: Why the European Way Is the Best Hope in an Insecure Age* (Berkeley, CA, 2010).

36. Timothy Garton Ash, *Free World: America, Europe, and the Surprising Future of the West* (New York, 2004).

37. Christof Mauch and Kiran K. Patel, eds., *The United States and Germany during the Twentieth Century: Competition and Convergence* (New York, 2010).

38. Timothy Snyder, *On Tyranny: Twenty Lessons from the Twentieth Century* (New York, 2017). Cf. Anne Applebaum, "A Warning from Europe: The Worst Is Yet to Come," *Atlantic*, October 2018.

39. Tony Judt, *Ill Fares the Land* (New York, 2010); Bob Woodward, *Fear: Trump in the White House* (New York, 2018).

Chapter 1. Peaceful Revolution

1. Thomas Roser, "DDR-Massenflucht: Ein Picknick hebt die Welt aus den Angeln," *Die Presse*, August 16, 2014.

2. Flyer, "Paneuropäisches Picknick in Sopron am Ort des 'Eisernen Vorhangs'"; Laszlo Nagy, "Das Paneuropäische Picknick und die Grenzöffnung am 11. September 1989," *Potsdamer Bulletin für Zeithistorische Studien*, nos. 23/24 (2001), 24–40.

3. Gyula Horn, *Freiheit, die ich meine: Erinnerungen des ungarischen Außenministers, der den Eisernen Vorhang öffnete* (Hamburg, 1991).

4. Hans-Dietrich Genscher and Karel Vodicka, *Zündfunke Prag: Wie 1989 der Mut zur Freiheit die Geschichte veränderte* (Munich, 2014). Cf. Karel Vodicka, *Die Prager Botschaftsflüchtlinge 1989* (Göttingen, 2014).

5. Vladimir Tismaneanu and Bogdan Jacob, eds., *The End and the Beginning: The Revolutions of 1989 and the Resurgence of History* (Budapest, 2012).

6. Sigrid Meuschel, *Legitimation und Parteiherrschaft: Zum Paradox von Stabilität und Revolution in der DDR, 1945–1989* (Frankfurt, 1992); Mary Fulbrook, *The People's State: East German Society from Hitler to Honecker* (New Haven, CT, 2005).

7. Mikhail Gorbachev, *Memoirs* (New York, 1996); Vladislav Zubok, *A Failed Empire: The Soviet Union in the Cold War from Stalin to Gorbachev* (Chapel Hill, NC, 2007).

8. Padraic Kenney, *A Carnival of Revolution: Central Europe 1989* (Princeton, NJ, 2002).

9. Bela Kiraly, *Lawful Revolution in Hungary, 1989–94* (Boulder, CO, 1995).

10. Michael Lemke, *Vor der Mauer: Berlin in der Ost-West-Konkurrenz 1948 bis 1961* (Cologne, 2011); Lorn Hillaker, "Presenting a Better Germany: Competing Cultural Diplomacies between East and West Germany, 1949–1990" (PhD diss., University of North Carolina at Chapel Hill, 2019).

11. Hope Harrison, *Driving the Soviets Up the Wall: Soviet-East German Relations, 1953–1961* (Princeton, NJ, 2005).

12. Konrad H. Jarausch, *The Rush to German Unity* (New York, 1994); Ilko-Sascha Kowal-czuk, *Endspiel: Die Revolution von 1989 in der DDR* (Munich, 2009).

13. Hans-Hermann Hertle, *Der Fall der Mauer: Die unbeabsichtigte Selbstauflösung des SED-Staates* (Opladen, 1996).

14. Timothy Garton Ash, *The Magic Lantern: The Revolution of '89, Witnessed in Warsaw, Budapest, Berlin and Prague* (New York, 1990); Michael Andrew Kukral, *Prague 1989: Theater of Revolution* (New York, 1997).

15. Venelin Ganev, *Preying on the State: The Transformation of Bulgaria after 1989* (Ithaca, NY, 2013).

16. Vladimir Tismaneanu and Marius Stan, *Romania Confronts Its Communist Past: Democracy, Memory, and Moral Justice* (New York, 2018).

17. Ash, *Magic Lantern*, 134ff.; Clemens Vollnhals, ed., *Jahre des Umbruchs: Friedliche Revolution in der DDR und Transition in Ostmitteleuropa* (Göttingen, 2011).

18. Stephen Kotkin, *Uncivil Society: 1989 and the Implosion of the Communist Establishment* (New York, 2009) versus Michael Richter, *Die friedliche Revolution: Aufbruch zur Demokratie in Sachsen 1989–90*, 2 vols. (Göttingen, 2009).

19. Mabel Berezin and Martin Schain, eds., *Europe Without Borders: Remapping Territory, Citizenship, and Identity in a Transnational Age* (Baltimore, 2003).

20. Andreas Rödder, *Deutschland einig Vaterland: Die Geschichte der Wiedervereinigung* (Munich, 2009).

21. Frederic Bozo, Andreas Rödder, and Mary Sarottee, eds., *German Reunification: A Multinational History* (London, 2017). Cf. the papers of the Two-Plus-Four Conference in Berlin, October 5–6, 2020, https://www.ifz-muenchen.de/en/events/event/datum////dreissig-jahre-zwei-plus-vier-vertrag/.

22. Anatol Lieven, *The Baltic Revolution: Estonia, Latvia, Lithuania and the Path to Independence* (New Haven, CT, 1999).

23. Timothy Snyder, *Bloodlands: Europe between Hitler and Stalin* (New York, 2010); Taras Kuzio, *Ukraine: Perestroika to Independence* (New York, 2000).

24. Patricia Levy and Michael Spilling, *Belarus* (New York, 2009).

25. Ronald Suny, *Revenge of the Past: Nationalism, Revolution and the Collapse of the Soviet Union* (Stanford, CA, 1993).

26. Leon Aron, *Boris Yeltsin: A Revolutionary Life* (New York, 2000).

27. Alexander Dallin, "Causes of the Collapse of the USSR," *Post-Soviet Affairs* 8 (1992), 279–302; Stephen Cohen, "Was the Soviet System Reformable?," *Slavic Review* 63 (2017), 459–88.

28. Stefan Wolle, *Die heile Welt der Diktatur: Alltag und Herrschaft in der DDR 1971–1989* (Berlin, 1996).

29. Konrad H. Jarausch, *Out of Ashes: A New History of Europe in the Twentieth Century* (Princeton, NJ, 2015).

30. Erich Honecker cited in *Neues Deutschland*, January 20, 1989. Cf. Kenney, *Carnival of Revolution*, 274ff.

31. Danken.feiern.beten, "Gott der Geschichte," https://www.3-oktober.de/30-jahre-deutsche-einheit.html; Kerstin Brückweh, Clemens Villinger, and Kathrin Zöller, eds., *Die lange Geschichte der "Wende": Geschichtswissenschaft im Dialog* (Berlin, 2020), 67–84.

32. Kieran Williams, *Václav Havel* (London, 2016); Gary Bruce, *The Firm: The Inside Story of the Stasi* (Oxford, 2010).

33. Klaus Hübschmann, *Trotzdem—(m)ein pralles Leben in der DDR* (Berlin, 2015); Nora Sefa, "Die ganze Welt schaut auf uns . . . ," *FAZ.NET*, October 3, 2019.

34. Alfred Kosing, *Innenansichten als Zeitzeugnisse: Philosophie und Politik in der DDR: Erinnerungen und Reflexionen* (Berlin, 2008). Cf. Rainer Eckert and Bernd Faulenbach, eds., *Halbherziger Revisionismus: Zum postkommunistischen Geschichtsbild* (Munich, 1996).

35. Jens Hacker, *Deutsche Irrtümer: Schönfärber und Helfershelfer der SED-Diktatur im Westen* (Berlin, 1992) versus Heinrich Potthoff, *Die 'Koalition der Vernunft': Deutschlandpolitik in den 80er Jahren* (Munich, 1995).

36. Ellen Schrecker, *Cold War Triumphalism: The Misuse of History after the Fall of Communism* (New York, 2004).

37. Francis Fukuyama, *The End of History and the Last Man* (New York, 1992); R. Bruce McColm, *Freedom in the World: Political Rights and Civil Liberties, 1989–1990* (Washington, DC, 1990).

38. Jan Zielonka, ed., *Democratic Consolidation in Eastern Europe* (Oxford, 2001).

39. Robert Skidelsky, ed., *Russia's Stormy Path to Reform* (London, 1995).

40. Stephen White, *Russia's New Politics: The Management of a Postcommunist Society* (Cambridge, 2000); Peter Eltsov, *The Long Telegram 2.0: A Neo-Kennanite Approach to Russia* (Lanham, MD, 2020).

41. Jana Hensel, "Laßt die Party ausfallen," *Die Zeit*, February 10, 2020; Charles S. Maier, *Dissolution: The Crisis of Communism and the End of East Germany* (Princeton, NJ, 1997).

42. President George Bush, "A Europe Whole and Free," May 31, 1989, http://usa.usembassy.de/etexts/ga6-890531.htm; Hans-Joachim Maaz, *Der Gefühlsstau: Ein Psychogramm der DDR* (Berlin, 1990).

43. Joachim von Puttkamer, Włodzimierz Borodziej, and Stanislav Holubec, eds., *From Revolution to Uncertainty: The Year 1990 in Central and Eastern Europe* (London, 2019).

44. Adam Roberts and Timothy Garton Ash, *Civil Resistance and Power Politics: The Experience of Nonviolent Action from Gandhi to the Present* (Oxford, 2009).

45. Jack A. Goldstone, "Rethinking Revolutions: Integrating Origins, Processes and Outcomes," *Comparative Studies of South Asia, Africa and the Middle East* 29 (2009), 18–32.

46. Valerie Bunce, *Subversive Institutions: The Design and the Destruction of Socialism and the State* (Cambridge, 1999).

47. Thomas Großmann, *Fernsehen, Revolution und das Ende der DDR* (Göttingen, 2015); Horn, *Freiheit*, 328.

48. George Lawson, *Negotiated Revolutions: The Czech Republic, South Africa and Chile* (London, 2004).

Chapter 2. Post-Communist Transformation

1. Bernhard Kislig, "Milliardärin bringt Kunst ins Engadin," *Berner Zeitung*, July 22, 2017; "Stary Browar—Ein Shopping Center voller Widersprüche," *Anlegen in Immobilien*, September 4, 2017.

2. Luiza Oleszczuk, "Poland's Richest Man and Legendary Investor Jan Kulczyk Dead at 65," *Forbes*, July 29, 2015; "Polen Nimmt Abschied: Sumpfland-Midas," *Radiodienst.pl*, September 3, 2015.

3. Adam Michnik, *Letters from Freedom: Post-Cold War Realities and Perspectives*, ed. Irena Grudzinska-Gross (Berkeley, CA, 1998), 117ff.

4. Leszek Balcerowicz, "Poland Must Stick to Winning Formula," *Financial Times*, June 3, 2014; Jeff Madrick, "Poland's 'Big Bang': Too Much Too Fast?," *New York Times*, May 20, 1990.

5. Philipp Ther, *Die neue Ordnung auf dem alten Kontinent: Eine Geschichte des neoliberalen Europa* (Berlin, 2014); John Connelly, *From Peoples into Nations: A History of Eastern Europe* (Princeton, NJ, 2020).

6. Norman Davies, *God's Playground: A History of Poland*, rev. ed. (New York, 2005).

7. Ben Slay, *The Polish Economy: Crisis, Reform and Transformation* (Princeton, NJ, 1994).

8. Lawrence Goodwyn, *Breaking the Barrier: The Rise of Solidarity in Poland* (New York, 1991); Maciej Bartkowski, "Poland's Solidarity Movement, 1980–1989," International Center on Nonviolent Conflict (2009).

9. Marek Jan Chodakiewicz, John Radzilowski, and Dariusz Tołczyk, eds., *Poland's Transformation: A Work in Progress* (Charlottesville, VA, 2003).

10. Leszek Balcerowicz, *Post-Communist Transition: Some Lessons* (London, 2002).

11. "Report for Selected Countries and Subjects," www.imf.org. Cf. Slay, *Polish Economy*, 86ff.

12. Zenon Wiśniewski, ed., *The Polish Economy on the Road to the European Union* (Toruń, 2003).

13. Jane Perlez, "Poland's New Entrepreneurs Push the Economy Ahead," *New York Times*, June 20, 1993.

14. "Poland: The Failure of Success," *New York Times*, September 23, 1993. Cf. Martin Myant and Terry Cox, eds., *Reinventing Poland: Economic and Political Transformation and Evolving National Identity* (London, 2008).

15. Rick Lyman, "With Robust Economy, Poland Navigates around Eastern Europe's Strains," *New York Times*, October 5, 2014; Balcerowicz, *Post-Communist Transition*, 14.

16. Tadeusz Kowalik, *From Solidarity to Sellout: The Restoration of Capitalism in Poland* (New York, 2011).

17. Wolfgang Merkel, "Plausible Theory, Unexpected Result: The Rapid Democratic Consolidation in Central and Eastern Europe," in Elisabeth Bakke and Ingo Peters, eds., *Twenty Years since the Fall of the Berlin Wall: Transitions, State Break-Up and Democratic Politics in Central Europe and Germany* (Berlin, 2011).

18. Konrad H. Jarausch, *The Rush to German Unity* (New York, 1994); Andreas Rödder, *Deutschland einig Vaterland: Die Geschichte der Wiedervereinigung* (Munich, 2009).

19. Konrad H. Jarausch, ed., *United Germany: Debating Processes and Prospects* (New York, 2013), 83–132; Philipp Ther, *Das andere Ende der Geschichte: Über die Große Transformation* (Berlin, 2020), 72–96.

20. Jack Reardon, "An Assessment of the Transition to a Market Economy in the Baltic Republics," *Journal of Economic Issues* 30 (1996), 629–38. Estonia was the most successful country of the three.

21. Colin Jones, "Czech Republic: Klaus Gets the Hard Seat," *Financial Times Business Limited*, September 1, 1996; Libor Zidek, *From Central Planning to the Market: The Transformation of the Czech Economy, 1989–2004* (New York, 2017).

22. Arpad von Klimo, *Hungary since 1945* (Abingdon, Oxon, 2018), 189–203. Cf. Ivan T. Berend, *Central and Eastern Europe, 1944–1993: Detour from the Periphery to the Periphery* (Cambridge, 1996).

23. Balcerowicz, *Post-Communist Transition*, 35ff.; Zidek, *From Central Planning to the Market*, 437.

24. Michael Alexeev and Shlomo Weber, eds., *The Oxford Handbook of the Russian Economy* (New York, 2013); Torbjörn Becker and Susanne Oxenstierna, eds., *The Russian Economy under Putin* (London, 2018).

25. Bertelsmann Transformation Index, nos. 152 and 153, http://bti2003.bertelsmann -transformation-index.de/152.0.html?&L=1, http://bti2003.bertelsmann-transformation-index .de/153.0.html?&L=1.

26. Taras Kuzio, ed., *Contemporary Ukraine: Dynamics of Post-Soviet Transformation* (Armonk, NY, 1998).

27. Jim Seroka and Vukašin Pavlović, eds., *The Tragedy of Yugoslavia: The Failure of Democratic Transformation* (London, 2015); Charles Ingrao and Thomas A. Emmert, eds., *Confronting the Yugoslav Controversies: A Scholars' Initiative* (West Lafayette, IN, 2009).

28. David A. Dyker, *Catching Up and Falling Behind: Post-Communist Transformation in His- torical Perspective* (London, 2004).

29. Ari Shapiro, "'Dancing Bears' Offers a Look into How Countries Adapted to Life after Communism," *NPR*, March 6, 2018. Cf. Slavenka Drakulić, *Café Europa: Life after Communism* (New York, 1997).

30. Adam Michnik, "Grey Is Beautiful: A Letter to Ira Katznelson," in *Letters from Freedom*, 317ff.; Robin Shepherd, "Why Plato Can't Run the Republic: Can Intellectuals Ever Be Politi- cians?," *New Statesman*, July 9, 2001.

31. Jane Perlez, "Poland's New Entrepreneurs Push the Economy Ahead," *New York Times*, June 20, 1993; Carter Dougherty, "Strong Economy and Labor Shortages Are Luring Polish Immigrants Back Home," *New York Times*, June 26, 2008.

32. "Contentment in a Post-Communist Society: Letter from Poland," *Guardian Weekly*, November 18, 2005; Leah Vatlin-Erwin, "The First Full Shelves: Grocery Shopping and Polish Pursuits of Normality after Communism" (master's thesis, University of North Carolina at Cha- pel Hill, 2018).

33. Henry Foy, "Young Rebels with a Cause Take on Region's Ageing Political Elite," *Finan- cial Times*, November 12, 2004; Jana Hensel, *After the Wall: Confessions from an East German Childhood* (New York, 2004). Cf. Volker Benkert, *Glückskinder der Einheit? Lebenswege der um 1970 in der DDR Geborenen* (Berlin, 2017).

34. Tina Rosenberg, "New Democracies, Old Wounds," *Foreign Affairs*, Spring 1995; Lavinia Stan, ed., *Post-Communist Transitional Justice: Lessons from Twenty-Five Years of Experience* (New York, 2015).

35. James Cox, "East Europe's Next Test: Capitalism Going through Growing Pains," *USA Today*, November 7, 1994; Ariane Tichit, "Analyse des divergences de chômage entre les pays en transition post-communistes," *Revue d'études comparatives Est-Ouest* 31, no. 4 (2000), 99–122.

36. Slavenka Drakulić, "How Women Survived Post-Communism (and Didn't Laugh)," *Eurozine*, June 5, 2015; Helen Frink, *Women after Communism: The East German Experience* (Lan- ham, MD, 2001).

37. Ivan T. Berend, *From the Soviet Bloc to the European Union: The Economic and Social Transformation of Eastern Europe since 1973* (Cambridge, 2009), 177–204.

38. Cox, "East Europe's Next Test"; Craig Whitney, "Eastern Europe, Post-Communism: Five Years Later," *New York Times*, September 30, 1994.

39. Whitney, "Eastern Europe"; Richard Rose and Christian Haerpfer, "Mass Response to Transformation in Post-Communist Societies," *Europe-Asia Studies* 46 (1994), 3–28.

40. Svetlana Alexievich, *Secondhand Time: The Last of the Soviets* (New York, 2016). Cf. Jarausch, *United Germany*, 1–21. Cf. Larissa Stiglich, "After Socialism: The Transformation of Everyday Life in Eisenhüttenstadt, 1975–2015" (PhD diss., University of North Carolina at Chapel Hill, 2020).

41. Hope Harrison, *After the Berlin Wall: Memory and the Making of the New Germany, 1989 to the Present* (Cambridge, 2020); Piotr Filipkowski, "Zwischen Geschichte der 'Transformation' und Transformation der (Zeit-) Geschichte: Einige Bemerkungen aus polnischer Sicht," in Brückweh, Villinger, and Zöller, eds., *Die lange Geschichte der "Wende,"* 87ff.

42. "The Atlantic Council Holds a Discussion on 25 Years of Transition: Post-Communist Europe's Economic Transformation," December 15, 2014. Cf. Richard Schröder, *Die wichtigsten Irrtümer über die deutsche Einheit* (Freiburg, 2007).

43. Filipkowski, "Zwischen Geschichte," 87ff.; Daniela Dahn, *Westwärts und nicht vergessen: Vom Unbehagen in der Einheit* (Berlin, 1996).

44. Egbert Jahn, ed., *Nationalism in Late and Post-Communist Europe* (Baden Baden, 2008); Connelly, *From Peoples into Nations*, 763–86.

45. Ivan T. Berend and Bojan Bugarič, "Unfinished Europe: Transition from Communism to Democracy in Central and Eastern Europe," *Journal of Contemporary History* 50 (2015), 768–85.

Chapter 3. European Integration

1. Kirsten Henton, "The Now-Renowned Schengen Agreement Was Signed in a Tiny Village in Luxembourg's South-East, a Location That Was Drenched in Symbolism," *BBC Travel*, December 3, 2018.

2. Charles S. Maier, *Once within Borders: Territories of Power, Wealth, and Belonging since 1500* (Cambridge, MA, 2016).

3. Jean-François Bellis, "Belgium–France–Federal Republic of Germany–Luxembourg–Netherlands: Schengen Agreement on the Gradual Abolition of Checks at Their Common Borders and the Convention Applying the Agreement," *EU International Legal Materials* (Brussels, 1991).

4. Angela Siebold, "Between Borders: France, Germany, and Poland in the Debate on Demarcation and Frontier Crossing in the Context of the Schengen Agreement," in Arnaud Lechevalier and Jan Wilgohs, eds., *Borders and Border Regions in Europe* (Bielefeld, 2013).

5. Roger Cohen, "Why I Am a European Patriot," *New York Times*, January 25, 2019. Cf. Steven Hill, *Europe's Promise: Why the European Way Is the Best Hope in an Insecure Age* (Berkeley, CA, 2010).

6. Douglas Murray, *The Strange Death of Europe: Immigration, Identity, Islam* (London, 2017). Cf. Thilo Sarrazin, *Deutschland schafft sich ab: Wie wir unser Land aufs Spiel setzen* (Munich, 2010).

7. Steve Erlanger, "A Fractured European Union Is Rudderless amid Turmoil," *New York Times*, December 12, 2018. Cf. Kiran Klaus Patel, *Projekt Europa: Eine kritische Geschichte* (Munich, 2018).

8. Desmond Dinan, *Ever Closer Union: An Introduction to European Integration*, 4th ed. (Boulder, CO, 2010).

9. Jacques Delors, *The Single Act and Europe: A Moment of Truth* (Luxembourg, 1986); Dennis Swann, *The Single European Market and Beyond: A Study of the Wider Implications of the Single European Act* (London, 1992).

10. "Single European Act," *Official Journal of the European Communities*, June 29, 1987, https://eur-lex.europa.eu/legal-content/EN/TXT/PDF/?uri=CELEX:11986U/TXT&from =EN; Dinan, *Ever Closer Union*, 80ff.

11. Douglas Hurd, *Memoirs* (London, 2003); Frederic Bozo, *Mitterrand, the End of the Cold War, and German Unification* (New York, 2009).

12. Council of the European Communities, "Treaty on European Union," February 7, 1992, https://europa.eu/european-union/law/treaties_en; Dinan, *Ever Closer Union*, 91ff.

13. Thomas Christiansen, Simon Duke, and Emil Kirchner, "Understanding and Assessing the Maastricht Treaty," *Journal of European Integration* 34 (2012), 685–98.

14. "Treaty of Amsterdam Amending the Treaty on European Union," October 11, 1997, https://eur-lex.europa.eu/legal-content/EN/TXT/HTML/?uri=CELEX:11997D /TXT&from=EN; Dinan, *Ever Closer Union*, 122ff.

15. "Euro at 20: Where Is It Heading?," *Pioneer*, February 3, 2019; Hans-Werner Sinn, *The Euro Trap: On Bursting Bubbles, Budgets, and Beliefs* (Oxford, 2014).

16. Michał Krzyżanowski and Florian Oberhuber, eds., *(Un)Doing Europe: Discourses and Practices of Negotiating the EU Constitution* (Brussels, 2007); Dinan, *Ever Closer Union*, 145ff.

17. "Treaty of Lisbon Amending the Treaty on European Union," December 13, 2007, https://eur-lex.europa.eu/legal-content/EN/TXT/?uri=celex:12007L/TXT; Finn Laursen, ed., *The EU's Lisbon Treaty: Institutional Choices and Implementation* (London, 2016).

18. Ulrike Guerot, "The European Paradox: Widening and Deepening in the European Union," *Brookings Institution*, June 2004; Patel, *Projekt Europa*, 342ff.

19. Andreas Wirsching, *Der Preis der Freiheit: Geschichte Europas in unserer Zeit* (Munich, 2012), 72ff.

20. Mikhail Gorbachev, *Memoirs* (London, 1996), 675. Cf. Joshua Itzkovitz Shifrinson, "NATO Enlargement—Was There a Promise?," *International Security* 42 (2017), 189–92.

21. Edwin T. Pechous, "NATO Enlargement and Beyond," *Connections* 7 (2008), 54–66.

22. Ivan T. Berend, *The History of European Integration: A New Perspective* (Abingdon, Oxon, 2016).

23. "Presidency Conclusions: Copenhagen European Council, 21–22 June 1993," http://www .europarl.europa.eu/enlargement_new/europeancouncil/pdf/cop_en.pdf; Dinan, *Ever Closer Union*, 147ff.

24. Miroslav N. Jovanović and Jelene Damnjanović, "EU Eastern Enlargement: Economic Effects on New Members," *Journal of Economic Integration* 29 (2014), 210–43; Ian Bache and Stephen George, *Politics in the European Union* (Oxford, 2006), 543ff.

25. "Germany Supports EU Membership for East European States," *Xinhua News*, April 1, 1994; Bruce Barnard, "EU's Flawed East Europe Policy," *Journal of Commerce*, October 25, 1994.

26. Alberto Quadrio Curzio and Marco Fortis, eds., *The EU and the Economies of the Eastern European Enlargement* (Berlin, 2008); Dinan, *Ever Closer Union*, 104ff.

27. "EU Puts Off Balkan Membership Talks as France Demands Reforms," *Voice of America*, June 26, 2018; Alon Ben-Meir, "Corruption in the Balkan Countries Is Impeding EU Membership," *Value Walk*, January 9, 2019.

28. "Washington: The Shifting Drivers of the AKP's EU Policy," *Plus Media Solutions*, May 31, 2017; Dinan, *Ever Closer Union*, 485–91.

29. Patel, *Projekt Europa*, 346ff.; Jovanović and Damnjanović, "EU Eastern Enlargement," 210.

30. Hartmut Kaelble, *A Social History of Europe, 1945–2000: Recovery and Transformation after Two World Wars* (New York, 2013).

31. European Commission, Migration and Home Affairs, "Border Crossing," https://ec.europa.eu/home-affairs/what-we-do/policies/borders-and-visas/border-crossing_en; "Border Checks Are Undermining Schengen," *Economist*, October 25, 2018.

32. David Marsh, *The Euro: The Battle for the New Global Currency* (New Haven, CT, 2011).

33. Eurostat, "Archive: From Farm to Fork—Food Chain Statistics," 2011; Karl Schlögel, "Europa neu vermessen: Die Rückkehr des Ostens in den europäischen Horizont," in Helmut König, Julia Schmidt, and Manfred Sicking, eds., *Europas Gedächtnis: Das neue Europa zwischen nationalen Erinnerungen und gemeinsamer Identität* (Bielefeld, 2008).

34. EMEA Research and Consulting, "How We Shop: Inside the Minds of Europe's Consumers," 2013, http://nrw.nl/wp-content/uploads/2015/02/CBRE-How-we-shop-inside-the-minds-of-europes-consumers-2013.pdf; Maria Dolores and Martin-Lagos Lopez, "Consumption and Modernization in the European Union," *European Sociological Review* 27 (2011), 124–37.

35. European Commission, "Erasmus+," http://ec.europa.eu/programmes/erasmus-plus/about_en; Miha Lesjak, Emil Juvan, Elizabeth M. Ineson, Matthew H. T. Yap, and Eva Podovšovnik Axelsson, "Erasmus Student Motivation: Why and Where to Go?," *Higher Education* 70 (2015), 845–65.

36. Council of Europe, "Higher Education and Research: The Bologna Process," https://www.coe.int/t/dg4/highereducation/EHEA2010/BolognaPedestrians_en.asp#P132_13851; Judith Marquand, *Democrats, Authoritarians and the Bologna Process: Universities in Germany, Russia, England and Wales* (Bingley, 2018).

37. Eurail, "Eurail Passes," https://www.eurail.com/en/eurail-passes; Ana Pereira, "An Intro to Rail Passes in Europe," TheBrokeBackpacker, November 22, 2020, https://www.thebrokebackpacker.com/train-travel-in-europe-guide/.

38. Hartmut Kaelble, "The European Public Sphere," Max Weber Lecture at the European University Institute, May 16, 2007.

39. UEFA, "Euro 2020," https://www.uefa.com/uefaeuro/index.html; Marc Theebom, Hans Westerbeek, and Paul De Knop, eds., *EU-Involvement in Sport: Between Inspiration and Regulation* (Brussels, 2013).

40. "Record Support for EU," Eurobarometer survey, May 23, 2018, https://www.youtube.com/watch?v=yTufHITtGBA; European Parliament, "2019 European Election Results," October 23, 2019, https://www.europarl.europa.eu/election-results-2019/en.

41. House of European History, "Permanent Exhibition," https://historia-europa.ep.eu/en/permanent-exhibition. Cf. Jennifer Rankin, "Brexit through the Gift Shop: Museum of European History Divides Critics," *Guardian*, August 12, 2018.

42. Florian Hartleb, *A Thorn in the Side of European Elites: The New Euroscepticism* (Brussels, 2015); Hanspeter Kriesi, "Rejoinder to Liesbet Hooghe and Gary Marks, 'A Postfunctional Theory of European Integration: From Permissive Consensus to Constraining Dissensus,'" *British Journal of Political Science* 39 (2009), 221–24.

43. Joschka Fischer, *Scheitert Europa?* (Cologne, 2014). Cf. Ulrike Guerot, *Warum Europa eine Republik werden muss: Eine politische Utopie* (Bonn, 2016).

44. Ivan Krastev and Stephen Holmes, *The Light That Failed: Why the West Is Losing the Fight for Democracy* (New York, 2019); Patel, *Projekt Europa*, 342ff.

45. Anne Applebaum, "A Warning from Europe: The Worst Is Yet to Come," *Atlantic*, October 2018, versus Jean-Claude Juncker, "Die Populisten irren sich fundamental," *Tagesspiegel*, February 19, 2019. Cf. John Connelly, *From Peoples into Nations: A History of Eastern Europe* (Princeton, NJ, 2020), 787ff.

Chapter 4. Sovereign Debt Debacle

1. Jon Henley, "Athens' Cashpoint Queues Lengthen in Face of Week-Long Bank Closures," *Guardian*, June 28, 2015; Robert Hackett, "See Greeks Line Up for Hours to Withdraw Just 60 Euros," *Fortune*, June 29, 2015.

2. Dimitris Dalakoglou, "Want to Know How Greeks See the Future? Get in the ATM Queue and Ask Them," *Conversation*, July 8, 2015; Andrew Higgins and James Kanter, "Europe Presses Greece to Agree to New Measures," *New York Times*, July 13, 2015.

3. Yannis Palaiologos, *The 13th Labor of Hercules: Inside the Greek Crisis* (London, 2014).

4. Paul Krugman, "'Eurozone Has Big, Big Problems' as Greek Debt Crisis Comes to a Head," MacNeil/Lehrer Productions, June 5, 2010; "Economic Conditions Greece," *Country-Watch*, February 11, 2019.

5. Uri Dadush, "Who Says the Euro Crisis Is Over?," *Wall Street Journal*, January 31, 2013; Joseph E. Stiglitz, *The Euro and Its Threat to the Future of Europe* (New York, 2016).

6. Adam Tooze, *Crashed: How a Decade of Financial Crises Changed the World* (New York, 2018), 321ff.

7. Figures from Eurostat and European Commission. Cf. Palaiologos, *13th Labor of Hercules*, 27ff.

8. Panagotis Sotiris, ed., *Crisis, Movement, Strategy* (Leiden, 2018), 1–12.

9. "Economic Conditions Greece," *CountryWatch*, February 11, 2019; Tooze, *Crashed*, 332ff.

10. Sebastian Jost, Anne Kunz, and Karsten Seibel, "Die Wahrheit über den Reichtum griechischer Reeder," *Die Welt*, July 14, 2015; Palaiologos, *13th Labor of Hercules*, 51ff.

11. Pavlos Roufos, *A Happy Future Is a Thing of the Past: The Greek Crisis and Other Disasters* (London, 2018).

12. Evdoxios Doxiadis and Aimee Placas, eds., *Living under Austerity: Greek Society in Crisis* (New York, 2018).

13. Christos Laskos and Euclid Tsakalotos, "From Resistance to Transitional Programme: The Strange Rise of the Radical Left in Greece," in Sotiris, *Crisis, Movement, Strategy*, 229–43.

14. Special report no. 7 on "Servicing the Greek Debt," *CountryWatch*, 137ff.; Yanis Varoufakis, *Adults in the Room: My Battle with the European and American Deep Establishment* (New York, 2017).

15. "Is the Greek Financial Crisis Over at Last?," *Economist*, August 21, 2018; Theodore Pelagidis and Michael Mitsopoulos, *Greece: From Exit to Recovery?* (Washington, DC, 2014).

16. Marcus Bensasson, "Greece's Financial Odyssey," *Bloomberg*, July 10, 2018; Theodore Pelagidis and Michael Mitsopoulos, eds., *Who's to Blame for Greece? Austerity in Charge of Saving a Broken Economy* (London, 2016).

17. Based on the bestseller by Michael Lewis, *The Big Short: Inside the Doomsday Machine* (New York, 2010).

18. Tooze, *Crashed*, 23ff.

19. George K. Zestos, *The Global Financial Crisis: From US Subprime Mortgages to European Sovereign Debt* (London, 2016), 42ff.

20. Philipp Ther, *Die neue Ordnung auf dem alten Kontinent: Eine Geschichte des neoliberalen Europa* (Berlin, 2014), 226ff.

21. Tooze, *Crashed*, 327; Sinn, *Euro Trap*, chap. 2.

22. José Manuel Pureza and Mariana Mortágua, "The European Neoliberal Order and the Eurocrisis: Blame It All on Germany?," *World Review of Political Economy* 7 (2016), 363–81; Peter A. Hall, "The Economics and Politics of the Euro Crisis," *German Politics* 21 (2012), 355–71.

23. Tooze, *Crashed*, 336ff.

24. Ther, *Neue Ordnung*, 233ff.

25. Adele Bergin, John Fitz Gerald, Ide Kearny, and Cormac O'Sullivan, "The Irish Fiscal Crisis," *National Institute Economic Review* 217 (2011), 47–59; Donal Donovan and Antoin E. Murphy, *The Fall of the Celtic Tiger: Ireland and the Euro Debt Crisis* (Oxford, 2013).

26. Tooze, *Crashed*, 372–438.

27. Tooze, Crashed, 438–46. Philip R. Lane, "The European Sovereign Debt Crisis," *Journal of Economic Perspectives* 26, no. 3 (2012), 49–67.

28. Go Tamakoshi and Shigeyuki Hamori, *The European Sovereign Debt Crisis and Its Impacts on Financial Markets* (London, 2015).

29. Caroline de la Porte and Elke Heins, eds., *The Sovereign Debt Crisis, the EU and Welfare State Reform* (London, 2016); Ira W. Lieberman, *In Good Times Prepare for Crisis: From the Great Depression to the Great Recession* (Washington, DC, 2018).

30. Pelagidis and Mitsopoulos, *Who's to Blame for Greece?*, 25ff.

31. Davie Rae and Paul van Nord, "Ireland's Housing Boom: What Has Driven It and Have Prices Overshot?," *OECD Economics Department Working Papers*, no. 492, 2006; Sylvia Poggioli, "Spain's Boom to Bust Illustrates Euro Dilemma," *NPR*, July 15, 2010.

32. Roufos, *A Happy Future Is a Thing of the Past*, 66ff.; Donovan and Murphy, *Fall of the Celtic Tiger*, 45ff.

33. Olivier Blanchard and Petro Portugal, "Boom, Slump, Sudden Stops, Recovery, and Policy Options: Portugal and the Euro," *Portuguese Economic Journal* 16 (2017), 149–68; Kaori Shigiya, "I Learned More Working for Oxfam in Less Than Three Years Than I Did in Nine Years at an Investment Bank," in Lilah Raptopoulos, "Weathering the Financial Crisis: How Seven Lives Were Changed," *Financial Times*, September 11, 2018.

34. Antonio Fatas, "What Has the Eurozone Learned from the Financial Crisis?," *Harvard Business Review*, September 28, 2018.

35. Joseph Stiglitz, "Austerity Has Been an Utter Disaster for the Eurozone," *Guardian*, October 1, 2014.

36. Story by Joseba Elola of *El Pais* in "My Eurozone Crisis: Personal Stories from around Europe," *Guardian*, October 18, 2012.

37. Joanna Ntoukaki, "I Learnt the Concept of Sovereign Debt Spread at the Age of 14," in "Weathering the Financial Crisis," and story by Federico Taddia, *La Stampa*, in "My Eurozone Crisis."

38. Stories by Randeep Ramesh, *Guardian*, and by Beatrice Gurrey, *Le Monde*, in "My Eurozone Crisis."

39. Lawrence C. Strauss, "To Culprit in the Financial Crisis: Human Nature," an interview with Carmen Reinhart and Kenneth Rogoff, *Barron's*, November 24, 2012.

40. Barry Eichengreen, "Europe, the Euro and the ECB: Monetary Success, Fiscal Failure," *Journal of Policy Modeling* 27 (2005), 427–39; Martin Feldstein, "The Failure of the Euro," *Foreign Affairs*, January/February 2012; Randall Germain and Herman Schwartz, "The Political Economy of Failure: The Euro as an International Currency," *Review of International Political Economy* 21 (2014), 1095–122.

41. The European Institute, "Austerity Measures in the EU—A Country by Country Table," updated on December 31, 2018, https://www.europeaninstitute.org/index.php/112-european -affairs/special-g-20-issue-on-financial-reform/1180-austerity-measures-in-the-eu.

42. Erik Jones, R. Daniel Kelemen, and Sophie Meunier, "Failing Forward? The Euro Crisis and the Incomplete Nature of European Integration," *Comparative Political Studies*, December 13, 2015. Cf. Matthias Matthijs and Mark Blyth, eds., *The Future of the Euro* (New York, 2015).

43. Jonty Bloom, "How Has Austerity Worked Out for Eurozone Countries?," *BBC News*, July 15, 2015; Helena Smith, "Greek Elections: Landslide Victory for Centre-Right New Democracy Party," *Guardian*, July 7, 2019.

44. European Commission, "European Integration," Eurobarometer Report, 2013, http://ec .europa.eu/commfrontoffice/publicopinion/topics/fs9_integration_40_en.pdf; Bruce Stokes, "Post-Brexit, Europeans More Favorable toward EU," *Pew Research Center Report*, June 15, 2017.

Chapter 5. Migration Wave

1. Jim Yardley and Elisabetta Povoledo, "Migrants Die as Burning Boat Capsizes off Italy," *New York Times*, October 4, 2013; "Italy to Hold State Funeral for Shipwreck Migrants," *BBC*, October 9, 2013.

2. "Lampedusa Boat Disaster: Aerial Search Mounted," *BBC*, October 9, 2013; Andrew Higgins, "For Migrants, Both Gratitude and Disillusion," *New York Times*, September 8, 2015.

3. Robert Press, "Dangerous Crossings: Voices from the African Migration to Italy/Europe," *Africa Today* 64 (2017), 2–27.

4. Roderick Parkes, "Nobody Move! Myths of the EU Migration Crisis," *Chaillot Paper* No. 143 (December 2017); Rita Chin, *The Crisis of Multiculturalism in Europe: A History* (Princeton, NJ, 2017).

5. Chin, *Crisis of Multiculturalism*, 9. Cf. Cornelia Wilhelm, ed., *Migration, Memory, and Diversity: Germany from 1945 to the Present* (New York, 2017).

6. Mark I. Choate, *Emigrant Nation: The Making of Italy Abroad* (Cambridge, MA, 2018), 1–20.

7. Pamela Ballinger, "A Sea of Difference, a History of Gaps: Migrants between Italy and Albania, 1939–1992," *Comparative Studies in Society and History* 60 (2018), 90–118.

8. Sue Reid, "Gaddafi's Diaspora and the Libyans Overwhelming an Italian Island Who Are Threatening to Come Here," *Mail on Sunday*, April 4, 2011; Guiseppe Campesi, "Frontex and the Production of the Euro-Mediterranean Borderlands," in Claudia Gualtieri, ed., *Migration and the Contemporary Mediterranean* (Oxford, 2018), 39–65.

9. Salvatore Coluccello, "Out of Africa: The Human Trade between Libya and Lampedusa," *Trends in Organized Crime* 10 (2007), 77–90; Andrea Mario Lavezzi and Eileen Quinn, "Migrant Smuggling Across the Mediterranean: An Economic Analysis," in Gualtieri, ed., *Migration and the Contemporary Mediterranean*, 159–76.

10. Fabio Caffio, "Governing Illegal Immigration by Sea: The Difficult Italian Challenge," in Gualtieri, ed., *Migration and the Contemporary Mediterranean*, 133–57.

11. Higgins, "For Migrants"; Felicity Lawrence, "Bitter Harvest," *Wall Street Journal*, December 19, 2006.

12. Martina Tazzioli, "Lampedusa as a Hotspot: Channels of (Forced) Mobility and Preventive Illegalization beyond the Island," in Gualtieri, ed., *Migration and the Contemporary Mediterranean*, 67–86.

13. Stefano Bellucci, "The International Political Economy of Immigration: The Changing Face of Italy," in Sante Matteo, ed., *ItaliAfrica: Bridging Continents and Cultures* (Stony Brook, NY, 2001), 85–103.

14. "Tidal Wave: Italy's Illegal Immigrants," *Economist*, July 5, 2014.

15. Lorenzo Tondo "'Migrant Menace': Salvini Accused of Targeting Refugees and Ignoring Mafia," *Guardian*, February 12, 2019; Art De Leon Tell, "A Disease in the Italian Body Politic: The Lega Nord, Identity, and Immigration, 1984–2014" (PhD diss., California State University, Fullerton, 2017).

16. Deborah Ball, "Hundreds of Migrants Believed Dead in Shipwreck off Libya," *Wall Street Journal*, April 19, 2015. Cf. Jill H. Casid, "Necropolitics at Sea," in Gualtieri, ed., *Migration and the Contemporary Mediterranean*, 193–214.

17. Allison Smale and Melissa Eddy, "Migrant Crisis Grows in Europe with Grisly Find," *New York Times*, August 28, 2015; Rick Lyman, "Migrants Widen Land Route to Europe," *New York Times*, July 19, 2015.

18. Campesi, "Frontex and the Production of the Euro-Mediterranean Borderlands," 43, 55ff.

19. Rick Lyman and Alison Smale, "Smuggling of Migrants through the Balkans Is Now 'Worth Billions,'" *New York Times*, September 4, 2015; and Smale and Eddy, "Migrant Crisis," *New York Times*, August 28, 2015.

20. International Rescue Committee, "Who We Are," 2021, https://www.rescue.org/who-we-are; Refugee Support, "Supporting Refugees and Local Communities with Dignity," https://www.refugeesupport.eu/about/.

21. Tom Stevens, "'Mix of Positive Feelings and Frustration': Readers on Refugees and the Mood in Sweden," *Guardian*, February 8, 2016; "Refugees in Sweden Seek to Rebuild Trust after Sexual Assaults," *Thai News Service*, March 24, 2016.

22. "Merkel's Refugee Policy Divides Europe," *Spiegel Online International*, September 21, 2015, https://www.spiegel.de/consent-a-?targetUrl=https%3A%2F%2Fwww.spiegel.de%2Finternational%2Fgermany%2Frefugee-policy-of-chancellor-merkel-divides-europe-a-1053603.html&ref; Jan Plamper, *Das Neue Wir: Warum Migration dazugehört: Eine andere Geschichte der Deutschen* (Frankfurt, 2019), 270ff.

23. "Asylum Seekers, Refugees Rekindle Debate on German Culture," *Handelsblatt Today*, October 2, 2015; William Booth, Antony Faiola, and Michael Birnbaum, "Europeans Retreat on Warm Welcome," *Washington Post*, September 18, 2015.

24. "Migrant Crisis: EU Ministers Approve Disputed Quota Plan," *BBC News*, September 22, 2015. Cf. "Drei Länder haben in der Flüchtlingskrise gegen EU-Recht verstoßen," *Tagesspiegel*, April 2, 2020.

25. "To Dissuade Migrants, Hungary Erects Balkan Fence," *Deutsche Welle*, July 13, 2015; Daniel McLaughlin, "Migration Crisis and New Border Fences Fuel Balkan Tension," *Irish Times*, November 14, 2015.

26. Lea Main-Klingst, "Refugees and the EU-Turkey Deal, Two Years On," *Newstex Blog*, March 29, 2018; Matina Stevis-Gridneff, Patrick Kingsley, and Hellen Willis, "Tear Gas, Gunfire and a Dash for the Border," *New York Times*, March 12, 2020.

27. "How Has the EU Mismanaged the Migrant Crisis?," *Financial Times*, March 12, 2016.

28. Marina Warner and Valentina Castagna, "Stories in Transit/*Storie in Transito*: Storytelling and Arrivants' Voices in Sicily," in Gualtieri, ed., *Migration and the Contemporary Mediterranean*, 223–43.

29. Jenny Erpenbeck, *Gehen, Ging Gegangen* (Munich, 2015); Gioanfranco Rosi, *Fuocoammare*, prize-winning Italian documentary, 2016.

30. Press, "Dangerous Crossings," 2–27; Yomi Kazeem, "The Harrowing, Step-by-Step Story of a Migrant's Journey to Europe, *Quartz Africa*, October 25, 2018. Cf. "A Syrian Refugee's Story," Caritas Aotearoa New Zealand, https://caritas.org.nz/newsroom/stories/syrian-refugees-story.

31. Kazeem, "Harrowing, Step-by-Step Story"; Press, "Dangerous Crossings."

32. Press, "Dangerous Crossings." Cf. Itayi Viriri, "Emmanuel, Ghana," in "Three Real Stories from Refugees," *World Economic Forum*, December 17, 2015.

33. Itayi Viriri, "Emmanuel, Ghana." Cf. Karl Penhaul and Vasco Cotovio, "Why I Fled: New Migrants in Italy Share Their Stories," *CNN*, April 24, 2015.

34. Caritas Aotearoa New Zealand, "A Syrian Refugee's Story," 2015, https://caritas.org.nz/newsroom/stories/syrian-refugees-story; "Five Migrant Stories from Greece: The Pull of Europe," *BBC News*, October 14, 2015.

35. Melissa Fleming, "Doaa, Syrian Refugee Living in Greece," in "Three Real Stories from Refugees," *World Economic Forum*, December 17, 2015.

36. For a documentary on the asylum process, see Benjamin Kahlmeyer, *The Invisibles* (2014).

37. "Deutschland gewährt am häufigsten Asyl," *Tagesspiegel*, April 25, 2019. Cf. Vera Hanewinkel, "Das Asylverfahren in Deutschland: Schema des Ablaufs," *Bundeszentrale für politische Bildung*, May 9, 2015.

38. "Ausländerfeindlichkeit nimmt zu," *ZdFheute*, November 7, 2019; Johannes Grunert, "Rechte jagen Menschen in Chemnitz," *Zeit Online*, August 27, 2019. Cf. Hajo Funke, "The

Radicalization of the Extreme Right: Charlottesville August 2017 and Chemnitz August 2018," *AICGS*, December 18, 2018.

39. "Stabiles Klima in der Integrationsrepublik Deutschland," *SVR-Integrationsbarometer* (Berlin, 2018).

40. Stories by Umar Silla, Mahmut Shubat, Idah Yaro, and Ajmal Sadiqi, "Why I Fled: New Migrants in Italy Share Their Stories"; International Organization of Migration, "Migrant Stories," https://www.iom.int/press-room/migrant-stories.

41. "Five Migrant Stories from Greece"; other testimonies in International Organization of Migration, "Migrant Stories."

42. "Five Migrant Stories from Greece"; testimonies in "Why I Fled: New Migrants in Italy Share Their Stories."

43. Figures from Eurostat, "Asylum and First Time Asylum Applicants," updated January 26, 2021, http:Europa.eu/Eurostat/en/web/products-datasets/-MIGR_ASYAPPCTZA).

44. Steven Erlanger, "Despite No Commitments in EU Migration Deal, Victory Is Declared," *New York Times*, June 30, 2018; "Sachverständige sehen deutsche Einwanderungspolitik 'in Balance,'" *Tagesspiegel*, May 7, 2019.

45. Nina von Hardenberg, Markus Schulte von Drach, and Henrike Roßbach, "Wie viele kamen, wer durfte bleiben, wie viele fanden Arbeit?," *Süddeutsche Zeitung*, September 4, 2020; Philip Oltermann, "How Angela Merkel's Great Migrant Gamble Paid Off," *Guardian*, August 30, 2020.

46. David Miller, *Strangers in Our Midst: The Political Philosophy of Immigration* (Cambridge, MA, 2016); Plamper, *Das Neue Wir*, 314ff.

Chapter 6. Brexit Self-Destruction

1. Tim Shipman, *All Out War: The Full Story of Brexit*, rev. ed. (London, 2017), 426–51.

2. Nigel Farage, *The Purple Revolution: The Year That Changed Everything* (London, 2015).

3. Stig Abell, *How Britain Really Works: Understanding the Ideas and Institutions of a Nation* (London, 2018), 84ff.

4. Harold D. Clarke, Matthew Goodwin, and Paul Whiteley, *Brexit: Why Britain Voted to Leave the European Union* (Cambridge, 2017), 61ff.

5. Duncan Weldon, "The British Model and the Brexit Shock: Plus ça change?," *Political Quarterly* 90 (2019); and Katrin Bennhold, "In Parliament Elections, Populists Seek to Break the EU from Within," *New York Times*, May 25, 2019.

6. Jeremy Black, *A History of Britain: 1945 to Brexit* (Bloomington, IN, 2017).

7. Desmond Dinan, *Europe Recast: A History of the European Union*, 2nd rev. ed. (London, 2014).

8. Matthew Goodwin and Caitlin Milazzo, *UKIP: Inside the Campaign to Redraw British Politics* (Oxford, 2015).

9. David Cameron, "EU Speech at Bloomberg," January 23, 2013, https:/www.government /speeches/eu-speech-at-bloomberg.

10. Shipman, *All Out War*, 116–45.

11. Shipman, *All Out War*, 146ff.; Sonia Purnell, *Just Boris: The Irresistible Rise of a Political Celebrity* (London, 2011).

12. Macer Hall, "Boris Johnson Urges Brits to Vote Brexit 'to Take Back Control,'" *Express*, June 20, 2016, https://www.express.co.uk/news/politics/681706/Boris-Johnson-vote-Brexit -take-back-control.

13. Campaign for "Britain Stronger in Europe," https://www.youtube.com/watch?v =1BMRq96sAwk.

14. "Brexit Bus" image, 2016, https://www.bing.com/images/search?q=Brexit+bus&id=0F EBABDD0D162EC0DC4BAAAD9A8035D8C2EF1253&form=IQFRBA&first=1&cw=1129&ch =859; Nicole Morley, "Here's How Spectacularly Wrong the Brexit Bus £350million Lie Was," *Metro News*, April 27, 2017, https://metro.co.uk/2017/04/27/heres-how-spectacularly-wrong -the-brexit-bus-350million-lie-was-6600987/?ito=cbshare.

15. Liesbet Hooge and Gary Marks, "Brexit," lecture at Chapel Hill, NC, April 8, 2019; Clarke, Goodwin, and Whiteley, *Brexit*, 146–74; Laurence Whitehead, "The Hard Truths of Brexit," *Journal of Democracy* 31 (2020), 81–94.

16. "Brexit: World Reaction as UK Votes to Leave EU," *BBC News*, June 24, 2016.

17. Anna M. Pusca, ed., *Rejecting the EU Constitution? From the Constitutional Treaty to the Treaty of Lisbon* (New York, 2009).

18. "Views from the Capitals: Europe Prepares for Article 50," *European Council on Foreign Relations*, March 2017; Alex de Ruyter and Beverley Nielsen, eds., *Brexit Negotiations after Article 50: Assessing Process, Progress and Impact* (Bingley, 2019).

19. Nick Whitney, "Rejecting Suicide, Britain Settles for Self-Harm on Brexit," *European Council on Foreign Relations*, August 30, 2017.

20. Hooge and Marks, "Brexit."

21. "Theresa May Says, 'Brexit Means Brexit,'" *Independent*, July 11, 2016, https://www .independent.co.uk/news/uk/politics/theresa-may-brexit-means-brexit; Mark Mardell, "What Does 'Brexit Means Brexit' Mean?," *BBC News*, July 14, 2016; and Shipman, *All Out War*, 508ff.

22. Florian Eder, "Europe's Brexit Greeting: Sorry and Good Riddance," *Politico*, June 23, 2016; Alan Barker, "Brussels on Brexit: What Michel Barnier Said and What He Meant," *Financial Times*, December 6, 2016.

23. European Commission, "Draft Agreement on the Withdrawal of the United Kingdom," November 14, 2018, https://ec.europa.eu/commission/sites/beta-political/files/draft _withdrawal_agreement_0.pdf.

24. UK Government, "How to Prepare if the UK Leaves the EU with No Deal," withdrawn on February 7, 2020, https://www.gov.uk/government/collections/how-to-prepare-if-the-uk -leaves-the-eu-with-no-deal; Serina Sandhu, "What Is a No-Deal Brexit? The Consequences of the UK Leaving the EU without an Agreement," *I News*, May 30, 2019.

25. Dan Sabbagh, "Theresa May Never Had a Grip on the Crown That Fell into Her Lap," *Guardian*, May 24, 2019; "Election 2017 Results," *BBC News*, https://www.bbc.com/news /election/2017/results.

26. Sabbagh, "Theresa May"; "Brexit Vote Lost in UK Parliament as EU Prepares for No-Deal Exit," *Deutsche Welle*, March 29, 2019, https://www.dw.com/en/brexit-vote-lost-in-uk -parliament-as-eu-prepares-for-no-deal-exit/a-48120892; Nika Shakhnazarova, "Tearesa Theresa May Resignation Speech," *Sun*, June 8, 2019, https://www.thesun.co.uk/news/9146569 /what-theresa-may-resignation-speech-quit-cry/.

27. "Brexit: All You Need to Know about the UK Leaving the EU," *BBC*, February 17, 2020; "Großbritannien droht mit Abbruch der Brexit-Gespräche," *Tagesspiegel*, February 28, 2020.

28. Steven Erlanger, "Deal Lets EU Preserve Core Ideals and Look to Future," *New York Times*, December 25, 2020; Albrecht Meier, "Nach der Einigung mit Brüssel," *Tagesspiegel*, December 24, 2020.

29. Björn Finke and Alexander Mühlauer, "Britische Bescherung," *Süddeutsche Zeitung*, December 24, 2020; Eshe Nelson, "A Week into Full Brexit, the Pain for UK Business Has Arrived," *New York Times*, January 9, 2021.

30. Luke McGee, "Fantasy Lives On: A Look at Theresa May's Time as Prime Minister," *CNN*, June 7, 2019; Francis Fukayama, *Identity: Contemporary Identity Politics and the Struggle for Recognition* (London, 2018).

31. Sam Knight, "In the Trenches with the True Brexit Believers," *New Yorker*, November 10, 2018; tweet from Hugh Norris on @peoplesvote_uk, April 15, 2018.

32. "Sunderland Voters Describe Why the Leave Vote There Was Resounding," *Channel 4 News*, July 7, 2019.

33. "Brexiteers' Opinions: Why They Voted Leave," *Sky News*, June 24, 2016, https://www.youtube.com/watch?v=rV-3U_YBP0E; "Do You Think People Who Voted Leave Are Thick?," *BBC Newsnight*, June 27, 2016, https://www.youtube.com/watch?v=Xdc2iX1B0AQ.

34. Bridget Brenan and Roscoe Whalan, "Many in Brexit Heartland Still Want to Leave the EU, Whatever It Takes," *ABC News*, January 6, 2019; Knight, "In the Trenches."

35. Christopher Kissane, "Historical Nonsense Underpins UK's Brexit Floundering," *Irish Times*, September 17, 2018; David Edgerton, *The Rise and Fall of the British Nation: A Twentieth-Century History* (London, 2018).

36. Brennan and Whalan, "Many in Brexit Heartland Still Want to Leave," https://www.remainernow.com/why_I_started_remainer-now; Josh "This Is Not the Brexit I Voted For, We Need a Peoples Vote on the Terms," https://www.remainernow.com/Josh_video_peoples_vote.

37. Remainer now statements on https://www.remainernow.com/we_won't_be_fooled_again_my_bregretter_letter; Tom Foudy, https://www.remainernow.com/brexit_isn_t_worth_it.

38. Gary Wrights, "We're Going to Be So Much Worse Off," *Remainer Now*, July 12, 2018; Simon Cowley, "Thoughts and Experience of Former Leave Voters, Now Remainers," *Remainer Now*, September 13, 2018.

39. Charles Gallaher, "NHS Doctor," *Remainer Now*, August 21, 2018; Emma Jane Manley, "Why I Voted Leave, by the MEP Candidate Fighting for Remain," *Remainer Now*, April 26, 2019; Ben, "I Voted Leave Because of Immigration: Why I Am Desperate to Change My Vote Now," *Remainer Now*, September 4, 2018.

40. Henry Saker-Clark, "From Jobs to Travel and Study: How Would Brexit Affect Young Britons," *Guardian*, June 22, 2016; "Our Brexit Fallacy and How We Must Move Forward," *Remainer Now*, September 7, 2018.

41. "European Citizens," in Linda Lewis, ed., "Telling Brexit Stories," https://tellingbrexitstories.co.uk/your-brexit-story/; "I Voted to Leave the EU: I Was Wrong," *Remainer Now*, July 13, 2018.

42. Brennan and Whalan, "Many in the Heartland Still Want to Leave"; Andrew James, "I Voted Leave . . . I Changed My Mind," *Remainer Now*, September 10, 2018; "If There Was

Another Referendum on Britain's Membership of the EU, How Would You Vote?," *What UK Thinks*, January 23, 2021, https://whatukthinks.org/eu/questions/if-a-second-eu-referendum-were-held-today-how-would-you-vote/.

43. European Parliament, "2019 European Election Results," https://www.election-results .eu/united-kingdom/. Cf. Steven Erlanger and Megan Specia, "European Parliament Elections: Five Biggest Takeaways," *New York Times*, May 27, 2019.

44. Linda Colley, *Britons: Forging the Nation, 1707–1837* (New Haven, CT, 2009).

45. "Brexiteers' Opinions: Why They Voted Leave," *Sky News*, June 24, 2016.

46. Sim, "Our Brexit Fallacy and How We Must Move Forward," *Remainer Now*, September 7, 2018. Cf. Bastian Jaeger and Joachim Krueger, "The Personality of Brexit Voters: Openness Predicts Best," *Psychology Today*, June 29, 2016.

47. Christopher Oram, "I Voted Leave. I Now Battle Alongside the 'First Generation Remainers' to Remain in the EU," *Remainer Now*, September 5, 2018; Celine-Agathe Caro, "Brexit and Populism: The Future of the 'European Project' from a German Perspective," http://clt.biz /bizprofile/eu-response-to-brexit/.

48. Caroline de Gruyter, "The Liberation of Europe," *European Council on Foreign Relations*, May 17, 2017; "The Future of Europe," *Special Eurobarometer Report* 479 (Brussels, October–November 2018); "Ende der Verhandlungen mit der EU?," *Tagesspiegel*, October 16, 2020.

Chapter 7. Economic Competitiveness

1. "Menschen, Autos und was sie bewegt . . . Eröffnung der 'Autostadt' in Wolfsburg," *Bau-Netz*, June 2, 2000; "Autostadt knackt Meilenstein: 40 Millionen Besucher," *Wolfsburger Allgemeine*, February 18, 2019.

2. Manfred Grieder and Markus Lupa, *Vom Käfer zum Weltkonzern: Die Volkswagen Chronik* (Wolfsburg, 2015); Bernhard Rieger, *The People's Car: A Global History of the Volkswagen Beetle* (Cambridge, MA, 2013).

3. Harry Menear, "Top 10 Biggest Companies in Europe by Revenue," *Business Chief*, April 13, 2018; Mark C. Schneider, *Volkswagen: Eine deutsche Geschichte* (Berlin, 2016), 209.

4. Elke Schulz, "Time Is Money—Understanding US Business Culture," *tcworld*, February 2007; Carmen M. Reinhart and Kenneth S. Rogoff, *This Time Is Different: Eight Centuries of Financial Folly* (Princeton, NJ, 2011).

5. Kirsty Hughes, ed., *European Competitiveness* (Cambridge, 1993), 1–8; Alexis Jacquemin and Lucio Pench, eds., *Europa im globalen Wettbewerb: Berichte des Rats für Wettbewerbsfähigkeit* (Baden-Baden, 1999).

6. Anthony J. Nicholls, *Freedom with Responsibility: The Social Market Economy in Germany, 1918 to 1963* (Oxford, 1984); Stefan Sorin Muresan, *Social Market Economy: The Case of Germany* (Springer, 2014).

7. Nils Heisterhagen, "Die Rückkehr zum deutschen Modell," *Cicero*, January 10, 2021.

8. "What Germany Offers the World: Germany's Economic Model," *Economist*, April 14, 2012; Bundesministerium für Wirtschaft und Energie, "Erfolgsmodell Mittelstand," https:// www.bmwi.de/Redaktion/DE/Dossier/politik-fuer-den-mittelstand.html.

9. Kees Gispen, *New Profession, Old Order: Engineers and German Society, 1815–1914* (Cambridge, 1990).

10. Bundesministerium für Bildung und Wissenschaft, *Vocational Training in the Dual System in the Federal Republic of Germany: An Investment in the Future* (Bonn, 1992).

11. Heiner Dribbusch and Peter Birke, *Les Syndicats du DGB depuis la crise: Évolutions, défis, stratégies* (Abidjan, 2014); Rebecca Page, "Co-Determination in Germany—A Beginner's Guide," *Hans Böckler Stiftung Arbeitspapier* 313 (November 2018).

12. Eric Solsten, *Germany: A Country Study* (Washington, DC, 1996), 305ff.

13. Konrad H. Jarausch, ed., *Das Ende der Zuversicht? Die Siebziger Jahre als Geschichte* (Göttingen, 2008); Herbert Giersch, Karl-Heinz Paqué, and Holger Schmieding, *The Fading Miracle: Four Decades of Market Economy in Germany* (Cambridge, 1992).

14. "Germany v. Germany," *Economist*, August 14, 1993; "Germany's Economy: The Sick Man of the Euro," *Economist*, June 5, 1999.

15. Tony Blair and Gerhard Schroeder, "Europe: The Third Way/*Die Neue Mitte*," *Internet Archive*, August 19, 1999, https://web.archive.org/web/19990819090124.

16. Speech of Chancellor Gerhard Schröder in the Bundestag, March 14, 2003, https://dipbt.bundestag.de/doc/btp/15/15032.pdf. Cf. Hans-Werner Sinn, *Ist Deutschland noch zu retten?* (Munich, 2003).

17. Wolfgang Wiegard, "Wirtschaft und Wettbewerbsfähigkeit—die Agenda 2010 im Rückblick," *ifo-Schnelldienst*, September 28, 2018; *Deutscher Bundestag Stenografischer Bericht 4. Sitzung*, November 30, 2005.

18. "Ready to Motor?—Germany's Economy," *Economist*, August 20, 2005; "Back Above the Bar Again—Germany's Economy," *Economist*, July 14, 2007.

19. Anthony Giddens, *Europe in the Global Age* (Cambridge, 2007).

20. Stuart Hall and David Soskice, *Varieties of Capitalism: The Institutional Foundation of Comparative Advantage* (Oxford, 2001); Abell, *How Britain Really Works*, 10ff.

21. James McWhinney, "The Nordic Model: Pros and Cons," *Investopedia*, June 25, 2019; Mary Hilson, *The Nordic Model: Scandinavia since 1945* (London, 2008).

22. Warren C. Baum, *French Economy and the State* (Princeton, NJ, 2016).

23. Guglielmo Meardi, "'Mediterranean Capitalism' under EU Pressure: Labour Market Reforms in Spain and Italy, 2010–2012," *Warsaw Forum of Economic Sociology* 3:1(5) Spring 2012.

24. David Lane and Martin Myant, eds., *Varieties of Capitalism in Post-Communist Countries* (New York, 2007).

25. Tore Fougner, "'The State,' International Competitiveness and Neoliberal Globalisation: Is There a Future beyond 'The Competition State'?," *Review of International Studies* 32 (2006), 165–85.

26. Carrefour, "Key Dates in Carrefour Group's History," http://www.carrefour.com/content/history; *Carrefour: Hypermarket Reinvention* (MarketLine, 2010).

27. Siemens, "Siemens Geschichte—Ein Überblick," https://new.siemens.com/global/de/unternehmen/ueber-uns/geschichte.html; Wilfried Feldenkirchen, *Von der Werkstatt zum Weltunternehmen* (Munich, 1997).

28. Shell, "Powering Industry with Help from the Sun," https://www.shell.com/; Joost Jonker, J. L. van Zanden, Stephen Howarth, and Keetie E. Sluyterman, *A History of Royal Dutch Shell* (Oxford, 2007).

29. European Commission, "EU Position in World Trade," January 15, 2021, https://ec.europa.eu/trade/policy/eu-position-in-world-trade/; Wilhelm Bartmann, *Zwischen Tradition*

und Fortschritt: Aus der Geschichte der Pharmabereiche von Bayer, Hoechst und Schering von 1935–1975 (Stuttgart, 2003).

30. Ben McPartland, "The Figures That Tell the Story of the State of France's Jobs Market," *Local*, July 5, 2017, https://www.thelocal.fr/20170705/the-figures-that-tell-the-story-of-the-french-jobs-market; Ulrich Beck, *Risk Society: Towards a New Modernity* (London, 1992).

31. Mike Stewart, "Business Turnaround Case Study," *CEO Worldwide Success Story*, no. 37; Jean-Luc Hauser, "Turnaround of a SMB Company Close to Insolvency," *CEO Europe Success Story*, no. 31.

32. Silvia Dahlkamp, "Alter Manager sucht Job. So hat's geklappt," *Spiegel Job und Karriere*, August 13, 2015, https://www.spiegel.de/karriere/bewerbung-50-plus-wie-aeltere-arbeitnehmer-jobs-finden-a-1045086.html; "Aussortiert," *Spiegel Job und Karriere*, October 15, 2015, https://www.spiegel.de/karriere/wenn-top-manager-ihre-macht-verlieren-a-1057484.html.

33. Géraldine Baraud, "Je suis dans la même entreprise depuis 20 ans, et alors?," *Welcome to the Jungle*, February 18, 2019, https://www.welcometothejungle.co/fr/articles/travailler-entreprise-anciennete.

34. ECB, "Labor Hoarding in the Euro Area," *Monthly Bulletin*, July 2003; Giulia Giupponi and Camille Landais, "Subsidising Labour Hoarding in Recessions: New Evidence from Italy's Cassa Integrazione," *VOX CEPR Policy Portal*, January 25, 2019.

35. Siemens XING, "Beste Areitgeber 2021," https://www.xing.com/company/siemensag/reviews.

36. Joshua Kelly, "France Wants to Make It Easier to Hire Workers So Employers Will Stop Harassing Them into Quitting," *PRI's The World*, May 13, 2016.

37. Ruth Berschens and Sandra Louven, "Young and Hungry for Work," *Handelsblatt*, May 1, 2017; Anders Melin, "Educated with a Dead-Beat Job—The Unseen Legacy of Europe's Crisis," *Reuters*, June 25, 2013.

38. Jessica Jones, "Spanish Millennials Are Reshaping Their Goals to Afford Life," *BBC News*, November 27, 2018; Andrew Stetsenko, "From Malta to the Netherlands: How to Land a Job and Relocate in 2 Months," *Relocate*, https://relocate.me, job 72.

39. Mary Loritz interviews with Chanyu Xu, June 26, 2019; Sebastian Siemiatkowski, June 18, 2019; and Shmuel Chafets, June 5, 2019, all at https://www.eu-startups.com/category/interviews/.

40. "Job Satisfaction in Europe—An International Comparison," *World of Labour*, April 28, 2013; Julian Baggini, "The Secret to Happiness? Health, Housing and Job Security," *Guardian*, February 14, 2019.

41. Muresan, *Social Market Economy*, 375–78; James C. Van Hook, *Rebuilding Germany: The Creation of the Social Market Economy, 1945–1957* (Cambridge, 2004).

42. Jeremy Leaman, *The Political Economy of Germany under Chancellors Kohl and Schröder: Decline of the German Model?* (New York, 2009); Thomas Hertfelder and Andreas Rödder, eds., *Modell Deutschland: Erfolgsgeschichte oder Illusion?* (Göttingen, 2007).

43. Richard Bronk, "Which Model of Capitalism?," *OECD Observer* 221/222 (2000), 12–15.

44. "So hätschen Konzerne ihre Mitarbeiter," *Focus Money Online*, https://www.focus.de/finanzen/news/unternehmen/daimler-vw-siemens-deutsche-bank-und-telekom-bayer-basf-und-siemens_id_3774350.html; "Arbeitszeiten und Urlaubszeiten in den USA," *USA Tipps*, https://www.usatipps.de/tipps/bevoelkerung/arbeitszeiten-und-urlaubszeiten/.

45. Daniel Tautz, "Soziale Ungleichheit weltweit gewachsen," *Zeit Online*, December 14, 2017; Clemens Fuest, "Soziale Marktwirtschaft: Exportschlager oder Auslaufmodell?," *ifoSchnelldienst*, November 8, 2018.

Chapter 8. Restructured Welfare State

1. "Borgana Bildar Gemensam Allians," *Aftonbladet*, August 31, 2004; "Program för Arbete," *Allians för Sverige*, August 31, 2005; "Alliance Manifesto Targets Jobs and Environment," *Local*, August 23, 2006.

2. "Narrow Win for Swedish Opposition," *BBC News*, September 17, 2006; Sarah Lyall and Ivar Ekman, "Sweden's Governing Party Voted Out after 12 Years," *International Herald Tribune*, September 18, 2006.

3. David Harsanyi, *Nanny State: How Food Fascist, Teetotaling Do-Gooders, Priggish Moralists and Other Boneheaded Bureaucrats Are Turning America into a Nation of Children* (New York, 2007); Alan Travis, "Thatcher Pushed for Breakup of Welfare State Despite NHS Pledge," *Guardian*, November 25, 2016.

4. Bernhard Ebbinghaus and Elias Naumann, eds., *Welfare State Reforms Seen from Below: Comparing Public Attitudes and Organized Interests in Britain and Germany* (Cham, 2018); Ian Ferguson, Michael Lavalette, and Gerry Mooney, *Rethinking Welfare: A Critical Perspective* (London, 2002), 2.

5. Nina Witoszek and Atle Midttun, eds., *Sustainable Modernity: The Nordic Model and Beyond* (Milton Park, 2018); Andreas Mulvag and Rune Stahl, "What Makes Scandinavia Different?," *Jacobin*, August 4, 2015.

6. Norbert Götz, "The Modern Home Sweet Home," in Kurt Almqvist and Kay Glans, eds., *The Swedish Success Story?* (Stockholm, 2004), 97–107.

7. M. Donald Hancock, "The Swedish Welfare State: Prospects and Contradictions," *Wilson Quarterly* 1 (1977), 111–26.

8. Hancock, "Swedish Welfare State"; Harold Wilensky, *The Welfare State and Equality: Structural and Ideological Roots of Public Expenditures* (Berkeley, CA, 1975).

9. Gøsta Esping-Andersen, *Social Foundations of Postindustrial Economies* (Oxford, 1999), 45ff. Cf. Karen Hagemann, Konrad H. Jarausch, and Cristina Allemann-Ghionda, eds., *Children, Families, and States: Time Policies of Childcare, Preschool, and Primary Education in Europe* (New York, 2011).

10. Richard B. Freeman, Brigitta Swedenborg, and Robert Topel, eds., *Reforming the Welfare State: Recovery and Beyond in Sweden* (Chicago, 2010), 1–2; "Arbeitslosenquote in Schweden bis 2025," *Statista*, 2021, https://de.statista.com/statistik/daten/studie/17328/umfrage/arbeitslosenquote-in-schweden/.

11. Subhash Thakur, Michael Keen, Balázs Horváth, and Valerie Cerra, *Sweden's Welfare State: Can the Bumblebee Keep Flying?* (Washington, DC, 2003).

12. Thakur et al., *Sweden's Welfare State*, 3–4, 12–13; Peter Starke, Alexandra Kaasch, and Franca van Hooren, *The Welfare State as Crisis Manager: Explaining the Diversity of Policy Responses to Economic Crisis* (Houndmills, 2013).

13. Thakur et al., *Sweden's Welfare State*, 6, 10–12

14. Peter S. Goodman, "The Nordic Model May Be the Best Cushion against Capitalism: Can It Survive Immigration?," *New York Times*, July 14, 2019.

15. Goodman, "Nordic Model"; Diana Mulinari and Anders Neergard, "We Are Sweden Democrats Because We Care for Others: Exploring Racisms in the Swedish Extreme Right," *European Journal of Women's Studies* 21 (2014), 43–56.

16. Carly Elizabeth Small, *The Rise and Fall of the Miraculous Welfare Machine: Immigration and Social Democracy in Twentieth-Century Sweden* (Ithaca, NY, 2016).

17. Evelyne Huber and John D. Stephens, *Development and Crisis of the Welfare State: Parties and Policies in Global Markets* (Chicago, 2001).

18. Anu Partanen, *The Nordic Theory of Everything: In Search of a Better Life* (New York, 2016), 47–62. Cf. Mary Hilson, *The Nordic Model: Scandinavia since 1945* (London, 2006).

19. Gøsta Esping-Andersen, *The Three Worlds of Welfare Capitalism* (Princeton, NJ, 1990). Cf. Gideon Calder, Jeremy Gass, and Kirsten Merrill-Glover, eds., *Changing Directions of the British Welfare State* (Cardiff, 2012).

20. John S. Ambler, ed., *The French Welfare State: Surviving Social and Ideological Change* (New York, 1991); Ilona Delouette and Yann Le Lann, "Troubles dans la protection sociale," *Revue Française de Socio-Economie* 20 (2018), 27–38.

21. Alfred Pfaller, "The German Welfare State after National Unification," *Digitale Bibliothek der FES* (Bonn, 1998). Cf. Hans-Günter Hockerts, *Drei Wege deutscher Sozialstaatlichkeit: NS-Diktatur, Bundesrepublik und DDR im Vergleich* (Munich, 1998).

22. Pau Marí-Klose and Francisco Javier Moreno-Fuentes, "The Southern European Welfare Model in the Post-Industrial Order," *European Societies* 15 (2013), 475–92.

23. Linda J. Cook, *Postcommunist Welfare States: Reform Politics in Russia and Eastern Europe* (Ithaca, NY, 2007).

24. Konrad H. Jarausch, ed., *Das Ende der Zuversicht: Die Siebziger Jahre als Geschichte* (Göttingen, 2008); Richard Musgrave, "The Tax Revolt," *Social Science* 59 (1979), 697–703.

25. John Kvist, "Activating Welfare States: Scandinavian Experiences in the 1990s," Research Programme on Comparative Welfare State, Research Working Paper no. 7 (2000).

26. Christoph Arndt, *The Electoral Consequences of Third Way Welfare State Reforms: Social Democracy's Transformation and Its Political Costs* (Amsterdam, 2013), 23–31, 153–82.

27. Freeman, Swedenborg, and Topel, *Reforming the Welfare State*, 19; Thakur et al., *Sweden's Welfare State*, 103–12; Sven Steinmo, *The Evolution of Modern States: Sweden, Japan, and the United States* (New York, 2010).

28. Nima Sandandaji, "So Long, Swedish Welfare State?," *Foreign Policy*, September 5, 2018; Jo Becker, "The Global Machine behind the Rise of Far Right Nationalism," *New York Times*, August 11, 2019.

29. Michael Tanner and Charles Hughes, "How European Welfare Discourages Work," *Politico*, August 28, 2015; Daniel J. Mitchell, "Lessons from Europe on Welfare, Dependency, and Self-Reliance," *Townhall Finance*, May 31, 2018.

30. "Welfare Fraud Complaints Often Dismissed," *Swedish Radio*, March 22, 2013; "Scammers Gonna Scam: Sweden Sees Big Rise in Benefit Fraud," *Sputnik International*, September 20, 2016.

31. Joanna Morehead, "Different Planets," *Guardian*, October 3, 2006; Partanen, *Nordic Theory of Everything*, 63ff.

32. Douglas Brown, "Why Nordic Nations Are the Best Places to Have Children," *World Economic Forum*, March 15, 2019. Cf. Hagemann, Jarausch, and Allemann-Ghionda, *Children, Families, and States*, 3ff., 137ff.

33. Siriku Kupiainen, Jarkko Hautamäki, and Tommi Karjalainen, *The Finnish Education System and PISA* (Helsinki, 2009); Pasi Sahlberg, "PISA in Finland: An Education Miracle or an Obstacle to Change?," *CEPS Journal* 1 (2011), 119–39.

34. Jan Magnussen, "The Scandinavian Healthcare System," *Medical Solutions*, May 2009, 63–68; Ian McAuley, "Creating a Better Health System: Lessons from Norway and Sweden," *Conversation*, September 1, 2014.

35. Alberto Alesina and Edward L. Glaeser, "Why Are Welfare States in the US and Europe so Different?," *Horizons Stratégiques*, 2006, 51–61; Jacob Holt, "Fighting for the Welfare State," May 6, 1998, http://www.american-pictures.com/english/racism/articles/welfare.htm.

36. Thomas Biegert, "A Generous Welfare State Can Help Reduce Unemployment," *LSE US Centre*, October 3, 2017; Torben M. Andersen and Michael Svarer, "Flexicurity in Denmark," *ifo DICE report*, no. 4 (2008).

37. Helen Davidson and others, "Which Are the Best Countries in the World to Grow Old In?," *Guardian*, March 3, 2015; Bernhard Ebbinghaus, "The Privatization and Marketization of Pensions in Europe," *European Policy Analysis* 1 (2015), 56–73.

38. OECD Data, "Poverty Rate," OECD (2019); Elise Gould and Hilary Wething, "US Poverty Rates Higher, Safety Net Weaker Than in Peer Countries," *Economic Policy Institute Brief*, July 24, 2012.

39. Partanen, *Nordic Theory of Everything*, 233–61.

40. Thakur et al., *Sweden's Welfare State*, 2ff., 103ff.

41. Thakur et al., *Sweden's Welfare State*, 3–7; Small, *Rise and Fall of the Miraculous Welfare Machine*, 125ff.

42. Kvist, "Activating Welfare States"; Robert Walker and Michael Wiseman, "Making Welfare Work: UK Activation Policies under New Labour," *International Social Security Review* 56 (2003), 3–29, https://onlinelibrary.wiley.com/doi/pdf/10.1111/1468-246X.00147.

43. Partanen, *Nordic Theory of Everything*, 327ff.; Esteban Ortiz-Ospina and Max Roser, "Happiness and Life Satisfaction," *Our World in Data*, May 2017, https://ourworldindata.org/happiness-and-life-satisfaction.

Chapter 9. Protected Environment

1. Jan Bierre Lauridsen and Søren Anderson, "Queen Says Good Wind to Giant Turbines," *Berlingske*, September 4, 2013; DONG Energy, "Anholt Offshore Wind Farm Newsletter," January 2012.

2. "30 Years of Policies for Wind Energy: Lessons from Denmark," https://www.irena.org/documentdownloads/publications/gwec_denmark.pdf; "Danish Energy Agreement for 2008–2011," *IEA Denmark*, May 12, 2014.

3. Mikael S. Andersen and Helle O. Nielsen, "Denmark: Small State with a Big Voice and Bigger Dilemmas," in Rüdiger Wurzel and James Connelly, eds., *The EU as a Leader in International Climate Change Politics* (London, 2016), 83–97.

4. Wurzel and Connelly, *EU as a Leader in International Climate Change Politics*; Henrik Lund et al., "Danish Wind Power: Export and Cost," *CEESA Paper*, June 13, 2009.

5. Sandra Chaney, *Nature of the Miracle Years: Conservation in West Germany, 1945–1975* (New York, 2008); Christof Mauch, "Slow Hope," *Rachel Carson Center Perspectives*, no. 1 (Munich, 2019).

6. Brett Smith, "Denmark: Environmental Issues, Policies and Clean Technology," *AZO-cleantech*, July 16, 2015.

7. "The Energy Movement OOA," http://www.ooa.dk/eng/engelsk.htm.

8. James Lyons (a US pioneer in wind power) email to author, September 2, 2019; "30 Years of Policies for Wind Energy," 59ff.

9. Andersen and Nielsen, "Denmark," 84–85; "Shedding Light on Energy in the EU," 2020 edition, https://ec.europa.eu/eurostat/cache/infographs/energy/bloc-2c.html.

10. Andersen and Nielsen, "Denmark," 84–85; Karl Sperling, Frede Hvelplund, and Brian Vad Mathiesen, "Evaluation of Wind Power Planning in Denmark: Towards an Integrated Perspective," *Energy* 35 (2010), 5443–54.

11. IEA, "Danish Energy Agreement for 2008–2011," *IEA/IRENA Renewables Policies Database*, November 5, 2017, https://www.iea.org/policiesandmeasures/pams/denmark/name-24487-en.php.

12. European Environment Agency, "Denmark Country Briefing 2015," https://www.eea.europa.eu/soer2015/countries/denmark.

13. "Denmark Passes Climate Change Act," *Offshorewind*, January 14, 2015; Andersen and Nielsen, "Denmark," 87ff.

14. BusinessGreen, "Denmark Aims to Get 50 Percent of All Electricity from Wind Power," *Guardian*, March 26, 2012; Andersen and Nielsen, "Denmark," 88ff.

15. Adele Peters, "How Copenhagen Plans to Reach Carbon Neutral Status in Just Six Years," *New York Times*, August 20, 2019.

16. Michael Booth, *The Almost Nearly Perfect People: Behind the Myth of Scandinavian Utopia* (New York, 2014).

17. Nigel Haig, *EU Environmental Policy: Its Journey to Center Stage* (London, 2016); Brundtland Commission, *Our Common Future: Report of the World Commission on Environment and Development* (Oxford, 1987).

18. "From Where Do We Import Energy and How Dependent Are We?," https://ec.europa.eu/eurostat/cache/infographs/energy/bloc-2c.html.

19. Wurzel and Connelly, "European Climate Leadership," in *The EU as a Leader in International Climate Change Politics*, 3–19.

20. "Kyoto Protocol to the United Nations Framework Convention on Climate Change," December 11, 1997, https://unfccc.int/resource/docs/convkp/kpeng.pdf; Susan R. Fletcher, *Global Climate Change: The Kyoto Protocol* (Washington, DC, 2005).

21. European Environment Agency, "Trends and Projections in Europe 2017," 1ff.; Charlotte Burns, Peter Eckersley, and Paul Tobin, "EU Environmental Policy in Times of Crisis," *Journal of European Public Policy*, January 11, 2019.

22. European Commission, Climate Action, "Paris Agreement," December 12, 2015, https://ec.europa.eu/clima/policies/international/negotiations/paris_en; Wurzel and Connelly, "European Climate Leadership," 8ff.

23. Sweden, "Saving the Climate," updated April 29, 2020, https://sweden.se/nature/sustainable-living/; Lars Peter Teigen, "Norway's Green Delusions," *Foreign Policy*, September 18, 2018; Jari Lyytimäk, "Environmental Protection in Finland," *ThisisFinland*, July 2014.

24. EEA, "Germany Country Briefing," February 18, 2015. Cf. Stephen Milder, *Greening Democracy: The Anti-Nuclear Movement and Political Environmentalism in West Germany and Beyond, 1968–1983* (Cambridge, 2017).

25. EEA, "France Country Briefing," February 18, 2015; Joseph Szarka, *The Shaping of Environmental Policy in France* (New York, 2002).

26. Brett Smith, "United Kingdom: Environmental Issues, Policies and Clean Technology," *AZOcleantech*, May 16, 2018; EEA, "United Kingdom Country Briefing," February 18, 2015.

27. Dave Keating, "Italy's Environment Policy," *Politico*, June 12, 2014; G. P. Thomas, "Environmental Policies in Spain," *AZOcleantech*, July 24, 2018.

28. EEA, "Poland Country Briefing" and "Czech Republic Country Briefing," February 18, 2015; National Academy of Sciences, "Environmental Policy in Eastern Europe," *Ecological Risks*, 2017.

29. European Commission, "The Habitats Directive," May 21, 1992, https://ec.europa.eu/environment/nature/legislation/habitatsdirective/index_en.htm; Arthur Neslen, "Conservationists Declare Victory for Wildlife as EU Saves Nature Directives," *Guardian*, December 7, 2016.

30. EEA, *Recycling Municipal Waste* (Brussels, 2008); Oliver Franklin-Wallis, "'Plastic Recycling Is a Myth': What Really Happens to Our Rubbish," *Guardian*, August 17, 2019; Rui Cunha Marques and Nuno Ferreira da Cruz, *Recycling and Extended Producer Responsibility: The European Experience* (London, 2016).

31. Alex Whiting, "Shoppers 'Can't Afford' Energy Efficient Cars, Homes," *Horizon*, July 25, 2019; EEA, "Progress on Energy Efficiency in Europe," February 20, 2019.

32. European Commission, "Reducing CO_2 Emissions from Passenger Cars before 2020," https://ec.europa.eu/clima/policies/transport/vehicles/cars_en; Jasper Jolly, "Carmakers Criticize 'Unrealistic,'" *Guardian*, December 18, 2018; William Boston, "EU Auto Makers Have to Sell More Electric Cars as New Emission Targets Loom," *Wall Street Journal*, June 21, 2019.

33. European Cycling Federation, "EU Cycling Strategy," https://ecf.com/eu_cycling_strategy; "Bike Culture: Europe vs. America," *Reliance Foundry*, June 22, 2017.

34. Jonathan English, "Why Public Transportation Works Better outside the US," *Citylab*, October 10, 2018; European Commission, "Clean Transport, Urban Transport," https://ec.europa.eu/transport/themes/urban/urban_mobility/urban_mobility_actions/public_transport_en.

35. European Food Information Council, "New Nutrition Guidelines for Europe, Halfway There," May 1, 2011; Livio Martucci, "Food Wellness in Europe," *International Nut and Dried Food Council*, July 20, 2018.

36. EU Science Hub, "Making the Most of Our Green Spaces," January 30, 2019; European Commission, "Urban Green Spaces Increase Happiness," *European Green Capital*, 2014.

37. EC, "Green Jobs—A Success Story in Europe," *Magazine Environment for Europeans*, November 14, 2016; "Jobs for a Green Future," *Magazine Environment for Europeans*, July 13, 2017.

38. Marion Solletty, Emma Diltz, and Gašper Zarvršnik, "Europe's Environmental Bad Guys," *Politico*, February 9, 2017.

39. Ricardo Garcia Mira, "Leading a Green Lifestyle Could Help Us Be More Satisfied," *Horizon*, November 4, 2015; Elizabeth Rosenthal, "What Makes Europe Greener Than the US?," *Yale Environment*, September 28, 2009.

40. Greta Thunberg, *No One Is Too Small to Make a Difference* (London, 2019); Jonathan Watts, "Greta Thunberg, Schoolgirl Climate Change Warrior," *Guardian*, March 11, 2019.

41. Conn Hallinan, "Climate Catastrophe Comes for Europe," *Foreign Policy in Focus*, September 5, 2019; Glenn Scherer, "Facing a Possible Climate Apocalypse: How Should We Live?," *Mongaby*, September 15, 2019.

42. Mat Hope and Eduardo Robaina, "How the Rise of Populism Is Fueling Climate Science Denial across Europe," *Desmog*, September 18, 2019; Stephen Pope, "Climate Change Divides Europe," *Forbes*, July 7, 2019.

43. EEA, "Climate Change Evident across Europe, Confirming Urgent Need for Adaptation," November 19, 2012; Nicola Davison, "The Anthropocene Epoch," *Guardian*, May 30, 2019.

44. EU, *Eurobarometer Special Report 468* (Brussels, 2017); "25 Everyday Techniques to Save the Environment," *One Cent at a Time*, January 11, 2017.

Chapter 10. Defense Disagreements

1. "Putin Reclaims Crimea and Bitterly Denounces the West," *New York Times*, March 19, 2014.

2. Timothy Snyder, *The Road to Unfreedom: Russia, Europe, America* (New York, 2018).

3. Jeffrey Mankoff, "Russia's Latest Land-Grab: How Putin Won Crimea and Lost Ukraine," *Foreign Affairs* 93 (2014), 60–68.

4. Petro Poroshenko, "Ukraine Involved in New Type of Warfare," *Interfax*, June 18, 2014. Cf. James J. Sheehan, *Where Have All the Soldiers Gone? The Transformation of Modern Europe* (Boston, 2008).

5. Sterling Michael Pavelec, *War and Warfare since 1945* (Milton Park, 2017); Wayne E. Lee, "Culture of War," in *Oxford Bibliographies* (New York, 2017).

6. Serhii Plokhy, *The Gates of Europe: A History of Ukraine* (London, 2015); Guido Hausmann and Tanja Penter, "The Uses of History Ukraine 2014: Ideology und Historiography," *Osteuropa* 93 (2014), 35ff.

7. Taras Kuzio, ed., *Contemporary Ukraine: Dynamics of Post-Soviet Transformation* (Armonk, NY, 1998).

8. Roman Solchanyk, *Ukraine and Russia: The Post-Soviet Transition* (Lanham, MD, 2001).

9. Andrew Wilson, *Ukraine's Orange Revolution* (New Haven, CT, 2005).

10. Neil McFarland and Anand Menon, "The EU and Ukraine," *Survival* 56 (2014), 95–101; Rilka Dragneva and Kataryna Wolczuk, *Ukraine between EU and Russia: The Integration Challenge* (Basingstoke, 2015).

11. Nadia Diuk, "Euromaidan: Ukraine's Self-Organizing Revolution," *World Affairs* 176 (2014), 9–16; David R. Marples and Frederick V. Mills, eds., *Ukraine's Euromaidan: Analyses of a Civil Revolution* (Stuttgart, 2015).

12. Douglas E. Schoen, *Putin's Master Plan: To Destroy Europe, Divide NATO, and Restore Russian Power and Global Influence* (New York, 2016).

13. Andrew E. Kramer, "Russian Military Supplied Missile That Shot Down Malaysian Jet, Prosecutors Say," *New York Times*, May 24, 2018.

14. "Ukraine Election: Comedian Zelensky Wins Presidency by Landslide," *BBC News*, April 22, 2019.

15. Viktor Yushchenko, "Whither Ukraine: Plotting Europe's Eastern Border," *New York Times*, September 10, 2014; Jussi Laine, Ilkka Liikanen, and James W. Scott, eds., *Post–Cold War Borders: Reframing Political Space in Eastern Europe* (London, 2018).

16. Anders Fogh Rasmussen, "NATO Must Increase Spending to Protect Europe's Eastern and Southern Borders," *Telegraph*, August 30, 2014.

17. William Safire, "Irregular Warfare," *New York Times Magazine*, June 8; 2008; John Hooper and Ian Black, "Anger at Rumsfeld Attack on 'Old Europe,'" *Guardian*, January 23, 2003.

18. Peter V. Jakobsen and Jens Ringsmose, "Victim of Its Own Success: How NATO's Difficulties Are Caused by the Absence of a Unifying Existential Threat," *Journal of Transatlantic Studies* 16 (2018), 38–58.

19. Robert J. Art, "Why Western Europe Needs the United States and NATO," *Political Science Quarterly* 111 (1996), 1–39; Frank Nagler, ed., *Die Bundeswehr 1955 bis 2005: Rückblenden, Einsichten, Perspektiven* (Munich, 2007).

20. Sabrina P. Ramet, *Balkan Babel: The Disintegration of Yugoslavia from the Death of Tito to the Fall of Milošević*, 4th ed. (Boulder, CO, 2002).

21. Steve Crenshaw, "Euro-Army Set to Advance from Words to Deeds," *Independent*, January 14, 1994; "Eurocorps: A Force for Europe and NATO," 2020, https://www.eurocorps.org/.

22. Martin Walker, "Post 9/11: The European Dimension," *World Policy Journal* 18 (2000/2001), 1–10.

23. PBS special report on "Terror in Europe," 2016; Petter Nesser, *Islamist Terrorism in Europe: A History* (New York, 2016).

24. "European Commission Outlines Main Achievements, Future Challenges of EU Counter-Terrorism Policy," *US Fed News Service*, July 21, 2010; Fiona de Londras and Josephine Doody, eds., *The Impact, Legitimacy and Effectiveness of EU Counter-Terrorism* (London, 2015).

25. Hae-Won Jun, "The European Public's Decision on the War in Iraq: Differences among the EU Member States," *International Area Review* 12 (2009), 47–63; Geoff Meade, "War on Iraq: European Divisions Still Remain," *Western Mail*, April 10, 2003.

26. Anand Menon, "European Defense Policy from Lisbon to Libya," *Global Politics and Strategy* 53 (2011), 75–90.

27. Julian E. Barnes and Robert Wall, "Mattis Presses Europe on NATO Defense Spending," *Wall Street Journal*, February 14, 2018; "Macron Hosts Trump amid Row over European Defense," *AFP International Text Wire*, November 10, 2018.

28. "UK Government: Iran/Nuclear: A Significant Step towards Confidence Building in Iran's Nuclear Programme," *M2 Presswire*, November 16, 2004; Paul K. Kerr, "Iran's Nuclear Program: Status," *Current Politics and Economics of the Middle East* 9 (2018), 151–250.

29. Chris Hedges, "From One Serbian Militia Chief, a Trail of Plunder and Slaughter," *New York Times*, March 25, 1996.

30. Elena Kostyuchenko, "The Story of a Russian Soldier's War in Ukraine: 'We All Knew What We Had to Do and What Could Happen,'" *Euromaidan Press*, March 2, 2015.

31. Kim Traill, "Propaganda Fuels Deadly Ukraine War on Europe's Eastern Border," *ABC Premium News*, November 19, 2019. Cf. Ivo Andric, *The Bridge on the Drina* (London, 1959).

32. Peter Finn, "Hamburg's Cauldron of Terror: Within Cell of 7, Hatred towards US Grew and Sept. 11 Plot Evolved," *Washington Post*, September 11, 2002.

33. "Paris Attacks: Who Were the Attackers?," *BBC News*, April 27, 2015; Angelique Chrisafis, "'It Looked Like a Battlefield': The Full Story of What Happened in the Bataclan," *Guardian*, November 20, 2015.

34. Brett Stephens, "What Is Anders Breivik?," *Wall Street Journal*, July 26, 2011; Sandra Laville, "Rightwing 'Lone Wolves' Kill More Than Islamic Terrorists Acting Alone, Report Says," *Guardian*, June 22, 2016.

35. Aida Cerkez, "Bosnian Woman Helped Make Rape a War Crime," *Christian Science Monitor*, March 8, 2013.

36. Michael Kaufman, "'Ethnic Cleansing': Europe's Old Horror with New Victims," *New York Times*, August 2, 1992; Norman Naimark, *Fires of Hatred: Ethnic Cleansing in Twentieth Century Europe* (Cambridge, 2001).

37. Rianne Letschert, Antony Pemberton, and Ines Staiger, eds., *Assisting Victims of Terrorism: Towards a European Standard of Justice* (Dordrecht, 2010).

38. European Report, "EU Tests Bush Administration at Washington Ministerial," March 3, 2001; Bruno Waterfield, "Ashton Draws Up Secret Plan to Run Bosnia," *Daily Telegraph*, July 28, 2010.

39. Rachel Kerr, "International Criminal Tribunal for the Former Yugoslavia (ICTY)," in *Oxford Bibliographies* (Oxford, 2018).

40. See the home pages of Doctors Without Borders, https://www.msf.org/; Greenpeace, https://www.greenpeace.org; Amnesty International, https://www amnesty.org; and the Association of European Journalists, https://www.aej.org/.

41. Ana Postlache, "The EU Security Continuum: The Interaction between Internal and External Spheres in Combating 'New Security Threats,'" *Sfera Politicii* 20 (2012), 149–57.

42. Michael Brenner, "EU Security Policy: What It Is, How It Works, Why It Matters," *Perspectives on Politics* 11 (2013), 348–49.

43. Antulio Echevarria, *Reconsidering the American Way of War: US Military Practice from the Revolution to Afghanistan* (Washington, DC, 2014). Cf. "Judy Asks: Will U.S. Troop Pullouts Accelerate European Defense Integration?," *Strategic Europe*, June 11, 2020.

44. Sebastian Sprenger, "Germany Sets Up European Defense Agenda with a Waning US Footprint in Mind," *DefenseNews*, July 15, 2020; Thomas L. Ilgen, ed., *Hard Power, Soft Power and the Future of Transatlantic Relations* (Aldershot, 2006).

45. Joseph S. Nye, *The Powers to Lead: Soft, Hard and Smart* (New York, 2008).

Chapter 11. Populist Backlash

1. Petition, "Les Citoyens de France," *Change.org*, May 29, 2018. Cf. Rosie Collyer, "A Year in the Life of Yellow Vest Protest Leader Priscilla Ludosky," *rfi*, November 15, 2019, https://www.rfi.fr.

2. "French Gilets Jaunes: Who Is Protest Leader Eric Drouet?," *BBC News*, November 18, 2019; John Lichfield, "Just Who Are the Gilets Jaunes?," *Guardian*, February 9, 2019. Cf. Timothy Garton Ash, "Time for a New Liberation?," *New York Review of Books*, October 24, 2019.

3. Albrecht Meier, "Es brodelt wieder in Frankreich," *Tagesspiegel*, November 17, 2019; "France's Macron Responds to Yellow Vests with Promise of Reform," *BBC News*, April 25, 2019.

4. Cas Mudde and Cristobal R. Kaltwasser, *Populism: A Very Short Introduction* (Oxford, 2017); Roger Cohen, "It's Time to Depopularize 'Populist,'" *New York Times*, July 13, 2018.

5. William A. Galston, "The Rise of European Populism and the Collapse of the Center-Left," *Brookings Institution*, March 8, 2018; "Europe and Right-Wing Nationalism: A Country by Country Guide," *BBC News*, November 13, 2019.

6. Marcos Ancelovici, Pascale Dufour, and Héloïse Nez, eds., *Street Politics in the Age of Austerity: From the Indignados to Occupy* (Amsterdam, 2016).

7. Pierre Poujade, *J'ai choisi le combat* (Saint-Cere, 1955); Jean Ruhlmann, "Le mouvement Poujade: De la défense professionelle au populisme nationaliste," *Revue d'Histoire Moderne et Contemporaine* 55 (2008), 222–29.

8. Dominique Renié, "'Heritage Populism' and France's National Front," *Journal of Democracy* 27 (2016), 47–57; Dominique Albertini and David Doucet, *Histoire du Front National* (Paris, 2013).

9. Marc Lazar, "The French Communist Party," in *The Cambridge History of Communism*, vol. 2 (Cambridge, 2017), 619–41; Gino J. Raymond, *The French Communist Party during the Fifth Republic: A Crisis of Leadership and Ideology* (Basingstoke, 2005).

10. David S. Bell and Byron Criddle, *Exceptional Socialists: The Case of the French Socialist Party* (Houndmills, 2014).

11. Immanuel Wallerstein, "France: The End of Gaullism?," *New York Times*, May 15, 2007; Serge Berstein, *Histoire de Gaullisme* (Paris, 2001).

12. Emmanuel Macron, *Revolution* (Brunswick, 2017); Jocelyn Evans and Gilles Ivaldi, *The 2017 French Presidential Elections: A Political Reformation* (Cham, 2018).

13. "Taking to the Streets: France's Big Protests," *AFP International*, March 22, 2018; Carly Read, "Paris Riots: Furious Clashes on the Streets of France as Protests Spiral Out of Control," *Express*, September 22, 2019.

14. Tristan Gaudiaut, "'Gilets Jaunes,' les origins économiques d'une colère," *Statista FR*, November 15, 2019.

15. Eberhard Spreng, "Wie sich die Gelbwesten verändern—und ihre Geschichte schreiben," *Tagesspiegel*, November 15, 2019; Lichfield, "Who Are the Gilets Jaunes?"

16. Simon Tormey, "The Contemporary Crisis of Representative Democracy," *Democratic Theory* 1 (2014), 104–12.

17. Mudde and Kaltwasser, *Populism*, 42ff.; Samir Gandesha, "Understanding Right and Left Populism," in Jeremiah Morelock, ed., *Critical Theory and Authoritarian Populism* (Westminster, 2018).

18. "Silvio Berlusconi: Italy's Perpetual Powerbroker," *BBC News*, May 29, 2019; Sergio Fabbrini, "The Rise and Fall of Silvio Berlusconi: Personalization of Politics and Its Limits," *Comparative European Politics* 11 (2014), 153–71.

19. Matt Schudel, "Jörg Haider: Politician Made Far-Right Party a Force in Austria," *Washington Post*, October 12, 2008; Lothat Höbelt, *Defiant Populist: Jörg Haider and the Politics of Austria* (West Lafayette, IN, 2003).

20. Jacques Paulus Koenis, "A History of Dutch Populism: From the Murder of Pim Fortuyn to the Rise of Geert Wilders," *Conversation*, March 14, 2017.

21. Olga Iakimova, "Exploring the Dynamics of Xenophobia in the Nordic Countries," *ResearchGate*, January 2018; Seri Berman, "Five Takeaways About the Swedish Election," *Washington Post*, September 12, 2018.

22. Kevin Ovendon, *Syriza: Inside the Labyrinth* (London, 2015); Giorgos Katsambekis and Alexandros Kioupkiolis, eds., *The Populist Radical Left in Europe* (Abingdon, Oxon, 2019).

23. Pablo Iglesias, "Understanding Podemos," *New Left Review* 93 (May–June 2015), 7–23. Cf. José Magone, *Contemporary Spanish Politics*, 3rd rev. ed. (London, 2017).

24. "Eastern Europe's Populist Scam," editorial, *New York Times*, November 6, 2019; Matina Stevis-Gridneff and Benjamin Novak, "EU Tries Gentle Diplomacy to Counter Hungary's Crackdown on Democracy," *New York Times*, March 31, 2020; Luke Waller, "Viktor Orbán Hungary: The Conservative Subversive," *Politico 28*, https://www.politico.eu/list/politico-28/viktor-orban/.

25. Norman Naimark, "Where Is Poland Heading?," *Hoover Digest*, 4 (2018), 121–28; Katharina Bluhm and Mihai Varga, eds., *New Conservatives in Russia and East Central Europe* (London, 2018).

26. Wolfgang Merkel and Robert Vehrkamp, "Warum der Populismus in Deutschland rückläufig ist," *Tagesspiegel*, September 6, 2020; Jay Julian Rosellini, *The German New Right: The AfD, PEGIDA and the Re-Imagining of National Identity* (London, 2019).

27. Cas Mudde, *Populist Radical Right Parties in Europe* (Cambridge, 2007); Mudde and Kaltwasser, *Populism*, 42ff.; Paul Krugman, "This Putsch Was Decades in the Making," *New York Times*, January 12, 2021.

28. Mark Baumgärtner et al., "Europas Saubermänner: Das wahre Gesicht der Rechtspopulisten," *Der Spiegel*, May 25, 2019, 16–27. Cf. Ash, "Time for a New Liberation?"

29. Suzanne Moore, "Jacob Rees-Mogg Isn't Old Fashioned, He Is a Thoroughly Modern Bigot," *Guardian*, September 6, 2017.

30. James McAuley, "Eric Zemmour Is France's Right-Wing Prophet of Doom," *Washington Post*, October 1, 2018; Scott McConnell, "Marion Marechal's Populism Is the Future of the French Right," *American Conservative*, October 3, 2019.

31. Dominik Owczarek, "The Roots of Populism in Poland: Unsustainable Growth and Cultural Backlash," *CIDOB*, April 2017; Darius Kalan, "A Tale of Two Polands," *Foreign Policy*, October 11, 2018.

32. Krisztina Than, "Fear of Migrants Galvanizes PM Orbán's Supporters in Rural Hungary," *Reuters*, March 21, 2018; Timofey Neshitov and Jan Puhl, "Im Labor des Populisten," *Der Spiegel*, December 28, 2019.

33. "Conversable Economist: Some Thoughts About Populism," *Newstex Global Business Blogs*, November 4, 2019; Thieß Petersen, "Ökonomische Wurzeln des Populismus," *Wirtschaftsdienst* 98 (2018), 638ff.

34. Armin Schäfer, "Return with a Vengeance: Working Class Anger and the Rise of Populism," *Items SSRC*, August 8, 2017; J. Rydgren, ed., *Class Politics and the Radical Right* (Abingdon, Oxon, 2012).

35. Yanis Varoufakis, *Adults in the Room: My Battle with Europe's Deep Establishment* (London, 2017); and review by Constantine P. Danopoulos, *Mediterranean Quarterly* 29 (2018), 120–23.

36. Thilo Sarrazin, *Deutschland schafft sich ab: Wie wir unser Land aufs Spiel setzen* (Munich, 2010); "German Election: How Right-Wing Is Nationalist AfD?," *BBC News*, October 13, 2017.

37. Benjamin Krämer, "Media Populism: A Conceptual Clarification and Some Theses on Its Effects," *Communication Theory* 24 (2014), 42–60.

38. Will Self, "The World Run by Comedians: But Is Anyone Laughing?," *Guardian*, August 25, 2019.

39. Colin Crouch, *Post-Democracy* (Cambridge, 2004), versus Klaus von Beyme, *From Post-Democracy to Neo-Democracy* (Cham, 2018).

40. Mudde and Kaltwasser, *Populism*, 79–96.

41. Paul Nolte, *Demokratie: Die 101 wichtigsten Fragen* (Munich, 2015), 141–43.

42. Jan-Werner Müller, *What Is Populism?* (State College, PA, 2016), 75–100.

43. Stephen Milder, *Greening Democracy: The Anti-Nuclear Movement and Political Environmentalism in West Germany and Beyond, 1968–1983* (Cambridge, 2017), 238–46.

Chapter 12. Global Role

1. Stanley Reed, "Climate Crisis Takes Center Stage at World Economic Forum," *New York Times*, January 21, 2020; Christina Garsten and Adrienne Sörbom, *Discreet Power: How the World Economic Forum Shapes Market Agendas* (Stanford, CA, 2018).

2. Ursula von der Leyen, "The European Green Deal," *Asia News Monitor*, December 16, 2019; Stephen Brown, "Von der Leyen Calls World Leaders to Action on Climate in Davos," *Politico*, January 22, 2020.

3. Chris Megerian, "At Davos, Trump Rejects Climate Crisis, Lauds US Economy and Fossil Fuels," *Los Angeles Times*, January 21, 2020.

4. Hannes Koch, "Merkel geht auf alle zu," *Die Tageszeitung*, January 24, 2020; Daniel Stelter, "Der Davoser Konsens ist eine Illusion," *Cicero*, January 28, 2020.

5. Anthony Giddens, Patrick Diamond, and Roger Liddle, eds., *Global Europe, Social Europe* (Cambridge, 2006).

6. Andreas Wirsching, *Der Preis der Freiheit: Geschichte Europas in unserer Zeit* (Munich, 2012); Konrad H. Jarausch, "'Partner in der Führung' oder zögerliche Mittelmacht? Das vereinigte Deutschland aus amerikanischer Sicht in den 1990er Jahren," https://www.ifz-muenchen.de/en/events/event/datum////dreissig-jahre-zwei-plus-vier-vertrag/, October 6, 2020.

7. Laura Silver, "Where Americans and Europeans Agree—and Differ—in the Values They See as Important," *Facttank*, October 18, 2019. Cf. Konrad H. Jarausch, "Drifting Apart: Cultural Dimensions of Transatlantic Estrangement," in Hermann Kurthen, Antonio Menendez, and Stefan Immerfall, eds., *Safeguarding German-American Relations in the New Century: Understanding and Accepting Mutual Differences* (Lanham, MD, 2006), 17–32.

8. "The American-Western European Value Gap," *Pew Research Center*, November 17, 2011; Jacob Poupshter and Mara Mordecai, "Americans and Germans Differ in Their Views of Each Other and the World," *Pew Research Center*, March 9, 2020.

9. Anna Dimitrova, "The State of the Transatlantic Relationship in the Trump Era," Fondation Robert Schuman, February 4, 2020; Donald E. Pease, *American Exceptionalism* (New York, 2018).

10. Xenia Wickett, *Transatlantic Relations Converging or Diverging?* (London, 2018); Frederiga Bindi, ed., *Europe and America: The End of the Transatlantic Relationship?* (Washington, DC, 2019).

11. "US Pressures EU to Ditch Iran at Mideast Conference," *RFI*, February 14, 2019; Conrad Smith, "EU 'Will Continue to Fight for Iranian Nuclear Deal,'" *PressReader*, January 9. 2020.

12. Timothy Snyder, *The Road to Unfreedom: Russia, Europe, America* (New York, 2018).

13. Klaus Larres, "Angela Merkel and China: Trade, the US, the South-China Sea and the Continuation of 'Ostpolitik,'" *CPG Online Magazine*, November 2015; Paul Gerwitz, "The Future of Trans-Atlantic Collaboration on China: What the EU-China Summit Showed," *Brookings*, June 26, 2020.

14. Simon Osborne, "EU Ignites Trump War," *Express*, February 20, 2018; "Trump to Impose Trade Tariffs on US-Allies Mexico, Canada, EU," *Asian News International*, May 31, 2018.

15. Dara Doyle and Aoife White, "Google's Ireland Tax Arrangement Draws More EU Scrutiny," *Bloomberg Wire Service*, April 15, 2019.

16. Simon Serfaty, "The Biden Transition," *Fondation Robert Schuman Policy Paper* no. 580, January 12, 2021; Erik Bratberg and David Whineray, "How Europe Views Transatlantic Relations Ahead of the 2020 U.S. Election," February 20, 2020, https://carnegieendowment.org /2020/02/20/how-europe-views-transatlantic-relations-ahead-of-2020-u.s.-election-pub -810492014.

17. Astrid Boening, Jan-Frederik Kremer, Aukje van Loon, eds., *Global Power Europe*, vol. 1 (Springer, 2013).

18. Wilfried Loth, *Building Europe: A History of European Unification* (Berlin, 2015).

19. Nicolai Wammen, "EU Enlargement," *Danish Foreign Policy Yearbook* (2014), 191–94.

20. Ulrich Krotz, Kiran Klaus Patel, and Federico Romero, eds., *Europe's Cold War Relations, 1957–1992* (London, 2019).

21. European Commission, "EU Aid Explorer," https://euaidexplorer.ec.europa.eu/content /homepage_en; Maurizio Carbone, *The European Union and International Development: The Politics of Foreign Aid* (New York, 2007).

22. Patrick Leblond and Crina Viju-Miljusevic, "EU Trade Policy in the Twenty-First Century," *Journal of European Public Policy* 26 (2019), 1836–46; https://ec.europa.eu/eurostat /statistics-explained/index.php?title=File:Value_of_international_trade_in_goods_and _services,_selected_countries,_2018_(billion_EUR)_GL2019.png.

23. Edith Drieskens and Louise G. van Schaik, eds., *The EU and Effective Multilateralism: Internal and External Reform Practices* (Abingdon, Oxon, 2014).

24. Thorsten Mumme, "Mit diesem Vertrag will die EU ihre Werte exportieren," *Tagesspiegel*, February 12, 2020; Felipe Gomez, Christina Churruca Muguruza, and Jan Wouters, eds., *EU Human Rights and Democratization Policies: Achievements and Challenges* (Abingdon, Oxon, 2018).

25. European Union External Action Service, "Military and Civilian Missions and Operations," March 5, 2019, https://eeas.europa.eu/headquarters/headquarters-homepage/430 /military-and-civilian-missions-and-operations_en; Isabelle Delpla, Xavier Bougarel, and Jean-Louis Fournel, eds., *Investigating Srebrenica: Institutions, Facts, Responsibilities* (New York, 2012).

26. Richard Milne, "EU Committed to Keeping the Peace," *Financial Times*, December 10, 2012; Josep Borrell, "Die EU muss die Sprache der Macht neu erlernen," *Tagesspiegel*, February 8, 2020.

27. Albrecht Meier, "Die Europäer bleiben auf die USA angewiesen—vorerst," *Tagesspiegel*, February 8, 2020; Wofgang Ischinger, "Helmut Schmidt würde sich im Grabe umdrehen," *Tagesspiegel*, February 9, 2020.

28. Bernd Polster, ed., *Westwind—die Amerikanisierung Europas* (Cologne, 1995).

29. Tim Leffel, "Moving beyond the Bullet Holes in Bosnia and Hercegovina," *perceptivetravel.com*, June 2018, https://www.perceptivetravel.com/issues/0618/bosnia.html.

30. "EU and US States by Population Density," *Stockingblue*, February 14, 2018, https://www.stockingblue.com/article/128/eu-and-us-states-by-population-density/; Joe Pinsker, "Why Are American Homes So Big?," *Atlantic*, September 12, 2019.

31. Aditi Shrikant, "Why US Public Transportation Is So Bad—And Why Americans Don't Care," *Vox*, September 26, 2018; Timothy Beatley, *Green Urbanism: Learning from European Cities* (Washington, DC, 2000).

32. Nurith Aizenman, "Gun Violence: How the US Compares with Other Countries," *NPR*, October 6, 2017, https://www.npr.org/sections/goatsandsoda/2017/10/06/555861898/gun-violence-how-the-u-s-compares-to-other-countries.

33. Zsolt Darvas, "This Is the State of Inequality in Europe," *World Economic Forum*, May 4, 2018; Lucas Chancel, "The Fairest of Them All: Why Europe Beats the US on Equality," *Guardian*, January 24, 2018.

34. Olga Khazan, "What's Actually Wrong with the US Health System," *Atlantic*, July 14, 2017; Katarina Janus and Etienne Minivielle, "Rethinking Health Care Delivery," *Health Affairs*, December 15, 2017.

35. Wojtek Baszczyk and Project Polska, "Everyday Reality of Employees in US vs. EU," *4LibertyEU*, February 20, 2019; statement by Ari Harjunmaa, comparing life in the United States and Germany, *Quora*, September 25, 2018.

36. Aldemaro Romero, "US vs. Europe in Higher Education," *Edwardsville Intelligencer*, January 10, 2018; and answers to "Is US Education Different from European Education?" on *Quora*, December 26, 2018.

37. Josephine Livingstone, "Why Are Americans So Hostile to State-Funded Art?," *New Republic*, May 28, 2017; Elisabeth Braw, "The Best Country for an Opera Singer to Live?," *Newsweek*, July 17, 2014.

38. Beverly Bird, "How Do US Taxes Compare to Other Countries?," *balance*, November 20, 2019; Eurofound, "European Quality of Life Survey 2016," https://www.eurofound.europa.eu/surveys/european-quality-of-life-surveys/european-quality-of-life-survey-2016.

39. Dietmar Rothermund, ed., *Memories of Post-Imperial Nations: The Aftermath of Decolonization, 1945–2013* (Cambridge, 2014).

40. Mark Langan, *Neo-Colonialism and the Poverty of 'Development'* (Cham, 2018); Godfrey Mwakikagile, *Economic Development in Africa* (Commack, NY, 1999).

41. Christin Archick and Rhoda Margesson, "The European Migration Crisis," *Congressional Research Service*, July 17, 2015; Jochen Oltmer, *Migration vom 19. bis zum 21. Jahrhundert* (Berlin, 2016).

42. European Union, "Culture in the European Union," October 26, 2020, https://europa.eu/european-union/topics/culture_en; Kai Chan, "These Are the Most Powerful Languages in the World," World Economic Forum, December 31, 2016.

Conclusion: A Progressive Alternative

1. Geir Moulson, "'Best Germany Yet' Marks 30th Anniversary of Reunification," *AP*, October 3, 2020.

2. Robert Ide, "Was sich aus dem rasanten Umbruch lernen läßt," *Tagesspiegel*, October 3, 2020. Cf. Markus Böick, Constantin Goschler, and Ralph Jessen, eds., *Jahrbuch Deutsche Einheit* 1 (2020).

3. Norkus Zenonas, "Catching Up and Falling Behind: Four Puzzles after Two Decades of Post-Communist Transformation," *Comparative Economic Research* 18 (2015), 63–79. Cf. Raj Kollmorgen, Hans-Jürgen Wagener, and Wolfgang Merkel, eds., *The Handbook of Political, Social, and Economic Transformation* (Oxford, 2019).

4. Philipp Ther, *Das andere Ende der Geschichte: Über die Große Transformation* (Berlin, 2020).

5. Konrad H. Jarausch, ed., *Das Ende der Zuversicht: Die siebziger Jahre als Geschichte* (Göttingen, 2008); Wolfgang Streeck, *Buying Time: The Delayed Crisis of Democratic Capitalism* (London, 2014).

6. Kathleen Thelen, *Varieties of Liberalization and the New Politics of Social Solidarity* (Cambridge, 2014).

7. Stephen Kotkin, *Uncivil Society: 1989 and the Implosion of the Communist Establishment* (New York, 2009). Cf. Donald J. Raleigh, *Soviet Baby Boomers: An Oral History of Russia's Cold War Generation* (Oxford, 2011).

8. Sławomir Dębski and Daniel S. Hamilton, eds., *Europe Whole and Free: Vision and Reality* (Washington, DC, 2019).

9. Konrad H. Jarausch, ed., *United Germany: Debating Processes and Prospects* (New York, 2013); Edgar Wolfrum, *Der Aufsteiger: Eine Geschichte Deutschlands von 1990 bis heute* (Stuttgart, 2020); Hartmut Kaelble, "The Crises in the EU and Germany, 2008–2020," lecture at the CES of the University of North Carolina at Chapel Hill, April 15, 2021.

10. Ivan T. Berend, *From the Soviet Bloc to the European Union: The Economic and Social Transformation of Central and Eastern Europe since 1973* (Cambridge, 2009).

11. Philipp Ther, *Europe since 1989: A History* (Princeton, NJ, 2016).

12. John Connelly, *From Peoples into Nations: A History of Eastern Europe* (Princeton, NJ, 2020).

13. Jacob Poushter, "Ten Key Takeaways About Public Opinion in Europe 30 Years after the Fall of Communism," *FactTank*, October 15, 2020.

14. "Angela Merkel Lays Out Vision to Unify European Union in Parliamentary Address," *Deutsche Welle*, July 8, 2020; Theresa Kuhn, "Grand Theories of European Integration Revisited: Does Identity Politics Shape the Course of European Integration?," *Journal of European Public Policy* 26 (2019), 1213–30.

15. World Economic Forum report, http://www.weforum.org/videos/europe-2020-report-jennifer-blank; "Competitiveness Report of the European Commission," https://www.wifo.ac.at/en/research/current_projects/competitiveness_report.

16. Erik Brattberg and Tomas Valasek, "EU Defense Cooperation: Progress amid Transatlantic Concerns," November 21, 2019, https://carnegieendowment.org/2019/11/21/eu-defense-cooperation-progress-amid-transatlantic-concerns-pub-80381; Maxime H. A. Larivé, *Debating European Security and Defense Policy: Understanding the Complexity* (London, 2014).

17. Matina Stevis-Gridneff, Patrick Kingsley, and Hellen Willis, "Tear Gas, Gunfire and a Dash for the Border," *New York Times*, March 13, 2020; Marco Scipioni, "Failing Forward in EU Migration Policy?," *Journal of European Public Policy* 25 (2018), 1357–75.

18. Selam Gebrekidan, "Scientists Urge Changes for Environmentally Damaging EU Farm Program," *New York Times*, March 11, 2020; Jos Delbeke and Peter Vis, *EU Climate Policy Explained* (London, 2015).

19. Katrin Bennhold, "A German Exception? Why the Country's Corona Death Rate Is Low," *New York Times*, April 4, 2020; Sarah Mervosh et al., "400,000 Deaths in a Year and Failure at Every Level," *New York Times*, January 18, 2021.

20. Richard Connor and John Silk, "Coronavirus: Germany Extends COVID Lockdown until February 14," *Deutsche Welle*, January 19, 2021; Sheryl Gay Stolberg, "Biden Announces National Effort to Counter Virus," *New York Times*, January 22, 2021.

21. David M. Herzenhorn and Lili Bayer, "EU Leaders Agree on €1.82T Budget and Coronavirus Recovery Package," *Politico*, July 20, 2020; Ferdinando Giugliano, "Why Europe's in Better Shape Than the U.S.," *Bloomberg Opinion*, July 6, 2020.

22. Matina Stevis-Gridneff, "'Protecting Our European Way of Life'? Outrage Follows New EU Role," *New York Times*, September 12, 2019; Annabelle Timsit, "Even Europeans Don't Agree on What the 'European Way of Life' Is," *Quartz*, October 16, 2019.

23. Francesco Piccinelli and Arnau Busquets Guardia, "The European Way of Life in Numbers," *Politico*, April 10, 2019. Cf. Hartmut Kaelble, ed., *The European Way: European Societies during the Nineteenth and Twentieth Centuries* (New York, 2004).

24. Javier Bilbao-Ubillos, "Is There Still Such a Thing as the 'European Social Model'?," *International Journal of Social Welfare*, May 31, 2015; Nicholas Kristof, "We're No 28! And Dropping," *New York Times*, September 10, 2020; John Purcell, "Why Is Europe More Progressive Than the USA?," *Quora*, May 25, 2019.

25. Roger Cohen, "The Future of Europe," lecture at the Center for European Studies at the University of North Carolina at Chapel Hill, September 29, 2020; and Andrew Gamble, *Open Left: The Future of Progressive Politics* (London, 2018).

SELECTED BIBLIOGRAPHY

Beatley, Timothy. *Green Urbanism: Learning from European Cities* (Washington, DC, 2000).

Bell, David S., and Byron Criddle. *Exceptional Socialists: The Case of the French Socialist Party* (Houndmills, 2014).

Berend, Ivan T. *Central and Eastern Europe, 1944–1993: Detour from the Periphery to the Periphery* (Cambridge, 1996).

———. *From the Soviet Bloc to the European Union: The Economic and Social Transformation of Eastern Europe since 1973* (Cambridge, 2009).

Black, Jeremy. *A History of Britain: 1945 to Brexit* (Bloomington, IN, 2017).

Carbone, Maurizio. *The European Union and International Development: The Politics of Foreign Aid* (New York, 2007).

Connelly, John. *From Peoples into Nations: A History of Eastern Europe* (Princeton, NJ, 2020).

Cousins, Mel. *European Welfare States: Comparative Perspectives* (London, 2005).

Crouch, Colin. *Post-Democracy* (Cambridge, 2004).

Dinan, Desmond. *Ever Closer Union: An Introduction to European Integration*, 4th ed. (Boulder, CO, 2010).

Eltsov, Peter. *The Long Telegram 2.0: A Neo-Kennanite Approach to Russia* (Lanham, MD, 2020).

Esping-Andersen, Gøsta. *Social Foundations of Postindustrial Economies* (Oxford, 1999).

Evans, Jocelyn, and Gilles Ivaldi. *The 2017 French Presidential Elections: A Political Reformation* (Cham, 2018).

Freeman, Richard B., Brigitta Swedenborg, and Robert Topel, eds. *Reforming the Welfare State: Recovery and Beyond in Sweden* (Chicago, 2010).

Garton Ash, Timothy. *Free World: America, Europe, and the Surprising Future of the West* (New York, 2004).

Giddens, Anthony. *Europe in the Global Age* (Cambridge, 2007).

Gomez, Felipe, Christina Churruca Muguruza, and Jan Wouters, eds. *EU Human Rights and Democratization Policies: Achievements and Challenges* (Abingdon, Oxon, 2018).

Goodwin, Matthew, and Caitlin Milazzo. *UKIP: Inside the Campaign to Redraw British Politics* (Oxford, 2015).

Gualtieri, Claudia, ed., *Migration and the Contemporary Mediterranean* (Oxford, 2018).

Hall, Stuart, and David Soskice. *Varieties of Capitalism: The Institutional Foundation of Comparative Advantage* (Oxford, 2001).

Hertfelder, Thomas, and Andreas Rödder, eds. *Modell Deutschland: Erfolgsgeschichte oder Illusion?* (Göttingen, 2007).

Hockerts, Hans-Günter. *Drei Wege deutscher Sozialstaatlichkeit: NS-Diktatur, Bundesrepublik und DDR im Vergleich* (Munich, 1998).

Hughes, Kirsty, ed., *European Competitiveness* (Cambridge, 1993).

Jarausch, Konrad H. *Out of Ashes: A New History of Europe in the Twentieth Century* (Princeton, NJ, 2015).

———. *The Rush to German Unity* (New York, 1994).

Kaelble, Hartmut. *A Social History of Europe, 1945–2000: Recovery and Transformation after Two World Wars* (New York, 2013).

Katsambekis, Giorgos, and Alexandros Kioupkiolis, eds. *The Populist Radical Left in Europe* (Abingdon Oxon, 2019).

Kenney, Padraic. *A Carnival of Revolution: Central Europe 1989* (Princeton, NJ, 2002).

Kershaw, Ian. *Roller-Coaster: Europe, 1950–2017* (London, 2018).

Kotkin, Stephen. *Uncivil Society: 1989 and the Implosion of the Communist Establishment* (New York, 2009).

Krastev, Ivan. *After Europe* (Philadelphia, 2017).

Krotz, Ulrich, Kiran Klaus Patel, and Federico Romero, eds. *Europe's Cold War Relations, 1957–1992* (London, 2019).

Langan, Mark. *Neo-Colonialism and the Poverty of 'Development'* (Cham, 2018).

Larivé, Maxime H. A. *Debating European Security and Defense Policy: Understanding the Complexity* (London, 2014).

Lemke, Christiane, and Helga Welsh. *Germany Today: Politics and Policies in a Changing World* (Lanham, MD, 2018).

Lipset, Seymour Martin, and Gary Marks. *It Didn't Happen Here: Why Socialism Failed in the United States* (New York, 2000).

Loth, Wilfried. *Building Europe: A History of European Unification* (Berlin, 2015).

Maier, Charles S. *Dissolution: The Crisis of Communism and the End of East Germany* (Princeton, NJ, 1997).

Marples, David R., and Frederick V. Mills, eds. *Ukraine's Euromaidan: Analyses of a Civil Revolution* (Stuttgart, 2015).

Marques, Rui Cunha, and Nuno Ferreira da Cruz. *Recycling and Extended Producer Responsibility: The European Experience* (London, 2016).

Marsh, David. *The Euro: The Battle for the New Global Currency* (New Haven, CT, 2011).

Milder, Stephen. *Greening Democracy: The Anti-Nuclear Movement and Political Environmentalism in West Germany and Beyond, 1968–1983* (Cambridge, 2017).

Mudde, Cas, and Cristobal R. Kaltwasser. *Populism: A Very Short Introduction* (Oxford, 2017).

Müller, Jan-Werner. *What Is Populism?* (State College, PA, 2016).

Murray, Douglas. *The Strange Death of Europe: Immigration, Identity, Islam* (London, 2017).

Naimark, Norman. *Fires of Hatred: Ethnic Cleansing in Twentieth Century Europe* (Cambridge, 2001).

Nesser, Petter. *Islamist Terrorism in Europe: A History* (New York, 2016).

Nolte, Paul. *Was ist Demokratie? Geschichte und Gegenwart* (Munich, 2012).

Nye, Joseph S. *The Powers to Lead: Soft, Hard and Smart* (New York, 2008).

Oltmer, Jochen. *Migration vom 19. bis zum 21. Jahrhundert* (Berlin, 2016).

Partanen, Anu. *The Nordic Theory of Everything: In Search of a Better Life* (New York, 2016).

Patel, Kiran Klaus. *Projekt Europa: Eine kritische Geschichte* (Munich, 2018).

Plamper, Jan. *Das Neue Wir: Warum Migration dazugehört; Eine andere Geschichte der Deutschen* (Frankfurt, 2019).

Plokhy, Serhii. *The Gates of Europe: A History of Ukraine* (London, 2015).

Ramet, Sabrina P. *Balkan Babel: The Disintegration of Yugoslavia from the Death of Tito to the Fall of Milošević*, 4th ed. (Boulder, CO, 2002).

Reinhart, Carmen M., and Kenneth S. Rogoff. *This Time Is Different: Eight Centuries of Financial Folly* (Princeton, NJ, 2011).

Rieger, Bernhard. *The People's Car: A Global History of the Volkswagen Beetle* (Cambridge, MA, 2013).

Rifkin, Jeremy. *The European Dream: How Europe's Vision of the Future Is Quietly Eclipsing the American Dream* (New York, 2004).

Rosellini, Jay Julian. *The German New Right: The AfD, PEGIDA and the Re-Imagining of National Identity* (London, 2019).

Roufos, Pavlos. *A Happy Future Is a Thing of the Past: The Greek Crisis and Other Disasters* (London, 2018).

Shipman, Tim. *All Out War: The Full Story of Brexit*, rev. ed. (London, 2017).

Small, Carly Elizabeth. *The Rise and Fall of the Miraculous Welfare Machine: Immigration and Social Democracy in Twentieth-Century Sweden* (Ithaca, NY, 2016).

Snyder, Timothy. *The Road to Unfreedom: Russia, Europe, America* (New York, 2018).

Stan, Lavinia, ed. *Post-Communist Transitional Justice: Lessons from Twenty-Five Years of Experience* (New York, 2015).

Ther, Philipp. *Die neue Ordnung auf dem alten Kontinent: Eine Geschichte des neoliberalen Europa* (Berlin, 2014).

Tooze, Adam. *Crashed: How a Decade of Financial Crises Changed the World* (New York, 2018).

von Klimo, Arpad. *Hungary since 1945* (Abingdon, Oxon, 2018).

Wilhelm, Cornelia, ed. *Migration, Memory, and Diversity: Germany from 1945 to the Present* (New York, 2017).

Wilson, Andrew. *Ukraine's Orange Revolution* (New Haven, CT, 2005).

Wirsching, Andreas. *Der Preis der Freiheit: Geschichte Europas in unserer Zeit* (Munich, 2012).

Wurzel, Rüdiger, and James Connelly, eds. *The EU as a Leader in International Climate Change Politics* (London, 2016).

Zidek, Libor. *From Central Planning to the Market: The Transformation of the Czech Economy, 1989–2004* (New York, 2017).

Zubok, Vladislav. *A Failed Empire: The Soviet Union in the Cold War from Stalin to Gorbachev* (Chapel Hill, NC, 2007).

INDEX

Milton Keynes UK
Ingram Content Group UK Ltd.
UKHW030410061224
452124UK00003B/140

9 780691 225531